Self and Non-Self in Early Buddhism

Religion and Reason 22

Method and Theory in the Study and Interpretation of Religion

MOUTON PUBLISHERS · THE HAGUE · PARIS · NEW YORK

Self and Non-Self in Early Buddhism

JOAQUÍN PÉREZ-REMÓN
Universidad de Deusto, Bilbao

MOUTON PUBLISHERS · THE HAGUE · PARIS · NEW YORK

ISBN: 90 279 7987 1

Printed in Great Britain

Preface

This book is based on a thesis submitted to the University of Bombay for the degree of Doctor of Philosophy. The title of the thesis was, '*The Anattavāda in the Suttapiṭaka*'. It was a voluminous thesis which had to be reduced to bearable proportions. In the process, important modifications have been introduced and the material has been more fittingly rearranged.

Most of the people who have written on the *anattā* doctrine, have done it after being thoroughly steeped in the mentality of later commentaries. We preferred to go straight to the original sources and to study the texts in their original setting. This book is the result of our endeavour. A perusal of the quotations will bear out that we have read up all the sources, from the first page to the last. Hence no opening is left for the accusation of presenting only a partial view of the problem.

We are duty bound to acknowledge our debt of gratitude to the following persons and institutions: to Dr. T. G. Mainkar, whose guidance in the writing of the thesis proved decisive; to Dr. A. Esteller, of St. Xavier's College, Bombay, for moral support and for his advice on some metrical passages which required textual elucidation; to the authorities and staff of the Library of the University of Bombay for the facilities they gave us; to Dr. T. E. Vetter, of the *Instituut Kern, Rijksuniversiteit,* Leiden, for carefully reading the manuscript, for his advice and valuable suggestions; to the Editors of the series 'Religion and Society', for accepting the book as part of their series; to the *Faculty of Theology* and *'Departamento de Investigación'* of '*Universidad de Deusto',* Bilbao, for subsidizing the publication of the book. May God bless them all.

Joaquín Pérez-Remón, M. A., Ph. D.

Contents

Part Two: The Metaphysical Self

List of Sources and Abbreviations

Note. The text chosen for reference is the *Nālandā-Devanāgarī-Pāli-Series,* published by the 'Pāli Publication Board' (Bihar Government), having as general editor, Bhikkhu J. Kashyap.

TITLE OF THE BOOK	YEAR OF PUBLICATION	ABBREVIATION
Vinaya-Piṭaka		
1. Mahāvagga	1956	Mvg
2. Cullavagga	1956	Clv
3. Pārājika	1958	Prj
4. Pācittiya	1958	Pct
5. Parivāra	1958	Prv
Sutta-Piṭaka		
1. Dīghanikāya, Vol. I	1958	D I
2. Dīghanikāya, Vol. II	1958	D II
3. Dīghanikāya, Vol. III	1958	D III
4. Majjhimanikāya, Vol. I	1958	M I
5. Majjhimanikāya, Vol. II	1958	M II
6. Majjhimanikāya, Vol. III	1958	M III
7. Saṁyuttanikāya, Vol. I	1959	S I
8. Saṁyuttanikāya, Vol. II (Containing Vols. II and III)	1959	S II-III
9. Saṁyuttanikāya, Vol. IV	1959	S IV
10. Saṁyuttanikāya, Vol. V	1959	S V
11. Aṅguttaranikāya, Vol. I	1960	A I
12. Aṅguttaranikāya, Vol. II	1960	A II
13. Aṅguttaranikāya, Vol. III	1960	A III
14. Aṅguttaranikāya, Vol. IV	1960	A IV

TITLE OF THE BOOK	YEAR OF PUBLICATION	ABBREVIATION
15. Khuddakanikāya, Vol. I,	1959	K I
i. Khuddakapātha		
ii. Dhammapada		K I, Dhp
iii. Udāna		K I, Ud
iv. Itivuttaka		K I, Itv
v. Suttanipāta		K I, Stn
16. Khuddakanikāya, Vol II,	1959	K II
i. Vimānavatthu		K II, Vmv
ii. Petavatthu		K II, Ptv
iii. Theragāthā		K II, Tha
iv. Therīgāthā		K II, Thi
17. Khuddakanikāya, Vol. III, part I, Jātaka	1959	K III, pt. I, J
18. Khuddakanikāya, Vol. III, part II, Jātaka	1959	K III, pt. II, J
19. Khuddakanikāya, Vol. IV, part I, Mahāniddesa	1960	K IV, pt. I, Mnd
20. Khuddakanikāya, Vol. IV, part II, Cullaniddessa	1959	K IV, pt. II, Cln
21. Khuddakanikāya, Vol. V, Paṭisambhidāmagga	1960	K V, Pṭs
22. Khuddakanikāya, Vol. VI, Apadāna (1)	1959	K VI, Apd 1
23. Khuddakanikāya, Vol. VII	1959	K VII
i. Apadāna (2)		K VII, Apd 2
ii. Buddhavaṁsa		K VII, Bhv
iii. Cariyāpiṭaka		K VII, Cpṭ

Introduction

We undertook the study of this subject, because from our first contacts with the original Pāli scriptures we got the impression that things were not as clear as some people would have us believe. We must admit that we did not expect to find such a huge mass of material in the texts themselves. This made it impossible for us to examine the development of the doctrine in the *Abhidhamma* and the Scholastic commentaries. All the same, our purpose was from the very beginning to go as close as possible to the fountain-head of Buddhism and to approach it as part of the Indian intellectual atmosphere prevailing in its world of origin. That is why we insist on the shramanic character of original Buddhism and on its affinities with other Indian systems, like original Sāṅkhya and Yoga, and Jainism. Not in vain whenever *samaṇas and brāhmaṇas* are mentioned together in the texts *samaṇas* come invariably first and when the Buddha is being addressed to by people not belonging to his faith is given the title of 'Gotama the samaṇa'. We must avow that the careful reading of the texts, even though many times dull and wearisome, has been rewarded with new insights and, to some extent at least, with real discoveries.

No one can deny that the *anattā* doctrine is and has been from early times a pillar of Buddhist dogma, together with all-pervading impermanence (*anicca*), and suffering (*dukkha*). No one can deny either that this doctrine is consistently propounded with great emphasis by orthodox Buddhists as one of the most outstanding characteristics of their system.

It has often been a topic of discussion whether the doctrine of the so-called *soullessness* was taught by the Buddha himself or was only a later development.[1] Individual texts or at most a limited number of them have been adduced while trying to prove that such was not the teaching of the Buddha, that he admitted the reality of the self. On the other hand, a great number of scriptural testimonies are ready at hand wherein the *anattā* doctrine is explicitly stated. There seem to be, in the earliest parts of the canon, texts which apparently at least conflict with one another. There are many, not just a few, passages, in the earlier parts of the Pāli canon, that express themselves as if *attā* were a reality, not discussed but taken for granted in the most natural way. A way out of the difficulty has been at times to distinguish between exoteric and esoteric teachings, between empirical and ultimate truth. But are such distinctions valid in this matter? The *anattā* doctrine raises many questions such as the reality of the moral agent and the existence and nature of moral responsibility, the continuity of individuality (personality?) in the rebirth-cycle, the nature of *kamma* and the way it works, the relation of *nibbāna* to the individual that attains to it. There are texts wherein the Buddha refuses to answer the question whether the liberated man exists or does not exist after death. Other texts seem to imply that the liberated man is a reality, in fact the quintessence, so to say, of all reality. All this comes to show that a systematic and complete study of the *anattā* doctrine and all its implications is a thing much to be desired.

We intend to undertake the study of the *anattā* doctrine as presented in the earlier parts of the Pāli canon, the *Suttapiṭaka* or *Five Nikāyas,* without neglecting any significant echo of the doctrine that might be found in the *Vinaya.* Even if we are aware that it would be uncritical to expect to find in the Nikāyas the very words (*ipsissima verba*) of the Buddha,[2] they are, nevertheless the documents that can bring us closest to the personal source of what later on came to be called Buddhism.

The reader should always keep in mind the distinction between the doctrine of relative or qualified *anattā* and the doctrine of absolute or unqualified *anattā*. It is undeniable that many passages in the Nikāyas teach that the aggregates (*khandhas*), the senses, the sense-objects, etc., are not the self, do not belong to the self, are not in the self, and the self is not in them. This denial, as it stands, constitutes for us the doctrine of *relative anattā.* On the other hand the opinion that simply denies the reality of the self in man is what we call absolute *anattā.*

A systematic and complete study of the *anattā* doctrine in the five Nikāyas cannot afford to overlook the positive side of the question. The *anattā* concept is a negative concept. A negative concept obtains its fundamental meaning from its positive counterpart. We do not agree with Piyadassi Thera when he writes:

...we must understand what the Buddha meant by *anattā.* He never

> meant anything in contradistinction to *attā.* He did not place the two terms in juxtaposition and say: 'This is my *anattā* in opposition to *attā'.* The term *anattā,* since the prefix '*an*' indicates non-existence, *abhāva,* and not opposition, *viruddha,* means literally *no attā,* that is the mere denial of an *attā,* the non-existence of *attā.*[3]

This is an issue that has to be decided not *a priori,* but after a careful study of the texts and after determining the way *attā* and *anattā* are used in them. *Anattā* is not the denial of something unreal, as when one denies the existence of 'the horns of a rabbit'. It is the denial of something positive. *Anattā* may be said to deny in the first place the *attā* of the heretics which is identified with the *khandhas* or the samsaric factors in man. But this is not all. Beyond that, we shall discover in the texts an irreconcilable opposition and polarity between *attā,* the true self, and *anattā,* which as a noun stands for something positive and opposed to *attā,* 'the non-self'. From this point of view, the opposition between *attā* and *anattā* is not the opposition between *mitra* (friend) and *amitra,* the latter meaning merely the absence of a friend, but the opposition between friend and enemy.

The study will have to be of a predominantly analytical nature. We shall quote the texts themselves and then make their exegesis following the criterion of a healthy criticism.

In the first part of the book we shall study the texts that refer to *attā.* The reason for doing so is mainly the following. If the belief in *absolute anattā* had been established right from the very beginning as one of the pillars of Buddhist dogma, and that in contradistinction to all existing systems, then tradition would have felt an instinctive abhorrence for the use of the term *attā,* which would have had a jarring effect on the ears and minds of the composers, the compilers and the reciters. If such had been the case, we may well argue that the use of the term *attā* would have been confined to a bare minimum and never extended beyond a scanty and conventional, and therefore not very meaningful, use of it. Does this apply to the Nikāyas? Only a complete analysis and classification of the passages wherein the term is used will provide us with the right answer.

There is an author that has made a direct reference to the problem raised by the use of the term *attā* in the Pāli canon. He says:

> The overwhelming refrain of the Tripiṭakas is that there is no soul or self

> as a substance. In the preceding pages we have cited explicit references which negate any notion of a transcendent 'I'. *Nevertheless, there are certain passages and statements which mention the word attā. These do create a problem.* Either it has to be accepted that there is inconsistency in the Tripiṭakas, which, considering the great bulk of this literature and also the fact that its different portions were composed at different periods, by several disciples, is not surprising, or it has to be accepted that the references to *attā* are to the empirical personality of man and not to a metaphysical substance.[4]

Several animadversions might be appended to this quotation. For the present we wish only to say that 'there are certain passages and statements...' should read 'there are *numerous* passages and statements...' as the first part of our book will demonstrate. In fact the references to *attā* in the five Nikāyas are as overwhelming, as regards their numbers, as the references to *anattā,* and plenty of those references are extremely significant.

N.B. Following the tendency prevailing in the Indian vernaculars not to pronounce the last vowel in adjectives such as *sāṁsarika* and *dhārmika,* we have instinctively transliterated them as 'samsaric' and 'dharmic' in the likeness of such English adjectives as 'symbolic, academic, etc.'. Then analogically, we have taken the liberty, which we hope will meet with the tolerant acceptance of the reader, to coin such adjectives as 'upanishadic, brahmanic, asmimanic, shramanic, etc.'. For the beautiful adjective 'nikayan' we are indebted to Mrs. Rhys Davids.

PART ONE

The Existential Self

1

Preliminary Remarks

The texts bearing on *attā* (and *anattā*) to be found in the Nikāyas fall into two categories, those that speak of the self in action, and those that in one way or other refer to the very nature of the self. The first kind of texts describe how the self either succumbs to the onslaughts of evil or conquers and suppresses it, attaining ultimate perfection and perfect freedom. The second kind of texts insist on what the self is not. The point at issue is whether or not the latter texts, with their negative references to *attā,* deny altogether the reality of the self. The self alluded to in the former set of texts may be called the existential self, while the self referred to in the latter set of texts may be called the metaphysical self. Whatever relation there may be between these two kinds of self, the existence of the texts that speak of them is a fact that no one can deny. That is why a separate study of the two groups of texts is something not only desirable, but even necessary if we want to have a complete view of the doctrine of self and non-self in primitive Buddhism.

HOW TO TRANSLATE THE TERM *attā*

The translation to be given to the term *attā* is to be fixed from the very outset.

The translation of *attā* as 'soul' ought to be discarded. The 'soul' is supposed to be wholly involved in all bodily and mental processes, vivifying the body and constituting the substrate of all intellectual and emotional phenomena. It is obvious that this kind of *attā* or 'soul' is emphatically rejected in many a passage of the Nikāyas. A term should be chosen general enough to fit in all contexts.

Mrs. Rhys Davids, in one of her works,[1] advocates the rendering of *attā* as 'spirit', not as 'soul' or 'self'. There are indeed many contexts where 'spirit' could be considered a convenient rendering of the term *attā.* For instance, the phrase, *sampassaṁ atthaṁ attano*[2] could very well be rendered as 'seing the good of his spirit'. The so often recurring *pahitatto* could very well be translated as 'a man of resolute spirit'. Similarly *bhāvitatto* could be considered equivalent to 'the man fully developed in spirit', etc. But 'spirit' is a concrete term which stands only for the immaterial aspect of man. There are passages in the Nikāyas where *attā* refers to man in general without any abstraction either from the material or the spiritual part of man. Thus we see the Buddha in one of his previous existences impersonating his father so as to be devoured by a Yakkha in his place. The expression used is, *nimminitvāna attanā* (v. 1. *attānaṁ*),[3] which may be translated as, 'impersonating [miraculously] [my father] by means of self'. It will not do to translate here *attanā* as: 'by means of my spirit'.

The word 'spirit' will not be able to convey the significant contrast between physical and 'spiritual' safety so fittingly expressed in the passage:

> It is as if there was for a man a house having eleven doors; if that house were on fire, he would be able to save himself (lit. *self*) by any of those doors. In the same way, can this man save the self by any of those eleven doors.[4]

We find in both the cases the same Pāli expression, *attānaṃ sotthiṃ kātuṃ,* which in the second case might well be translated as 'he can save his spirit', but not in the first case. Many more illustrations of this type could be given.

There is still one more difficulty. *Attā* is often used to denote what may be said to be the core of man's personality. The word 'spirit' does not appear fully to convey this meaning, at least not in the context of Indian philosophy, where 'self' seems to have a more marked philosophical connotation.

Therefore it seems better to choose 'self' as the English equivalent to *attā.* 'Self' connotes primarily 'identity' or being what a man is, and therefore it connotes also separation from other individuals. It has a sufficiently general meaning applicable in all contexts, whether *attā* is conceived as related or unrelated to the empirical world, be it interior (*ajjhattaṁ*) or exterior (*bahidhā*). It can also be applied to the moral nature of man and to his ontological reality, or, we may add, unreality, if absolute *anattā* proves to be the only acceptable doctrine in the Buddhist context. It can be applied, finally, even in those cases where the physical nature of man is alluded to either alone or as a part of the whole man.

Mrs. Rhys Davids' reluctance to accept 'self' as a translation for *attā* springs from the 'debasement', which according to her the term 'self' has undergone in the English language.[5] In Mrs. Rhys Davids' words one can detect an implicit contention, made explicit by her in other parts of her writings, that the original *attā* of Buddhism coincided with the *ātman* of the Upaniṣads. Early Buddhism accepts the reality of the 'individual' self as a matter of fact. Early Buddhism speaks of the individual self in a way similar to that of Sāṅkhya and Yoga, Jainism, etc. In all these systems the individual self was held in great esteem when considered the agent and recipient of salvation. This self may be something metempirical, but not something 'divine' or exhibiting a universal cosmic character.

Even if the self in man is one, it displays in primitive Buddhism a wealth of existential vitality which precludes any simplification. This existential wealth is expressed in this book, in relation to the moral self, by saying that it is ambivalent, and that in several ways. Firstly, it is ambivalent in the spontaneous freedom of choice that it can exercise, either for better or worse. Secondly, it is ambivalent because it has the power of introspection, and thus the Nikāyas speak of the self reproving the self. Thirdly, it is ambivalent inasmuch as the self is at once the subject of the action and the recipient of its results, even in the case of the highest perfection. Hence to say, as the 'conventionalists' are wont to say, in order to dismiss as little significant the oblique cases of *attā,* that they have a reflexive sense, is to say nothing new. What other sense could they have? 'Reflexive,' according to the Oxford Dictionary is an adjective 'implying agent's action on himself'. The oblique cases of *attā* have a reflexive sense, precisely because they are oblique cases of *attā*, and represent it in its different grammatical functions.

Now a difference in idiom is to be noted between Pāli and English. In English we speak of 'myself, yourself, himself or herself', which correspond to *attā* or *attānaṁ,* as the case may be, but a translation like that will often weaken the expressive force of the Pāli term, which literally means 'self', or 'the self', that is to say the very personal individuality that justifies in the first place the use of possessive adjectives like, 'mine, your, his or her', and of personal pronouns such as 'I, me, etc.'. Similar is the case with the translation of *attano* as, 'of myself, of yourself, etc.', and of *attanā* as, 'by myself, by yourself, by himself, etc.'. That is why we shall in our translations stick, as far as possible, to the original even at the cost of sacrificing good English idiom. Let us illustrate this point with an example. We have the passage where the two chamberlains of king Pasenadi tell the Buddha:

> Well, Lord, at that time the elephant is to be guarded, the ladies also are to be guarded, and even *the self* is to be guarded (*attā pi rakkhitabbo hoti*).[6]

The last phrase alludes to the care to ward off temptation while attending to the king's wives of so delicate a complexion and extremely attractive. This temptation tends to sully the self, which has to be kept in check and absolutely pure. This, F. L. Woodward, yielding to the 'conventionalist' way of expressing things, translates:

> Well, Lord, at such times we have to ward the elephant, and we have to ward the ladies, and ward *ourselves* as well. (Italics ours).

The expressive force of *attā* (thus in the nominative) in the text seems to have vanished in F. L. Woodward's translation, where the self as a moral *reality* does not get any prominence.

HAS THE TERM *attā* A MERE CONVENTIONAL SENSE IN THE NIKĀYAS?

It is convenient to dwell now on the so much bandied about distinction between the conventional use of *attā* and its real use, the latter being summarily dismissed from the Nikāyas by the 'conventionalists'. K. N. Upadhyaya deals with this and quoting some passages whose import will be discussed later on, with a stroke of the pen, dismisses as mere conventional talk all the usages of *attā* to be found in the Nikāyas.[7] B. C. Law introduces in this context the distinction between *sammutisacca* (apparent truth) and *paramatthasacca* (real truth).[8] The quotation given by him is taken from a much later work, the *Milindapañha,* but such distinction of truths is absent from the Nikāyas. Buddhism, as presented in the Nikāyas is, above everything else, a soteriology, that is to say, a system of moral training (taking the term moral in its broadest sense) having as its aim the gradual purification of beings and their final liberation in *nibbāna* . Buddhism in the Nikāyas is no Cosmology or Metaphysics. It distinguishes between three levels of attainments, *diṭṭhadhammikattha, samparāyikattha,* and *paramattha,*[9] that is to say, 'moral attainment' (*attha*) to be had in this very life, in other worlds (but still within the transmigratory cycle), and *nibbāna.* That *paramattha* is *nibbāna* we have it in:

> The highest aim (*paramattha*) is said to be the undecaying *nibbāna* (*amataṁ nibbānaṁ*).[10]

We also meet in the Nikāyas with *paramatthasuññaṁ,* which is not metaphysical but 'moral', and is described as an utter purification culminating in *parinibbāna,* with the concomittant cessation of all sensorial activities.[11] But the distinction between *sammutisacca* and *paramatthasacca* is of later origin.

Another way of stating the distinction between two kinds of self refers to the empirical personality of man and to a metaphysical substance, as we have seen it done by Vishwanath Prasad Varma in a passage quoted in the Introduction, and that is why we have divided our book into two parts, the first dealing with the existential self (which will represent the self in action and therefore working on the empirical level) and the second dealing with the ontological or metaphysical self as such. Let it be clear that this distinction is not propounded in so many words in the Nikāyas and that the empiricality of the moral self does not prejudice in any way its reality.

Th. Stcherbatsky, the great champion of absolute *anattā,* is ready to agree that:

> Buddhism never denied the existence of a personality, or soul, in the empirical sense, it only maintained that it was no ultimate reality (*dharma*).[12]

Nevertheless we have Buddhagosa's words in the *Visuddhimagga:*

> For there is ill but none to feel it;
> For there is action but no doer;
> And there is peace, but no one to enjoy it;
> A way there is, but no one goes it (*gamako*).[13]

It seems pretty clear that in this passage the reality of the moral self is utterly denied. Coming back to Stcherbatsky, it must be said that the Buddhism described by him in the work just quoted is not the Buddhism of the Nikāyas. We have already remarked that the Buddhism of the Nikāyas is above everything else a soteriology, i.e., a system of salvation, while Stcherbatsky calls the type of Buddhism he describes 'a metaphysical theory'.[14] But after reading through 'Apendix II', entitled, 'Classification of all elements of existence', with so many divisions and subdivisions whose soteriological value a reader of the Nikāyas is likely to question, one is inclined to call the system not Metaphysics but Phenomenology. Phenomenology dealing with things empirical, how could the empirical self be denied? But is the self of the Nikāyas wholly empirical? We deem it enough for our purpose to discuss the point whether or not the term *attā*, when used in the Nikāyas, has got a mere conventional sense, without any reality to back it, a reality, that is, of the highest order.

We see four ways in which one may try to weaken and even to nullify the meaning of the term *attā* as used in the Nikāyas.

1. In the first place, one might say that the Buddha made use of the term *attā* only when speaking to laymen and unlearned people, who could never understand the doctrine of absolute *anattā*. As a matter of fact, many passages of those that are going to be quoted in the first part of our book are taken from exhortations of the Buddha to his bhikkhus and from the utterances of learned bhikkhus communicating their feelings for the benefit of the rest.

2. Another escape sought by those who wish to empty the *attā* texts of any deep and real meaning is to say that the Buddha delivered two kinds of teaching, esoteric and exoteric, the former meant only for the few and the latter for the rank and file. Happily we have against this a direct testimony attributed to the Buddha himself:

> I have taught the doctrine, Ānanda, without making a distinction between esoteric and exoteric teaching. There is not, Ānanda, in the case of the Tathāgata any close-fistedness as regards the teachings.[15]

An appeal may also be made to the less quoted simile of the three fields and the three water pots, which, taken as it stands, proves that the Buddha did not make any difference in his preaching, not only between monks and monks, between monks and nuns, between them and his layfollowers, but even between all these and the wanderers samaṇas and brāhamaṇas of other sects. The Buddha says that in all three cases the dhamma preached by him is the same:

To them I preach the dhamma auspicious and morally helpful (*kalyāna*) from beginning to end, absolutely perfect in letter and spirit [and] explain [also] the utterly pure brahma-life (*brahmacariya*).[16]

3. There is a third way of attempting to water down the significance of the *attā* passages to be found in the Nikāyas, by searching for texts in the Nikāyas that apparently do so.

K. N. Upadhyaya, who is a convinced 'conventionalist', adduces four texts, which, so he thinks, prove that the term *attā* in the Nikāyas has a mere conventional meaning. He quotes in the first place a passage from the *Dīghanikāya,* saying:

Buddha himself states in this connection that 'they are merely popular expressions, popular terms of speech, designations in common practice and usages prevalent in the world, which the Tathāgata makes use of without being mislead'.[17]

The quotation is taken from the *Poṭṭhapādasutta,* which, like many other suttas, is a composite work where several different and seemingly unrelated topics are put together. The quoted words of the Buddha occur in the last part of the sutta. In this part, the Buddha himself, without being questioned about it, introduces the topic of the three planes of worldly existence (*attapaṭilābho*); physical (*oḷariko*), mental (*manomayo*), and formless (*arūpo*), saying that he teaches dhamma for the giving up of all those planes of existence and for the attainment, here and now, of complete wisdom being personally realized and conducive to perfect happiness. Then Citta asks the Buddha whether while one of the three kinds of existence is going on, that existence is true (*sacco*) and the others sould be considered false (*mogho*). The Buddha answers that, while one of the three existences is going on, it cannot be designated by the names of the other two (*na saṅkhaṁ gacchati*). The Buddha then makes Citta declare that when he existed in the past he could not say that he did not exist; that when he will be existing in the future he will not be able to say that he will not be existing; and that when he exists in the present he cannot say that he does not exist. He makes him also confess that the past existence, while it was going on, was true and the other two false, etc. Then the Buddha applies this reasoning to the three planes of existence saying that, while one of them is going on, it cannot be designated by the names of the other two.

And he winds up the discussion with the following simile:

> In the same way, Citta, as milk proceeds from the cow, curds proceed from milk, fresh butter proceeds from curds, clarified butter proceeds from fresh butter, and cream of clarified butter proceeds from clarified butter. At the time when it is milk, it cannot be called fresh butter, etc., etc., but it is called at that time just milk. At the time when it is curds, it cannot be called milk, it cannot be called fresh butter, etc., etc. (And so of all the rest).
>
> In that very way, at the time, Citta, when there is a physical acquisition of rebirth, it cannot be called a mental acquisition of rebirth or a formless acquisition of rebirth. At the time, Citta, when there is a mental acquisition of rebirth, it cannot be called a physical acquisition of rebirth, etc., etc. And these, Citta, are common names, common expressions, common usages, common designations which the Tathāgata utters without grasping at them.

I fail to see how the last words underrate all the usages of *attā* to be found in the Nikāyas, when in the context they apply directly only to *oḷāriko attapaṭilābho, manomayo attapaṭilābho,* and *arūpo attapaṭilābho,* terms which the Buddha uses without any sort of attachment to them, when precisely he professes to teach the way that leads to their cessation.[18] I do not see either how in this sutta:

> Citta Hatthisāriputta raised a question about the nature of 'identity' of the self in course of transmigration from one plane of existence to another,

and that:

> This was explained with the simile of milk in course of fermentation, which elucidates the law of Universal Flux, and proves that the identity is to be accepted only for practical consideration, not as a metaphysical truth.[19]

This certainly is reading into the text something that does not seem to be there. If at all, the simile, as similar ones found in the Upanishads, would illustrate the opposite, namely that the difference is merely nominal while the reality remains the same. In fact, G. C. Pande thinks that the words, *Iti imā kho Citta lokasamaññā*... are a corrective to the simile of the transformation of milk, establishing an unchanging identity behind changing appearances, which is clearly un-Buddhistic.[20] The least therefore that can be asserted is that it is not at all clear that this passage settles the conventional use of the term *attā* all through the Nikāyas.

The second passage adduced by K. N. Upadhyaya to prove the conventional use of *attā* in the Nikāyas says that a bhikkhu who is an Arahant, who has done what was to be done, has destroyed the *āsavas* and is bearing a body for the last time, without the least remnant of conceit:

He may use expressions such as 'I speak',
He may also use expressions such as 'mine',
He, an expert, knowing the designation among people,
Will utter this merely as a conventional way of talking.[21]

The whole context of the passage deals with moral, not metaphysical matters. All the qualifications of the bhikkhu in question are moral, the one that is more to the point being the absolute freedom from asmimanic feelings,[22] which obviously will enable him to use the same expressions used by other people concerning 'I' and 'mine' without any meaning of conceit. Keeping as a background other teachings of the Nikāyas to be explained later on, the passage just quoted may be paraphrased as follows. All conceit is based on the *sakkāyadiṭṭhi,* that is to say on the identification of the *attā* with the empirical man. One who is perfect is one who has put aside the *khandhas* and broken thereby all the ties with the empirical man. Therefore he cannot use truthfully expressions that for other people imply such identification, wherein 'I' and 'mine' are included. But if he wants to speak and be understood he will have to use the same language as the common people use but never with the same inner meaning. To say that this proves the 'conventional' use of *attā* in every case is equivalent to identifying adequately 'I' with the 'self'. But 'I' cannot be uttered in the absence of any empirical impressions, while we are told in so many passages that *attā,* as such, ought to be never conceived as having any ontological relation to the empirical man. Therefore the text adduced may be said to prove that one who has attained perfection has realized that *attā* is by nature disconnected from whatever is empirical, even though in his communication with others may be bound to use expressions that seem to gainsay such disconnection. The text cannot be appealed to as a proof for absolute *anattā* or that the term *attā* is always used with a mere conventional meaning.

There remain two other texts quoted by K. N. Upadhyaya in order to prove the conventional use of *attā* in the Nikāyas. But the texts do not refer directly to *attā*, the self, but to *satto*, being. This seems to imply that in the Nikāyas the terms *attā* and *satto* are, for all practical purposes, synonyms, but such is not by any means the case. Let us take the second text brought forward, the famous verses of the nun Vajirā:

> Just as by the assemblage of parts there arises the term 'chariot',
> Even so, when the *khandhas* exist [together] there arises the conventional term *satto* [being].[23]

These lines obviously refer to the empirical man, who is a mere congeries of physical and psychical phenomena. We are often told in the Scriptures that these phenomena, the *khandhas*, are not the self, do not belong to the self, the self is not in them, and they are not in the self. Māra, who has been introduced in this context as giving the empirical man the designation of *satto*, is explicitly accused of holding the heretical view that identifies *attā* with the *khandhas* in '*Māra diṭṭhigataṁ nu te*'. Māra is reputed to perceive only the empirical man as it becomes clear from a number of passages where we are told that he is unable to see the man that has put aside his empirical adjuncts.[24] Hence the reality of *attā* is not challenged in this context. All this will become clearer in the second part of the book.

There is another problem that should not be left unmentioned. To try to belittle the importance in meaning of so many texts that speak of *attā* on the strength of one text here and one text there, besides giving the impression of overstepping all limits of proportion, involves the fallacy of supposing that all the teachins of the Nikāyas reproduce exactly the original words of the Buddha, so that we cannot find in them different currents of thought or different strata in the building up of tradition that may be the result of a changing mentality and a development of doctrine. Taking this into account, a critically minded man will try first to ponder every *sutta* or passage as standing on its own, without ever forgetting the context, and then only to see whether or not all of them can be said to form a system harmonious in all its parts.

4. The last way of invalidating the usages of the term *attā* is by opposing them to the texts where the *anattā* doctrine is propounded. In this case, the texts referring to *attā* would constitute the thesis, while the texts referring to *anattā* would provide us with the antithesis. The problem will be whether, in this case, the antithesis annuls the thesis or whether there

is a possibility of synthesis and of what kind. This can be decided only after a careful study of the *attā* and *anattā* texts found in the Nikāyas.

THE NIKAYAN APPROACH TO THE TERM *attā*

If the distinction between *sammutisacca* and *paramatthasacca,* with reference to *attā,* was introduced at a much later time, what is the Nikayan approach regarding the term *attā*? Fortunately for us we get in the Nikāyas themselves some commentarial material (the *Mahāniddesa* and *Cullaniddesa*), and we can see for ourselves the way those early commentators deal with the term *attā.* The only kind of criticism those early commentators knew of is the use of the term *attā* with a '*diṭṭhi* mentality', that is to say a mentality that identifies in some way or another the self (*attā*) with the *khandhas* and falls thereby a prey to conceit. Thus we never meet in the *Mahāniddesa* and *Cullaniddesa* with expressions like, '*attā vuccati lokiyasammuti*' or '*attā vuccati lokiyavohāro*', that would mean that *attā* is used merely in a conventional sense. On the other hand, we come several times across a sentence that reads, *attā vuccati diṭṭhigataṁ,* and in every case we can see that the use of the term smacks of conceit.

We find several passages where the commentarial censure of the term *attā* being used with a *diṭṭhi* mentality, or what is the same with a feeling of conceit, occurs.

1. While commenting upon:

   that profit that he sees in self (*attani*),

we are warned:

   attā is used with a *diṭṭhi* mentality (*diṭṭhigataṁ*).[25]

2. Again, commenting on the same words in a different context, we are told:

   attā is used with a *diṭṭhi* mentality. Drawn by that *diṭṭhi* mentality (*diṭṭhiyā*) he sees two kinds of profit of self (*attano*).[26]

3. Commenting upon:

   there is for him neither *attā* nor *nirattā,*

we are given two possible explanations for *attā* and *nirattā,* the first one being:

attā means that he does not profess the heresy of eternalism (*attānudiṭṭhi*)...

Nirattā, that is to say the heresy of annihilationism (*ucchedadiṭṭhi*)...[27]

4. Commenting upon:

giving up *attā* he has nothing to do in this world,

two possible explanations are given again, the first being:

attañjaho means giving up the heresy of eternalism (*attadiṭṭhi*).[28]

5. Finally, while commenting upon:

giving up *attā,* not grasping at anything,

the same two possible explanations are indicated the first one being expressed as:

giving up *attā* means giving up the heresy of eternalism (*attadiṭṭhi*).[29]

It is therefore evident that the only distinction in the use of the term *attā* in which the Buddhism of the Nikāyas is interested is the distinction between the orthodox and unorthodox use of it. From the texts just quoted any one can see that the unorthodox use of *attā* is the one that has as its ideological background the *attānudiṭṭhi,* as opposed to annihilationism (*ucchedadiṭṭhi*) and which on the other hand coincides with the *sakkāyadiṭṭhi*[30] that is the identification of the *attā* with the *khandhas* or the admission of any ontological relationship between the two.

The only way left to contradict this line of thought is to say that the unorthodox use of *attā* singled out by early commentators coincides exactly with the conventional use of the term, which will be equivalent to saying that whenever the term *attā* is used it has an unorthodox sense. This is utterly inadmissible, because if such were the case, then the Buddha would be introduced as using heretical language when he speaks of the self, and that regarding his own person. He is, for instance, reported to have said of himself:

My age is fully ripe,
My life is at an end,
I shall depart leaving you,
I have made a refuge for the self
(*kataṁ me saraṇaṁ attano*).[31]

The very thought that the Buddha was resorting here to a heretical way of thinking and talking is revolting and even blasphemous, when the very kernel of his teaching, as presented in the Nikāyas, contradicts and forcefully condemns any identification of *attā* with the *khandhas.*

Thus it is well established that the only kind of disapproval shown by the early commentators regarding the term *attā* refers to its asmimanic or heretical use, paying no attention to the later distinction between the conventional use of the term and its *paramatthika* use. On the other hand, it is also well established that the so-called conventional use of the term does not correspond with its asmimanic or heretical use.

The commentators have taught us another very important lesson. The conventionalists dismiss all the oblique cases of *attā* as having merely a reflexive sense, as if they never had any direct relation to *attā* as 'the self'. In two of the passages quoted, the commentary bears on *attani,* an oblique case of *attā.* The commentators do not dismiss it as having a merely reflexive sense, but they refer it expressly to *attā* in its asmimanic sense.

No one will deny that the term *attā* is sometimes used with a merely reflexive sense, but no emphasis is then laid on *attā* as the innermost reality in man, the subject and beneficiary of all soteriological activities. We may find sayings like, 'With his own means' (*attano dhamena*),[32] where *attā* has obviously a merely reflexive sense. What is to be denied is that *attā* is always used in this sense and that the distinction between the conventional (*vyāvahārika*) and the real (*pāramārthika*) use of the term *attā* was given any relevance in the Nikāyas. We may admit that this distinction is applicable to a certain degree to the existential self as opposed to the metaphysical self, but without in any way denying the reality of the former.

In fine, the basic distinction between the different usages or meanings of the term *attā* in the Nikāyas, the one that was considered relevant and important, is the distinction between its asmimanic and heretical sense (*diṭṭhigataṁ*) and its non-asmimanic and non-heretical sense.

2

Attā as Man's Highest Value

Confident of having established the fact that the distinction between the conventional and the real use of *attā* is not given relevance in the Nikāyas, and that the only valid distinction recognized in them is that between the orthodox and unorthodox sense of the term (which in no way corresponds with the former distinction), we now proceed to the analysis of a good number of texts where *attā* stands for something of the greatest importance, this being incompatible with a mere conventional use of the term. Raising *attā* to the rank of the highest value in man, lays such emphasis on it that it seems irrelevant to say that for those who gave it such importance it stood merely for something conventional, without any reality behind it.

THE SELF AS REFUGE

Let us now occupy ourselves with the famous expressions:

> Therefore, Ānanda, stay as those who have the self as island, as those who have the self as refuge, as those who have no other refuge; as those who have dhamma as island, as those who have dhamma as refuge, as those who have no other refuge.[1]

This is one of the best known utterances of the Buddha and seems to assert, implicitly at least, the reality of *attā*.[2]

How should the compounds *attadīpā,* etc., be translated? They are *bahubbihi* compounds containing two nouns in apposition, and therefore to be explained as, 'those who have the self as island, those who have the self as refuge, etc.'. In times back the word *dīpa* in the first compound was generally translated as 'lamp', a possible translation if we pay attention only to the word itself, but 'island' seems to be a more likely rendering in the context. It is a well known fact that a distinguishing characteristic of Nikayan style consists in piling up synonyms, doubtless to make clearer and more forceful what is being explained. Hence it will not do to say that if *attadīpā* already meant, 'those who have the self as island', (island meaning a refuge from the current of *samsāra*)[3] it would have been a useless repetition to add immediately *attasaraṇā*, which obviously means, 'those who have the self as refuge'. Besides, if the meanings of *attadīpā* and *attasaraṇā* are entirely different, then the structure of the sentence ought to have been, *attadīpā anaññadīpā viharatha attasaraṇā anaññasaraṇā*. The absence of *anaññadīpā* shows that *anaññasaraṇā* comes at the end with a sense of finality that affects both *attadīpā* and *attasaraṇā*, which thereby are considered as having the same fundamental meaning. One thing seems to be certain, that *attasaraṇā* cannot be translated as 'be a refuge unto yourselves', because in that case *dhammasaraṇā* which follows immediately as part of the same sentence would have to be analogically translated as 'be a refuge unto dhamma', which clearly does not fit. Our position is confirmed by a passage where the Buddha is reported to refer to his bhikkhus and bhikkhunīs as people who 'abide having him as their island, their cave of shelter, their stronghold, their refuge'.[4]

The passage under discussion occurs in the *Mahāparinibbānasutta*. In the context, Ānanda expresses his fear that the Tathāgata might pass away without making some pronouncement for the benefit of the Order, we might say he expected a kind of spiritual last will and testament. Buddha replies that he has nothing more to say, that he has been a teachter who has not kept anything undisclosed. He adds that no one has a right to say that the Order will be under his care, and this applies even to the Tathāgata who is about to complete his course through life. Then it is that he utters those memorable words:

> Therefore, Ānanda, stay as those who have the self as island,
> as those who have the self as refuge,
> as those who have no other refuge, etc.

It is difficult to conceive that a believer in absolute *anattā*, denying to *attā* any objective reality, would advice his disciples to take their stand on something that he taught was entirely unreal. The *attā* of the context, together with dhamma and intimately connected with it, was expected to make up for the absence of the Buddha, who was about to leave the world.

That this exhortation advocates reliance on the self and personal maturity, so as not to be in need of the physical presence of the Buddha even for reaching to the peak of immortality, is brought out by the concluding passage:

> And whoever, Ānanda, either now or after my end will stay as those who have the self as island, as those who have the self as refuge, as those who have no other refuge; as those who have dhamma as island, as those who have dhamma as refuge, as those who have no other refuge, they among my bhikkhus shall reach the peak of immortality, provided they are desirous of training themselves.

An intimate relationship is proclaimed here between *attā* and *dhamma,* a relationship hinted at by the parallelism established in the text: *attadīpā-dhammadīpā*; *attasaraṇā-dhammasaraṇā*; and in both cases, *anaññasaraṇā.* One might say that what the text proposes is a self in which dhamma inheres as in its natural abode, practically identified with it.

And how to be one who has the self as island, as refuge, who has no other refuge, and has, as well, dhamma as island etc.? This is described as follows:

> Herein, bhikkhus, a bhikkhu dwells contemplating the body in the body, strenuous, self-possessed, mindful, restraining the hankering and dejection to be found in the world.

Therefore, in this context, in order to act as one who has the self as island, as refuge, who has no other refuge, etc., one should withdraw from all wordly craving and dejection, in perfect conscious mastery over the body and all subjective phenomena. The body and all subjective phenomena are precisely the non-self, as we are told in numberless passages of the Nikāyas. One can see here a real opposition between the self and the non-self; if one term of the opposition, namely the non-self, is something real, so the other term, i.e. the self, will also be real.[5]

In another context, we find 'having the self as refuge' and the consequent practice of the stations of mindfulness (*satipaṭṭhāna*) set in opposition to *dukkha,* a summary of whatever is samsaric and therefore non-self. No one will deny that *dukkha* in the Nikāyas is presented as something very real, hence the refuge that enables one to make an end of *dukkha* ought also to be real:

> Therefore, be those who have the self as island,
> moving about the stations of mindfulness.

Developing the seven limbs of wisdom,
you will make an end of Pain.[6]

This opposition between having the self as refuge (*attadīpā, bhikkhave, viharatha,* etc.) and the non-self, in the form of the *khandhas* constitutes the main topic of the *Attadīpasutta* of the *Saṁyutta.*[7] The *sutta* tells us that those who have the self as refuge etc. are qualified to inquire thoroughly into the question as to what is the origin of grief, lamentation, pain, dejection and disturbance and what keeps them going on. Then we are told that the origin of grief, lamentation, etc. consists in regarding the *khandhas* as the self, or as attributes of the self, or as being in the self or the self being in them. The impermanence and instability of the *khandhas* makes one who identifies them with the self experience trouble, vexation, worry, etc. The self as island is shown here as the 'terra firma' in contradistinction to the *khandhas.*

In the *Theragāthā* we meet with a striking passage wherefrom it becomes clear that the right translation for *dīpa* is 'island'. The realities opposed here are the self on one side and birth and old age on the other:

Like a surge of the great ocean,
So also birth and old age will roll over you.
Do make a firm island out of the self,
Since there is no other refuge to be found for you.[8]

Note the meaningful line, *so karohi sudīpamattanā tvaṁ.* Could such words, with the emphasis revealed by the term *sudīpaṁ,* 'a firm island', be attributed to one who professed the unreality of the self? Can *attā* be taken here as something merely conventional? Would anyone be able to build a 'firm island' having as material, so to say, a mere word? No one who has read even superficially the Nikāyas can deny the reality of old age and death, that summarize *dukkha* and *saṁsāra.* To such agonizing and gripping reality is the author of those lines going to oppose a remedy which existed only in his imagination and he being conscious of it?

At other times, the texts do not speak of the self as island or refuge, but of making an island or refuge for the self. They too have their rôle to play in building up the correct image of *attā* as reflected in the teaching of the Nikāyas.

There is a personal utterance of the Buddha about making a refuge for the self. He is taking his final leave, before his death, from his disciples and tells them that all component things are subject to decay (*vayadhammā saṅkhārā*), exhorts them to strive to attain their aim with diligence and announces his impending death. Then it is that we are given the following lines as uttered by the Buddha:

My life is fully ripe, my life is at an end,
I shall depart leaving you, I have made a refuge for the self.[9]

The two remaining ślokas are an exhortation to work with diligence and make an end of Pain. Therefore the context seems to suggest that making a refuge for the self and making an end of Pain are somehow equivalent. Let us ponder the words, *kataṁ me saraṇaṁ attano. Me* is here the agent of the passive participle *kataṁ,* and *attano* is a dative that stands for the beneficiary of the action of the verb. The Buddha is about to die and reveals his inner disposition when about to attain *parinibbāna.* He does not say that he has left the self aside as if it were only a hindrance, he does not say either that he has waged war against the self and finally destroyed it. On the contrary he seems to give as an equivalent of his readiness to pass into utter *nibbāna* the fact that he has made a refuge for the self. The ambivalence of the term *attā* becomes clear from the fact that in this sentence *me,* the active agent, and *attano,* the beneficiary of the action, are not two different entities but one and the same, that is, the Buddha who is about to attain utter *nibbāna.* The reality of *attā* is linked here with the reality of *nibbāna.*

In the *Pheṇapiṇḍūpamasutta* of the *Khandhasaṁyutta* the advice that the bhikkhu should make a refuge for the self (*kareyya saraṇamattano*) is also connected with the obtention of *nibbāna,* the *accutaṁ padaṁ.* The reality of *attā* is enhanced here by the illusory nature of the *khandhas* as opposed to it. *Rūpa* is likened to foam, *vedanā* is likened to a bubble, *saññā* is likened to a mirage, the *saṅkhārā* are likened to a plantain-tree that has no pith, *viññāṇa* is likened to a juggler's creation. By seing the *khandhas* in this light, the Aryan disciple grows disgusted at them, disgust produces repulsion, and repulsion leads to freedom. The metrical part of the sutta repeats the ideas of the prose part and ends up with the thought of ultimate liberation expressed in the following way:

Thus considering the *khandhas* [as pithless], the bhikkhu, displaying energy,
Day and night self-controlled, mindful,

Should cast off all fetters, should make a refuge for the self (*kareyya saraṇattano*),
Should behave like one whose head is ablaze, aspiring to the unfailing state (*accutaṁ padaṁ*).[10]

'Making a refuge for the self' is here connected with 'casting off all fetters' (*jaheyya sabbasaṁyogaṁ*), which is mentioned before, and the 'aspiration for the unfailing state' (*patthayaṁ accutaṁ padaṁ*), which comes soon after. All this, added to the consideration of the *khandhas* as something illusory is an implicit but definite assertion of the reality of *attā.*

In the *Dhammapada* we find two more stanzas where the idea of making an island for the self finds an echo:

Do make an island for the self (*so karohi dīpaṁ attano*), strive fast, be wise,
Having removed all stain, flawless, you will come to the divine ariyan land.[11]

The same stanza is repeated with the ending:

...you will not come again to birth and old age.[12]

In these stanzas, making an island for the self is connected with final liberation expressed as 'the divine ariyan land' and 'the cessation of birth and old age'. If liberation is subsequent to making an island for the self or equivalent to it, how can anyone say that the *attā* referred to here is a mere conventional name, when it stands for the person who is liberated, liberation being a most appealing reality in the Nikāyas?

That 'making a refuge for the self' is the right disposition for the attainment of *nibbāna,* or an equivalent to it is forcefully expressed in the *Therīgāthā:*

Even among the gods there is no other refuge for the self apart from the happiness of *nibbāna.*[13]

Akin to *saraṇaṁ attano,* 'a refuge for the self', is *bhavanaṁ attano,* 'an abode for the self', found in a passage of the *Suttanipāta* which reinforces whatever the previous texts have taught us by denying that the self can find its abode in anything samsaric:

The world is essenceless all around,
the quarters are quaking.
Desiring an abode for the self (*icchaṁ bhavanaṁ attano*),
I saw none unoccupied (*anositaṁ*).[14]

The commentator, in the *Mahāniddesa,* gives as synonyms of *bhavanaṁ: tāṇaṁ, leṇaṁ, saraṇaṁ, gatiṁ, parāyanaṁ,*[15] and explains the occupancy that prevents the *attā* from finding any shelter in the world by saying:

> All youth is tenanted by old age, all health is tenanted by illness, all life is tenanted by death, all acquisitions are tenanted by loss, all glory is tenanted by defamation, all praise is tenanted by blame, all happiness is tenanted by pain.

Here, too, we find *attā* introduced as being utterly incompatible with whatever is *anicca* and *dukkha,* and that is why it cannot find a fitting dwelling place in the world which is entirely occupied by them. And here, too, the reality of *attā* is again contrasted with the unreality of the world, which is said to be essenceless (*asāro*),

Finally, to wind up this section on 'the self as refuge or island', we shall turn towards a stanza in the *Suttanipāta* where those who have the self as island are said to be unattached, entirely free, i.e. aloof from whatever is samsaric which is utterly repugnant to the self:

> The brāhmaṇa who intent on gaining merit would offer sacrifices,
> Should bestow an offering, at the proper time,
> On those who fare in the world with the self as island (*ye attadīpā vicaranti loke*),
> Possessing nothing, freed in every way (*akiñcanā sabbadhi vippamuttā*).[16]

THE SELF IS BEST

Few passages seem more suitable to show the eminent place held by *attā* in the Nikāyas as those centred on the idea that the self is the best and dearest thing for man, and therefore to be preferred to everything else, to be preserved at all costs. In fact *attā* is conceived as having an absolute existential value to which all else ought to surrender, something that becomes the measuring rod for everything that pertains to man. All this seems to point to an inner reality that gives man all the value he has, not a mere conventional idea. While reading such testimonies one finds it impossible to think they were uttered by people who believed in the doctrine of absolute *anattā.*

Let us first take for our consideration that gem of a dialogue between king Pasenadi and his queen consort Mallikā. Mrs. Rhys Davids remarks, 'the Commentary pictures the king seeking a confession of love for himself from the woman he had so benefited, and a confirmation of mutual trust'.[17] He asks her:

Is there by any chance any other dearer to you,
Mallikā, than the self?

The answer is unequivocal:

There is not by any chance any other dearer to me than the self
(*Natthi kho me, mahārāja, kocañño attanā piyataro*).[18]

The queen returns the question to the king who answers in the same strain. After that the king reports the conversation to the Buddha who corroborates the sentiments of the royal couple. The sutta ends with the stanza:

Going around all quarters with the mind,
Not a thing was found dearer than the self
(*nevajjhagā piyataramattanā kvaci*).
In this way the self of every one is dear to others,
Therefore one who loves the self (*attakāmo*) should never hurt another.

It is evident that in the prose part of the sutta the term *attā* has an overwhelming 'spiritual ' implication; otherwise, Mallikā's reply would have been only a mean confession of selfishness, unworthy of the implicit approval that sorrounds the narrative. A true lover is expected, as a matter of course, to say that he or she loves the beloved more than 'himself' or 'herself'. This shows that the translation of *attanā* as 'myself' (which would be the translation preferred by the 'conventionalists') would disfigure the inner meaning of the passage. The only thing that prevented Mallikā and Pasenadi to give an affirmative answer is that they chose to look at *attā,* 'the self', as what ought to be cherished above everything else, without incurring the blame of inordinate 'self-centredness', but as doing what any sensible person ought to do. The same is to be said of *attakāmo,* 'in love of the self', in the metrical part of the sutta. One who loves himself selfishly will not worry about hurting or not hurting others.

The same considerations will apply to a passage where we are told that a deity comes to the Buddha and gives expression to four utterances of worldly wisdom, the first being:

There is no love comparable to that of a son.

The Buddha is reported to have said as repartee:

There is no love comparable to that of the self
(*natthi attasamaṁ pemaṁ*)[19]

If there is no love comparable to the love of the self, then in the matter of 'spiritual' profit *attā* should come first. This is not selfishness but the right order of things. We are told in other parts of the Nikāyas that the ideal is that one should work for the welfare of the self and for the welfare of others,[20] but if one has to choose between the two the welfare of the self ought to get priority:

One should not impair the good of the self,
for the sake of the good of others, however great,
Having ascertained the good of the self,
let him be ever intent on it.[21]

This objective excellence of the self above everything and everybody else makes the ideal of the *paccekasambuddhas* acceptable even though they look only after the self, unconcerned for others, without thereby incurring the blame of selfishness:

The *paccekasambuddha* is given only to the good of the self (*attānaṁ eva poseti*), not of others.[22]

The attā that is looked after exclusively by a *paccekasambuddha* cannot possibly be the merely conventional self, since this would betray a reprehensible selfishness, nor the self of the *sakkāyadiṭṭhi,* which is utterly destroyed in them, but the self that is the highest value in man and which by the very nature of things ought always to get preference.

One watches zealously over what he holds to be dearest. This should apply to the self better than to anything else:

If a man were to think the self dear
(*attānaṁ ce piyaṁ jaññā*),
he would guard it well guarded,
The wise man should be watching in every one
of the three watches of the night.[23]

And what does it mean 'to guard the self', but to preserve it immune from all moral harm, from all samsaric contamination? That is how king Pasenadi explains it while addressing the Buddha:

Lord, while I was meditating in solitude, there arose in my mind the following thoughts. 'By whom is the self guarded, by whom is the self not

> guarded (*kesaṁ nu rakkhito attā, kesaṁ arakkhito attā*)' Then it occurred to me, 'Whoever misbehave by action, by word, or by thought, are those by whom the self is not guarded. Even if they were guarded by a troop of elephants, or of horses, or of chariots, or of infantry men, even so their self would not be guarded by them. Why so? Because their guard is external, not internal, that is why the self is not guarded by them. All who behave properly by action, by word, or by thought, are those by whom the self is guarded. Even if they are not guarded by a troop of elephants, or of horses, or of chariots, or of infantry men, even so the self would be guarded by them. Why so? Because their guard is internal not external, that is why the self is guarded by them.'[24]

The Buddha makes his own Pasenadi's words and adds a short metrical utterance, but the term *attā* does not occur in it.

The translation of *kesaṁ nu rakkhito attā* consonant with the merely conventional value of *attā* would be something like this, 'Who are those who guard themselves?' Would that be a fitting rendering of the passage? The reality to be guarded here is not the external man, but the inner man, who is nothing else but the self

We behold this guard over the self practiced by the two chamberlains of Pasenadi, who come to explain to the Buddha what they call an oppression most annoying. The passage is beautifully translated by F. L. Woodward, but for one important detail, to which reference has been made in the first chapter:

> Here, Lord, when king Pasenadi wants to go ariding in the Park, we have to deck the riding-elephant and set thereon the favourite lovely wives of his majesty, one before and one behind. Now the fragrance of their bodies is so sweet. It is just as if a casket of scent were open, – these royal ladies are so sweetly scented. Lord, the touch of those ladies is as soft to the hand as a tuft of cotton-wool, so delicately are they nurtured. Well, Lord, at such times, we have to ward the elephant, and we have to ward the ladies, and ward ourselves as well (*attā pi rakkhitabbo hoti*). In spite of that, Lord, we are not conscious of calling up any evil thoughts about those ladies. Now, Lord, this is [what we meant by] another oppression still more oppressive, nay, most oppressive.[25]

As any one can see, Woodward has yielded here to the conventionalist way of looking at things and has translated *attā pi rakkhitabbo hoti,* as 'we have to ward ourselves as well', as if the chamberlains had say *attāno pi rakkhitabbā homa.* The text does not give us an oblique case of *attā,* but the very term *attā* (nominative) in all its meaningful splendour. It stands for the spiritual reality of man that is to be kept aloof from any sort of moral perversity.

This guard of the self is illustrated in the *Saṁyutta* by means of the parable of the acrobat and his young attendant, and is given at the same time a social projection. It is by keeping the self safe that we restrain from doing harm to others, thus keeping them also safe.

Before balancing on the bamboo pole, the main acrobat tells his young attendant:

> Now, Medakathālika, my lad, you care for my safety and I shall take care of your safety. Thus we, protected by one another, shall display our tricks, shall get our fee, and climb down safe and sound from the bamboo pole.

The pupil answers:

> No, master, it shall not be thus. You, master, take care of yourself (*attānaṁ rakkha*), and I shall take care of myself (*ahaṁ attānaṁ rakkhisāmi*). Thus we, self-protected (*attaguttā*), self-guarded (*attarakkhitā*), shall display our tricks, shall get our fee, and shall climb down safe and sound from the bamboo pole.

The Buddha's comment on the pupil's words is:

> That pupil was intelligent, inasmuch as he spoke thus to his master.

Then the Buddha applies the physical import of the parable to the 'spiritual' life:

> Bhikkhus, 'I shall keep the self safe' (*attānaṁ rakkhisāmi*), this means that the stations of mindfulness ought to be dwelt upon. 'I shall keep another safe' (*paraṁ rakkhisāmi*), this means that the stations of mindfulness ought to be dwelt upon. Keeping the self safe, bhikkhus, one keeps others safe; keeping others safe, one keeps the self safe. And how, bhikkhus, keeping the self safe one keeps others safe? It is by dwelling upon, by cultivating, by making to grow. And how, bhikkhus, keeping others safe one keeps the self safe? Through forbearance, through harmlessness, through goodwill, through compassion...[26]

Anyone can see the difference between the *attānaṁ* of the first part of the parable and that of the second part. The first *attānaṁ* stands for the physical man, while the second stands for the 'spiritual' man, who has been our concern in the previous pages. No one will object to saying that the first *attānaṁ* is used in a reflexive sense, even though no one can deny that it stands also for a physical reality. The disapproval falls on saying that the *attānaṁ* of the second part has a merely reflexive sense, without referring to a spiritual objective reality. That the second *attānaṁ* has also a reflexive sense is but natural, since such sense is of the very nature of *attā* as explained in the first chapter. It may be said that the first *attānaṁ* has a derivative meaning, while the second one exhibits the primary sense of the word.

The value of the self is asserted in a negative way by the injunction never to despise it. Thus five qualites are given, endowed with which a hearer of the true faith (*saddhamma*) is able to enter on the Way, on the correctness of things;

> He does not despise talk (on *saddhamma*), he does not despise the talker, he does not despise the self (*na attānaṁ paribhoti*), he listens to dhamma with undistracted mind, with one-pointed mind he revolves it systematically in his mind.[27]

This will mean, if given in a positive way, that the appreciation of *attā* is one of the requirements to profit by the teaching of dhamma. One is tempted to ask whether the votaries of absolute *anattā* possess such appreciation of the self.

The self, the dearest thing for man, becomes an absolute value, which has to be preserved by all means and in preference to everything else:

> What should a man desirous of his own good never give up?
> What should mortal man never surrender?

The answer is:

> Man should never give up the self (*attānaṁ na dade poso*),
> he should never surrender the self (*attānaṁ na pariccaje*).[28]

Being the absolute value for man, *attā* becomes the measure of things moral, and in that sense it appears equated with *dhamma,* an undercurrent of thought present in other parts of the Nikāyas.

> One should not transgress against the self (*attānaṁ nātivatteyya*),
> One should not undertake any wrong (*adhammaṁ na samācare*),
> He should not cross where there is no crossing place,
> He should not apply himself to evil.[29]

The absolute value of *attā* makes it a foregone conclusion that it should be sufficient for man. Man ought to find satisfaction in it, without looking for gratification in things external to it,

He for whom the self alone is not enough (*yassattā nālameko va*),
Who procures for himself the taste of all sensual pleasures,
Even if the whole world were his,
He would not obtain happiness.[30]

The second *pāda, sabbakāmarasāharo,* can very well be applied to *attā* as 'one that brings with itself the taste of all desires', i.e. is fully satisfying. All things without the self are unable to bring happiness, the self alone, without anything else can bring it. How to give to *yass'attā n'ālam'éko va* the merely reflexive sense that the conventionalists attribute everywhere to *attā?* They would have to translate the *pāda* as, 'he for whom he himself alone is not enough'. This translation would not reproduce the subtle distinction that the text makes between *yassa* an *attā. Attā* here is rather something that stands by itself, an objective reality even in its essential subjectivity. This will apply also to several of the testimonies that follow, where *attā* occurs in the nominative case.

Another reference to *attā*'s full sufficiency is found in the *Therīgāthā,* where it is given as a compelling reason to return to a life of celibacy by a wanderer who had abandoned it.

If the self is sufficient for me (*yadi me attā sakkoti*),
I have had enough of this (*alaṁ mayhaṁ*),
I cannot bear to stay in one house with Isidāsī.[31]

This intrinsic 'self-sufficiency' of *attā* leads us to consider its relation to other external acquisitions. Properly speaking, the only real possession of the self is the self itself. All else is external to it as we shall see in the second part of the book where we shall meet time and again with testimonies saying that nothing else can be said to belong to the self in the deepest and ultimate sense. The ontological autonomy of the self is the foundation of its moral autonomy and furnishes the ultimate reason for the absolute detachment preached by the Nikāyas. In practice this is the only ontological consideration regarding the self in which the Nikāyas are interested. We may say it is the principle and foundation of the moral training preached by the Nikāyas.

I have sons, I have wealth, thus the fool hurts himself,

> But since the self [in him] is not the possession of the self (*attā hi attano natthi*], how can sons, how can wealth [be his possessions]?[32]

In all this we can detect an implicit avowal of the doctrine of relative *anattā.*

External acquisition can have some value, a relative value of course, only after one has secured the self:

> 'This is not pleasing to me', a man who says this,
> Repudiating the self (*attaṁ niraṅkatvā*) cherishes what he finds dear,
> The self is the best (*attā va seyyo*) and the best is the highest,
> Acquisitions can be dear after having secured the self (*ocitattena pacchā*).[33]

Due to the excellence of the self, as compared to all other acquisitions, no loss, however great, can be compared to the loss of the self,

> Insignificant is this bad luck,
> When one playing dice looses his wealth.
> This is the greatest bad luck,
> The loss of everything together with the self
> (*sabbasā pi sahā pi attanā*),
> Of one who makes his mind inimical to the saints.[34]

If the self is the best and highest in man, and that is so on the ontological order of things, it is utterly absurd that one should behave as if the self were his enemy by practicing evil.

> Lord, while I was meditating in solitude, there arose in my mind the following thoughts. 'For whom is the self a dear friend, for whom is the self a hateful enemy (*kesaṁ nu kho piyo attā, kesaṁ appiyo attā*)?' Then it occurred to me, 'Whoever misbehave by action, by word or by thought, are those for whom the self is a hateful enemy. Even if they were to say, "the self is our dear friend", even so the self would be to them a hateful enemy. Why so? Whatever one who hates would do to the one he hates, that is what they themselves (*attanā*) do to the self (*attano*). That is why the self is a hateful enemy to them. Whoever behave properly by action by word or by thought, are those for whom the self is a dear friend. Even if they were to say, "the self is our hateful enemy", even so the self would be their dear friend. Why so? Whatever one who loves would do to the one he loves, that is what they themselves do to the self. That is why the self is a dear friend to them.'[35]

One of the important characteristics of primitive Buddhism stands out here. Primitive Buddhism did not approve either of a merely speculative interest in the self or of an uncommited love for the self above everything else. Genuine love for the self ought to be shown not in feelings or in words but in deeds. This is concisely expressed in the first line of the metrical part of the same sutta:

If he would recognize the self as a dear friend (*attānaṁ ce piyaṁ jaññā*),
he would not associate it with evil.

Quite clearly, in this line, *attānaṁ* has no mere reflexive sense. The pronoun *naṁ* that substitutes for it in the second pāda (*na naṁ pāpena saṁyuje*) has no reflexive sense, but shows the *attā* in the preceding *attānaṁ* as something objective.

Similar is the lesson taught in:

The fool and unwise get on with a self that is like an enemy (*amitteneva attanā*),
While they practise evil deeds, that have a bitter fruit.[36]

And in:

He whose evil conduct is exceeding great, like a sal-tree overspread by a creeper,
Causes the self to be such as his enemy would wish it to be.[37]

The love for the self above everything else supplies the rationale for the virtue of *ahiṁsā.* The principle involved here is that *attā* is the dearest thing for every being. Therefore one should never do harm to others, seing that they feel in the same way, regarding their own respective selves, as he feels regarding his own self. This is called the *ātmaupamya bhāva.*[38]

It is only proper that the self should be considered the dearest thing for man, but such love should be free from any admixture of 'selfishness', untarnished by any asmimanic feeling. *Asmimāna* is the primary product of the identification of the self with the *khandhas,* i.e. the non-self.

IN LOVE WITH THE SELF

If the self is the dearest thing for man, it naturally follows that love of self, barring of course any admixture of *asmimāna,* is something commendable. One term used to convey this idea is *attakāmo,* which may be translated as 'one who is in love with the self'. The compound is made up of two parts highly offensive to later Buddhist thought. This alone seems to guarantee its antiquity. *Attā* is a term brought into disrepute by the later belief in absolute *anattā*. *Kāma* is a term of which we read in the *Pāli Text Society's Pāli-English Dictionary:* 'In all enumerations of obstacles to perfection or of general divisions and definitions of mental conditions, *kāma* occupies the leading position'.[39] The term *kāma* is used also to connote desirable worldly and heavenly bliss, but always within the circle of rebirth and therefore to be spurned by the wise. The term *atthakāma* may very well be acceptable to Buddhism by all standards, not so *attakāma* when placed on the background of later Buddhist thought.[40] *Attakāma,* inasmuch as it points to a man of lofty aspirations is more in line with the upanishadic epithets, *ātmakriḍa, ātmarati*[41] and, of course, *ātmakāma.*[42] That in spite of so many difficulties the compound *attakāma* should have been preserved gives it a very special value.

Attakāma occurs in a context where Brahmā Sahampati refers to the fact that it is the norm of the Buddhas to show respect and veneration for the true norm (*saddhamma*). He concludes:

> Therefore the true norm should be respected by the lover of the self (*attakāmena*),
> By one who aspires to greatness, recalling the teaching of the Buddhas.[43]

The same śloka is found somewhere else, with exactly the same context, but with the difference that a prose colophon is appended to it.[44] The words of the colophon are attributed to the Buddha and are such as to confirm the higher meaning of *attakāmena:*

> Then, bhikkhus, finding this was Brahmā's will and that it was fitting to the self (*attano ca patirūpaṁ*), I dwelt honouring, paying homage to, serving that very dhamma that had been fully comprehended by me.[45]

The *śloka* that is now occupying us shows a very special relationship between *attā* and dhamma, a relationship to which reference has already been made. The lover of the self ought, just because he is a lover of the self, to show great respect to the dhamma. This close relationship is also brought out by the words, *attano ca patirūpaṁ,* where dhamma seems to be considered the counterpart (that is the literal meaning of *patirūpaṁ*) of *attā.* All this gives a positive sensation that the term *attā* is endowed in the text with a more meaningful connotation than just the merely conventional one.

This close affinity between *attā,* as the highest value in man, and dhamma is also exhibited in another context, where it is spoken of taking advantage of a Buddha having come into the world, of the good norm being preached and of having been born as a man in such auspicious circumstances,

> To be sure, effort has to be made by the lover of the self (*attakāmena*),
> How he may come to know the good norm and not let the opportunity (lit. 'moment') pass.[46]

The significant appelation *attakāmarūpā* is used by the keeper of the Bamboo Grove in relation to Anuruddha and his companions. He tried to prevent the Buddha, unknown to himself, from entering the grove so that he might not disturb the three holy men. He speaks of them as:

> Three young men of good families stay here in the likeness of those who are in love with the self (*attakāmarūpā*).
> Do not disturb them.[47]

Here the term is meant to summarize the motives that three young men of noble birth had to leave the world and dedicate themselves with ardour and resolution to an intense purification of the highest degree. They did so because they were lovers of the self. Would it do to say that those three young men had chosen that lofty manner of life just because they were 'lovers of themselves'?

Lastly there occurs another compound of similar import as that of *attakāma,* used in a very suggestive context. The compound is *ajjhattarato,* which may be very well translated as, 'in love with the inner self'. The context speaks of the very moment when the Buddha entered into parinibbāna.

> Thereupon the Exalted One, at Cāpāla Shrine, mindful and self-possessed let go his life's aggregate (*āyusaṅkhāraṁ*). And when the life's aggregate was let go by the Blessed One there was a mighty earthquake, and there burst a terrific hair-raising thunder. And then the Blessed One, knowing this to be its meaning, at that time, uttered these solemn words,
> Weighing the immeasurable and becoming, the sage rejected the aggregate of his becoming,

> In love with the inner self (*ajjhattarato*), well composed, split his individual existence (*attasambhavaṁ*) as if it were an armour.[48]

At the very moment when the Buddha was about to attain the highest aim of the holiest of existences, we are told that he was *ajjhattarato,* 'in love with the inner self', and therefore integrated with it (*samāhito*). This is naturally opposed to what he consciously rejected there and then, to wit the aggregate of his becoming and his individual existence (*attasaṁbhava*) which he split as if it were an armour. The simile is that of a man encased in an armour, as in a metal shell, who breaks the armour, makes it fall in pieces, and sets himself free. Who is here set free but the one who is in perfect communion with the self (*ajjhattarato*), perfectly integrated (*samāhito*) and what from is he set free but from what is the non-self? Another flash of light is made to converge here on the polarity between the self and the non-self, that constitutes the main theme of the Nikāyas.
Obviously the one who is set free in perfect communion with the self is not in the last analysis different from the self itself. We cannot express this things unless we avail ourselves of this ambivalent way of speaking, which is not meant to destroy the essential unity of man. In fine, we are confronted here with someone, the Buddha, the muni, setting himself (his self!) free from the aggregate of existence, and we are told that he was at that very moment "in love with the inner self," a strange disposition indeed for one whose main message is supposed to have been that of absolute *anattā.*

LOOK FOR THE SELF

Another context where *attā* is used with such emphasis as to convey quite naturally the meaning of a deep reality, not of a merely conventional idea, is the one of the *Mahāvagga,*[49] where a group of young people are made to confess that it would be better for them to go in search of the self than in search of a prostitute, who had run away after stealing their belongings. Here, as in other contexts, we find a very meaningful transition from the physical to the 'spiritual', and the reality of the former seems to point to the reality of the latter.
The words of the Buddha are:

Then what do you think, yougsters, what is the best for you, that you go in search of a woman or that you go in search of the self (*yaṁ vā attānaṁ gaveseyyatha*)?

The youngsters reply:

This, Lord, is the best for us, that we go in search of the self (*yaṁ mayaṁ attānaṁ gaveseyyāma*).

This is one of the cases where clearly enough the translation of *attānaṁ* as 'yourselves' and 'ourselves' cuts the edge off the meaningful expression and renders it colourless. Such text like this, read without prejudice and taken in the natural way in which it was uttered, implies the highest possible reality of the self, a reality diligently to be sought and found and the finding of which, as we are going to see is equivalent to liberation. A strange way of preaching for a master who had come, according to many, first and foremost with the message of absolute *anattā*. In fact, as we shall see in the second part of the book, the *anattā* doctrine which he preached is meant to help the chosen ones better to find *attā,* since it shows what is not *attā* and how to discard it.

There have been scholars who have singled out this text as possibly teaching the reality of *attā,* but I know of no one who has called the attention of the reader to the whole context of the passage. The conclusion drawn by the Buddha in the dialogue quoted above is:

Therefore, youngsters, sit down, I shall teach you *dhamma.*

Does this not imply that hearing *dhamma* and putting it into practice leads to the finding of the self? Another implicit reference to the already mentioned affinity existing between the self and *dhamma.* And what kind of *dhamma* did the Buddha teach to those young people who had agreed to go in search of the self? If we are going to believe the narrator, the Buddha explained to them the whole of dhamma in a systematic manner, not only the 'popular' part of the dhamma, but also its superior part that leads to realization. The first part would be constituted by talk on charity (*dāna*), virtue and morality (*sīla*), heavenly rewards (*saggo*). The second part would comprehend talk on the Way (*maggo*), on the dangers of sense pleasures, on the degradation of sinfulness or impurity, on the advantages of renunciation. And when the Buddha knew that they had developed the right disposition of mind, he taught them the four Noble Truths, and the teaching developed in the young men, while still sitting there, the *dham-*

macakkhu, whereby they saw that 'whatever is of a nature to arise, all that is of a nature to cease (*yaṁ kiñci samudayadhammaṁ, sabbaṁ taṁ nirodhadhammaṁ*)'. They understood the dhamma and were freed from all doubt, fully satisfied, not relying on anybody else as regards the teaching. Finally they asked for renunciation and ordination, which were granted to them by the Master with the words, 'Well preached is the dhamma, live the holy life (*brahmacariya*) for the complete extermination of Pain (*sammā dukkhassa antakiriyāya*)'.

If there is to be a logical sequence of ideas in the passage, this will mean that by understanding the dhamma, renouncing the world, being ordained, and going towards the complete destruction of pain, those young people had found the self or were set on the right path to find it. Is it not a paradox that the arisal of the *dhammacakkhu* with the full comprehension that 'whatever is of a nature to arise, all that is of a nature to cease', a formula always considered to be the dogmatic basis for universal impermanence and therefore for the denial of *attā,* should have been in this instance instrumental for the finding of the self?

Akin to the above exhortation to look for the self is the exhortation imparted by the Buddha to Paṭācārā, who had lost her closest relatives in death:

Then the master told me:
'Daughter, be not afflicted, console yourself,
Look for your self (*attānaṁ te gavesassu*). Why are you feeling miserable to no purpose?
There is no refuge in children, in relatives and acquaintances,
For one who has been seized by death there is no refuge in relatives'.[50]

The text seems to suggest again that the only refuge providing real security is the self. Here too the result of the exhortation, 'look for your self', is the attainment of the highest, just as in the account of the *Mahāvagga.* The result here is:

Hearing that utterance of the sage, I obtained the first fruit,
Having renounced the world not long after, I attained arahantship.

In line with the preceding texts is that in which Ubbiri tells us how she was remonstrated by the Buddha when she could not be consoled at the death of her daughter:

'My dear Jīvā', thus saying you bewail in the forest,

Find the self (*attānaṁ adhigaccha*), Ubbiri,
Eighty four thousand, all named Jīvā,
Have been cremated in this cemetery, for whom among them are you mourning?[51]

Here again we have someone looking for other people and being advised by the Buddha to search for the self. And here too the final result of the search for the self is the highest attainment:

He pulled out my dart, difficult to see, rooted in the heart,
He expelled from me the sorrow for my daughter, by which I was overcome,
And today, with the dart pulled out, I am desireless, having attained perfect *nibbāna* (*parinibbutā*).

Are these striking points of similarity between the three passages studied in this section mere random coincidence or more than that?

PACCATTAṀ

Paccattaṁ is one of those compounds that must needs be taken into account when trying to give a complete evaluation of the usages of the term *attā* in the Nikāyas. The corresponding term in Sanskrit has what may be called 'a distributive sense', i.e., 'for every soul or in every soul'. The *P.T.S.*'s *Pāli-English Dictionary* lists the following meanings for the word, 'separately, individually, singly, by himself, in his own heart'. By adding 'in his own heart', the compilers betray the conviction that a mere distributive sense does not exhaust the meaning of the term in the Pāli texts, that it connotes at times an idea of intimacy, which may be said to be of the highest degree, referring 'to the very self'. According to G. C. Pande, 'in Paccatta Attā seems to have the sense of the individual', but adding in a note a passage of which he says, 'the following passage seems to support Mrs. Rhys Davids' interpretation...'[52] There are also other passages similar to the one quoted by G. C. Pande and another set of passages can be pointed out that are much more expressive.

That *paccattaṁ* in Pāli does not necessarily have a distributive sense is evident from a passage in the *Pācittiya.* A rule found there says:

Whatever bhikkhunī should curse self (*attānaṁ*) or another with reference to hell and with reference to the holy life, incurs an offence of expiation.

The commentary or *vibhaṅga* explains:

attānaṁ ti paccattaṁ.[53]

Here *paccattaṁ* is given as equivalent to *attānaṁ* and referring therefore to an individual as opposed to others, where no distributive sense can be discovered.

The passage of which G. C. Pande says that it seems to support Mrs. Rhys Davids' interpretation is found in the *Nidānasaṁyutta.* There, Paviṭṭha questions Musila:

Is it so that independently from faith, independently from any bias, independently from tradition, independently from examination of reasons, independently from the acceptance of understanding of speculations, there is for the venerable Musila in his very self (*paccattameva*) the knowledge that old age and death are conditioned by birth?[54]

The question is addressed to a single bhikkhu, hence the possibility of the distributive sense of *paccattaṁ* does not arise. On the other hand, the emphatic *paccattam' eva* demands the highest kind of intimacy, to be found nowhere but in the very self, to which the *attā* in *paccattaṁ* refers. This reference to the self is found in a noteworthy context. The self is presented here as the ultimate subject of realization, by means of superior wisdom, regarding the *paṭiccasamuppāda* presumed to be one of the strongest foundations for absolute *anattā.*

The same kind of innermost, 'personal' realization is demanded by contexts that speak of the dhamma to be experienced by the wise in their very self:

And besides, Mahānāma, the ariyan disciple brings to mind *dhamma,* 'Well explained has been the *dhamma* by the Blessed One, the *dhamma* that bears fruit here and now, not subject to time [for results], that invites every man to come and see for himself, leading to the highest good, to be experienced by the wise in their very self (*paccattaṁ veditabbo viññūhi*).[55]

We find again the emphatic expression, *paccattaññeva,* in:

Bhikkhus, wise and mindful, develop a boundless concentration. A fivefold knowledge arises in their very self (*paccattaññeva*) in the case of

> those who, wise and mindful develop a boundless concentration. What fivefold knowledge? 'This concentration is pleasant at present and will yield a pleasant karmic result (*sukhavipāko*) in the future', such knowledge arises in their very self, 'This concentration is noble, entirely "spiritual"', such knowledge arises in their very self; 'This concentration is not practiced by an unworthy man',...; 'This concentration is peaceful, excellent, obtained by the pacified man, attained by means of mental fixity, not subject to the blame of the saṅkhāras',...; 'I too mindful enter into it and mindful I emerge from it', such knowledge arises in their very self.[56]

The same value as to *paccattam'eva* or *paccattañ'ñeva* is to be attributed to *attapaccakkha.*

> The dhamma that has been known in a personal way (*sāmaṁ*), all by oneself (*sayaṁ*), perceived in the very self (*attapaccakkhaṁ*) does not rest on faith to others, be they samaṇas, brāhmaṇas, a deva, Māra, or Brahmā.[57]

As indicated above, there are still much more expressive texts where the emphatic *paccattam'eva,* or a similar one, is used. In them, by means of the said expression the attainment of *nibbāna* is linked with the very self. Let us not forget that we have already reviewed, in the preceding sections of this chapter, other texts where the self was involved in attaining the highest good.

> He [thus] dwelling contemplating impermanence in those feelings, contemplating dispassion, contemplating cessation, contemplating renunciation, does not grasp at anything in the world, and not grasping he is not perturbed, not being perturbed he attains utter *nibbāna* in his very self (*paccattaṁyeva parinibbāyati*). He knows 'Destroyed is birth, lived is the holy life, done is what was to be done, there will be no more of thus-conditioned existence'.[58]

It appears wholly unacceptable to translate *paccattaṁyeva parinibbāyati* as, 'he attains utter nibbāna just individually', while the translation 'attains nibbāna in the very self', seems to do full justice to the context.[59]

> Singular importance is to be ascribed to the following *paccattaññeva,*
> Even so, brother, a bhikkhu does not see the self or what pertains to the self in the six spheres of sense. So seing he is not attached to anything in the world. Not being attached he is not perturbed. Not being per-

> turbed he attains utter *nibbāna* in his very self (*paccattaññeva parinibbāyati*). 'Destroyed is birth...', this he knows.[60]

The singularity of the context consists in that the assertion of *attā* contained in *paccattaññeva* follows a clear admission of what we have termed relative *anattā,* as if there was no contradiction between the two.

AJJHATTAṀ

Ajjhattaṁ is another compound whose study is a must for one who aspires to a complete view of the use and meaning of the term *attā* in the Nikāyas. As an introduction to our study let us quote G. C. Pande:

> The conclusion that Buddha believed in the Ātman has been sought to be enforced by the argument that there are some compound words which there is some reason to suppose early and yet in which the word Attan seems to be used in a sense different from that of the man as a complex of body and mind only. Such are Ajjhatta, Paccatta, Attabhāva, Pahitatta and Bhāvitatta. In the case of the first compound alone, however, has the argument some weight. Although later Ajjhatta came to be just the inner as opposed to the outer and condemned equally along with it, in some uses, apparently early, it is given a place of value. Man in withdrawing into himself obviously neared something which was prized. This would be difficult to understand were the man no more than an impermanent aggregate.[61]

Pande's assertion that only in the case of *ajjhatta* has the argument for the Buddha's belief in the Ātman some weight should be counterbalanced by the evidence just adduced in the foregoing section regarding *paccattaṁ* and by the evidence that will be adduced in the rest of the book, regarding other compounds. Such evidence should not be valued in isolation from, but together with, all the evidence accumulated throughout this book, which should induce scholars to display a more positive approach to this subject than has been customary in the past.

The second point that Pande makes is of importance. 'Man in withdrawing into himself obviously neared something that was prized.' Why should man's intimacy become the rallying point for his highest 'spiritual' aspirations and activities if there was nothing in man beyond an impermanent assemblage of samsaric factors, physical as well as mental, when he is continually being told in the Nikāyas to shun whatever is impermanent, and therefore painful, and hence not the self? Nevertheless we have reported above that it is said of the Buddha, when he was just attaining utter nibbāna that the *muni*, 'in love with his inner self (*ajjhattarato*), well composed, split his individual [samsaric] existence (*attasambhavaṁ*), as if it were an armour'.[62] It is clear that in this text *ajjhattarato* or better the *ajjhatta* of *ajjhattarato* is the opposite of *attasambhava,* which in the context stands for the samsaric phenomena in man's existence.

The *P.T.S.'s Pāli-English Dictionary* translates *ajjhattarato* as 'with inward joy'. That would be, if at all, the translation of *ajjhattaratī. Rato* means 'attached to, in love with'. If man is merely an unstable bundle of *khandhas,* what is there within him that can justify the complete attachment and dedication conveyed by *ajjhattarato,* specially when the man in question, here the Buddha, is about to attain *nibbāna?*

Ajjhattarato occurs also in the definition of a bhikkhu found in the *Dhammapada,* which doubtless refers to an ideal and perfect bhikkhu:

Controlled as to his hands, controlled as to his feet,
Controlled as to his speech, the best among those practising control,
In love with the inner self (*ajjhattarato*), well composed,
Satisfied in solitude, him they call a bhikkhu.[63]

Similar in character is the expression, *ajjhattaṁ ramaye mano* in:

When the mind is gladdened it becomes alert, well balanced,
And that is the time of quietude, let him make the mind disport in the inner self (*ajjhattaṁ ramaye mano*).[64]

Whatever has been said of *ajjhattarato* can be applied to *ajjhattacintī.* We read in the *Suttanipāta,*

With a mind turned to the inner self (*ajjhattacintī*),
he should not let his mind go forth to outward things,
He who by character is controlled as to the self (*saṅgahitattabhāvo*).[65]

We seem to have here the self on one side, outward things on the other side, and the mind in the centre being directed towards the self, and that is how one becomes controlled as to the self.

Ajjhattacintī is again used in a context where the one who is such is supposed to be in a condition to cross the current of saṁsāra and attain salvation:

Proficient in morality in every way, full of wisdom, well composed,
With a mind turned to the inner self (*ajjhattacintī*), watchful, he goes across the current difficult to cross.[66]

Mention should also be made of part of a text to be quoted in full when dealing with the purity of the self:

I, leaving side the burning of wood, brāhmaṇa,
Cause to burst only the flames of a fire which is the very self (*ajjhattame-vujjalayāmi jotiṁ*),
With fire constantly burning, always with a self well composed,
I, an arahant, live my brahma-life.[67]

That *ajjhattam'eva* refers to the very self is proved by the words that come not long after, 'the self well tamed is the flame of man' (*attā sudanto purisassa joti*).

In the previous context, a contrast was drawn between outward ritualism and inner spiritual reality. Similar to this in import is a passage from the *Saṁyutta* where *ajjhattaṁ* seems to stand also for the inner 'spiritual' reality in opposition to the outward man. Nandaka, minister of the Licchavis came to see the Buddha. While he was listening to the Master's teaching there came one to announce that the time for his bath had come. The minister's reply was:

I say, let alone for the present that sort of external bath. I will be satisfied with this 'spiritual' bath of the very self (*ajjhattaṁ*), to wit, faith in the Blessed One.[68]

To the external man we find here opposed the inner man, the agent and beneficiary of salvation, the source and aim of all 'spiritual' activities.

One thing is certain, *ajjhattaṁ* always implies some degree of interiority or intimacy and in this sense is always liable to be opposed to *bahiddhā* or *bāhira*. But it is left to further appreciation to determine the degree of interiority or intimacy that the term assumes in a given context. Does it refer to the innermost core of man's personality or merely to the inner layers of his existential periphery? We have so far adduced some texts where the interiority or intimacy connoted by the term seems to be the deepest one, corresponding to the Sanskrit *adhyātma*, which as a noun means 'the indwelling supreme Spirit', as an adjective means 'belonging to the self', and as an adverb means 'concerning the self'. In the Nikāyas the usual form is *ajjhattaṁ*, which even though at times seems to be an adjective (*ajjhattaṁ nahānaṁ* in the last quoted text as opposed to *bāhirena nahānena*), at other times is clearly an adverb (as in *viharati ajjhattaṁ vūpasantacitto*[69]). When indisputably used as an adjective it assumes the form *ajjhattika.* Therefore it should be kept in mind that the presence of *ajjhattaṁ* near an accusative or a neuter noun does not thereby make it an adjective, it may very well be an adverb to be understood as 'concerning the self or in the very self', if the greatest degree of intimacy seems demanded by the context.

Nothing is more intimate to man, on the experiential level (not the ontological one) than the mind, and nothing affects him existentially more than his mental activities, which in our case embrace not only his intellectual operations but also his emotional and volitional reactions. Many an instance may be singled out of *ajjhattaṁ* being used in connection with the mind. In those cases, when *ajjhattaṁ* is explicitly opposed to *bahiddhā,* it may have just the meaning of 'inwardly', and nothing more. Such may be the following passage, where the context speaks of seven qualities that make a monk in a short time realize by himself (*sayaṁ*) the fourfold analytical knowledge. Two of the items are:

> When the mind is inwardly recollected (*ajjhattaṁ saṅkhittaṁ*) he knows as it really is, 'my mind is inwardly recollected'; when his mind is outwardly distracted (*bahiddhā vikkkhittaṁ*) he knows as it really is, 'my mind is outwardly distracted'.[70]

But in this case, too, one might say that even as *bahiddhā* has a meaning of direction, indicating the trend of the mind when it is dispersed among, or distracted with the things of sense, so too, analogically, *ajjhattaṁ* will also have a sense of direction, indicating the trend of the mind when it is focussed inwards, that is towards the innermost man, 'towards the very self', this being etymologically the meaning of *ajjhattaṁ.*

When *ajjhattaṁ* is used with reference to the mind, without being opposed to *bahiddhā,* one may say that there is no obvious need to tell us that the mind and its activities are inner to man. Therefore if *ajjhattaṁ* is used in those cases merely with the meaning of 'inwardly', 'interiorly', etc., it becomes just a redundant expression that adds no shade of meaning to the passage. If any specific meaning is to be attributed to it, it ought to be no other than its primary meaning, 'concerning the self'. But this alone will not persuade a convinced 'conventionalist'. Take, for instance:

The paccekasambuddha is one who enjoys solitude, a lover of solitude, addicted to peace of mind in the very self (*ajjhattaṁ*), diligent in meditation, endowed with insight, one who takes keen delight in solitude, a contemplative, a lover of contemplation, addicted to [inward] integration (*ekattaṁ*), gravid with the highest good.[71]

Here we have a perfect man who has discarded all that is samsaric, who has suppressed all mental dissipation, and ever given to meditation is entirely intent on 'oneness' (*ekattaṁ*). What can this 'One' be on which he is intent. Certainly not anything belonging to the *khandhas* which he has repudiated. Of him we are told that he is, *ajjhattaṁ cetosamatham'anuyutto.* If we translate this as, 'addicted to inward peace of mind', the word 'inward' becomes redundant, since, from the point of view of the paccekasambbhuda, there cannot be any 'outward' peace of mind. Will it not be preferable to translate the phrase as, 'addicted to peace of mind in the very self'?

The aforesaid considerations will apply with greater cogency to the emphatic form, *ajjhattam'eva* or *ajjattañ'ñeva.* Thus we find in F. L. Woodward's translation:

Once more, your reverences, a monk's mind is utterly cleared of perplexities about Dhamma. That is the time, your reverences, when his thought (*cittaṁ*) stands fixed in the very self (*ajjhattameva*), settles down, becomes one pointed, is composed.[72]

And again:

By the thought, 'I shall complete the higher practice of the training where incomplete, or if complete I shall supplement it here and there by wisdom'-mindfulness in the very self (*ajjhattaṁyeva*) is well set up.[73]

There are other usages of *ajjhattaṁ* in connection with good and bad qualities, with virtues and vices, which have the same value as the corresponding usages of *attā* as the moral agent, i.e., as related to moral good and moral evil, with which we shall deal later on in the book. That *ajjhattaṁ* from this point of view is synonymous with *attā* is proved in the following text, where *ajjhattaṁ* is opposed to *añño,* an opposition typical of *attā* in so many passages of the Nikāyas:

Let the bhikkhu become calm in the self (*ajjhattaṁ*),
Let him not look for quietude from another,
For one who is calm in the self (*ajjhattaṁ*),

> Nothing is assumed nor therefore rejected.[74]

A number of illustrations could be brought in of *ajjhattaṁ* standing for *attā* as the moral agent.[75] We shall bring into focus just one, where *ajjhattaṁ* stands for the self entirely purified in its relation to *nibbāna,*

> Then feeling disgust for the body, freeing myself from passion as regards the self (*ajjhattaṁ*),
> Not slothful, fully detached, entirely calmed, I attained *nibbāna.*[76]

3

The Self as the Moral Agent

The self as the moral agent is not being introduced here for the first time. The self has been shown acting as the moral agent practically all throughout the preceding chapter. It is incontrovertible that we shall be able to speak of the self in positive terms only in so far as we experience it involved in the realm of the empirical. What is metempirical is, by its very nature, inexpressible. On the other hand, this involvement of the self in what is empirical is radically the cause of our samsaric existence. To try to break this involvement and attain liberation constitutes what may be called the 'moral' activity of the self, taking the term 'moral' in its broadest sense, not identical with the term 'ethical'. Such moral activity of the self is meant to lead, through an ever more refined purification and detachment (both things are ultimately the same) to the summit of purification and detachment that is *nibbāna.*

We have already spoken of the multiple ambivalence of our experience of the self. One of the aspects of this ambivalence is that the self can freely choose to follow either the right or the wrong path. Therefore it will be necessary to study separately, following the testimony of the Nikāyas. the relation of the self to moral evil and the relation of the self to moral good and perfection.

The denial of the reality of the metaphysical self led, very logically indeed, to the denial of the reality of the moral self. The final attitude in this respect is unambiguously expressed in the *Visuddhimagga:*

For there is ill but none to feel it;
For there is action but no doer;
And there is peace but none to enjoy it;
A way there is, but no one goes it (*gamako*).[1]

Let us see whether the way of speaking of the Nikāyas leaves any room for this conclusion of a sophisticated system that in course of time arrived at the denial of all reality in the man who had been established from the beginning at the centre of things.

MORAL ENERGY OF THE SELF

In the first place, we shall turn our attention to some passages that speak openly of the moral energy of the self in general.

Kassapa, the heretical teacher, denied the existence of sin and merit. Both are referred in a negative way to the self in a *śloka* that succintly gives an exposition of the heresy:

Herein in mutilating or slaying, in killing or plundering,
Kassapa does not see either sin or merit for the self (*puññaṁ vā pana attano*).[2]

Considering that the *śloka* describes a heresy and the heresy denies either sin or merit for the self, it follows that, according to orthodox doctrine, *attā* as the moral agent, can be the cause of sin or of merit.

We find also a summary description in verse of Makkhali Gosāla's heresy where explicit reference is made to the deeds of the self:

Those who say there is no energy, those who teach the absence of cause,
Those who proclaim as vain other people's actions and the actions of the self (*parakāraṁ attakārañ'ca*),
Are bad men in the world, foolish held to be wise,
A man like them will commit sin and make others commit it.[3]

In the *Sandakasutta* of the *Majjhima* we have the reaction of Buddhism to the four heretical opinions of Ajita Kesakambala, Purāṇa Kassapa, Makkhali Gosāla, and Pakudha Kaccāyana. All of them deny either the moral causality of the self, or his inner strength and freedom of choice as regards good an evil. Thus we are told by Kesakambala that 'there is no fruit or result of good or bad actions... both fool and wise men, after the dissolution of the body, are annihilated, are destroyed, do not exist beyond death'. Kassapa is of opinion that 'no sin is committed by one who acts or makes another act, by one who mutilates or makes another mutilate, etc.', and, after mentioning other sinful actions tells us that 'there is no sin as a result of that, no sin takes place', adding that 'there is no merit regarding charity, self-control, and restraint, no merit takes place'. Gosāla asserts that 'there is no reason, no cause, for the defilement of beings... there is no reason, no cause, for the purification of beings, there is no [inner] strength, no [inner] potency... living beings are powerless, strengthless, devoid of vigour, evolving in a series of existences ruled by necessity; through the six types of men they experience pain and happiness'. Finally, Kaccâyana comes to the conclusion that 'both fool and wise men, having transmigrated, after going through one existence after another, will make an end of pain'. The reaction of Buddhism in every case is the same:

> If the word of this good master be true, then what is done in this respect is done without me, what is accomplished in this respect is accomplished without me. Besides, both of us are the same in this respect, when both of us may have embraced the condition of a samaṇa, although I do not say that 'after the dissolution of the body, both of us will be annihilated, will perish, will not come to be after death', (or 'although I do not say that sin is not committed in the case of both of us doing [what is wrong]', or 'although I do not say that both of us will be purified without reason, without cause', or 'although I do not say that both of us, [merely] after having transmigrated, after going through one existence after another will make an end of pain'). And then it surpasses all measure in the case of this good master the state of nudity, of being shaved, of exerting while squatting, of plucking the hair and beard; while I, occupying a couch crowded with sons, enjoying Kāsi's sandalwood, being adorned with garlands, perfumes, and unguents, acquiring gold and silver, will fare the same as this good master regarding a future destiny. What knowing, what seing, would I myself undertake the brahma-life under this master? This life is a non-brahma-life'. Realizing this, he goes away disgusted with that brahma-life.[4]

This is an eloquent admission of the reality of the moral agent as depositary of inner strength and freedom of choice. Without this, a life of renunciation and spiritual endeavour becomes senseless and even absurd.

The Nikayan view of the case is given us in those lines of the *Suttanipāta*:

> It is by the self that evil is done, it is by the self that one is impure,
> It is by the self that one avoids evil, it is by the self (*attanā*) that one is purified,
> Purity and impurity depend on the self (*paccattaṁ*), no one could purify another.[5]

In a passage of the *Aṅguttara,* the Buddha is introduced confronting those who say: (1) whatever we experience, either weal or woe, or neither weal nor woe, is due to some previous action (*pubbekatahetu*); (2) whatever we experience..., is due to the creative activity of a supreme deity (*issaranimmānahetu*); and (3) whatever we experience..., happens without any previous cause or condition (*ahetuappaccaya*). He argues against these views saying that, if they were true, man would commit sinful deeds either through the irresistible influence of a previous *kamma,* or through the necessitating will of a creator, or sinful actions would happen by themselves, without there being any reason for their coming into existence. And, in every case, he concludes with the same forceful expressions:

> Now, bhikkhus, for those who have recourse to previous *kamma* (or to the creative volition of a god, or to the absence of all cause or condition), as to the truth of the matter (*sārato*) there is neither will (*chando*), nor effort (*vāyamo*), nor 'this ought to be done this ought not to be done' (*idaṁ vā karaṇīyaṁ idaṁ vā akaraṇīyaṁ*). Thus there not being truly and verily the possibility of [freely] doing or not doing, the title 'samaṇa' cannot be applied personally (*paccattaṁ*) and according to *dhamma* to you who dwell [thus] bewildered and unguarded.[6]

These views are collectively catalogued at the beginning of the sutta as 'doctrines of non-action' (*akiriyā*), the greatest 'ethical' heresy in the Buddhism of the Nikāyas. Obviously, the outcoming conclusion is that right view admits of a real moral action, which implies a doer as the *hetu* or the *paccaya* of such action. Besides, the quotation tells us that the action presupposes desire, effort, obligation and possibility to do or not to do (both being implied in the potential passive participles, *karaṇīyaṁ, akaraṇīyaṁ*), and all such attributes belong not to the action as such but to the moral agent, who only thus can be accounted 'responsible' for doing or not doing. How can these statements be harmonised with the view that there is action, but there is no doer?

Five heterodox doctrines are rejected in an interesting passage of the *Jātaka.* They are: (1) everything proceeds of natural necessity, a rigid determinism rules over nature and man, hence there is no good and no evil; (2) the deterministic theory that makes everything dependent on a creator, who would be the one to commit sin, not man; (3) everything has its roots in previous actions, therefore, if I kill someone it will be a consequence of my *khamma* and I shall not be held responsible; (4) every creature is formed out of the four elements and there is nothing else in them; at death creatures disintegrate into their component elements, there being no other world and no stain of sin; (5) the kṣatriyas hold that one can kill anyone provided it suits his own purpose, hence there is no sin in killing; and (6) there is no inner strength and freedom in the moral agent, hence there is no moral activity and things happen without a cause.[7]

If these positions are presented as heretical it means: (1) that there is no natural necessity or rigid determinism, hence there is moral good and evil; (2) that we are not puppets of a superior being, but are endowed with the power of self-determination; (3) that *khamma* does not impair our present freedom of choice; (4) that there is in man more than meets the eye, something that can be affected by the stain of sin and for which there is another world; and (5) that there is inner strength and freedom in the moral agent.

These positive conclusions obtained by contrast with the heterodox opinions lead unmistakably to the final view that the moral agent, the innate energy and freedom of the moral agent, the moral result of the action affecting the moral agent, all these, are to be considered as so many realities. Later speculation came to the conclusion, on the basis of absolute *anattā,* that the moral agent is not real, while retaining as real other factors like innate freedom of action and moral responsibility. The obvious result of such discrimative denial of the reality of the moral agent is that there is in man operative energy and freedom of action without any subject of attribution, that there is moral responsibility without any subject of retribution, an opinion not found in the Nikāyas either explicitly or implicitly.

Intense effort with a view to attain moral perfection presupposes the possibility of action on the part of the self. This is reported as propounded by the Buddha in a dialogue between him and a brāhmaṇa recorded in the Aṅguttara. The dialogue begins with the words of the brāhmaṇa:

> I, friend Gotama, am of this opinion, of this view,
> 'There is no action of the self (*natthi attakāro*) and no action of another (*natthi parakāro*)'.[8]

The Buddha answers that he had never seen or heard anyone having such opinion and view. The opinion seems to refer mainly to moral matters, but the Buddha argues by propounding some external actions which no one could deny without making a fool of himself:

> How can one who himself (*sayaṁ*) goes forward, who himself (*sayaṁ*) goes backward speak thus, 'There is no action of the self and no action of another'?[9]

Then the Buddha asks the following questions to which an affirmative answer is given, as expected, by the brāhmaṇa:

> What do you think, brāhmaṇa, is there any potentiality (*dhātu*) for initiative (*ārabbha*)?
>
> There being a potentiality for initiative are there beings known to exercise it?

The conclusion is:

> There being a potentiality for initiative and when beings are known to exercise it, that is the action of the self and the action of another as regards beings.

It is important to note that the potentiality referred to here is not self-subsisting but subsisting in the agent that transforms the potentiality into an accomplished actuality. This militates against the denial of the doer proclaimed in the *Visuddhimagga.* The same argument is applied to *nikkamadhātu* (potentiality for exertion), *parakkamadhātu* (potentiality for endeavour), *thāmadhātu* (potentiality for effort), *ṭhitidhātu* (potentiality for steadfastness), *upakkamadhātu* (potentiality for undertaking).

These are some excerpts of what Mrs. Rhys Davids has to say of this sutta, which is very significantly entitled, *Attakārīsutta*:

> ...In it we have a man (said to be a brāhman – which is obviously impossible) stating as his opinion, that in man's actions the doing is not rightly to be called 'by the self' or 'by another'. The statement might be equally well rendered 'there is no self-agent, no other-who-is-agent...'... Gotama's refutation of the opinion is of the bedrock of his teaching, and wipes out the doctrine of *anattā,* no-self, as being his! He gives 'initiative', literally the 'datum of having started', or 'begun' an act *as the criterion of the active presence of the very man or self.* Here is verily a very live-wire of teaching, here is a very doctrine of will, of choice,... This [the opponent's doctrine] is a denial of the causer, the man, of effective causation. This is a denial of the causer, the man, the invisible spiritual being, the self. And we have Gotama denying all knowledge of this denial, which he is declared by most writers to have made his central doctrine! But the chief interest lies in the testing of agency by 'initiative'. This was a great word.[10]

Once settled that moral dynamism does not stand by itself, but is an attribute of the self, a moral agent exercising it, a testimony may be offered of such dynamism in action from among the numerous ones that could be adduced:

> How faring, carpenter, is he faring towards the cessation of wrong moral behaviour? Herein, carpenter, a bhikkhu engenders desire, exerts himself, displays energy, forces his mind, strives for the non arising of wrong sinful states of mind that have not yet arisen; ...for the getting rid of evil states of mind that have arisen; ...for the preservation, maintenance, increase, expansion, furtherance, completion of right states of mind that have arisen.[11]

The moral agent's inherent energy for action can be also illustrated, expressly referred to the self, by a passage of the *Aṅguttara* where the sovereignty of the self (*attādhipateyya*) is described:

> Herein, bhikkhus, a bhikkhu gone to the forest, to the root of a tree, to a lonely spot, reflects thus, 'Not for the sake of robes did I leave home for the homeless life. Not for the sake of alms, of residence, or for the sake of becoming or not becoming thus [in a future existence] did I leave home for a homeless life. But for the thought: here am I beset by birth, old age, death, sorrows, lamentations, pains, despair and tribulations, affected by pain, overcome by pain. If only I came to know the end of at least some of this mass of pain! And if having given up the pleasures of the senses I, who left home for the homeless life, were to look for similar or still worse pleasures of the senses, that would not befit me.' He reflects thus, 'My unsluggish effort shall be put to action, my undisturbed mindfulness will be established, my body will be calm not turbulent, my mind will be well composed, one-pointed'. He, making the self the sole sovereign (*attānaṁyeva adhipatiṁ karitvā*), abandons what is evil, fosters what is good, abandons what is blameful, fosters what is blameless, he preserves the self pure (*attānaṁ suddhaṁ pariharati*). This is called sovereignty of the self.[12]

We are shown here not a mere figure-head a nominal leader, but a true sovereign that imposes his will, becoming the one and absolute master of the situation. It is difficult to conceive how can anyone say, after having read statements like this one, that for those who composed them *attā* was no more than a conventional term or a merely empirical phenomenon without roots in the deepest layer of man's reality, a merely empirical datum of no ultimate value.

Finally we shall direct our attention to an emphatic passage in the *Theragāthā* wherein the inconstancy and wantonness of the mind is beautifully described. The moral agent reacts against this inconstancy and wantonness of the mind and vows to bring the mind under complete subjection. For the sake of brevity only those verses will be quoted, which describe in eloquent terms the final decision of the moral agent,

O formless one, moving far, wandering alone,
I shall not do your bidding now,
Because sensual pleasures are bitter, full of great dangers,
I shall fare on thinking only of *nibbāna*.(v. 1125)

Formerly this mind wandered wantonly,
As it wished, as it desired, as it pleased,
Now I shall restrain it thoroughly,
As the holder of the goad restrains an elephant in rut. (v. 1133)

It is not as it was for you before,
I am not ready to go back to your influence,
I have renounced the world under the teaching of the great sage.
Those like me are not subject to destruction. (v. 1135)

Verses 1141-1142 begin with the words, 'I shall exercise my dominion as being the absolute master' (*Tathā tu kassāmi yathā pi issaro*).[13]

Doubtless the Nikāyas put forward a moral agent as a personal reality endowed with a large amount of moral energy and as exercising it.

SALVATION IN GENERAL AND THE SELF

That salvation spoken of in a general way is related to the self becomes evident from the following quotations.

We meet several times with the root *uddhṛ,* from which derives the word *uddhāra,* which in the vernaculars means above all salvation. Thus:

Be fond of diligence, guard well your mind,
Drag out the self from evil pass (*duggā uddharathattānaṁ*), as if it were an elephant sunk in the mire.[14]

Also:

> A Buddha has arisen in the world, the doctrine of the Buddhas is at present being taught,
> The self can be saved (*sakkā uddharituṁ attā*) by a man desirous of virtue.[15]

Salvation in general is also described as pulling out the dart from the self:

> Indolence is a defilement, impurity follows in the wake of indolence,
> Through diligence and wisdom, one should pull out the dart from the self (*abbahe sallamattano*).[16]

Also:

> The dart arising from the self (*sallaṁ attasamuṭṭhānaṁ*), whatever is produced by what leads to renewed existences,
> For the non setting in motion of these, he taught the excellent way.[17]

Finally:

> Whoever looks for the happiness of the self (*attano sukhaṁ*), should pull out the dart of the self (*abbahe sallamattano*),
> Lamenting, vain desires and self-dejection (*domanassaṁ ca attano*).[18]

Some texts may be added here that speak of 'establishing the self' or setting it on a firm footing.

> From mental application indeed is wisdom born, from lack of mental application is wisdom destroyed,
> Knowing this twofold way to becoming and to destruction,
> Let him there establish the self (*tathāttānaṁ niveseyya*), where wisdom is made to grow.[19]

Also:

> One should first of all establish the self on what is befitting (*attānameva pathamaṁ patirūpe nivesaye*),
> Then he could advise others, being wise, without spoiling them.[20]

THE CHARIOT AND THE CHARIOTEER

Man's moral activity, implying as it implies spiritual advancement through control of the lower passions and inclinations, is very fittingly compared to a chariot. A chariot is meant for travelling fast, but it requires on the part of the driver good controlling skill to keep the horses galloping on the right way.

The simile is used several times in the Pāli canon. The central point to be investigated (keeping in mind the *anattā* doctrine) is the question as to who is the master of the chariot.[21]

The simile occurs in the *Dhammapada* in a very simplified form. After saying that the man tamed as to self (*attadanto*) is better than the finest tamed animals like horses and elephants, we are given the reason for it:

> Not by means of those mounts would one go to the unexplored region (*agataṁ disaṁ*),
> As by means of a well trained self (*attanā sudantena*) the trained man goes by virtue of his training.[22]

Here the well trained self is the mount or vehicle (*yāna*) by means of which the well trained man goes to the *agataṁ disaṁ,* which doubtless stands for *nibbāna.*[23] But who trains the self but the very self? And who can be said from the context to reach the unexplored region but the 'selfsame' self? This is in keeping with what we are told in the simile that the self is at the same time the person that goes and reaches the unexplored region and the vehicle by which the going takes palce (*attanā sudantena danto...gacchati*). Who is here *danto*? The one who is tamed as to self (*attadanto*). How does he reach the end of his journey? By means of a well trained self (*attanā sudantena*). Is this instrument for journeying, the well trained self, in any way extrinsic to the person who makes the journey, represented by the word *danto*? By no means, it is the person itself. Another illustration of the ambivalence of the self in man. And will it be coherent to say that the end of the journey is real, but the person who is said to reach it has a merely conventional value?

In a simplified form too we find the simile of the charioteer in the *Theragāthā,* where the subservience of the mind to the moral agent is again forcefully expressed,

> I shall restrain you mind, as an elephant [is restrained] with a bolted gate,
> I shall not incite you to evil, net of sensual pleasures, body-born.
> Thus restrained, you will not go away, as an elephant [does not go away] not finding the door opened.
> Witch-mind, in love with evil, you will not forcibly run away again and again.
> As the strong holder of the hook makes a newly caught, untamed ele-

phant turn round against his will, thus shall I make you turn round.
As an excellent charioteer, skillful in taming magnificent horses, tames a thoroughbred horse, thus shall I tame you, in full control of the five powers.
I shall fasten you with mindfulness. I, being restrained as to the self (*pay-atatto*), shall tame you.
Checked by the yoke of energy you will not wander away far from here, mind.[24]

That *attā* is the charioteer is made clear by the epithet *payatatto* applied to the moral agent active here. This moral agent is set forth as superior to the mind and in full control of it. None but the self is superior to the mind, the last of the *khandhas*.

The *Saṁyutta* provides us with a detailed allegory of the chariot. The question that introduces it has obviously a metaphorical meaning:

There is a wilderness called 'infatuation', resounding with companies of Apsaras, frequented by troops of demons, how will the journey be made through it?

The answer is as follows:

The way is called 'straight', the direction is called 'free from fear',
The chariot is called 'the uncreaking', well fitted with the wheels of *dhamma*.
Conscientiousness is its break, mindfulness its protective board,
I say that *dhamma* is the charioteer, having as forerunner right view.
Whosoever possesses such vehicle, be it a man or a woman,
Such a one, with this vehicle, will reach the confines of *nibbāna*.[25]

Here, two persons occupy the chariot, the driver or charioteer and the owner and traveller. *Dhamma* is the controlling power, the guiding principle, the charioteer. The traveller that arrives at *nibbāna* by means of the vehicle is stated to be either a man or a woman possessing it. The term *attā* is not explicitly stated but the 'personal element' is present in 'the man or the woman'.

The allegory of the chariot, still richer in details, occurs again in the *Saṁyutta*. Here the chariot is called '*brahmaratha*'. When Ānanda went for his alms-round in the morning his eyes beheld a glorious sight. He saw the brāhmaṇa Jāṇusoṇi being led through Sāvatthi in a large van entirely white. Everything about it was white: the horses, their harness, the coach, the protecting board, the reins, the goad-stick, the umbrella, the turban, the clothes, the sandals and the fan. Such dazzling vision made Ānanda exclaim in amazement, '*Brahmaṁ vata, bho, yānaṁ! Brahmayānarūpaṁ vata, bho!*' When Ānanda reports his experience to the Buddha, the latter applies the term *'brahmayāna'* or what is given as its equivalent *'dharmayāna'* to the Eightfold Noble Path. After a detailed exposition of the Path, the Buddha is supposed to have uttered the verses:

Whose faith and wisdom are always properly fitted to the yoke,
Conscientiousness is the pole, mind the yoke-straps, mindfulness the guard and charioteer,
The chariot having all the accesories of good conduct, knowledge as the axle, energy as the wheels,
Equanimity the fitting peg for the axle, desirelessness the protective board,
Good will, non-violence, seclusion, the weapons,
Endurance the leathern armour, it proceeds towards utter security (*yogakkhemāya*).
Such is the unsurpassed brahma-chariot, produced in the self (*etadattani sambhūtaṁ*).
The sages are led out of the world. Whatever happens, victory is sure.[26]

No prejudice can be discovered here against *attā*. In fact we meet here with the very telling expression, '*etadattani sambhūtaṁ*' referring to the chariot, which Woodward translates as 'built by the self', but which more accurately should be translated as 'built in the self', or 'built of the self', an interpretation confirmed by the variant found in the Roman edition, *etadattanīyaṁ bhūtaṁ*. Mindfulness is the charioteer, and here, too, two persons are contemplated as occupying the chariot, the charioteer and the sage that is led out of the world. But what is mindfulness but a production of the sage himself? And really speaking there is no difference between the sage and the chariot, since the latter is made out of the sage's self. Another clear illustration of the ambivalence of *attā,* who is not different from the person but the person itself.

The simile of the chariot makes its appearance again in the *Jātaka.* The passage seems to bear testimony to the later struggle to substitue the mind for the self. In fact we find together two descriptions of the chariot. In one we are told that the body which is deemed to be the chariot is *'manosā-*

rathiko', i.e., 'having the mind as the charioteer'; while in the other the contention is that *attā* is the charioteer, *'tattha attā va sārathi'.* This contradiction is a clear clue leading to the fact of the later interpolation of the description where the mind is asserted to be the charioteer. There is a difference in style which has a decisive value. The interpolated description is written in a very ornate style redolent of later craftmanship, while the other description is written in the simple popular style of the early *Pāli* verses. In the interpolated description, almost every *pāda* consists of one single compound, while in the second description there are no compounds to be seen. The interpolated description runs from verse 1333 to verse 1338. Verse 1339 is one of transition, where except for the first *pāda* that is formed by a single compound, the rest is written in simple and popular style. The description, beginning with this verse, runs as follows:

> The unattached mind (*citta*) is the rug, resorting to spiritual growth is the dust-fender,
> Mindfulness is the goad of the sage, steadfastness the yoke and the reins,
> The mind leads the self-controled man along the way (*mano dantaṁ pathaṁ neti*), by means of well tamed horses,
> Passion and greed are the wrong way, and self-control is the right way,
> Wisdom, O king, is the driving force of the vehicle that runs through the objects of sense, there the self is certainly the charioteer (*tattha attā va sārathi*).[27]

There seems to be a conflict here between two expressions, namely, *mano dantaṁ pathaṁ neti* (where the mind seems to be given the rôle of charioteer) and *tattha attā va sārathi* (where the self (*attā*) is explicitly said to be the charioteer). The conflict may be solved by keeping in mind that, as was the case with some of the descriptions already given, there were two persons occupying the chariot. In such case, the mind may be taken here as being the charioteer who drives the horses under the mastery of *attā* which would then be the traveller and owner of the chariot (*rathin*), as it was expressly said in the description of the *Katha Up.* One thing stands unchallenged, the author of such emphatic statement as *tattha attā va sārathi* had no kind of prejudice against *attā.* The simile of the chariot is used also in the *Mahāniddesa* while commenting on:

> A man who having formerly fared as a celibate (*eko*), gives himself to sexual practices,

> Common men consider him a man fallen in the world, like a cart that has lost the way.[28]

First, a list of different vehicles is given to explain the word *yānaṁ,* and then it is said in connexion with *yānaṁ*:

> When deviating, out of control, unrestrained, unmastered, takes up a wrong course, climbs on uneven ground, on a stump of a tree, on a rock, and the cart is destroyed as well as the driver, and even may fall down a cliff.

These physical events of the uncontrolled cart are applied to some moral shortcomings. And then coming to describe the effects of those shortcomings on the rider it is said:

> Even as a deviating cart, out of control, unrestrained, unmastered, destroys both the cart and the rider, in the same way the strayed man, like a deviating cart, destroys the self (*attānaṁ bhañjati*) in hell, destroys the self in animal rebirth, destroys the self in the realm of wandering spirits, destroys the self in the world of men, destroys the self in the world of gods.[29]

If all forms of rebirth are considered to destroy the self, it follows that the only way of saving the self is either to set the self in a condition immediate to the achievement of *nibbāna* or to make it actually attain to it. In this description, too, we have an explicit reference to *attā.*

In the *Rathopamasutta* of the *Saḷāyatanasaṁyutta,* three topics are treated, the first one being how does one become a keeper of the doors of the senses. First of all we are instructed how to proceed in order to control every one of the senses (*cakkhu, sota, ghāna, jivhā, kāyo, manas*). Then the simile of the chariot is given as an illustration. Here is F. L. Woodward's translation of it:

> Suppose, brethren, on level ground at the crossing of the four highways a car drawn by thoroughbreds, with a goad set in rest therein, and a clever trainer, a driver who trains steeds. He mounts thereon, with his left hand holding the reins, and in his right hand he takes the goad, and drives the car forward and backward, wither he wills. Just so, brethren, a brother practises the guard over the six faculties, he practises for their restraint, for their taming, for their calming. That, brethren, is how a brother keeps guard over the faculties.[30]

There is here no explicit reference to *attā,* but we can observe the moral agent, the man, in full control, different from, and superior to the senses including the mind, and exercising full mastery over them.

In the *Devaputtasaṁyutta* we see described the dire consequences of an inept driving:

> The fool and unwise go through life having the self as a real enemy (*amitteneva attanā*),
> Doing sinful deeds that produce a bitter fruit,
> That deed is not well done, of which, once done, one repents,
> Whose karmic result one experiences crying with a face covered with tears.
> That deed is well done, of which, once done, one does not repent,
> Whose karmic result one experiences delighted and with a happy mind.
> Cautiously one should do that which he thinks is beneficial to the self (*yaṁ jaññā hitamattano*).
> The thoughtful wise should advance not having a carter's thoughts.
> Even as a carter, leaving a soft, level highway, takes to an uneven road and broods like one whose axle is broken,
> Thus the ignorant, diverting from the good norm and turning to what is wrong,
> Having reached the mouth of death, broods like one whose axle is broken.[31]

The activity of the moral agent as a real person pervades the whole passage and we find in it two references to *attā.*

The doctrine of absolute *anattā* does not seem to have had any operative influence in the treatment of the chariot metaphor.

KNOWLEDGE OF THE SELF

We are contemplating the picture of the moral self as depicted by the Nikāyas. Now the power to reflecting upon itself, which the self has, is precisely the root cause of all moral responsibility. Responsibility requires power of choice and freedom of decision. This power of choice and freedom of decision cannot work unless the moral self has the power to reflect upon itself, weighing the relative moral value of an action as compared to another, either before performing it or after having performed it. This also implies that the self knows the self, that the self can approve or disapprove of what the self is going to do or has done, that the self is the witness of the self.

Thus we are told that in case of a rebuke given by a bhikkhu to another who has committed an offence, both should examine the self by the self (*attanā attānaṁ paccavekkhati*), otherwise a protracted strife between the bhikkhus may ensue and the peace of the Order will be disturbed.[32] The introspective power of the self is indicated by the reduplication *attanā attānaṁ,* where *attanā* was not necessary from the grammatical point of view in order to make perfect sense by any 'conventionalist' standards.

In the *Anumānasutta* of the *Majjhima* we find the same insistence on the reflective activity of the self upon the self with the same reduplication.

First of all, the sutta speaks of making an inference on the self by the self (*attanā va attānaṁ anuminitabbaṁ*)[33] in the following way: If I see a man who is a slave of evil desires, that man displeases me, in the same way I shall displease others if I am a slave of evil desires. The bhikkhu so reflecting resolves never to be such. The same applies to other bad qualities.

Then the self reflects upon the self to see whether or not he is in the grip of those bad qualities (*attanā va attānaṁ evaṁ paccavekkhitabbaṁ*).[34]

The sutta closes very fittingly with the simile of the mirror (which applies so well to the reduplication *attanā attānaṁ* where a person sees his or her face in order to improve upon its appearance. In the same way, if a bhikkhu sees in his self (*attani samanupassati*) all those evil qualities not yet suppressed he ought to exert himself in suppressing them. If he sees in his self all those evil qualities already suppressed, then with a glad heart he will train himself in good qualities.[35]

That this power of introspection is to be used for the spiritual benefit of the practitioner is clear from:

> If, your reverences, a bhikkhu while reflecting does not see in the self (*attani na samanupassati*) all these good qualities, then that bhikkhu, for the obtention of all these good qualities has to put forth a special desire, effort, endeavour, exertion, unrestrained impulse, mindfulness, attention.... And if, your reverences, a bhikkhu, while reflecting, sees in the self (*attani samanupassati*) some good qualities and does not see in the self some other good qualities, that bhikkhu, your reverences, for the stability of those good qualities that he sees in the self and for the ob-

> tention of those good qualities that he does not see in the self has to put forth a special desire.... And if, your reverences, a bhikkhu, while reflecting, does see in the self all those good qualities, he has to apply himself to stability in those good qualities, and further still to the destruction of the *āsavas*.[36]

We have here again a patent reference to the intense dynamism of which the self as the moral agent is capable. Such dynamism either has to be considered as having no cause or has to originate in the self working for its own liberation.

This power of introspection of which the Nikāyas speak makes possible the knowledge of the self. Among the seven qualities that make a bhikkhu worthy of offerings and gifts so that he becomes in this regard an unsurpassed field of merit in the world, the quality of being *attaññu* is mentioned.

> And how is one a knower of the self (*attaññu*)? Herein, bhikkhus, a bhikkhu knows the self (*attānaṁ jānāti*). Just this much am I as regards faith, virtue, learning, detachment, wisdom, intelligence....[37]

The self referred to here is the moral self. The verbal opposition *bhikkhu-attānaṁ* makes it clear that the moral self is taken to be the inward existential reality of the bhikkhu, the moral substrate of those qualities. This is the natural way of talking. The denial of the reality of the moral self shows itself in this context as an irrelevant metaphysical subtlety of doubtful soteriological value.

We find the power to reflect combined with the witnessing of the self in:

> ... and ariyan disciple reflects thus, I am set on the way to the uprooting, to the abandonment of those fetters which were the cause of my being one who harms creatures. If I were such a man, the self would upraid me (*attāpi maṁ upadeyya*) as a result of that, and even wise men after due consideration would blame me as a result of that, and after the breaking up of the body, after death, a bad destiny would be expected as a result of that....[38]

A 'conventionalist' would have to translate *attā pi maṁ upadeyya* as 'I would blame myself'. Would such translation convey fully the meaning of *attā* in the nominative and the distinction between *attā* and *maṁ*? *Attā* here stands for the highest existential authority in man, the ruling moral power.

We read also:

> ... some bhikkhu is not one that carries out in full the teacher's instructions.... As he is staying aloof in this way, the teacher upraids him, and, when they have examined him, his learned fellow brahma-farers upraid him, and *devatās* upraid him, and the self upraids the self (*attā pi attānaṁ upavadati*).[39]

Again:

> Does perhaps the self, Vakkali, reproach you as to morals (*taṁ... attā sīlato na upavadati*)?
>
> In no way, Lord, does the self reproach me as to morals.[40]

This last *attā* has a special value, on account of being found in a context where the *khandhas* being *anattā* is taught almost in every page, thus showing that the *anattā* doctrine of the composer had, in his mind, no absolute value.

Herein, *attā* constitutes the 'Supreme Court' for man:

> Not by another's attribution is the deed of mortal man evil.
> He should not perform it by the self (*attanā*), as mortals are kinsmen of their deeds,
> One is not a thief by another's word, one is not a sage by another's word.
> As the self knows him (*attā ca naṁ yathāvedi*), so the deities know him also.[41]

The self is an all-knowing judge, not subject to any kind of bribe or corruption:

> There is no hiding place in the world for one who commits sin,
> Your self, man, knows (*attā te purisa jānāti*), whether it be true or false,
> For sure, friend, you despise the self (*attānaṁ atimaññasi*), who is an auspicious witness,
> You who, although there is sin in the self (*attani*), try to conceal the self (*attānaṁ parigūhasi*).
> Devas as well as Tathāgatas see
> The fool who in the world walks crookedly.[42]

On a closer scrutiny of this text one can see a difference in meaning between the *attā* of the second line, the ever undeceived witness and judge, and the *attā* of the third and fourth lines. The first *attā* shines forth in a region of pure light, untainted by deceit and hypocrisy, while the second *attā* shows itself involved in the samsaric process, a prey of sin. Man tries unsuccessfully to hide the second self from the first. A better token of the ambivalence of the self could not be given us.

It is quite within this line of thought we are now pursuing that the Scriptures should speak of (shall we say a *religious*?) fear of the self:

> There are, bhikkhus, these four fears. What four? Fear of reproach coming from the self (*attānuvādabhayaṁ*), fear of reproach coming from others, fear of punishment and fear of a bad destiny. And what, bhikkhus, is fear of reproach coming from the self? Herein, bhikkhus, a bhikkhu reflects thus, 'Were I to practice evil bodily conduct, evil conduct in speech, and evil mental conduct, would not the self reproach me as to morals' (*kiñca taṁ yaṁ maṁ attā sīlato na upavadeyya*)?[43]

As a consequence of every one of the four fears, the moral agent shuns misconduct in body, speech and thought and preserves the self pure (*suddhaṁ attānaṁ pariharati*). The fear of punishment by a human authority and the fear of a bad destiny after death are sufficient motives to deter one from committing sinful actions. The fear of reproach on the part of others is based on the dread all of us feel for shame and exposure. But can one feel a reverential fear for the self unless the self is felt to be a superior witness whose disapproval makes one feel uncomfortable and even disconfitted? For this, there must be some distinction between 'ourselves' and 'the self', i.e., the witness, the judge and reproving authority qualified to take us to task. All this seems to point out to the reality of the self.

MANIFESTATION OF THE SELF

We have just studied the 'self-knowledge' of the moral self in its double aspect of reflection and witnessing. Now comes the question of revealing the self to others, a question dealt with in different parts of the canon.

We shall consider, first of all, the contrasting case of a bad bhikkhu who, prompted by hypocrisy and a desire of temporal advantages, tries to conceal the real condition of his self:

> Whoever professes the self to be different from what it is (*aññathā santamattānaṁ, aññathā yo pavedaye*),
> What is enjoyed by him is the result of theft, as by the fraud of a cheat.[44]

The words obviously refer to a sanctimonious monk who makes a show of virtue, having none, so as to attract the generosity of people towards himself. He is a thief and a cheat.

The opposite attribute is considered an ornament of a good bhikkhu. Among the five qualities he is expected to possess, one is:

> He is not deceitful or hypocritical, but manifests his self as it really is (*yathābhūtaṁ attānaṁ āvikattā*) to his master, or to the wise, or to his companions in the godly life.[45]

Now we turn to the texts that speak of a positive and wilful manifestation of the virtuous self. The attitude of the Nikāyas in this respect appears to be somehow hesitant, due to the danger of *asmimāna* found therein. Let us begin with the Selasutta of the *Majjhima*. Sela was a brāhamaṇa who knew the thirty-two marks of a superior man. He saw all of them in the Buddha.

> Then it occurred to Sela the brāhamaṇa 'The Lord is endowed with the thirty-two marks of a Great Man in full, not partially, but yet I do not know whether he is an Awaken One or not. All the same I have heard it said by aged brahmans, full of years, teachers of teachers: "When their own praises (*sake vaṇṇe*) are being spoken, those that are perfect ones (*arahanto*) fully Self-Awaken Ones (*sammāsambuddhā*) reveal the self (*attānaṁ pātukaronti*)"'.[46]

I. B. Horner appends to this her translation a footnote that says, '*Attānaṁ pātukaronti:* cf. Vin. ii, 186, A. ii, 186, A. iii, 123, i.e., manifest, or make visible, exhibit, bring to light, 'betray' (G. S. iii, 98) the self. But in the Buddha's teaching that is what a foolish person does, e.g., Devadatta, not arahants, and, at D. iii, 115 not the Tathāgata'.

It is not so. The manifestation of the self refers explicitly in the context to arahants and sammāsambuddhas. In fact, if we continue reading the passage we see that in order to make Gotama reveal the self, Sela sings, in the verses that follow, Gotama's praises beginning with:

> You have a perfect body, beautifully complexioned, nobly born, lovely to behold,
> You are gold-coloured, O Blessed One, you are one who has resplendent teeth, fully strong, etc., etc.

In answer to those praises, the Buddha declares the self in no ambiguous terms. He says among other things:

I am a king, Sela, a peerless *dhamma*-king....
The wheel has been set arolling by me, the matchless *dhamma*-wheel....
What is to be known is known by me, and what is to be developed has been developed by me,
What is to be left aside has been left aside by me, therefore, brāhmaṇa, I am a Buddha.
[...]
Of those whose appearance is extremely rare in the world,
I am, brāhmaṇa, a Perfectly Illumined One, a physician without peer,
Brahma-become, without compare, the destroyer of Māra's hosts.
Having subjected all foes, I rejoice, all fear vanished.

It is therefore evident that the Buddha is presented in these verses proclaiming the self, that is to say what made him a Buddha different from, and far above the rest of men. It is difficult to think that those who composed and compiled a passage like this did not believe in the reality of the Buddha's self, this being for them a mere name, not an abiding reality.[47]

It is on this background that a passage of the *Buddhavaṁsa* should be placed:

Knowing their mind, the sage skilful in similes,
The destroyer of doubts, the great hero, spoke of the qualities of the self (*kathesi attano guṇaṁ*).[48]

In the account that follows the Buddha is shown using expressions such as,

[...]
The knowledge of a Buddha is immeasurable, they are unable to comprehend it.
[...]
There is no coming to the world equal to mine, I have escaped new births,
I am supreme as regards enlightenment, as regards the rolling of the *dhamma*-wheel.

The *Dīghanikāya* gives us what is called the lion's roar of the Buddha. It goes like this:

There are, Kassapa, some samaṇas, brāmaṇas preachers of virtue. They in different ways speak in praise of virtue. But regarding the ariyan su-

> preme virtue I do not see anyone entirely equal to self (*attano samasamaṁ*) much less superior. Therefore I myself am better in this respect, that is in what is further virtue.[49]

Somehow or other, when reading such statements of self-praise one experiences certain apprehension and inclines to think that they reflect more the high appreciation of the Buddha professed by his followers than the very way he spoke. Be it as it may, such words ought to be considered free from all asmimanic feelings, which could not abide in the Buddha's mind. But what of this self-manifestation when other people are those who manifest their self?

Some texts seem to reflect a certain misgiving about the proclamation of the self by virtuous people, on the ground, doubtlessly, that it may be a sign of asmimāna or may foster it. In the *Mahāvagga* we hear Soṇa declaring some spiritual achievements, even the highest, as having been attained by himself. Then the Exalted One is made to comment in the presence of the bhikkhus:

> Thus, bhikkhus, the sons of noble families declare their wisdom, the goal is spoken of, and the self is not referred to (*attho va vutto, attā ca anupanīto*). But then I think some worthless men declare their wisdom in a light way , they afterwards get into trouble.[50]

I. B. Horner translates *attā ca anupanīto* as 'the self is not obtruded'.[51] She quotes the *Commentary* explaining 'the self is not obtruded' as 'if (the profound knowledge) is declared thus, "I am an arahant", the self is not obtruded (or mentioned, or brought forward, *na upanīto*)', Well if profound knowledge is proclaimed by saying, 'I am an arahant', it is clear that, in the literal sense at least, the self is brought forward, as 'I' stands for the self as far as the latter becomes the subject and to a certain extent the object of experience. Has the Commentary in mind that what does not really exist cannot be said to be brought forward? The truth is that in the present context the phrase *attā ca anupanīto* has nothing to do with the doctrine of absolute *anattā*, but has a literal meaning. The whole declaration of profound knowledge is done by Soṇa in a general way, not in the first, but in the third person. The phrase points rather to the absence of conceit, not to the unreality of *attā*.

The saying, *attho ca vutto attā ca anupanīto*, is found again in the *Aṅguttara*.[52] The context is as follows. A certain disciple of the Ājīvakas comes to Ānanda and puts three questions to him: 'Who are those whose dhamma is well explained? Who in the world are well accomplished? Who in the world are virtuous?' Ānanda answers in all simplicity that those who preach the riddance of *rāga, moha* and *dosa* are those whose dhamma is well preached. That those who have achieved the riddance of *rāga, moha* and *dosa* are those who are well accomplished. That those who have cut *rāga, moha* and *dosa* to the root, making them like a stump of a palm tree never to rise again, are really virtuous. The questioner agrees with all this and says:

> It is wonderful, sir, it is marvellous! Here is no trumpeting of one's own creed, no depreciation of another's creed, but just teaching of Dhamma in its proper sphere. You have spoken of man's welfare, and the self is not brought into question.

The translation given is of F. L. Woodward's (*The Book of the Gradual Sayings,* I, pp. 197-198), who appends to the passage the following footnote, '*Attho ca vutto attā ca anupanīto, Comy.* takes this to mean, 'You have given an answer to my question, but you do not say "I myself have such virtues"'. The same phrase occurs at A III, 359 (where *Comy.* says nothing). There is, I think, no reference here to the soul theory.' These last words mean to say that there is no reference here to the *anattā* doctrine. If the self is not brought forward here is because, 'here is no trumpeting of one's own creed, no depreciation of another's creed'. *Attā ca na upanīto* conveys the total absence of *asmimāna.* It was a common practice in dialogues between members of opposite sects to show one's own creed to advantage while detracting from the opponent's creed. This is not done by Ānanda and he is praised for that by the Ājivaka follower.

Another context where the words, *attho ca vutto attā ca anupanīto* occur and yield the sense of avoidance of conceit is also found in the *Aṅguttara.* Khemo and Sumano tell the Buddha respectively that an arahant does not think either 'He is better than me, he is equal to me, he is inferior to me;' or 'He is not better than me, he is not equal to me, he is not inferior to me'. The Buddha commends such utterances with the words:

> Thus, bhikkhus, the sons of noble families declare their wisdom; the goal is spoken of, and the self is not referred to. But then I think, etc.[53]

In spite of the vacillation evinced by some texts regarding any explicit reference to the self in matters of spiritual achievement, it is evident that other texts regard this explicit reference to the self as legitimate. Thus:

> Inasmuch as, householder, the five dreads and hostilities have been appeased in the ariyan disciple, and inasmuch as he is endowed with the four limbs of stream-winning, and the Ariyan Way is well seen and penetrated by him, he may, if he so desires, manifest the self by the self (*attanā va attānaṁ byākareyya*), saying 'I am one for whom hell has been brought to an end, I am one for whom birth as an animal has been brought to an end, I am one for whom the realm of the Petas has been brought to an end, I am one for whom the state of woe, the bad destiny, the downfall has been brought to an end. I am a stream-winner, one whose nature is not to go to the downfall, secure, one who is bound for enlightenment.'[54]

There is an adjective etymologically connected with *upanīto* and *anupanīto* of the preceding texts. The adjective in question is *attūpanāyika.*

On a certain occasion a great number of Kosalans came to see the Buddha. They told him that their ideal was to live a life where their worldly desires for children, for Benares sandalwood, garlands, unguents, gold and silver, and after death to be reborn in heaven, would be fulfilled. They asked the Buddha to explain to them such dhamma as would be instrumental in the materialization of these wishes. The Buddha answered, as translated by Woodward (*The Book of the Kindred Sayings,* V, p. 308):

> I will teach you, householders, the Norm-method that brings profit to the self (*attūpanāyikam*). Listen to it. Fix it well in your minds, I shall speak.

The passage whose translation has just been given begins with the words, *attūpanāyikaṁ vo, gahapatayo....* It seems better to translate *vo* as 'rather', as being a particle that shows the opposition between the teaching actually imparted by the Buddha and the teaching the Kosalans were demanding. Woodward's phrase, 'that brings profit to the self', would be the translation of *attatthūpanāyikaṁ,* but the original is *attūpanāyikaṁ,* which keeping in mind the words *upanīto* and *anupanīto* in the preceding texts will rather mean, 'that leads the practitioner to make an explicit reference to the self', as it becomes clear from what follows. The Buddha begins by teaching the practice of the commandments. Then he explains those virtues that lead to 'the attainment of the stream' (*sotāpatti*). As a result of the practice of those virtues, the Buddha says that,

> he may, if he so desires, manifest the self by the self (*attanā va attānaṁ byākareyya*), saying, 'I am one for whom hell has been brought to an end, etc. [as given above]'.[55]

This winding up of the passage makes clear the sense of *attūpanāyika* as implying an explicitly reference to the self to whom the attainment of the stream is attributed.

Following on the study of the manifestation of the self looked upon as legitimate by the Nikāyas we come to that of Ugga, the householder, who had been declared by the Exalted One to be the possessor of eight wonderful qualities. When a certain bhikkhu came to see him, Ugga declared to him those eight qualities as he himself knew them. The eighth one is:

> Of all those five lower fetters that have been explained by the Exalted One, I do not see anything of them in the self (*attani*) that has not been abandoned.[56]

The *Saṁyutta* speaks of the 'mirror of *dhamma*' (*dhammādāso*) which enables one to declare the self by the self (*attanā va attānaṁ byākareyya*), proclaiming that one has attained to the spiritual degree of *sotāpatti*, meaning that one is free from all forms of reincarnational punishment and is sure to obtain the highest enlightenment.[57]

We find the 'mirror of *dhamma*' mentioned in the *Theragāthā*:

> Leaving aside the five hindrances (*nīvaraṇe*) for the obtention of utter security (*yogakkhema*),
> Taking up the mirror of *dhamma* for the knowledge and vision of the self (*ñāṇadassanamattano*),
> I observed this body both within and without,
> Interiorly as well as exteriorly the body appeared to be empty.[58]

The mirror of *dhamma* is a technical term that stands for a condition that enables one to see and proclaim the self as being a *sotāpanno*. From that height of perfection the Thera was able to see the vacuity of the body. One may see here an implicit statement of the doctrine of relative *anattā*, forasmuch as the knowledge and vision of the self is opposed to the vacuity of the body, which thereby is declared to be empty of the self or of what belongs to the self, a doctrine that will be studied in the second part of this book.

Disapproval at a manifestation of the self that is to all appearances asmimanic is to be seen in:

> The man who manifests to others the virtues
> And observances of self (*attano*), not being asked,
> Wise men call that an anariyan way of behaviour,
> That one himself should manifest the self
> (*yo ātumānaṁ sayameva pāva*).[59]

We find in the *Saṁyutta* a kind of manifestation of the self on the part of Sāriputta given in a number of answers called forth by the corresponding questions of the Buddha. One of the questions and its ensuing answer are problematic, at least when one reads the translation that Mrs. Rhys Davids gives of them:

> But if, Sāriputta, they should ask you: – By what deliverance is it, friend Sāriputta, that you have confessed that saving knowledge: – 'Perished are intoxicants, lived the divine life, done what was to be done, nothing further of these conditions: – this I know': – how would you make an answer?
>
> If I were thus asked, Lord, I should thus make an answer: – By deliverance from self (*ajjhattaṁ vimokkhā*), friend, by the destruction of all grasping I live with such a clear mind that the intoxicants flow no more and I admit no [immutable] Soul (*attānaṁ ca nāvajānāmi*). Thus asked thus would I make an answer.
>
> Well done, well done, *Sāriputta....*[60]

According to this translation we have apparently here an explicit denial of the self. Is that so? Some animadversions offer themselves readily when scrutinizing the translation.

In the first place, the translation reflects rather an original text that would read, *kena vimokkhā* ('by what deliverance'), but the text has it, *kathaṁ vimokkhā,* which corresponds in the answer to, *ajjhattaṁ vimokkhā.* But *ajjhattam* stands in the text for an adverbial adjunct (not an adjective, that would be *ajjhatikena*) which answers to *kathaṁ* of the question, which means 'how, in what way'. The correct translation should therefore be 'by a deliverance regarding the self', that is to say 'by a deliverance *of* the self' (never *from* the self), where the self is not the thing from which one is liberated, but the innermost part of man, his existential reality, that is the beneficiary of such deliverance.

In the second place, we see *attānaṁ ca nāvajānāmi* translated as 'and I admit no [immutable] Soul'. This could be the translation of a phrase like, *attānaṁ ca nānujānāmi.* But the verb used here is not *anujānāti* but *avajānāti,* 'to despise', as it is clear from:

He who extols self (*attāṇaṁ*), and despises (*avajānāti*) others....[61]

Therefore the phrase, as it stands, should be translated as 'and I do not despise the self',[62] which contains no denial of the self.

Before closing the section, and with it the chapter, there comes for discussion an obscure passage in which the introspection of the self by the self is apparently denied by the Buddha:

Who does not contemplate the self of self (or, by the self) (*attano attānaṁ,* v. 1. *attanā attānaṁ*),
Concentrated, straight-gone, with self well poised (*tiṭhatto*),
He indeed faultless, unobstructed, doubt-free,
The Tathāgata is worthy of sacrificial offering.[63]

The *first* possible reading of the first line is:

Yo attano attānaṁ nānupassati.

The expression *attano attānaṁ* is unusual. The only possible explanation of this line within the thought-frame of the Nikāyas would be, 'He who does not see the true self of the *attānudiṭṭhi*-self'. But even in this case there would be no assertion of absolute *anattā.* The passage would run parallel to all those passages of the Nikāyas that deny *attā* being the *khandhas* or being in any way ontologically related to them. But if this thought were to be expressed in a way consonant with the constant teaching of the Nikā yas, it would sound something like, *yo anattani attānaṁ nānupassati.*

The *second* possible reading of the first line is:

Yo attanā attānaṁ nānupassati.

The combination *attanā attānaṁ* is of frequent occurrence in the Nikāyas. E. M. Hare accepts this reading. He translates, 'He who perceiveth not self by self', and appends to his translation the following footnote, '... *cf.* the Vedānta view: *Ātmānaṁ ātmanā paśya,* "See the self by the Self" (Max Müller, *Collected Works,* XV, 81)',[64] as if the line were an explicit contradiction of the vedantic view. But it seems that an isolated contradiction of an alien system, not explicitly or implicitly contradicted anywhere in the Nikāyas is out of place here, where 'positive' reasons are given why the Buddha should be the recipient of sacrificial offerings. The whole setting of the sutta, its introduction included, points rather to the ever present polemics about caste and ritual, not about creed and doctrine. Therefore it seems more plausible to look in this line for something genuinely Buddhist, something in agreement with *samāhito* (concentrated) and *tiṭhatto* (with self well poised) in the next line.

Keeping this in mind, the best possible reading would be:

Yo attanāttānaṁ anupassati,

which has the advantage of providing the line with the correct number of syllables, eleven, and would make of it a kind of *satipaṭṭhāna* regarding the self, an attitude that could very well be summed up in what we read in the following line:

> well concentrated, straight-gone (or 'straightened' *ujjugato*),[65] with self well poised.

The initial '*n*' of *nānupassati* could very well be a case of dyplologia, a well known phenomenon in texts handed down by mechanical recitation, where a consonant that is found twice together, *naṁ ānu,* is introduced once more, *naṁ nānu.* The conclusion of all this will be that in all probability we have in this line neither a denial of *attā* nor a contradiction of an unpaniṣadic view.[66]

4

The Self and Moral Evil

Repeated reference has been made to the ambivalence of the moral self as described in the Nikāyas. One aspect of this ambivalence is the freedom of choice between good and evil that the moral self is able to exercise. At the beginning of this chapter we should consider the fact that the misery of man is radically due to the involvement of the self in the samsaric process. The training proposed in the Nikāyas has as its aim the utter disengagement of the self from the samsaric process and the consequent attainment of liberation or *nibbāna.* If liberation and *nibbāna* are real, we are bound to admit by force of contrast that the self's involvement in the samsaric process and its dire consequences are also real in a negative sort of way. The reality of this involvement and its dire consequences is the theme of the present chapter.

THE METAPHYSICAL SELF, AS SUCH, IS ABOVE MORAL GOOD AND EVIL

It is an altogether different question the elucidation of what kind of relation there can be between the self and moral evil. A few words on this matter will not be out of place so that the reader may have the right frame of mind while reading what is going to follow on the subject.

One thing is certain, the relation between the self and moral evil is not an ontological relation. The same applies to moral good. This means to say that the self is ontologically, that is to say by its very nature, above moral evil and its effects, as well as above moral good and its effects. This follows from what we are told in several passages of the scriptures which will be presently quoted:

> No brāhmaṇa ever claimed purity from a different source [than the self] (*aññato*),
> Either in things seen, heard, thought, or in morality and observances.
> Unattached both to good and evil (*puññe ca pāpe ca*)
> Disclaiming whatever is obtained, he should be inactive here.[1]

The ultimate purity which is the ideal of the enlightened man, here called a (true) brāmaṇa, is a purity that is unaffected both by moral good and by moral evil, belonging to a plane superior to both, consisting in a condition that is reflected in the total absence of wilful moral activity, in the absolute desirelessness to do evil and to obtain merit. This is the absolute isolation of the self which brings about liberation. The improvement caused by moral practices is meant first of all to detach the self from what is evil, and this is mainly done by the counterpractice of good. This is not enough; any attachment of the self to whatever is not the self itself is wrong from the ultimate point of view. Moral good and the subsequent merit is not the self, even though it takes the self towards an ever more perfect detachment from worldly things. Finally the self has to be detached from moral good and merit and be freed with a freedom that is its very nature.

Herein lie some metaphysical questions that the Buddha did not deign to discuss. The first question will be a fundamental one. If the self is by its very nature absolutely unaffected by the samsaric process, how is it in the first place that we find ourselves (our selves!) immersed in such samsaric process? How could the whole thing possibly start? This is a problem which the main Indian philosophical systems have in common. In the second place one can speculate on the possibility of the self being affected by whatever tends either to keep it caught in, or to disentangle it from *saṁsāra*. We shall see that this last question crops up twice in the canon, but the Buddha does not give any answer to it.[2]

Buddha's position was eminently practical. We may or may not succeed in explaining the fundamental metaphysical questions involved in our present condition; but one thing is certain without any possibility of doubt, we experience ourselves as caught in the *samsāra* and as victims of *dukkha,* the all pervading everlasting existential pain. The Buddha's attitude was that of a teacher who does not want to waste time in discussing the metaphysical questions involved in this issue, but prefers to apply all man's resources to the breaking up of the *saṁsāra* and come thereby to the destruction of Pain.

There are at least two other contexts where this 'pristine' purity of the self is asserted:

> One who here has escaped from attachment both to good and evil, free from pain, rid of defilement, pure, him I call a brāhmaṇa.[3]

And:

One who intent on the holy life, having done away with both good and evil,

Fares in the world with full deliberation, is said to be a true bhikkhu.[4]

It is on the moral level that good and evil really affect the self. The opposition between the metaphysical level and the moral level is not the opposition between the real and conventional. Both of them are real in their own right and at their proper sphere. From what we have seen and what we are going to see it is clear that the Nikāyas speak of the moral self and the effects of good and evil on it as so many realities.

All this may be illustrated by the phenomenon of the defraction of light. In it the uniform light is deflected and decomposed into bands of different colours. The incidence of the light on the object which is the cause of the deflection and decomposition of the light will stand for the involvement of the self in the samsaric process. On the yonder side of the process we have the ontologically pure light of the self. On this side of the process we have the light of the self decomposed into different 'moral' hues. The purpose of all moral training is to 'integrate' the decomposed moral self into the colourless simplicity of the original light where all ambivalence ceases.

A merely 'reflexive sense' will not exhaust the fullness of meaning of the term *attā* as used in passages to follow. Let us take, for instance, a passage where after praising the life of one who leaves home for the homeless state, it is said:

If he is scurrilous by character, given to worry, dull,

The life of such is sinful, it increases the impurity of the self (*rajaṁ vaḍḍheti attano*).[5]

Shall we translate the last *pāda* as, 'it increases his own impurity'? But what kind of impurity is that? All will agree that it is not physical but 'spiritual'. Hence the *pāda* will be more fittingly translated as, 'it increases the impurity of the self'.

The same will apply in the case of:

Easy to do are evil deeds, and harmful to the self (*attano ahitāni ca*),

That which is beneficial and good, that indeed is extremely hard to do.[6]

The harm mentioned here affects the 'spiritual' man. Therefore we cannot see in *attano* a merely reflexive pronoun which will refer to man in a general way, but a term that stands for the 'spiritual' man or self.

THE MORAL SELF AS THE CAUSE OF MORAL EVIL

After the foregoing considerations we shall be better disposed to appreciate in all their worth the testimonies we are going to adduce.

We meet a number of times with the assertion that moral evil arises from the self. The term used is *attasambhūta*.

> Greed and ill-will and infatuation, born of the self (*attasambhūtā*),
> kill an evil-minded man, as the fruit kills the bamboo plant.[7]

The simile is significant. As the fruit of the bamboo plant means the death of the latter, so greed, ill-will and infatuation, born of the self (*attasambhūtā*) cause man's utter 'spiritual' ruin.

The self as the source of moral evil is explicitly mentioned in the *Dhammapada:*

> By the self is evil done (*attanā hi kataṁ pāpaṁ*), (evil) is born of the self (*attajaṁ*), proceeding from the self (*attasambhavaṁ*),
> It crushes the foolish man, like a diamond reduces to powder a precious stone.[8]

We find in the *Theragāthā* a very interesting statement that seems to imply that all moral evil proceeds from the wrong notion of self, that of the *sakkāyadiṭṭhi,* as its immediate source. This would confirm the contention that the only valid distinction in the Nikāyas regarding the self is between *attā* as being *diṭṭhigataṁ* and its opposite the true *attā,*

> Climbing on the terrace of the stations of mindfulness, I looked around
> At the people in love with their samsaric individuality (*sakkāyaṁ*), of whom much I had thought before.
> And when I saw the Way, the climbing on the boat,
> Not relying on self (*anadiṭṭhāya attānaṁ*), I discovered the supreme crossing point.
> The dart that arises form the self (*attasamuṭṭhānaṁ*), produced by whatever leads to new existences,
> For the not setting in motion of these, the excellent Way was taught.[9]

We have here a bhikkhu who climbs on the terrace of the stations of mindfulness and from there contemplates the misery of those fully immersed in their samsaric notion of the self. In the *śloka* that follows the lines just quoted and is the end of the poem the author says, 'the Buddha removed from me the so long latent, the so long standing bond...'. There is therefore a forcefull contrast between those in love with their samsaric self and the bhikkhu who confesses that the Buddha had removed from him all samsaric bond. This *me* (he speaks in the first person) undoubtedly stands for the true self, the self that works his way towards salvation. Another thing worth noticing is that in this passage we come across a phrase that at least in its literal form contradicts the famous *attadīpā, attasaraṇā anaññasaraṇā.* The latter expressions tell us to rely on no other than the self for refuge, while *anadhiṭṭhāya attānaṁ* excludes any reliance on the self or climbing on it as on a boat fit to cross the current of *saṁsāra.* Therefore, both these selves cannot be equated. The second one stands for the self that is *diṭṭhigataṁ,* as becomes clear from the context, the first one will stand, as a result of the contrast, for the true self. Another contrast can still be pointed out. We are told here of people that are in love with their samsaric individuality (*sakkāyābhirataṁ pajaṁ*) and ought to be pitied for their misery. We came across such appelations as *attakāma, ajjhattarato,* and Queen Mallikā confessed that there was for her nothing dearer than the self. Again these both selves cannot stand for one and the same thing. The latter passages ought to refer to an *attā* different from, and opposed to, the *attā* of the *sakkāyadiṭṭhi.*

The doctrine underlying this passage should be well pondered. The immediate source of good and the immediate source of evil cannot be one and the same without any distinction. Whenever there is any activity which tends to final release, the self involved there as the immediate source of such activity is the true self. But the immediate source of any activity that tends to confirm or prolong the samsaric involvement of the self cannot be the true self as such but the moral self working under the wrong notion of its mistaken identity with what is non-self. This wrong notion of self is at work as long as there is any remnant of attachment to those things that are not the self. After all *avijjā* is the first link in the chain of the samsaric process, the *avijjā* that keeps the moral self under the spell of the erroneous and harmful idea of its indentification with things worldly.

THE MORAL SELF UNDER THE INFLUENCE OF MORAL SHORTCOMINGS

We shall now survey some passages that speak of the self as affected by moral shortcomings.

In the first place, the self may be found bad by default, when certain good states are missing in it:

> If, bhikkhus, a bhikkhu, while reflecting, does not see in the self (*attani*) all these good states, then that bhikkhu, for the attainment of all these good states, has to put forth an overwhelming desire, effort, endeavour, etc.[10]

The self may be also the substrate of moral imperfections and vices:

> In the same way, bhikkhus, a bhikkhu beholds these five hindrances (*nīvaraṇe*) in the self (*attani*), when they have not yet been abolished, as a debt, as a disease, as prison, as slavery, as a road in the wilderness.[11]

On a certain occasion, the Buddha met a bhikkhu who was going on his alms round delighting in exterior things and forgetful of mindfulness and composure. He gave him a stern rebuke,

> Do not make the self impure, bhikkhu (*mā kho tvaṁ, bhikkhu, attānaṁ kaṭuviyamakāsi*). That flies will not fall upon, will not stream into a self thus made impure, oozing out with the stench of rotten flesh, this is not possible.[12]

It is to be noted that the phrase, 'that flies will not fall upon, will not stream into a self thus made impure...' gives to the term *attānaṁ* an objective value which can be ill expressed by the use of a merely reflexive pronoun in the translation. Covetousness is said soon after to be the impurity of the self; malevolence, the foul smell of rotten flesh; and evil desires, the flies.

The self is also presented as the active moral agent of evil:

> Applying the self to a wrong endeavour (*ayoge juñjamattānaṁ*), not applying the self to the right endeavour (*yogasmiṁ ca ayojayaṁ*),
> Neglecting his welfare, grasping what is attractive, he should envy one who applies himself to the self.[13]

What can possibly mean *attānuyoginaṁ*? The text seems to demand rather *atthānuyoginaṁ,* 'one who applies himself to what is profitable', as a sequence to the previous *pāda, atthaṁ hitvā piyaggāhi,* but there is no *varia lectio* in favour of *atthānuyoginaṁ.* If one who applies himself to the self is to be envied it will be so because he is doing the right thing. Therefore, the *attā* to which he applies himself cannot be the *attā* of the *sakkāyadiṭṭhi,* but the true *attā.* In *attānuyoginaṁ* the self shows itself as the reality that man ought to love above all other things, of which so much has been said in the preceding chapters.

THE MORAL SELF 'WOUNDED AND KILLED' BY EVIL

Morally wrong actions harm the self at times with a harm that is expressed occasionally with very strong language, connoting a kind of spiritual death. This harm is of a moral nature and affects what we call the 'spiritual' nature of man. It does not refer directly to the evil consequences or different kinds of punishment that may follow the practice of evil; it refers to the immediate damaging effect that ensues from practising evil or allowing evil conditions to prevail over the self. Such emphatic language describes the harm done to the self as something real, even if it can be only expressed under the guise of metaphorical language. We do not see how a merely conventional notion of the self as the object of such 'spiritual' harm can do justice to such descriptions.

> Possessed of three qualities, the foolish imperfect man carries about a self that is injured and wounded (*khataṁ upahataṁ attānaṁ pariharati*), and he comes to be blameworthy, censured by the wise, and produces great demerit. What three? Evil bodily conduct, evil conduct in speech, evil mental conduct.[14]

The sentence, 'carries about a self...' is worth pondering. It distinguishes between man in general and the *attā* as the wounded spiritual reality that is carried about by him, suggesting the objective reality of the latter. This distinction comes out more prominently in a passage where *attā* is in the nominative and preceded by the genitive of possession, *assa:*

> and first of all indeed his self is injured and wounded
> (*assa attā khato ca hoti upahato ca*).[15]

Here the translation that would give *attā* a merely reflexive sense is simply impossible.

A similar harmful effect regarding the self is attributed to Ariṭṭha's wrong view that 'following the things declared stumbling blocks by the Lord, there is no stumbling block at all'.

Buddha's reprimand to the recalcitrant bhikkhu is severe:

> And yet you, foolish man, not only misrepresent me with this being wrongly grasped by your self (*attanā duggahitena*),
> but also injure the self (*attānaṁ khaṇasi*) and give rise to much demerit,
> which for a long time will be for you a cause of discomfort and sorrow.[16]

One who sins against the *pañcasīla* here itself is 'digging out the root of the self' (*mūlaṁ khaṇati attano*).[17] We are afraid a 'conventionalist' would find some difficulty in translating this phrase. He would have to translate it as, 'he digs up his own root'. Would this convey the full meaning of the original?

The canon insists often on the avoidance of evil language. In a passage that occurs several times the tongue is compared to a hatchet which splits the self by means of evil language,

> For every man that is born a hatchet is formed in the mouth,
> By means of which the fool splits the self (*yāya chindati attānaṁ*) speaking evil language.[18]

The *Parivāra* gives us a description in verse of the bhikkhu not possessed of the qualities that qualify one to reprove others and every one of the 14 stanzas ends with the same line:

> such a reproving man brings the self to ruin
> (*tadiso codako jhāpeti attānaṁ*).[19]
> The spiritual harm done to the self by the practice of evil is expressed at times in terms of sickness and death:
>
> > Men in great numbers set on a path consisting of sensual pleasures, leading to an unhappy end,
> > Follow it for a long time, bringing illness to the self (*attano rogamāvahaṁ*).[20]

Also:

> Gains, honour, and fame accrued to Devadatta for the slaughter of the self (*attavadhāya*),
> gains, honour, and fame accrued to Devadatta for his ruin.[21]
> Possessions kill the foolish, not the seekers of the further shore,
> By his craving for possessions, the fool kills, as well as others, the self (*hanti aññeva attanaṁ* [sic]).[22]

Referring to an impostor who pretends to lead a simple life in order to be honoured by people, it is said:

First he kills the self (*hanati attānaṁ*), then he kills others.
He kills the self thoroughly (*suhataṁ hanti attānaṁ*), as with a net is killed a bird.[23]
The fool who resorting to evil views, reviles the teaching of the arahants, the dharmic life of the ariyans,
Like the fruit of the *kaṭṭha* plant, he bursts open for the destruction of the self (*attaghātāya phallati*)[24]

ASMIMĀNA AS THE ROOT OF ALL MORAL EVIL

From the moral point of view there is no other disposition more harmful to the self than conceit or *asmimāna.* As a matter of fact, asmimāna is at the root of all evil and is the fundamental cause for the maintenance of the cycles of birth and death, the *samsāra.* The reason behind this is not difficult to find. *Asmimāna* basically consists in the Buddhist system in the wrong idea of the *sakkāyadiṭṭhi* self, which identifies the self with the *khandhas,* and is therefore the first born child of *avijjā.* Asmimāna casts its shadow on the moral life of man in the form of undue attachment to things that are not the self. Any action that goes counter to liberation is in the last analysis an action inspired by inordinate 'self-attachment' strengthening thereby the hold on man of *asmimāna* and contributing to a perverse 'self-assertion' wherein the self that asserts itself is not the pure, ontologically independent self but the wrong idea of it projected on the samsaric experience. We can discover this asmimānic self, connoted by the term *attā* in a passage of the *Aṅguttaranikāya.*

There are, bhikkhus, these four anariyan quests.
What four? Herein, bhikkhus, a certain man, being as regards self (*attanā*) by nature subject to decay (*jarādhammo*) he seeks precisely (*eva*) after that which is by nature subject to decay; being as regards self (*attanā*) by nature subject to disease he seeks precisely after that which is by nature subject to disease; being as regards self (*attanā*) by nature subject to death he seeks precisely after that which is by nature subject to death; being as regards self (*attanā*) subject to defilement he seeks precisely after that which is by nature subject to defilement. These, bhikkhus, are the four anariyan quests.

> There are, bhikkhus, these four ariyan quests. What four? Herein, bhikkhus a certain man being as regards self (*attanā*) by nature subject to decay seing wretchedness in what is by nature subject to decay he seeks after the undecaying, the unsurpassed utter security, *nibbāna*; being as regards self (*attanā*) by nature subject to disease seing wretchedness in what is by nature subject to disease he seeks after the unailing, unsurpassed utter security, *nibbāna*; ... he seeks after the deathless, unsurpassed utter security, *nibbāna*; ... he seeks after the undefiled, unsurpassed utter security, nibbāna.[25]

A careful survey of this passage will bring out the following points:

1. There is a marked difference between the first part and the second part of the passage. We may say that the first part concerns a person called in many other parts of the canon *assutavā putthujjano,* while the second part describes the activity of the opposite *sutavā ariyasāvako.*

2. The *attanā* in both parts refers to one and the same thing. Obviously it cannot be the *attā* of *attadīpā attasaraṇā anaññasaraṇā,* or the one indicated in the compounds *attakāmo, ajjhattarato,* or the *attā* that leaves aside all the things mentioned in the unariyan quests and seeks after *nibbāna,* the one specified for instance in the compound *nibutatto,* which we shall study later on. The *attā* of this passage is the one that is commented upon in the *Niddesa* as *attā vuccati diṭṭhigataṁ.* This is equivalent to saying that the *attā* of this passage is the *attā* of the *sakkāyadiṭṭhi,* the one that identifies itself with the khandhas. It is this identification that makes this *attā* be by nature decay, disease, death, defilement.

3. The three first paragraphs in both parts of this passage refer to *attā* as something rather objective, as they speak of decay, disease and death as opposed to the undecaying, the unailing, the deathless, *nibbāna.* The fourth paragraphs in both parts of the passage attribute to *attā* a moral import, as they speak of defilement and its opposite, the undefiled, *nibbāna.* On account of the four paragraphs in both parts speaking of the same *attā* we come here to the same conclusion as the one drawn from the passage of the *Theragāthā* mentioned above, namely, that the self of the *sakkāyadiṭṭhi,* the one identified with decay, disease, death, and what leads to it, is the immediate source of defilement, impurity, attachment to worldly things, i.e. of all moral evil.

4. In the first part of the passage there is an unbroken continuity be-

tween what a man is 'as regards self' and what he seeks after. This continuity is expressed by the particle *eva,* translated as 'precisely'. Man, in this first part considers himself to be by nature decay, disease, death and defilement and seeks precisely after what is by nature decay, disease, death and defilement. In the second part, the continuity between what he is as regards self and what he seeks after is broken. It is obvious that the *attā* of the *sakkāyadiṭṭhi* is not competent to see the wretchedness of whatever is by nature decay, disease, death and defilement (being identified with it) and still less to seek after liberation from those things in the undecaying, unailing, deathless, undefiled *nibbāna.* Therefore the moral self that exercises its activity in the second part of the passage has to be the true self. No one will object to saying that these four ariyan quests coincide in spirit with the famous *attānaṁ gaveseyyātha.*

Given the fundamental depravity of asmimāna it is no wonder to read that the victory over it is like the final victory:

> How, bhikkhus, is a bhikkhu an ariyan with flag lowered down (a sign of victory), with the burden laid down, entirely detached? Herein, bhikkhus, a bhikku whose conceit (*asmimāno*) has been abandoned, entirely uprooted, turned into a palm-tree stump never to sprout again, of a nature never to arise in the future; that is how, bhikkhus, a bhikkhu is an ariyan with flag lowered down, with the burden laid down, entirely detached.[26]

That is why to the question:

> What is that one thing that should be abandoned?

The answer given is:

> Conceit (*asmimāna*) is the one thing that should be abandoned.[27]

A compound that expresses this asmimanic 'self-attachment' is *attahetu,* where again the *attā* referred to cannot be the true pure self but its distorted samsaric image:

> Not for the sake of self (*na attahetu*), not for the sake of others should one desire a son, wealth or a kingdom,
> One should not desire prosperity for self (*attano*) in a way contrary to dhamma.
> Let him be virtuous, wise, proceeding according to *dhamma.*[28]

One of the most common manifestations of *asmimāna* is the feeling of proud superiority regarding others:

That advantage that he sees in self (*attani*),
As regards what is seen, heard, thought, as regards morality and observances,
Being therein attached only to that,
He considers all others to be inferiors.[29]

That this *attani* stands for the asmimanic self is clear from the commentary to this lines found in the *Mahāniddesa,* where, as noted in the first chapter, it is said of it, *attā vuccati diṭṭhigataṁ.*[30]

That is why *asmimāna* is not found in the Buddhas, who are free from pride of self and contempt for others:

Fearless are those Buddhas, like a lion the king of beasts,
They neither praise self (*nevukkaṁsenti attānaṁ*), nor despise other beings.
Free from pride and contempt, equal to all beings,
The Buddhas are not given to self-glorification (*anattukaṁsakā*), such is the eternal law of the Buddhas.[31]

The Thera Jenta confesses that before he met the Buddha he was proud of his birth, possessions and appearance, and he did not consider anyone to be his equal or superior (*nāttano samakaṁ kañci atirekaṁ ca maññisaṁ*). But after meeting the Buddha, all his conceit was eradicated (*asmimāno samucchinno*).[32]

One betrays conceit not only when he praises himself and despises others, but also when he is in the grip of an unhealthy obsession regarding self and tries to see whether he is superior, equal or inferior to others. Among the different kinds of conceit we find these three mentioned in the *Mahāniddesa,* 'the conceit, "I am better", the conceit, "I am equal", the conceit, "I am inferior"'.[33] Somewhere else we read:

Let him not think, 'I am better than he is',
'I am inferior', or even 'I am equal',
Under the impression of manyfold forms,
He should not persist in speculating on self
(*ātumānaṁ vikappayaṁ*).[34]

This disastrous self-centredness, being wholly immersed in sense impressions (cf. above, 'under the impression of manyfold forms') and overpowered by them, is directed towards the empirical factors, which are erroneously treated as 'the self'. Herein lies the error of such attitude and the source of all the harm that this kind of obsession does to man. Here lurks what, as we shall see in the second part of the book, is the *diṭṭhi* of all *diṭṭhis* and their common bedrock, the *sakkāyadiṭṭhi.* We may call this doctrine the moral doctrine of *anattā* which corresponds with the metaphysical doctrine of *anattā* to be studied in the second part of the book.

That this morbid attention given to self is intimately connected with what is called a *diṭṭhi,* i.e. a self-centred view on any subject, becomes manifest from:

Let him not form a *diṭṭhi* in the world,
As regards knowledge, morality or observances,
He should not bring in self (*attānaṁ anupaneyya*) saying 'I am equal';
He should not consider [himself] inferior or superior.[35]

And:

By what he calls another a fool,
By that he considers himself (*ātumānaṁ*) an expert
[He himself being called an expert by himself (*sayaṁ attanā*)],
And proclaims others contemptible.
When he is proficient in a view of exceeding quality (*atisāradiṭṭhiyā*),
Mad with pride, considering himself perfect,
He himself crowns self (*sayameva sāmaṁ*) in his mind,
So perfect is that view of his indeed.[36]

This chapter should convince us that whenever something goes morally wrong in man, the spirit at work is the fallacious, erring spirit of the *sakkāyadiṭṭhi,* which practises a kind of samsaric 'self-assertion', which is only a distorted caricature of the real 'Self-assertion'. The latter is expressed in any true effort to clear away *avijjā,* to subdue all wrong inclinations, to master the senses and the mind, in fine, to detach the Self from whatever is non-self and establish it on that supreme region which is the abode of supreme security and peace, not subject to change, beyond the reach of *dukkha,* and out of boundaries from the perpetual recurrence of birht and death.

Seing things in this light, the preceding considerations confirm the assertion that the only distinction of consequence recognized by the Nikāyas regarding the use of the term *attā* is the distinction between the *attā* of the *sakkāyadiṭṭhi* and the true *attā.*

5

Towards Perfection

Mention has just been made of two kinds of "self-assertion", the illusory and harmful one that asserts the asmimanic self, and the beneficial and authentic one that tries to detach the Self from all samsaric influences and bring about its perfect integration. In broad lines, the process of salvation may be said to comprehend the following steps,

1. Suppression of moral evil.
2. Practice of virtue, which is both, a means to suppress moral evil by the insertion of the contrary and a predisposition for the attainment of final liberation, as it runs in the direction of utter detachment.
3. Final attainment of liberation, which is the supreme kind of purity, by means of which, the Self, detached from even what is considered morally good and meritorious, establishes itself on its independent metaphysical reality.

This chapter is going to deal with the salutary activity undertaken by man in order eventually to bring about the establishement of the Self in its own metaphysical hypostasis.

THE SELF AS RELATED TO MORAL GOOD

We have contemplated the self as affected by bad moral qualities and imperfections. We are to see now the other side of the coin. The moral self is also exhibited in the Nikāyas as the doer and possessor of good actions and qualities.

A bhikkhu who beholds in the self (*attani samanupassati*) certain good qualities but does not see others has to put forth 'a vehement desire, effort, determination, exertion, unrestricted impulse, mindfulness and circumspection' for stability (*patiṭṭhāya*) in those good qualities he has, for the attainment of the good qualities that he finds missing in the self and furthermore for the destruction of the *āsavas,* this being the final step towards perfection.[1]

The stability of good conditions in the self demands stability or permanence in the moral self. Good conditions are not contemplated as subsisting by themselves, but as inherent in the self that sets in motion the moral activity called for and reaps its fruits, as it is shown in the following text:

> Whoever, your reverences, be it a bhikkhu or a bhikkhunī beholds in the self (*attani samanupassati*) four conditions, ought to come to this conclusion, 'I am not declining in good conditions. This has been declared by the Blessed One to be non-decay'. What four conditions? Paucity of lust, paucity of ill-will, paucity of infatuation, and the eye of wisdom of such an one operates as regards profound questions on propriety and impropriety (*ṭhānāṭhānesu*).[2]

The discussion of the painful effects of evil on the self has been one of the topics in the preceding chapter. Now we are told that the lack of evil and the presence of good make the self happy and contented.

> As if it were freedom from debt, as health, as freedom from bonds, as freedom from slavery, as a land of security, that is how a bhikkhu beholds the five hindrances (*nīvaraṇe*) when abolished in the self (*pahīne attani samanupassati*).[3]

The elation produced by the abolishment of the *nīvaraṇas* (sensuality and passion, ill-will, torpor, worry, perplexity or doubt), similar to the elation of one who has set himself free from debt, one who feels healthy after a spell of sickness, one who experiences freedom from past bonds, one who finds himself a free man after having been a slave, or one who reaches a secure land after traversing a region infested by robbers, such elation does not apply to the 'suppressed' *nīvaraṇas,* but to the self that sees them abolished in itself. This again demands the permanence of the self through the process of abolishement and after they have been abolished.

We met frequently with the expression, *khataṁ upahataṁ attānaṁ pariharati,* 'He carries about a self that is wounded and injured or uprooted and half dead'. The possessor of the good qualities contrary to the vices that were the cause of the self's miserable condition, 'carries about a self that is not wounded (*akkhataṁ*) nor injured (*anupahataṁ*)'. This is, as indicated on another occasion, a negative way of talking that expresses a flourishing spiritual health, as the Buddhist texts are fond of such negative expressions.[4]

This impression of well-being consequent to the suppression of bad qualities and the acquisition of their contraries demands also the permanence of the moral self. The same will apply to the following:

> One thing more, Mahānāma, the ariyan disciple brings to mind the virtues of the self (*attano*), unbroken, flawless, spotless, unblemished, freedom-giving, commended by the wise, undefiled and leading to *samādhi,*

whence follows the purification of the mind from lust, ill-will and infatuation, the attainment of knowledge and the experience of great joy. And:

> One thing more, Mahānāna, the ariyan disciple brings to mind the liberality of the self (*attano*), thinking, 'It is an acquisition for me, that I myself (*yo'haṁ*) among people possessed of the stain of stinginess live the family life with a mind free from the stain of stinginess'.[5]

We have here a self-centredness that cannot be identified with the inordinate self-centredness described in the preceding chapter. This self-centredness is directed towards the true self, that is why it does not run counter to liberation from the three fundamental blemishes of character (lust, ill-will and infatuation). The same will apply to:

> Thus these good qualities that I see planted in the self (*ṭhite passāmi attani*),
> Hence joy arises for me, and great mental ease.[6]

Finally the self is shown as the substrate of virtues in another passage of the *Jātaka*:

> One who beholds in the self (*attani passati*) virtue, knowledge and insight,
> Attains both to the welfare of self (*attano*) and of others.[7]

We find another type of passages where both the active moral agent as well as the moral substratum of virtues is indicated by the use of the term *attanā.*

> Bhikkhus, a bhikkhu possessed of five qualities is fit to converse with his fellow-farers in the brahma-life. What five? Herein, bhikkhus, a bhikkhu is endowed with virtue as regards the self (*attanā*) and replies to questions bearing on information about the obtention of virtue.[8]

Parallel passages follow where the same applies to perfect concentration (*samādhi*), wisdom (*paññā*), liberation (*vimutti*), and perfect knowledge of liberation (*vimuttiñāṇadassana*), which are counted among the highest achievements in the Buddhist training.

This *attanā* is used ten times in passages similar to:

There are, bhikkhus, ten praiseworthy conditions. What ten? Herein bhikkhus, a bhikkhu is as regards the self (*attanā*) a man of few wants (*appiccho*), and is a maker of speeches to the bhikkhus about wanting little.[9]

Parallel passages follow about being contented, secluded, shunning company, strenuous, perfect in virtue, perfect in concentration, perfect in wisdom, perfect in liberation, perfect in the complete knowledge of liberation.

Moral good in general is often expressed by the term *attha,* which may be translated as 'spiritual welfare or spiritual acquisition'. There are three levels of attainment, attainment in this very life (*diṭṭhadhammikattha*), attainment in a life to come (*samparāyikattha*), and *paramattha*[10] this being none other than *nibbāna*.[11] We shall take into account here some passages where *attha* is explicitly connected with the self (*attā*). One of the most general and comprehensive statements is:

Hence, let the wise man, discerning the welfare of the self (*sampassaṁ atthaṁ attano*),
Thoroughly investigate *dhamma,* thus thereby he will be purified.[12]

That *attha* in this sense has an entirely 'spiritual' value and as such affects the 'spiritual' man is clear from the preceding text and also from:

One who beholds in the self (*attani passati*) virtue, wisdom and knowledge of tradition,
He attains both the welfare of the self (*attano*) and of others.[13]

Self-restraint or self-mastery is a means, the most universal one, to achieve this 'spiritual welfare' of the self:

I shall restrain the self (*sanniggaṇhāmi attānaṁ*),
having in mind the spiritual welfare of the self
(*sampassaṁ atthaṁ attano*).[14]

A singularly fine example of what has often been referred to as ambivalence of the self. *Attānaṁ* is the first *pāda* stands for the moral self as involved in worldly phenomena, that is likely to go wrong if not kept in check. *Attano* in the second *pāda* stands for the moral self as the beneficiary of such self-mastery, as the subject of purification and final liberation to which all self-mastery is directed.

Attha or spiritual achievement is explicitly connected with the self in the first three items listed in a catalogue of ten 'proper aims or achievements' (*yathatthā*) given in the *Paṭisambhidāmagga.* They are, 'the aim or achievement of self-mastery' (*attadamathattho*), 'the aim or achievement of self-quietude' (*attasamathattho*), and 'the aim or achievement of the *nibbāna* of the self' (*attaparinibbāpanattho*).[15]

SELF-EXERTION

The practice of virtue and the attainment of final purification and consequent liberation are not to be had for the asking. They demand an unrelenting striving, a continual output of energy, an unbroken perseverance. Passages where this kind of exertion is recommended or described at work are of very frequent occurrence.[16] Such passages contain an implicit assertion of the reality of the moral agent. To say that there is exertion and no one to produce it is entirely un-Buddhistic, because it fails to assign a cause to such exertion. Such effort, such endeavour, such unremitting dedication to purification and final liberation is not a spontaneous phenomenon but something to be deliberately produced and maintained. Inner states such as those described in the above footnote do not just happen but are intentionally induced and kept going. Therefore we have to look for their cause. They cannot be deemed to be the creation of anyone of the *khandhas,* since the existence and permanence of the latter depend on the *paṭiccasamuppāda,* while all and everyone of the links of the *paṭiccasamuppāda* are in their totality factors of samsaric existence, not of liberation. The *paṭiccasamuppāda* cannot in any way be said to be an *asaṅkhatagāmimaggo,* but runs counter to it. Liberation consists in the breaking of the chain which has to be effected forcibly, by a factor exterior to the chain itself, as the tendency of the chain left to itself is to perpetuate itself. If final liberation were the spontaneous result of the *paṭiccasamuppāda,* it would take place all by itself and that is precisely Makkhali Gosāla's heresy.[17] The factor outside the *paṭiccasamuppāda* which strives for the breaking of the latter ought to be real, for the effect of its action is also real, namely the bringing to an end of the round of samsaric existences. This factor, exterior to the *paṭiccasamuppāda*-chain cannot be but the *attā,* which is independent from it and the agent of purification and liberation, as we can see from so many testimonies of the Nikāyas.

Let us see now how moral exertion is explicitly connected with the self.

Before a display of energy as has been described above, there has to be present what is called *attasammāpaṇidhi,* 'right aspiration of the self'. We read in the *Kuddakapātha:*

> Dwelling in a befitting place, and merit acquired from previous works, And right aspiration of the self (*attasammāpaṇidhi*), this is the supremely good omen.[18]

Exertion as explicitly related to *attā* is found in the compound *pahitatto,* of frequent use. F. L. Woodward translates it as, 'with self established',[19] and gives a footnote refering to Mrs. Rhys Davids' comments on the commentarial explanation of the compound, where Mrs. Rhys Davids also translates the compound as, 'with self well established':

> A parallel term *pahitatta,* 'one who has the self established', is, it is true, in a frequently occurring formula. But it is by the Commentary bent into conformity with the anatta teaching, by the philologically improbable exegesis: 'who has the self sent away' (*pesitatto*).[20]

The term *pahitatto* is explained in the *Mahāniddesa* when commenting on the words, *pahitattassa bhikkhuno.* Two explanations are given. The first one consists in piling up synonyms that imply effort, exertion, strength, etc.,

> 'of the self exerting (*pahitattassa*)' this means of one displaying energy, of one engaged in steadfastness, of one given to strong effort, of one who has an acute desire, of one who does not put down the burden regarding good qualities.

The second explanation, the one repudiated by Mrs. Rhys Davids, reads:

> 'of him whose self is incited (*pesitattassa*)' means whose self (*yassattā*), (following the Siamese and Roman editions, the other editions read *yassatthāya*) is impelled (*pesito*) as regards the benefit of the self (*attatthe*), and as regards right conduct (*ñāye*), and as regards marks (*lakkhaṇe: anicca, dukkha, anattā*?), and as regards performance (*karaṇe*), and as regards questions of propriety or impropriety (*ṭhānāṭhāne,* which may mean also as regards good and bad destiny).

Instead of a disavowal of the self we find here a full recognition of it in the use of *yassattā* and *attatthe. Pesito* means not only 'sent away' but also 'sent forth, impelled', and this second meaning is the one best fitting the context of this second explanation. It makes little difference whetter *pesito* is commented upon with reference to *padahati* (to strive, to exert) or *pahiṇati,* which corresponds with the Sanskrit root *prahi,* whose passive participle *prahita* means not only 'sent away, expelled', but also and mainly, 'urged on, incited, stirred up'. It is to be noted that the Sanskrit *preṣita* has as the first acceptation, 'set in motion, urged on, impelled', even though it may also mean 'banished'. After the second explanation of *pahitattassa,* where *pahito* is explained as *pesito* there follow several formulas that are thought to be suited for impelling the self in one or other of the ways just pointed out (*attatthe, ñāye,* etc.). It is here that some may have been misled to think that *pesito* means 'sent away, banished'. If that might be a right translation in *sabbe dhammā anattā ti pesitattassa,* it will not do justice to other slogans like, 'this is the way conducive to the cessation of the *āsavas*', 'these things ought to be known', 'these things ought to be realized', (*ayaṁ āsavanirodhagāminī paṭipadā ti pesitattassa, ime dhammā abhiññeyyā ti pesitattassa, ime dhammā sacchikātabbā ti pesitattassa*), where it is obvious that the *attā* is not 'banished or disowned', but 'sent forth, impelled, urged', to follow the way, to know, to realize.[21]

No, the authors and compilers of the *Niddesa* were by no means partisans of absolute *anattā,* they kept a very balanced attitude between acceptance of *attā* and profession of relative *anattā,* as it is apparent in this very text where no embarassment is felt in the use of *yassattā* and *attatthe,* while on the other hand the doctrine of relative *anattā* is clearly stated in *sabbe dhammā anattā.* As a matter of fact, this balanced attitude is one of the outstanding characteristics of the *Niddesa.*

Pahitatto is the theme of the *Sīlasutta* of the *Aṅguttara.* In the prose section one who whether walking or standing, or sitting, or lying down is free from covetousness and ill-will, free from torpor, free from worry, having suppressed doubt, one who has undertaken the effort to be diligent, one who has established in himself an ever watchful mindfulness, one whose body is serene, not violent, one whose mind is well composed and concentrated, one who is such, is called, 'ardent, scrupulous, ever concentrated, one who has undertaken effort, self-exerting (*pahitatto*)'. In the metrical part of the sutta we read:

He should walk exerting himself, he should stand exerting himself,
He should sit down exerting himself, he should lie down exerting himself,
He should bend it (the arm, etc.) exerting himself, he should stretch it out exerting himself.

Whether above, in the middle or below, while existing in the world lasts,
He should consider the rising and ceasing of the *dhammas* and *khandhas,*
Always keeping in mind the way to calm the mind proper to those that train themselves.
Such a bhikkhu is said to be one who is ever self-exerting (*satataṁ pahitattò*).[22]

Another context speaks of one who at the news of a calamity or death befallen some person or relative, or at the actual sight of such occurrence gets a moral shock and starts applying himself methodically to moral exertion. The text continues:

Self-exerting (*pahitatto*), when still in his body (*kāyena c'eva*), realizes the highest truth and sees it, having penetrated it by means of insight.[23]

Self-exertion is but a means to an end, that is the realization of the highest truth. A self-exerting bhikkhu, wholly given to self-exertion does not pay attention to outward comforts:

Eating four or five morsels, let him drink water,
That should be enough for living in comfort for a self-exerting bhikkhu (*pahitattassa bhikkhuno*).
If one allowable robe covers him and that obtained as an alms,
That should be enough ... .
If just the rain does not fall on the knees of him who is sitting cross-legged,
That should be enough ... .[24]

Māra tempted the Buddha who was practising self-exertion by the river Nerañjarā with thoughts of giving up his exertion, which seemed to endanger his life, and to lead a more bearable life trying to get merits by means of sacrifice. The Buddha replies that merit is of no use to himself, and continues:

There is faith for me and strength and wisdom,
Why do you worry about my life when I am thus self-exerting (*pahitattaṁ*)?
This wind might dry even the currents of the rivers,
Even my blood may dry up while I am thus self-exerting (*pahitattassa*).
With blood dried up, bile and phlegm also dry up,
With muscles withered, the mind gets calmed all the better.[25]

The life of a good buddhist bhikkhu is depicted in the Nikāyas as a life of continuous dedication, unremitting effort, endless tension towards self-realization even in the midst of an unperturbed calm and apparent inactivity. This is what secures for him the attainment of the ultimate peace (*nibbāna*) even in this very life (*diṭṭhe dhamme*). In line with the importance given in the canon to good company as a source of encouragement to persevere in such excellent pursuit, we read:

> Let him dwell with the solitary, self-exerting, meditative noble ones, with the wise who are ever displaying energy.[26]

SELF-CONTROL

Among the moral activities of the self in its way towards perfection, one that obtains pre-eminence in all systems of moral training is the struggle for self-control.

Just at the outset, it is of the outmost importance that we decide the question about who is the controller of the self. It cannot be any other than the self itself. Here we have another instance of the ambivalence of the moral self, which consists this time in the action of the self upon itself. Indeed all moral actions of the self are 'reflexive' in this primary sense, as all of them bear some kind of fruit for the very self that is their agent. This action, the result of which remains in the agent is called 'immanent action', and all the actions of the self are basically immanent for the reason already given. We read:

> Impel the self by means of the self (*attanā codayattānaṁ*), control the self by means of the self (*paṭimaṁsettha attanā*),
> Being with guarded self (*attagutto*), mindful, you, bhikkhu, will dwell in bliss.[27]

Thus it is clear that any use of the term *attā* (and not only the oblique cases, as the 'conventionalists' are wont to say) has basically a reflexive sense. This gives us the clue for the interpretation of so many compounds where *attā* is one of the elements. When we say of someone, using the compound occurring in this very text, that he is *attagutto,* 'a man with guarded self', it is to be understood that the *attā* is both the guardian and the guarded.

The main characteristics of the self, as revealed in its moral activity, is that of self-possession, which is equivalent to self-determination, without any outward hindrance. That is precisely the reason given in the *Mahāvagga*[28] to prove that the khandhas are not the self, they are not self-possessed and cannot be changed according as one wishes. Self-control is precisely what gives the self the unobstructed freedom of action necessary for the attainment of perfection.

At times, the excellence of self-control is joyfully sung:

> One might defeat in battle thousands upon thousands of men,
> He who would conquer one, the self (*attānaṁ*), he indeed is the best of warriors.
> The conquered self (*attā*) is certainly better than conquering other people,
> For the man whose self is tamed (*attadantassa*), who fares ever mindful.[29]

There is a stanza that, judging from the number of times it occurs became very popular:

> Irrigators have mastery over the waters, fletchers have mastery over the shaft,
> Carpenters have mastery over the wood, the wise bring the self under subjection (*attānaṁ damayanti*).[30]

The main thing to be subdued when trying for self-control is the mind always bent on reckless wandering. Both these types of control are mentioned together in a stanza that insists on the simile of the fletcher:

> Straightening the self (*samunnamayaṁ attānaṁ*), as the fletcher does with the shaft,
> Making the mind straight, pierce ignorance, O Hārita.[31]

Those who later on substituted for all practical purposes *citta* for *attā*, making the former the ultimate constituent of human personality could draw from this text an argument in favour of their view calling attention to the parallelism between *samunamayamattānaṁ* and *cittaṁ ujuṃ karitvāna.* But such parallelism suffers from an essential dissimilarity. Self itself straightens the self, while the mind does not straighten itself, but is straightened under the initiative and energy of the moral agent. In the text, it is Hārita who straightens himself (his self!), a purely reflexive and immanent action, and he is also who straightens the mind in order to pierce through ignorance, an action that is immanent as regards the total moral agent, as the piercing through ignorance devolves ultimately to the benefit of the self, while the mind is a mere instrument of the moral agent.[32]

It is from the perspective just shown that the following text should be viewed:

> On four occasions, bhikkhus, earnestness, mindfulness and watchfulness of mind should be exercised by the very self (*attarūpena*). What four?
>
> 'Let not the mind become for me lustful in things leading to lust', thus earnestness, mindfulness and watchfulness of mind should be exercised by the very self (*attarūpena*).
>
> 'Let not my mind be full of ill-will in things leading to ill-will, …'. 'Let not my mind be infatuated in things leading to infatuation, …'. 'Let not my mind be conceited in things leading to conceit, …'.[33]

The subsidiarity of the mind to the self and the role of mind's control in the acquisition of self-control is expressed in:

> The bhikkhu, having obtained his alms at the proper time,
> Going alone, let him sit apart.
> With a mind turned to self (*ajjhattacintī*), he should not let his mind go forth to outward things,
> He who by character is controlled as to self (*saṅgahitattabhāvo*).[34]

Control of the self includes not only control of the mind but of the senses as well. It is by means of the senses that the mind runs riot. A text tells us explicitly that this control of the senses ought to be practiced for the benefit of the self:

> By following what method, by keeping what observance by what kind of conduct would one
> Be a doer of what ought to be done for the self (*attano kiccakārī'ssa*), and not hurt it in any way?
> Man's senses may be for his benefit or harm.
> If unguarded, they are for his harm, if guarded, for his benefit.
> Guarding the senses, protecting them, one would
> Be a doer of what ought to be done for the self, and would not hurt it in any way.[35]

Self-control, though absolutely necessary, is not an easy thing:

> If he were to make his self (*attānaṁ*), as he teaches others to be,
> Then being tamed he could try to tame others, because the self, as it is

well known, is difficult to tame (*attā hi kira duddamo*).[36]

Akin to control of the self is the guarding of the self:

Like a frontier town, well guarded within and without,
Even so you should guard the self (*evaṁ gopetha attānaṁ*), let not the opportunity pass by.[37]

One whose self is guarded is called *rakkhitatto* in the *Theragāthā*:

He should occupy solitary beds and seats,
He should procure release from fetters,
If he does not pursue sexual love,
He may dwell in the Order with guarded self (*rakkhitatto*), ever mindful.[38]

The moral qualification of self-control is also expressed by means of several compounds. In finding out their true meaning, the rule already given should be kept in mind, that in such cases the self is controller and controlled, all in one, because as the *Suttanipāta* says:

The self is the master of the self (*attā hi attano nātho*), who else could be his master?
For by reason of having a well tamed self (*attanā hi sudantena*), one obtains a master difficult to obtain.[39]

Thus we meet with *attavasī,* 'one who has obtained mastery over the self';[40] *attadanto,* 'one whose self is tamed',[41] which, as the quotations given in the footnote show, is frequently combined with *samāhito,* 'recollected integrated'. We find also the last quality indicated with the compound *samāhitatto,* 'with a self well composed', which is fully explained in the *Mahāniddesa,*[42] *saññatatto,*[43] translated by E. M. Hare as 'restrained-of-self', *saṁyatatto*[44] and *susaṁvutatto*[45] which mean practically the same thing.

Yatatto, 'restrained as to the self', is given as a qualification of a true brāhmaṇa in a very interesting description of him given at the request of a member of that caste:

He is a brāhmaṇa who has ousted all evil dispositions, not rough (*nihuṁhuṁko*), free from impurity, with a self well controlled (*yatatto*),
A knower of the highest knowledge (*vedantagū*), who has lived the brahma-life (*brahmacariya*),
He would explain the highest doctrine (*brahmavādaṁ*) according to truth (*dhammena*),

For whom there is no arrogance in the world.[46]

This definition is interesting because it seems to contain some vedantic echoes. But are they really vedantic echoes or ritualistic references? It must be assumed as a rule that the passages where there is some tendencious reference to the brāhmaṇas, unless proved to be otherwise, relate to the brāhmaṇas' ritualistic life or and to their pride of caste. We meet here not merely with *vedagū,* used in other passages of the canon, but with *vedantagū.* Even so, the only Sanskrit word corresponding to the latter seems to be *vedāntaga,* which according to Monier-Williams (*A Sanskrit-English Dictionary*) occurs in the *Mahābhārata* with the meaning, 'one who has gone to the end of the veda or who has complete knowledge of the veda', having therefore the same meaning as *vedagū.* Besides, the line *vedantagū vūsitabrahmacariyo,* which we have translated, 'a knower of the highest knowledge who has lived the brahma-life', is also found at S I, p. 167, *Brāhmaṇasaṁyutta,* 9, where it occurs in a context with an explicitly sacrificial background, and where, again *vedantagū* does not seem to imply either more or less than *vedaguṁ* in the stanza that immediately follows. The same line is found at K I, p. 336, Stn 3, 4, 61, in a part of the metrical composition that seems to be a later addition, as the original refrain of the poem seems to have been all through, *Tathāgato arahati pūraḷāsaṁ,* and not *Yo brāhmaṇo puññapekkho yajeta* (which is the refrain of the interpolated stanzas, being also the refrain of a poem found at K I, pp. 341 f., Stn 3, 5, from which the two stanzas beginning with *Ye kāme hitvā* and *Ye vītarāga* have been literally borrowed). In any case the background is always a ritualistic one, not philosophical. As regards the term *brahmavāda,* also contained in the definition we are discussing, the references given by Monier-Williams (Ibid.) are the *Taittirīya Brāhmaṇa* and the *Brahma Purāṇa,* and is translated by him as 'discourse or explanation of sacred texts', which gives the term once more a ritualistic significance. It is worth noticing the Buddhistic twist given to *brahmavāda* by means of the word *dhammena* in *dhammena so brahmavādaṁ vadeyya.* The word *nihuṁhuṁko* may also be an intentional pun of ritualistic origin. The word may mean either, 'one who does not utter *huṁ huṁ*', this being a sacred ritual utterance, or 'one who is gentle, not rough, not grumbling'. The last line of the definition contains an open reference to the pride of caste of the brāhmaṇas so often disapproved and even ridiculed in the canon.

In the *Suttanipāta, yatatto* occurs in a description of a muni, together with *saññatatto,* which is, doubtless, similar in meaning.[47]

We may ask, before closing this section on controlling and restraining the self, what is the place of painful striving in the task of bringing the self under control. This point is discussed in the *Devahasutta* of the *Majjhima.* There is a passage in the *sutta* where *attā* is mentioned in this regard:

> And how, bhikkhus, is effort fruitful, how is striving fruitful? Herein, bhikkhus, a bhikkhu does not sully the purified self (*anaddhabhūtaṁ attānaṁ*) by means of pain (*dukkhena*), he does not give up joy which conforms to dhamma, and he does not develop any attachment to such joy.[48]

The background against which this passage is projected is the Jaina mentality according to which salvation is to be obtained mainly, if not exclusively, by severe asceticism, which is the exercise most immediately connected with the annulment of accumulated kamma. Happiness does not seem to get any place in the Jaina system excepting of course the eschatological condition of the liberated soul.[49] Not so in Buddhism, which as it is well known follows a middle way between extreme severity and indulgence. There are practices in Buddhism like the one of the four *jhānas* which are expected to produce intense happiness. The only necessary condition for the non-refusal of happiness and joy is that there should be no inordinate attachment to it. We read in the same sutta:

> And again, bhikkhus, a bhikkhu reflects thus, 'Dwelling as I please unworthy states increase, worthy states decrease, but if I exert my self (*attānaṁ padahanto*) by painful deeds unworthy states decrease and worthy states increase. Suppose I were to exert my self (*attānaṁ padaheyyaṁ*) by painful deeds?' He exerts his self by painful deeds .... At other time he does not exert his self by painful deeds. What is the reason for that? The purpose for which he had exerted his self by painful deeds, such purpose has been attained. Therefore, at other time he does not exert his self by painful deeds.[50]

Painful striving is in Buddhism a means for a definite end to be achieved (*idha*) here and now, not something applied for an unseen purpose. As a consequence of that, painful striving can be applied to measure, as against what happens in Jainism.

PURIFICATION OF THE SELF

The process of purification of the self is given great importance in the Buddhist system of training. As Buddhagosa says in his introductory discourses to his *Visuddhimagga,* 'Here by purity is meant *Nibbāna,* which is free from all taints and exceedingly pure'.[51] And he quotes the *Dhammapada*:

> All aggregates are impermanent, when one sees by means of wisdom,
> Then he gets disgusted at grief. This is the path of purity.[52]

But 'purity' is not an absolute entity and, as such, admits of degrees. Only that purity is absolute that takes one to *anupādāparinibbāna,* i.e. 'utter nibbāna without rebirth-basis'.[53]

A text has already been quoted attesting that purity and impurity depend on the self, another instance of the ambivalence of the moral self. The last line of the text reads:

> Purity and impurity depend on the self (*paccattaṁ*),
> no one could purify another.[54]

Purification of the self is not a task to be done at a stroke, it is a task that requires the patience and skill of the artisan:

> The wise man, methodically, little by little, moment after moment,
> Removes the impurity from the self (*attano*), as a silver-smith removes the impurity from silver.[55]

The simile is very appropriate. The silver-smith stands for the moral agent, the silver stands for the self, the physical impurities of the silver stand for the moral impurities of the self. The latter are meant to be discarded so that the self may stand clean and resplendent.

The stanza quoted in the foregoing note is commented on in the *Mahāniddesa. Kammāro* is explained as *suvaṇṇakāro,* 'gold-smith', and *rajataṁ,* as *jātarūpaṁ,* 'gold in its natural state'.

> As the gold-smith melts, dissolves, removes the gross impurities of gold, and melts, dissolves, removes also the average impurities, and melts, dissolves, removes even the subtlest impurities, even so the bhikkhu melts, dissolves, removes, leaves aside, dispels, exterminates, destroys the gross impurities (*kilese*) of the self (*attano*), and the average impurities of the self, and the subtlest impurities of the self. Or, the bhikkhu melts, dissolves, removes, leaves aside, dispels, exterminates, destroys

the impurity of lust from the self (*attano*), the impurity of ill-will, of infatuation, of conceit, of wrong view, of the *kilesas,* of evil conduct, whatever is blinding, obstructing sight, depriving of knowledge, hampering higher wisdom, having its part with distress, not conducing to *nibbāna,* etc.[56]

The mind is, doubtless, the innermost instrument of the moral agent. That is why purity of the mind is insisted upon in so many passages of the Nikāyas. In several passages we find the following verses:

Leaving aside dark works, the wise man should practise bright works,
Going from home to the homeless state, in solitude, where worldly joys are difficult,
There, let him desire for the outstanding joy; setting aside sense-pleasures, possessing nothing,
Let the wise man cleanse the self (*pariodapeyya attānaṁ*) from the impurities of the mind (*cittaklesehi*).[57]

The last two lines offer the right perspective, namely that the mind is not purified for its own sake but for the sake of the self, who is the ultimate beneficiary of all moral purity.

The expression *visuddhaṁ attānaṁ samanupassati,* 'he beholds the self purified', (where, let us not forget, the seer and the seen are one and the same), appears in a context of the *Majjhima,* which explains the purity of the self in great detail:

And how bhikkhus, a bhikkhu is one who has attained the proper way and method of a samaṇa? Covetousness is abandoned by the bhikkhu who was covetous, malevolence is abandoned by the bhikkhu who was malevolent, anger is abandoned by a bhikkhu who was given to anger, grudge is abandoned by a bhikkhu who had any grudge, hypocrisy is abandoned by the bhikkhu who was a hypocrite, spite is abandoned by the bhikkhu who was spiteful, envy is abandoned by the bhikkhu who was envious, stinginess is abandoned by the bhikkhu who was stingy, craftiness is abandoned by the bhikkhu who was crafty, deceit is abandoned by the bhikkhu who was deceitful, evil desires are abandoned by the bhikkhu who had them, wrong view is abandoned by the bhikkhu who had it. I say that by the abandonment of these impurities of a samaṇa, of these defects, of these vices, of these miserable conditions to be punished with an unhappy destiny, one becomes an attainer of the right way and method of the samaṇas. He beholds the self purified (*visuddhaṁ attānaṁ samanupassati*) from all these evil and unworthy conditions.[58]

Another expression that proclaims the purity of the self is, *suddhaṁ attānaṁ pariharati,* 'he preserves the self pure'. It is repeated seven times in the *Nagaropamasutta* of the *Aṅguttara,* where the Buddha describes the seven good qualities that adorn the ariyan disciple, one with whom Māra has nothing to do.[59]

A peculiar usage in this connection is that of *sucibhūtena attāna viharati,* 'he dwells with a self made pure', regarding the second precept, that of not taking what is not given, not with any other precept. The reason for such peculiarity is not apparent.[60]

A fitting conclusion for this section is afforded to us by the *Saṁyutta* in a beautiful passage where the real inner purity of the self is contrasted with the outward purity of the ritual:

By heaping up fire-wood, do not, brāhmaṇa,
Dream of purity. That is something external.
Because, so the wise say, purity is not obtained by him,
Who wishes to get it by external means.
I, leaving aside the burning of wood, brāhmaṇa,
Make only burst the flames of a fire attached to the self (*ajjhattaṁ*).
With fire constantly burning, always with a self well composed (*samāhitatto*),
I, an arahant, live my brahma-life.
A shoulder-yoke is, brāhmaṇa, your conceit,
Anger is your smoke, your false words are ashes.
The tongue of man is his sacrificial spoon, the heart his fire-altar,
The self well tamed (*attā sudanto*), the fire.
Dhamma, brāhmaṇa, is a lake with virtue as the bathing place,
Pure, undefiled, praised by the good,
Where the wise (*vedaguno*), bathing,
With selves detached (*anallagattā*) cross to the further shore..."[61]

One who speaks of a fire attached to the self (*ajjhattamevujjalayāmi jotiṁ*), one who says that the very self of man is the fire of sacrifice that is life itself (*attā sudanto purisassa joti*), one who in the same context calls himself, 'always with a self well composed' (*niccasamāhitatto*), and who calls those taking their bath in the lake of *dhamma,* 'those with self detached' (*anallagattā*) does not seem at all to be a votary of absolute *anattā.* When he opposes to the physical, ritual fire the inward fire that is the self he is trying to substitue what he deems a reality for what he deems a shadow. To the ritual conventionality of sacrifices and ablutions he opposes the spiritual reality of the self and *dhamma.*

6

The Self and Perfection

Through the preceding chapters we have enjoyed a rather complete view of the display of energy set forth by the self on its way to perfection. In this chapter we are to contemplate the self in full possession of perfection, called liberation and *nibbāna*. The reality of the supreme stage of the moral life should be a token of the reality of the moral self that is said to encounter it.

PERFECTION OF THE SELF

The perfect man is called in the Pāli canon an arahant. The moral perfection of the arahant is beautifully described in a passage of the *Aṅguttara*. Soṇa after having won arahantship came to the Buddha and said:

> He who is an arahant, with *āsavas* destroyed, who has lived the life, done what was to be done, laid down the burden, attained the good aim, whose bonds of becoming have been scattered, freed by perfect wisdom, one such is intent on six respects: he is intent on desirelessness, on solitude, on not harming, on the destruction of craving, on the destruction of grasping, on non-infatuation.
>
> Perhaps, Lord, herein, it might occur to some venerable one, 'Is it then so that only just out of faith this reverend one has applied himself to desirelessness?' That should not, Lord, be viewed in this way. The bhikkhu, Lord, who with *āsavas* destroyed, has lived the life, done what was to be done, who does not see anything [else] to be done for the self (*karaṇīyaṁ attano asamanupassati*), or to be added to what has been done, by the destruction of passion, due to dispassion, is given to desirelessness, by the destruction of ill-will, due to the absence of ill-will, is given to desirelessness, by the destruction of infatuation, due to the absence of infatuation, is given to desirelessness.[1]

The phrase to be emphasised here is *karaṇīyaṁ attano asamanupassati,* 'who does not see anything [else] to be done for the self or by the self', which means complete perfection and refers such perfection explicitly to the self. This self, obviously, cannot be the self of the *sakkāyadiṭṭhi,* but the true self. It is in this context that the full meaning of a verse of the *Dhammapada* can be perceived:

> One endowed with virtue and insight, who stands on *dhamma,* knower of the truth,
> who does the deeds of the self (*attano kamma kubbānaṁ*), such is the one people hold dear.[2]

How would a 'conventionalist' translate the words, *attano kamma kubbānaṁ*? Would he be satisfied with, 'who does his own deeds'? Is that the full sense of the phrase? Certainly not. Here *attā* even though represented by an oblique case, holds the rank of the innermost and uttermost value in man, the supreme criterion for discerning the worth of all other values. This gives *attā* a definite existential reality.

SELF-STABILITY

We are going to study successively three ways to express man's existential perfection relating it explicitly to *attā,* namely, *ṭhitatto, brahmabhūtena attanā viharati,* and *bhāvitatto.*

We may translate *ṭhitatto* as 'one whose self is well established'.

Leaving aside some usages of *ṭhitatto,* where the term is applied to a man who is perfect but not yet with the ultimate perfection,[3] we shall concentrate on those texts where the epithet applies to one who has attained *nibbāna,* thereby implying absolute perfection. Such is the case when the title is applied to the Buddha by one of his questioners, calling him, 'one who has crossed, gone beyond, who has attained nibbāna, whose self is well (or permanently) established (*ṭhitatto*)'.[4] Again, a bhikkhu who leads the life of renunciation in a perfect way is said to be *danto, parinibbuto, ṭhitatto,* 'self-controlled, who has attained *nibbāna,* one whose self is perfectly established'.[5] We also find *ṭhitatto* used together with *parinibbuto* in the *Theragāthā*:

> He who was hard to tame is tamed by discipline, worthy, satisfied, crossed over doubt,

> A conqueror, with fears gone, that Dabba has attained *nibbāna,* being one whose self is perfectly established (*ṭhitatto*).[6]

Ṭhitatto is used in a 'Buddhist' definition of a true brāhmaṇa given to Sabhiya by the Buddha. Here again the connection of *ṭhitatto* with the obtention of *nibbāna* is clearly indicated,

> Having expelled all sin,
> Purified, well concentrated, of self perfectly established (*ṭhitatto*),
> One who having crossed the *saṁsāra* is a fully accomplished one (*kevalī*),
> Unattached, such a one is called a brāmaṇa.[7]

Before passing on to another topic, it will not be irrelevant to insist on an entirely forgotten aspect of Buddhism, with which the term *ṭhitatto* is connected. *Ṭhitto,* the first part of the compound implies steadfastness, steadiness, stability, that is to say *moral permanence.* This moral permanence is not something that arises and endures by itself, is not something either that inheres in the moral condition alone irrespective of the moral agent, but something that is produced and upheld by the moral agent and inheres in it as the substrate of moral qualities. Such kind of moral permanence demands the permanence of the moral agent whose attribute it becomes. Therefore man's moral personality, when brought to perfection, is not something momentary and changeable, but something durable and permanent. Following this line of thought, we find the word *ṭhito* explained as:

> Who is not disturbed either at gain or loss, either at glory or ignominy, either at praise or insult, either at pleasure or pain, one who is not inconstant, who is not shaken, who does not waver.[8]

In another passage we find *ṭhito* given as an equivalent to *tiṇṇo* (one who has crossed the *saṁsāra*) in expressions like, 'passing beyond all turbulence (or craving) he stands firm, having extinguished the fire of the *kilesas* he stands firm etc.'. And at the end we are shown the man in question, who, we are told, is an arahant bearing the body for the last time (*antimadehadharo arahā*), standing firm when everything saṁsaric crumbles down around himself, namely, the *khandhas,* the *dhātus,* the spheres of sense, saṁsaric existence and transmigration.[9]

The truth of impermanence is insisted upon to satiety in all works on Buddhism, and it is made into the main argument for the non-existence of *attā,* which if existent, ought to be permanent. Herein, as well as regarding other aspects of Buddhism, there lurks the danger of one-sidedness. Is the impermanence taught by primitive Buddhism an absolute one so as to exclude any sort of permanence? As a matter of fact it is not. We may say that the Buddhist way of perfection goes from what is impermanent to what is permanent. That the point of departure is what is impermanent, which precisely on that account ought to produce disgust and ought to be rejected in order to achieve liberation, is attested by many passages to be adduced in the second part of the book. But why should impermanence, precisely as impermanence, so impress a man with disgust, a disgust that leads to abhorrence and liberation, unless the man in question be convinced that permanence and unchangeability are the ideal thing and a possibility?

Certainly permanence was the ideal from the very beginning. In a comparison between the khandhas and *nibbāna* instituted in the *Paṭisambhidāmagga,* it is said that if the *khandhas* are to be considered impermanent (*anicca*), *nibbāna* is to be considered permanent (*nicca*), and the same kind of opposition is said to exist between the *khandhas* being unstable (*adhuva*) and *nibbāna* being stable (*dhuva*), the *khandhas* being liable to change *vipariṇāmadhamma*) and *nibbāna* being unchangeable (*avipariṇāmadhamma*).[10]

In between the impermanence that one wishes to leave behind and the permanence towards which he is striving there extends a constant effort for the acquisition of moral permanence or imperturbability. Thus we read in the *Aṅguttara:*

> It is as if there was a rock, Lord, a mountain without fissures, unperforated, of one solid mass. Then mighty winds and rains were to come from the east, but they would not shake it, or make it totter or quake; then mighty winds and rains were to come from the west..., from the north..., from the south, but they would not shake it, or make it totter or quake, even so, Lord, if many forms to be recognized by the eye come within the range of the bhikkhu's eye, whose mind is thus perfectly free, they do not overpower his mind. The mind of him is pure, stable, having acquired steadfastness and sees the end of it.

The same applies to the other objects of sense.[11] A pertinent question occurs here. How can the mind which is ontologically impermanent and morally utterly unstable come to possess such steadfastness? All by itself or as a result of the moral agent's mastery over it? Nowhere in the Nikāyas is the mind endowed with the faculty of self-determination. Even in the passage just quoted, the mind is not considered an ultimate but something subsidiary belonging to the bhikkhu in question expressly stated or represented by *assa,* 'of him'. Commenting on *anejo sabbadhī samo* (unmoved, unperturbed in every way) we are told:

> Turbulence (*ejā*) is craving … . He whose turbulence has been abandoned, uprooted … burnt in the fire of knowledge is called unmoved (*anejo*). He is not disturbed either at gain or loss, at glory or ignominy … (as above).

And the commentary on *sabbadhī samo* ends with the words:

> He is in everything the same, he is in everything unaffected, in everything he possesses equanimity. That is how one is unperturbed in every way.[12]

This moral permanence which is the ideal of Buddhism as a fitting preparation for the impermanence of *nibbāna* develops into the moral unchangeability of the arahant described in the *Dīghanikāya:*

> It is possible, Candu, that the wanderers of other faiths might speak thus, 'The samaṇas sons of the sakyas dwell with unsteady virtues'. The wanderes of other faiths speaking like this should be admonished thus, 'There are, your reverences, conditions proposed, pointed out to the disciples of the Blessed One, the Arahant, the Perfectly Enlightened One, who knows and sees, not to be transgressed while life lasts. In the same way as Indra's column, an iron post, deeply rooted, well dug in is immovable, unshakable … . The bhikkhu who is an arahant, with *āsavas* destroyed, who has lived the life, done what was to be done, laid down the burden, attained the good aim, scattered the bonds of becoming, who has been freed by proper wisdom, it is [morally] impossible that he should commit nine sins. It is [morally] impossible, your reverences, that a bhikkhu who has destroyed the *āsavas* should intentionally deprive any living being of life, that he should take possession of what is not given, that he should tell intentional lies, that the should store up in order to enjoy it at will even as before when he was a householder, that he should go the wrong way in excitement, that he should go the wrong way in ill-will, that he should go the wrong way in infatuation, that he should go the wrong way in fear.'[13]

It is thus clear that the impermanence taught in the Nikāyas is not an absolute one. Impermanence is predicated only of the factors of rebirth as such. Man is expected not to identify himself (his self!) with that impermanence, but to feel a violent distaste for it, to detach himself (his self!) from it and through such detachment to win liberation. The end that is *nibbāna* is not impermanent, but just the opposite, and the way that leads to *nibbāna* goes through the achievement of an ever greater moral steadfastness and stability and even eventual moral immutability. There is no samsaric factor that can be pointed out as the cause either of the tendency towards *nibbāna* or of the quest for moral stability that leads to it. No samsaric factor can of its very nature dissolve itself into *nibbāna,* otherwise, *nibbāna* would be a spontaneous attainment open to all men. Besides, what is essentially impermanent cannot be said to possess or to be able to produce a tendency towards moral permanence and eventual immutability. These have to be forcibly induced by a superior agent, which cannot be any other than the self as the moral agent. The impermanence taught in the Nikāyas has always a moral implication and is never presented as a metaphysical truth. The impermanence taught in the Nikāyas is not something metempirical like the momentariness (*kaṇikattā*) of later Buddhism.[14] The impermanence taught in the Nikāyas is something obvious, that falls within the realm of experience and fit to disillusion us about the value of things worldly and to push us to a complete detachment from them and finally to liberation.

'HE DWELLS WITH A SELF BRAHMA-BECOME'

Before undertaking the discussion of the value of this expression in the Nikāyas we should see whether we have in it a token of upaniṣadic influence in the Pāli canon. The compound *brahmabhūta* does not occur in the *Upaniṣads.* The references given by Monier-Williams in his Dictionary point to later works like the *Manusmṛti, Mahābhārata,* and *Viṣṇu Purāṇa.* The first time that the compound occurs in the *Bhagavadgītā* is in:

Yo'ntaḥsukho'ntarārāmas tathā 'ntarjyotir eva yah, sa yogī brahmanirvāṇaṁ brahmabhūto'dhigacchati.

R. C. Zaehner discusses the compound *brahmabhūto* while commenting on this verse in his work *The Bhagavadgītā* (London, 1973: 212-215). His reasoning starts with the assumption that the term *nirvāṇa* is essentially Buddhist. Then he takes into consideration the compound *brahmanirvāṇa,* which he classifies as an adoption cum adaptation of the Buddhist term, and he therefore translates as, 'Nirvāṇa that is Brahman too'. Then taking as the immediate basis for his conclusion that, in the quoted verse of the *Bhagavadgītā, brahmabhūto* is used along with *brahmanirvāṇa,* and that the whole chapter five, in which the verse is found, is influenced by Buddhist ideas and Buddhist terminology, he concludes that *brahmabhūto* which is a stock phrase in the Pāli canon was originally Buddhist and was borrowed from the Pāli scriptures by the author of the *Bhagavadgītā.*[15]

It is a well known fact that *brahma* is used in the Nikāyas as an adjective indicative of 'eminence, greatness, excellence', as in *brahmajāla* (the divine net), *brahmadaṇḍa* (the highest penalty), *brahmadeyya* (a most excellent gift), etc.

Brahmabhūto may be explained in two different ways. The first explanation will make *brahma* to be an adjective indicative of excellence, while *bhūto* will mean 'a being'. The second explanation will take *brahma* for a noun (Brahmā or Brahman?), while *bhūto* will be the passive participle of *bhavati.* If the second explanation be accepted, the compound *brahmabhūto* will be an irregular formation. It ought to have been *brahmibhūto* or *brahmībhūto.*[16]

The oldest texts in this respect are those that speak of bhikkhus having attained by right of merit to a state like that of the gods and like that of the brahma gods (*devappattā* and *brahmappattā*).[17] Then we have the question, 'And how, Doṇa, does a brāmaṇa become similar to Brahmā?', followed by the corresponding answer that a brāhmaṇa who leaves the world, cuts his hair and beard, dons the saffron robe, leaves home for the homeless state and practises the *brahmavihāras,* is a brāhmaṇa who becomes similar to Brahmā (*brahmasamo*).[18] Here *brahmasamo* seems to mean very much the same as *brahmappattā* in the previous text. Then follows a discussion of how one becomes similar to a god (*devasamo*).

These usages of *Brahmā* in compounds such as *brahmappattā* and *brahmasamo,* indicative of spiritual achievement may explain the arisal of the compound *brahmabhūto* within the ideological frame of the Pāli canon, although a borrowing cum adaptation of the later vedantic *brahmabhūto* cannot be entirely discarded. *Brahmabhūto* is first of all a title of the Buddha:

> The Blessed One knows to perfection (*jānaṁ jānāti*), sees to perfection (*passaṁ passati*), [he who is] vision incarnate (*chakkhubhūto*), dhamma incarnate (*dhammabhūto*), Brahman (or Brahmā?) incarnate (*brahmabhūto*), a preacher, a teacher, a purveyor of [spiritual] welfare a giver of immortality, the lord of *dhamma*, the Tathāgata.[19]

Here it seems far better to take the *Brahma* of *brahmabhūto* as referring to Brahman (a case of adoption cum adaptation), because within the ideological frame of the Pāli canon to say that Buddha was Brahmā incarnate would not be emphatic enough. That the passage is late seems very probable from the fact that it appears always in cases where the teacher is not the Buddha, but someone else who explains extensively what the Buddha had uttered in short, this being perhaps a literary device to canonize teachings traditionally attributed to disciples of the Buddha. Further, *chakkhubhūto, ñāṇabhūto, dhammabhūto, brahmabhūto* offers the semblance of a later interpolation, because what follows such dithyrambic epithets seems to be an anticlimax. Compare specially *dhammabhūto*, where the Buddha is shown as dhamma personified, and *dhammassāmī*, where he appears merely as the lord of *dhamma*.

When predicated of other people than the Buddha, *brahmabhūto* qualifies persons endowed with the highest perfection:

> Happy indeed are the arahants, there is in them no craving,
> their conceit has been rooted out, the net of infatuation has been torn for them,
> They have gained immovability, their mind is undisturbed, they are untainted in the world, brahma-become, rid of the *āsavas*.[20]

The important fact for us to note is that the highest perfection indicated by the term *brahmabhūto* is explicitly applied to *attā* in a number of passages by means of the expression, *brahmabhūtena attanā viharati*. Thus in the *Aṅguttara*, when speaking of a man whose mind is freed from the *āsavas*, and knows that 'birth has been destroyed, the holy life has been lived, what was to be done is done, there will be no more living in these conditions', it is added:

> There was formerly greed, which was said to be harmful, that is no more, thus this is beneficial. There was formerly ill-will.... There was former-

ly infatuation.... He in this very life, being satisfied, quenched (*nibbuto*), cooled, experiencing happiness, dwells with a self brahma-become (*brahmabhūtena attanā viharati*).[21]

The formula, 'He in this very life, being satisfied... dwells with a self brahma-become', is used in the case of a man 'who is neither a self-tormentor, addicted to the practice of self-torture, nor a tormentor of others, addicted to the practice of tormenting others'.[22] The description of this type of men, the best among the four kinds of men enumerated in the passage, is very lengthy. It beings with the appearance of a Buddha in the world and his preaching of *dhamma,* that moves a man to leave the world and embrace the holy life. He keeps the precepts and the rules of the Order, he is satisfied and happy with a poor mendicant's life, keeps his senses under control, practises mindfulness in all his actions, gets rid of the five *nīvaraṇas,* practises the four *jhānas,* calls to mind previous existences, with the heavenly eye he sees the rise and fall of beings. The description ends with the following passage.

When the mind is thus composed, thoroughly purified, unblemished, free from defilements, rendered soft and pliable, stable and steadfast, he bends his mind to the knowledge of the destruction of the *āsavas.* He knows as it really is, 'this is suffering', he knows as it really is, 'this is the origin of suffering', ... 'the cessation of suffering', ... 'the way conducing to the cessation of suffering', ... 'these are the *āsavas*', ... 'this is the origin of the *āsavas*', ... 'this is the cessation of the *āsavas*', 'this is the way conducing to the cessation of the *āsavas*'. The mind of him who knows thus, who sees thus is rid from the *āsava* of sensual desires, ... from the *āsava* of becoming, ... from the *āsava* of ignorance. In one thus freed, there arises the knowledge, 'I am free'. He comprehends, 'Destroyed is birth, lived is the holy life, done is what was to be done, there will be no more life in these conditions'. This is said to be, bhikkhus, a man who is neither a self-tormentor, a man addicted to the practice of self-torture, nor a tormentor of others, a man addicted to the practice of tormenting others. He in this very life, being satisfied, quenched (*nibbuto*), cooled, experiencing happiness, dwells with a self brahma-become (*brahmabhūtena attanā viharati*).[23]

Thus, one who dwells 'with a self brahma-become' is endowed with all the highest attainments envisaged by the Buddhist training, including freedom from rebirth and liberation in *nibbāna.* It would be a disappointing anticlimax to have to think at the conclusion of such brilliant description that such a self is not a reality but a merely conventional name.

The phrase, *brahmabhūtena attanā viharati,* occurs at least five times in the *Niddesa.* Thus, when commenting on the term *ananugidho,* 'not covetous', the text continues:

> Greed (*gedho*) means craving (*taṇhā*), that is passion, infatuation... (there follows a long list of equivalents and different kinds of craving like craving for the objects of sense, the different types of reincarnational craving and even the inordinate craving for *nirodha*)... which are the root of all evil. He whose greed has been set aside, extirpated, appeased, quieted, not likely to rise again, consumed in the fire of knowledge, is called a non-covetous man. He is without greed as regards material forms, as regards sounds ... (as regards all the other objects of sense), without greed as regards things to be seen, heard, imagined or known, not enslaved, not infatuated, unattached, free from greed, having foregone greed, having given up greed, having expelled greed, having cast out greed, having abandoned greed, having renounced greed, free from passion, having foregone passion.... He in this very life, being satisfied, quenched (*nibbuto*), cooled, experiencing happiness, dwells with a self brahma-become.[24]

It should not pass unnoticed that, in the passage just quoted and a little before that, there is an obvious imitation of a vedantic expression, 'burnt with the fire of knowledge', (*ñāṇagginā daḍḍhā*), not found anywhere else in the Nikāyas. It corresponds to *jñānāgnidagdhakarmānaṁ* in the *Bhagavadgītā* (IV, 19).[25]

In a passage of the *Cullaniddesa, brahmabhūtena attanā viharati* is applied to the Buddha:

> The desires for attractive things are entirely known and the desire as a stain of character has been abandoned by the Buddha, the Blessed One. On account of this knowledge of desires for attractive things and of the abandonment of desire as a stain of character, the Blessed One does not cherish desires, does not long for desires, does not wish for desires, does not strive after desires. Those who cherish desires, who long for desires, who wish for desires, who strive after desires are passionate, affected by passion, given to fancies. The Blessed One does not cherish desires...

> therefore the Enlightened One is desireless, free from longing, one who has given up desire, one who has expelled desire, one who has cast out desire, one who has abandoned desire, one who has renounced desire, free from passion, having foregone passion,... satisfied, quenched, cooled, experiencing happiness, he dwells with a self brahma-become.[26]

It is evident that all the passages where, *brahmabhūtena attanā viharati* is used, refer to a self that is free from all attachment and has attained to the quenching of *nibbāna.* Such a usage of *attā* gives the term a prominence that could not be expected from people utterly convinced that the basic teaching of early Buddhism was that of absolute *anattā.* This is something remarkable specially in the case of the authors and compilers of the *Niddesa,* who knew very well the authentic teaching of the Nikāyas and nevertheless betray no scruple in making use of the term *attā* in this and other significant ways, when, as it has been noted, they were conscious of certain usages of *attā* that were *diṭṭhigataṁ,* and as such to be avoided by orthodox thinking people. And it is not so that they fail to convey 'the other side of the coin', that is to say the doctrine of relative *anattā.*[27] This confirms what has already been asserted that the *Niddesa* keeps an ideal balanced attitude between acceptance of *attā* and profession of relative *anattā.*

FULL BLOSSOMING OF THE SELF

Another expression that links moral perfection with *attā* is the compound *bhāvitatto,* which may be translated as 'one whose self is fully developed', and indicates a person who has actuated all the moral potentialities for moral perfection hidden in man.[28]

The Pāli-English Dictionary of the *P. T. S.* translates it as 'one whose attan (ātman) is bhāvita, i.e. well trained or composed. Attan here-citta (as PvA 139), thus "self composed, well balanced",' One has to go to the commentaries to find out that *attā* is *citta,* but never care to discuss why the composers and compilers of the Nikāyas stuck to *attā* all through in the use of so many compounds as have been already noted and will be noted hereafter, if they were convinced that *attā* stood in all of them for *citta.* The fact of this later substitution reveals a change in mentality, undoubtedly under the influence of the doctrine of absolute *anattā.*

Let us first of all go to the *Niddesa* to find out the meaning of *bhāvitatto* towards the end of the Nikayan period. *Bhāvitatto* is the title given to the Buddha in the *Suttanipāta, maññāmi taṁ vedaguṁ bhāvitattaṁ,* 'I deem you are the possessor of knowledge, one whose self is fully developed'.[29] This line is commented on in the *Cullaniddesa.* As an answer to the question, *kathaṁ bhagavā bhāvitatto*? we are told:

> The Blessed One is one who has developed the body (*bhāvitakāyo*), who has developed virtue (-*sīlo*), who has developed the mind (-*citto*), who has developed wisdom (-*pañño*), who has developed the stations of mindfulness (-*satipaṭṭhāno*), who has developed the right exertions (-*sammapadhāno*), who has developed the bases of psychic power (-*iddhipādo*), who has developed the faculties (-*indriyo*), who has developed the powers (-*balo*), who has developed the limbs of wisdom (-*bhojjhaṅgo*), who has developed the way (-*maggo*), who has abandoned the impurities, who has known the immovable (*paṭividdhākuppo*), who has realized cessation.[30] Grief is well known to him, [its] origination has been abandoned, the way has been developed, cessation has been realised, what was to be known has been known, what was to be thoroughly known has been thoroughly known, what was to be abandoned has been abandoned, what was to be developed has been developed, what was to be realised has been realised, unlimitted, profound, immeasurable, etc.[31]

It is evident that *bhāvitatto* does not correspond exactly with *bhāvitacitto,* which is shown here to be merely one of the items included in the 'spiritual' development of one who has reached the condition of *bhāvitatto.* This development takes into account the whole man, including the body and all the items of 'spiritual' perfection. It is a development of the moral agent as a whole, who actively fosters the unfolding of his higher potentialities and on whom devolves the 'spiritual' perfection that is the result of so many efforts. It has already been noted that nowhere is the mind shown to be endowed with the attribute of self-determination implied in this striving after the best. There is someone higher than the mind, which is after all only a samsaric factor, who is responsible for this 'spiritual' progress. This someone cannot be other than the self.

Let us single out some passages where *bhāvitatto* clearly implies the highest possible perfection.

First of all, *bhāvitatto* is predicated of the Buddha:

He whose lust, ill-will and ignorance are discarded,
Him, among many, they call one whose self has been developed (*bhāvit-tattaṁ*), brahma-become, Tathāgata,
Buddha, one who is beyond enmity and danger, one who has left aside, everything.[32]

Several passages, besides the last two quoted in note 32 (p. 339) show the link existing between being *bhāvitatto* and bearing a body for the last time, another indication that the term *bhāvitatto* indicates the highest perfection:

Knowing the body as perishable, and consciousness as something that fades away (v. 1. *pabhaṅgunaṁ* = impermanent),
Seing the danger in the bases for rebirth, having gone beyond birth and death,
Having obtained the supreme peace, the man who is of a fully developed self (*bhāvitatto*), awaits his time.[33]

Also the arahants, credited with the highest perfection, are called *bhāvi-tattā*:

Even the arahants, with a self fully developed (*bhāvitattā*), having done whatever was to be done, rid of the *āsavas,*
Cast out their body, by exhaustion of their merit and demerit.[34]

Some texts speak of the reverence due to those that are *bhavitattā* and the advantage of giving them veneration above the offering of sacrifices.

One who would offer thousand of sacrifices every month for hundred years,
If he were to venerate even for a moment one who is fully developed as to the self (*bhāvitattānaṁ*),
He would fare better by reason of this veneration, than by reason of the sacrifices lasting one hundred years.[35]

We are also reminded of the saving power of those who are *bhāvitattā*. First the simile is given of one who will be able to carry many across the current by means of a strong boat. The text continues:

In the same way, one possessed of knowledge (*vedagū*), whose self is fully developed (*bhāvitatto*),
Greatly learned and unshakable,
Having full knowledge of tradition, will persuade others,
Who are endowed with readiness to pay attention.[36]

We are here still very far from salvation through faith in the Bodhisattas and through their merits. It is only by their example and power of persuasion that perfect men will be able to help spiritually those who show readiness to be helped. Even in the case of the Buddha, the only thing he can do is showing the way, it is for others to follow it by themselves and be saved.[37]

As opposite terms to *bhāvitatto,* we get *anavositatto,* 'he whose self is unfulfilled'[38] and *avyositattā,* 'those not perfected as to the self'.[39] In both the cases it is said that such people go on from one existence to another. This is equivalent to saying that liberation from *saṁsāra* is achieved only by the perfection and fulfilment of the self.

The term *bhāvitatto* does not represent an isolated concept in the teaching of the Nikāyas. It is important to call attention to it because there has been a tendency to present Buddhism as a system pre-eminently negative in outlook. The Buddhism of the Nikāyas is not a system wholly consisting in abstention, eradication, suppression, cessation etc. There is another aspect to it, wherein furthering, developing, perfecting are given full scope and considered necessary. Many quotations could be given to substantiate this statement. Let us give at least one of the most comprehensive. It is a part of the *Mahāsakuludāyisutta* of the *Majjhima:*

> And besides, Udāyin, a method has been explained by me to my disciples, following which my disciples develop (*bhāventi*) the four stations of mindfulness. Herein, Udāyin, a bhikkhu dwells contemplating the body in the body, ardent, attentive, mindful, putting aside the covetousness and dejection [prevailing] in the world,... he dwells contemplating feelings in feelings, ... he dwells contemplating the mind in the mind,... he dwells contemplating mental objects in mental objects, ardent, attentive, mindful, putting aside the covetousness and dejection [prevailing] in the world. And in this way many of my disciples dwell having attained to the highest perfection in wisdom.
>
> And besides, Udāyin, a method has been explained by me to my disciples, following which my disciples develop (*bhāventi*) the four right strivings. Herein, Udāyin, a bhikkhu generates desire, endeavours, undertakes effort, exerts his mind, strives after the non-arising of sinful evil states not yet arisen,... strives after the arising of right states not yet arisen,... strives after the stability, not falling out of, further increase, enhancement, development, completion of right states already arisen.

> And in this way many of my disciples dwell having attained to the highest perfection in wisdom.[40]

The sutta continues describing how the disciples of the Buddha develop (*bhāventi*) the four bases of psychic power (*iddhipāde*), the five controlling faculties (*indriyāni*), the five powers (*balāni*), the seven limbs of awakening (*bojjhaṅge*), the eight items of the Way, the eight deliverances (*vimokkhe*), the eight spheres of mastery (*abhibhāyatanāni*), the ten spheres of meditative devices (*kasiṇāyatanāni*); the four *jhānas.*

This is a rather comprehensive picture of the possibilities for spiritual development opened to a dedicated bhikkhu. This passage and many others that could be quoted should be taken as the ideological background for the complete understanding of the term *bhāvitatto.*[41] The mind cannot be the main performer in this display of energy and zest for an all round perfection. There are certain stages, for instance the last *vimokkha,* where the mind is wholly left behind and nevertheless even of the man come to this condition it is said, 'And in this way many of my disciples dwell having attained to the highest perfection in wisdom'.

We must distinguish in Buddhism between two sorts of becoming: samsaric becoming (*bhava*) which is ruled by the *paṭiccasamuppāda* and where the moral agent remains in the grip of spiritual passivity and inertia, and spiritual becoming (*bhāvanā*), which goes counter to the current of the *paṭiccasamuppāda* and is a product of the moral agent's energy and subject to the latter's activity. The former (*bhava*) presupposes a disintegration of man's moral personality, which is left to drift in the current of *saṁsāra,* while the latter (*bhāvanā*) is a creative and integrating process culminating in the *bhāvitatto,* the man who while developing all his spiritual capacity crosses to the yonder shore. The final and culminating *nirodha* is not something purely negative, but a result of a perfect plenitude and of an accomplished development.

THE SELF AND NIBBĀNA

Let us examine now the relationship existing between *attā* and *nibbāna* in those texts in which both are explicitly mentioned. This will cast still more light on the use of the term *attā* in the Nikāyas.

A striking and explicitly stated connection between *attā* and *nibbāna* is found in a verse of the *Theragāthā,*

Go on the right path announced [to you] and never turn back,
Inciting the self by the self (*attanā codayattānaṁ*), one should win *nibbāna.*[42]

One aspect of what has been called ambivalence of the self is clearly expressed here. In *attanā codayattānaṁ,* the *attā* stands at the same time for the impelling agent and the impelled. This is equivalent to self-determination in the immanent sense of the self determining itself to follow a line of conduct or to pursue an ideal. In this instance neither the first nor the second *attā* can in any way be said to be the *attā* of the *sakkhāyadiṭṭhi,* the asmimanic self, which cannot either take the initiative to go towards *nibbāna* or be the winner of it. Does all this indicate that the self is the one that attains *nibbāna*? It is so with reference to the *attā* which is the real agent and producer of perfection as well as the beneficiary of it. About the metempirical condition of *attā* in *nibbāna,* the Buddha revealed nothing.

There is a passage connecting *attā* with *nibbāna* which is most problably an echo of an upanishadic passage, where Brahman's transcendence with relation to the physical world is asserted.[43] As a rule, vedantic influences on the Pāli canon are traceable to later vedānta. That this is a special case seems guaranteed by the literal affinity of the texts. In the corresponding passage of the Pāli canon it is the transcendence of *nibbāna* that is taught. As a result of an instruction imparted to him by the Buddha, Bāhiya was freed from the *āsavas* and soon after was gored to death by a young cow. The bhikkhus wanted to know what Bāhiya's destiny was in the other world and the Buddha told them that he had attained *nibbāna.* Then the Buddha is said to have exclaimed:

Where water and earth, fire, air, do not find any footing,
There the stars do not glimmer, the sun does not shine,
The moon does not gleam, no darkness is found there,
And when the sage, the brāhmaṇa, has come to knowledge by the self (*yadā ca attanā vedi*),
He is freed from form and the formless, from pleasure and pain.[44]

There are three reasons to assert the upanishadic character of this passage: (1) It reflects the cosmic significance that the Brahman has in the *Upaniṣads,* and applies it to *nibbāna,* which originally was a moral condition not a cosmic substrate. (2) On account of the paradoxical description of *nibbāna* that it contains. In spite of the lack of any cosmic luminaries there is no darkness there. The *Upaniṣads* are fond of this type of language. (3) The very mention of a brāmaṇa as the one who attains *nibbāna* becomes significant in this context. As a matter of fact, in order to restore to the passage its upanishadic character only a very small alteration is needed, which precisely shows the difference between vedānta and Buddhism. The change would consist in substituting *attānaṁ* for *attanā* in *yadā ca attanā vedi.* This substitution has the grammatical advantage of making explicit the object of knowledge which is left out in the Pāli passage, because in Buddhism *attā,* the transcendental or metaphysical *attā,* is never an object of knowledge, this applies only to the active moral agent who has to obtain the liberating knowledge. One thing is clear in the Pāli text, the direct connection of *attā* with liberation from name-and-form and from pleasure and pain. The wording of the text leaves no doubt as to the fact that *yadā ca attanā vedi* and *pamuccati* refer to one and the same person.[45]

In the *Suttanipāta* we find Sabhiya asking the Buddha what attainment entitles one to be called a bhikkhu. The answer is:

One who by the path made by the self (*pajjena katena attanā*),
Is gone to utter coolness (*parinibbānagato*), has crossed all doubt.
Leaving aside becoming and non-becoming,
One who has lived the life, who has suppressed all rebirth, such a one is called a [true] bhikkhu.[46]

Note that the way for going to *nibbāna* and crossing all doubt is not proposed here as something objective to be followed, but as something that one has to make out of the self. It is in this subjective sense that the Way can be said to be developed or fostered and thus justify expressions such as *maggabhāvanā* and *bhāvitamaggo.* This seems to contradict the saying of the *Visuddhimagga,* 'A way there is but no one goes it'. If at all, the text just quoted would compel us to say, 'There is a goer, but there is no way, inasfar as the way is made as the goer goes'. Commenting on, *nāhaṁ sahissāmi pamocanāya,* we read in the *Cullaniddesa:*

No other can become a liberator. If they want to be liberated they will do it by following with their self (*attanā*) the proper course, the favourable course, the suitable course, the course leading to the aim, the course of complete righteousness, [following it] by their own (*sakena*) strength, by their own (*sakena*) power, by their own (*sakena*) vigour, by their own (*sakena*) exertion, by their own (*sakena*) manly strength, by their own (*sakena*) manly power, by their own (*sakena*) manly vigour, by their own (*sakena*) manly exertion.[47]

Attanā comes in the original after the eightfold repetition of *sakena,* the most natural word to use for one who positively excluded all *attā. Attanā* in the original summarizes emphatically whatever has preceded, being besides a term that a staunch believer in absolute *anattā* would instinctively avoid. The value of *attanā* as an emphatic expression related to the very self is warranted by the fact that it was not necessary in any way to make perfect sense.

Attā is connected with *nibbāna* as the agent responsible for the attainment of such state and as the beneficiary of such attainment in:

It is as if there was for a man a house having eleven doors; if that house were on fire, he would be able to make himself safe (*attānaṁ sotthiṁ kātuṁ*) by anyone of the doors. In the same way I (*ahaṁ*) will be able to make the self safe (*attānaṁ sotthiṁ kātuṁ*) by anyone of those eleven doors that lead to immortality *(amatadvārānaṁ)*.[48]

In this text we find the same words used with reference to man saving his physical being as with reference to a man saving his 'spiritual' reality by crossing the door to the *amata,* 'the deathless', (*nibbāna*): *attānaṁ sotthiṁ kātuṁ*. The parallelism of the simile seems to postulate that the *attā* that is saved by entering into immortality be a reality even as the former one is. To say that *attā* in the second case is a merely conventional name, without any objective 'spiritual' reality behind it, is to deprive the passage of its expressive power.

In the *Therīapadāna* we find at least an indirect connection between the self and *nibbāna* in the following verses:

As the fire that burns in a mass of iron that is being hammered,
Gradually subsiding, its destiny is not known,
Thus the destiny of those thoroughly liberated cannot be indicated,
Of those who have crossed over the flood of the fetter of sensual pleasures, of those who have attained to happiness immovable.
Therefore, be of those who make a refuge of the self (*attadīpā tato hotha*), of those who live within the stations of mindfulness,
Cultivating the seven limbs of wisdom, you will make an end of Pain.[49]

Therefore those who 'make a refuge of the self', who withdraw from everything else and live only for the self, are those who attain to happiness immovable and make an end of Pain.

Attānaṁyeva parinibbāpeti exhibits again the self as the agent and the beneficiary of the obtention of *nibbāna* in:

> But, bhikkhus, the law of decay brings about old age for the learned man, the disciple of the Noble One. When the law of decay brings about old age, he reflects thus, 'The law of decay does not bring about old age exclusively for me; while there takes place coming and going, passing away and arising of beings the law of decay brings about old age for all beings. And if, when the law of decay brings about old age, were I to grieve, to weary, to bemoan, to beat the breast, to fall into confusion, food would not be tasteful to me, uggliness would come upon my body, affairs would not be attended to, enemies would be pleased and friends would be mentally afflicted.' When the law of decay brings about old age he does not grieve, he is not wearied, he does not bemoan, he does not fall into confusion. Of him, bhikkhus, it is said, 'The learned disciple of the Noble One has pulled out the poisoned dart of grief, transfixed by which the unlearned common man just torments his own self (*attānaṁyeva paritāpeti*).' The disciple of the Noble One free from grief, relieved from the dart, makes his own self come into nibbāna (*attānaṁyeva parinibbāpeti*).[50]

As it has already been pointed out the pulling out of the dart from the self is an equivalent for salvation.[51]

Finally the connection between the self and *nibbāna* may be formulated by means of *paccattaṁ.*

> By not fostering his mental predispositions, by not fostering his mental inclinations, he does not cling to anything in the world, not clinging to anything in the world he is not perturbed, not being perturbed he attains to utter *nibbāna* as regards the self (*paccattaññeva parinibbāyati*). He knows, 'Birth is destroyed, lived is the holy life, done is what was to be done, there will be no more living in these conditions.[52]

Some times the relation between *attā* and *nibbāna* is given by the words *nibbānaṁ attano.* The phrase in itself is ambiguous. We may consider *attano* either a subjective genitive or an objective genitive. In the first case *attano* will stand for the subject of the verbal action denoted by *nibbāna,* and *nibbāna* will be taken as having the positive meaning of ultimate attainment. In the second case *attano* will stand for the object of the verbal action, and then *nibbāna* will have the negative meaning of blowing out or extinguishing. If *attā* is what is extinguished, in that case *attā* will stand for the asmimanic self that has to be destroyed in order to be liberated. If *attā* stands for the subject of such positive attainment as the ultimate perfection of *nibbāna* then *attā* will represent the true self.

A case where *attano* seems to stand for the agent and beneficiary of the obtention of *nibbāna,* and the latter to stand for the highest obtainable perfection will be:

> He dwells having attained to the first *jhāna,* for the satisfaction of the self, for the peace of the self, for the living in comfort of the self, for the entering into *nibbāna* of the self (*attano... okkamanāya nibbānassa*).[53]

In this text, *attano* precedes all the datives following, which are more or less synonymous expressions, whose ultimate meaning is clarified by the last one, *okkamanāya nibbānassa.* It is obvious that *attano* stands here for the beneficiary of 'satisfaction, peace (literally non-trouble), living in comfort', all of which are positive perfections, hence it has to stand also for the beneficiary of 'entering into *nibbāna',* which ought to be considered a positive perfection, the one that sums up all of them. The same seems to be the case in:

> Mindfulness as regards the body well established,
> Restrained in the six spheres of the senses,
> The bhikkhu who is well composed,
> Would know the *nibbāna* of the self (*nibbānamattano*).[54]

We move on a different ground when the Scriptures speak of the extinction of the impurities of the self, as a preliminary to *nibbāna.* If in this case, the self is thought to be identified with such impurities and therefore extinguished with them, the self involved there will be the asmimanic self. But there is another way of looking at this. The self affected by impurities may be the moral agent as involved in the samsaric process and becoming thereby a victim of its impurities. and to be purified from them if *nibbāna* is to be won. Then what is really extinguished is not the self but its impurities and the self is what attains *nibbāna* as liberation. Thus we read:

> Cut off the attachment of the self (*sinehamattano*), like an autumnal lotus with the hand,

Foster the Way that is peace. *Nibbāna* has been shown by the Blessed One.[55]

Commenting on 'How seing a bhikkhu attains *nibbāna*? (*Kathaṁ disvā nibbāti bhikkhu*)', the commentary elaborates:

How seing that is how considering, how pondering, how judging ... he extinguishes the lust of self (*attano rāgaṁ nibbāpeti*), extinguishes the ill-will of self, extinguishes the infatuation of self, etc.[56]

Here the extinction applies directly to lust, ill-will, infatuation, etc. that affect the self. We read also:

Whatever fetters are there in the world,
He should not be attached to them, knowing thoroughly the pleasure of the senses,
He is to train himself in the *nibbāna* of the self.[57]

The commentary proceeds in the following way:

For the extinction of the lust of self, for the extinction of ill-will, for the extinction of infatuation, for the extinction of anger, for the extinction of enmity ... for the calming down, the quiescence, the cessation, the extinction, the giving up, the allaying of the accumulation of evil states ... .

Here too what is extinguished is not the self but its impurities. Thus far, the commentary has given us only the negative side of the process. In what follows it gives us the positive side:

... he should train himself in higher morality, and he should train himself in higher contemplation, and he should train himself in higher wisdom, he should practice these trainings consciously, knowingly, attentively, with due reflection, he should train himself in them straightening the mind, he should train himself in putting forth faith, he should train himself exercising vigour, he should train himself establishing mindfulness, he should train himself concentrating the mind, he should train himself understanding with higher wisdom, he should train himself knowing thoroughly what is to be known, he should train himself leaving aside what is to be left aside, he should train himself developing what is to be developed, he should perform, carry out, press forward [what he has] once undertaken, realizing what should be realized. This is the meaning of 'let him train himself in the *nibbāna* of the self (*sikkhe nibbānamattano*)'.[58]

It is therefore evident that the expression *nibbānaṁ attano,* 'the nibbāna of the self', does not stand in the mind of the commentators for the extinction of the self, but for the extinction of the moral depravities and imperfections which tarnish the self. But even this gives only the negative side of the picture. There is a positive side that consists of all sorts of spiritual achievements of which *nibbāna* is the final aim and crowning accomplishment, where the self is not extinguished but developed and raised to a plane of absolute perfection. Therefore in *nibbānaṁ attano,* the term *nibbāna* exhibits more a positive meaning of completion and consummation than a negative meaning of quenching or extinguishing, a meaning undoubtedly contained in the etymological root of the word and originally, perhaps, its only meaning.

NIBBUTATTO

What precedes gives us the right frame of mind for the proper understanding of the meaning of *nibbutatto* and *abhinibbutatto,* which will have a positive significance, as 'one whose self has reached (the perfection of) *nibbāna',* not a negative one, as 'one whose self has been extinguished'. This being the case, the *attā* in *nibbutatto* cannot stand for the mind which certainly ought to be quenched and extinghuished so as to open the door to *nibbāna.* Thus we have here another cogent reason to assert that the *anattā* doctrine taught in the Nikāyas has not an absolute value, but only a relative one, as it will be explained in the second part of the book. All the same it should be noted that practically all the passages where the compound is to be found insist more on the obliteration of imperfections than on fostering spiritual accomplishments. Thus:

In whom no delusion dwells, no pride,
One who has done away with avarice, selfishness, desire,
One who has put away anger, with a self utterly cooled (*abhinibbutatto*),
He indeed is a brāmaṇa, a samaṇa, a bhikkhu.[59]

Abhinibbutatto is commented on in the *Mahāniddesa.* The commentator does not say that what is cooled or extinguished is the self, but lust, ill-will, infatuation, etc., that is those moral vices or imperfections that prevent one from becoming *abhinibbutatto*:

> By the active extinction of lust [man becomes] one whose self is utterly cooled (*abhinibbutatto*), by the active extinction of ill-will..., by the active extinction of infatuation... of wrath... of enmity... of anger... of malice... of envy... of niggardliness ... of deceit... of treachery... of obstinacy... of impetuosity... of conceit... of arrogance... of pride ... of indolence... of all impurities... of all wrong conduct... of all anxieties... of all fever of passion... of all afflictions..., by the extinction of all the accumulation of wrong dispositions [man becomes] one whose self is utterly cooled (*abhinibbutatto*).[60]

There is another *attā* compound linking *attā* with *nibbāna, attaparinibbāna.* It occurs as the last member in a list of three, viz. *attadama, attasama* and *attaparinibbāna,* that is, 'mastery of the self, equanimity of the self, and utter cooling of the self'. As the first two refer to two positive perfections of the self, namely mastery and equanimity, so must the third one refer to the utmost perfection of the self, confirming our opinion that the self is not what is extinguished but the beneficiary of the extinction that is *nibbāna,* an extinction that carries the moral agent to the utmost perfection.[61] These three compounds give in a more concise way what is explained in a passage of the *Aṅguttara,* where the Buddha gives to a brāhmaṇa his spiritual explanation of the sacrificial fires. When he comes to explain the *dakṣiṇa* or southern fire, he says:

> Herein, brāhmaṇa, those samaṇas and brāhmaṇas who abstain from false teaching, who are given to forbearance and meekness, whose single purpose is to master the self, whose single purpose is to make the self calm, whose single purpose is to make the self attain to utter coolness, this is called, brāhmaṇa, the southern fire.[62]

Finally to confirm the opinion that the extinction of *nibbāna* does not apply to the self but to the imperfections to be abolished so that the self may reach *nibbāna* we may ponder:

> ...having left out lust, having renounced lust, desireless, quenched (*nibbuto*), cooled (*sītibhūto*), he dwells with a self brahma-become.[63]

The words *brahmabhūtena attanā viharati,* which may be translated as 'he dwells with a self brought to the utmost perfection', could in no way come after *nibbuto* and *sītibhūto* if *nibbāna* implied the extinction of the self.

7

The Self as Related to Kamma and Rebirth

We have just contemplated the self as the moral agent struggling for its own purification and through a constant and relentless effort coming finally to the purity that is its own, when utterly purified and totally perfect. But this self is in most men caught in the cycle of birhts and deaths that constitute *saṁsāra,* being reborn time and again according to its *kamma.* We would not have a complete treatment of the usages of *attā* in the Nikāyas if we were to neglect this existential migration of man from one birth to another and the relation that this and the presiding *kamma* bear to the moral agent.

THE SELF AND KAMMA

The position of later Buddhism in this matter is made sufficiently clear in the *Visuddhimagga:*

> Beyond the cause he sees not a doer, beyond the proceeding of results he sees no one to enjoy the results. And by means of right understanding he sees clearly that, to say there is a doer, when there is a cause, there is some one to enjoy when there is proceeding of results, is, among the wise, only a concept, a mere usage. Hence said the ancients,
>
> Of karma there is no doer; nor is there
> Somebody to experience its results.
> It's nothing but mere states that come to pass....[1]

Let us see how the Nikāyas express themselves in this matter. One thing is sure, that the antiquity of the saying quoted in the *Visuddhimagga,* 'Of karma there is no doer, etc.' does not go back in time to the early period of the Nikāyas. On the other hand, there seem to be in the Nikāyas a number of texts that plainly contradict such statements. If anyone were to say that the *Visuddhimagga* points only to the metaphysical self, he will have to be reminded that the denial of a metaphysical substrate in man's personality led, quite logically indeed, to the denial of the reality of the moral agent, which became merely 'a concept, a mere usage'. The reality of the moral agent cannot stand without a corresponding metaphysical substrate. With the denial of the latter, the moral agent is reduced to a merely phenomenal congeries of factors, a mere succession of phenomena, a simple appearance without any abiding identity. This is not reflected in the way of talking of the Nikāyas.

Those texts will be quoted first, where both the assertions that there is no doer of *kamma* and no experiencer of results are contradicted.

We turn our attention first of all to the emphatic words of Yama, repeated three times, and addressed to one who in spite of the so called messengers of the gods being sent to him, out of negligence and carelessness did not act rightly:

> That evil action of yours was not done by mother, father, brother, sister, friends and companions, relatives and kinsmen, devas, samaṇas and brāhmaṇas but by yourself alone (*tayā'va*) was that evil action done, and it is you yourself (*taññ'eva*) who will experience its result.[2]

Will anyone demand a clearer assertion of the doer and experiencer and their mutual identity? Also:

> For one seized by death, leaving this human existence,
> What is his very down (*sakaṁ*)? What having taken he goes?
> What is that follows him like a pursuing shadow?
> Both good actions and bad actions that the mortal being does here,
> That is what is his very own. That is what he having taken goes.
> That is what follows him like a pursuing shadow.
> Therefore one should do good, taking provisions for the other world.
> In the other world good actions are the support of beings.[3]

The *Dhammapada* not only asserts the existence of the doer and experiencer, but links the karmic purity and impurity with *attā*.

> Here he is unhappy, having died he is unhappy,
> Both there and there the evil-doer is unhappy.
> He is unhappy, he grieves,
> Seing the karmic impurity of self (*attano*).
> Here he is happy...
> Seing the karmic purity of the self (*attano*).[4]

In two different places of the *Jātaka* we find the same text in which *kamma* is also linked with *attā* and by means of the simile of the sower and the reaper the reality and identity of the doer and experiencer is implicitly asserted:

> Whatever a man does, that is what he discovers in his self (*attani passati*),
> The doer of good sees good, the evil-doer sees evil,
> As is the seed he sows, such is the harvest he reaps.[5]

Subha, a young brāhmaṇa, comes to ask the Buddha for the reason and cause of inequalities observable in human beings as regards birth, station in life, length of existence, etc. The Buddha replies:

> Beings are those who have *kamma* as their own (*kammassakā*), heirs to their *kamma,* those who have *kamma* as their birth-source, those for whom *kamma* is a kin, those who have *kamma* as their prop. *Kamma* divides human beings, that is to say by lowness and excellence.[6]

And in the *Therīgāthā,* as an introduction to the recollection of her own seven previous existences, whose karmic consequences she was suffering in the current existence, Isidāsī tells us:

> I know seven existences of my self (*attano*), of which this one is the fruit and karmic result.[7]

In the *Saṁsappanīyasutta* of the *Aṅguttara* we find a concise formula which may be useful as a corrective to later dogma, *yaṁ karoti tena upapajjati,* 'whatever a man does, according to that he rises again'. If we examine in the light of this formula the statement of the *Visuddhimagga*:

> From karma come to pass results,
> Result has karma as its source,
> From karma comes a future life,
> And in this way the world proceeds,[8]

we shall see that these lines give us the truth but not the whole truth. Once *kamma* is there (*yaṁ karoti*) the result of a future life cannot but be realised (*tena upapajjati*). But what is the reason for the existence of *kamma*? It is most un-Buddhistic to leave any reality without any cause being assigned to it. The cause of *kamma* itself is the activity of the moral agent, based on the latter's freedom of choice. *Kamma* needs for its existence and specification the activity of the moral agent. Thus the above formula gives the lie to those lines of the *Visuddhimagga*:

> Of karma there is no doer, nor is there
> Somebody to experience its result.

If we divide the above given formula into two parts, the first part, *yaṁ karoti,* contradicts the statement that 'of karma there is no doer'. The second part, *tena upapajjati,* considering that the subject of *karoti* and *upapajjati* is one and the same, and that the arising is governed by the previously collected *kamma,* means that the one who experiences *kamma* was previously the doer of it. Hence this second part of the formula contradicts the statement, 'nor is there somebody to experience its result'. The identity of subject for the two verbs implies also some kind of real personal continuity through transmigration.

The existence of an experiencer and the unfailing experience of *kamma* is again asserted by the Buddha in an explicit way in:

> I do not teach, bhikkhus, the coming to an end of accumulated *kamma* intentionally done without being experienced, and this has to occur either is this very life or in another turn of existence. And I do not teach that there is any making an end of pain without having experienced the accumulated *kamma* intentionally done.[9]

The words, 'intentionally done' (*sañcetanikaṁ*) presuppose the freedom of choice of the moral agent and his consequent responsibility.

In the *Itivuttaka* the Buddha asserts his knowledge of having enjoyed for long periods of time the lovely fruit of his good deeds.[10]

The existence of an experiencer, and implicitly even that of a doer are also asserted in the *Suttanipāta,* linking karmic pain with *attā*:

> For the *kamma* of no one perishes,
> One dies having it as his lord,
> The fool evil-doer, in the world to come,
> Sees pain in his self (*attani*).[11]

In the *Petavatthu* we find a testimony that very emphatically insists on the identity of doer and experiencer and at the same time links *kamma* with *attā*:

> In former times I was stingy,
> I did not give even though having abundant wealth,
> In [the practice of] holy gifts, I did not make an island for the self (*dīpaṁ nākāsimattano*),
> I, that very person (*svāhaṁ*), experience remorse, in the grip of the *kamma* of my self (*attakammaphalūpago*).[12]

There are some texts that at their face value might seem to confirm the opinion that there is no doer of *kamma.* Let us make an impartial evaluation of them.

The clearest exposition of the question is to be found in a dialogue between Mahākoṭṭhika and Sāriputta:

> What now, friend Sāriputta, are old-age and death made by oneself (*sayaṁkataṁ*), are they made by another (*paraṅkataṁ*), are they made by oneself and by another, or are they made neither by oneself or by another, arisen by chance?
>
> Old-age and death, friend Koṭṭhika, are not made by oneself, are not made by another, are not made both by oneself and another and do not arise by chance, but conditioned by birth arise old-age and death.[13]

The first thing to be noted here is that *kamma* is an ambiguous term, it may stand either for the deed of self or for the result of that deed. Obviously in this text the second meaning of the term is to be accepted. What is excluded here is the need to postulate any immediate intervention of an intelligent agent in the uninterrupted flow of natural phenomena that constitute *saṁsāra,* which are the fruit of previous deeds. The intervention of an intelligent subject may be of two kinds, namely, the intervention of self or of another. This 'another' excludes primarily any sort of creator, be it the *issara* (creator) of other texts or any deva. Such a tenet was a basic one in the non-brahmanic systems like Buddhism and Jainism as well as in original Sāṅkhya, which did not feel the need of a creator and admitted only the natural evolution of pre-existing elements. On the other hand, chance was also excluded by the fact that every phenomenon ought to have a cause or pre-existing condition. This is a fundamental frame of mind for the interpretation of texts such as the present one.

The same reasoning applies to *kamma* as the result of previous deeds, since the cyclic evolution of the individual in *saṁsāra* is nothing else but the maturing of his *kamma.* The individual that undergoes the result of his *kamma,* as previous deeds done by himself, does not exercise any kind of immediate efficient causality in its realisation. A creator has nothing to do either with such realisation, since the fruit of a previous *kamma* does not depend on the will of any being, but operates autonomously, forming a system of retribution complete in itself. Chance is also excluded, as any pleasure or pain that the individual experiences can be traced down to some natural cause. This is a fundamental doctrine propounded in other passages like:

> It is impossible for a man of right view to fall back on the opinion that pleasure and pain are made by self, are made by another, are made both by self and by another, arise by chance not made by self, arise by chance not made by another, arise by chance not made by self and another.

The reason for these impossibilities is immediately given:

> And what is the reason for that? The cause has been seen properly by that man of right view and also that all things proceed from a cause.[14]

Clearly, then, two extreme possibilities are considered here for the actual existence of pleasure and pain, either a personal agency or efficient cause or a fortuitous origin. Both these extremes are rejected and a 'middle way' chosen, namely, the opinion that the actual existence of pleasure and pain has its cause in the chain of natural phenomena,[15] but what may be called 'moral causality', that is causality of the moral agent, who with his previous deeds made this origin of pleasure and pain necessary, is neither asserted nor denied here. It is explicitly asserted in the following:

> It was not gotten by me by chance, nor was it the result of any evolution (*transference of merits? – pariṇāmajaṁ*),
> It is not made by self (*sayaṁ*) or given by the gods,
> This mansion was gotten by me out of merit,
> Through the virtuous deeds of my onw.[16]

In the production of the fruit of kamma we find here excluded:

a) 'Chance' (*nādhiccaladdhaṁ*), but the opposition to chance seems to have here a wider connotation that in the previous texts. There chance was excluded on the strength of every natural phenomenon having its natural cause. Here we are implicitly told that the qualitative action of natural causes is not left to chance either. The kind of birht to be had by a given individual, the amount of pleasure to be enjoyed by him, the amount of pain to be suffered is not left to chance, not only in the sense that pleasure and pain owe their origin immediately to natural causes, but also that they have their karmic *raison d'être* in the 'moral causality' of the individual. That is why we are told, 'This mansion was gotten by me out of merit, through virtuous deeds of my own'.

b) We are also told that the obtention of the fruit of *kamma* is not the result of *pariṇāma*. This word may mean 'evolution', and might exclude the type of deterministic evolution taught by Makkhali Gosāla. But *pariṇāmanā* (or *parivarta*) came to mean in the Mahāyana system the application by the Bodhisattva of his own merits for the welfare and spiritual progress of others. Is, this the meaning to be given to the word *pariṇāma* here?[17] For one thing the term occurs in texts which are evidently of later origin.

c) Finally any efficient causality either on the part of self or of another is excluded as having any immediate influence in the obtention of the fruit of kamma.

d) The only causality admitted is the one we have called 'moral causality' which is exercised by means of good and bad actions previously done by the moral agent and for which he is fully responsible, 'This mansion was gotten by me out of merit, through virtuous deeds of my own'.[18]

Two suttas are still to examined that introduce their topic with a dialogue in which the matter being explained is dealt with.

In the first dialogue the naked ascetic Kassapa questions the Buddha:

- What now, friend Gotama, is pain made by self?
- Then what, friend Gotama, is pain made by another?
- Then what, friend Gotama, is pain made both by self and by another?
- Then what, friend Gotama, is pain not made by self, not made by another, arisen by chance?

Every time the Buddha answers in the negative. The dialogue continues:

- Then what, friend Gotama, pain does not exist?
- It is not so, Kassapa, that pain does not exist, pain certainly exists.
- Then is it that the venerable Gotama neither knows nor sees pain?
- It is not so, Kassapa, that I neither know nor see pain. I certainly know pain, Kassapa, I certainly see pain, Kassapa.

Kassapa shows bewilderment at the answers given him by the Buddha and asks for a clarification.[19] The same dialogue is given in the introduction to the following sutta (18), but this time the topic of discussion is not *dukkha* alone but both *sukhadukkha.* As it is evident, the problem, as posited here, remains within the limits already discussed.

In both the dialogues the fundamental solution to the problem is made to lie in the *paṭiccasamuppāda.* The *paṭiccasamuppāda,* as solution to the problem is presented in the two-fold formula that deals first with the origination (*samudaya*) of *dukkha* and after that with the cessation (*nirodha*) of *dukkha.* One might say that in the introductory dialogue where the problem is posited the question of the cessation of *dukkha* does not come in and therefore the second formula is out of place here. But the composers of the Nikāyas were not creating a written text but a text meant for recitation and expediency made them include as many stock passages as possible, which by reason of their frequent occurrence became a great help to the memorizing of the reciters. This mechanical addition of stock passages without effecting in them the changes needed to make them fit perfectly well in the new context does not at times make things as clear as one would wish them to be. Another example of inadaptability of stock passages to the new context may be seen in the second sutta of those discussed here, which purpots to deal with the origin of *sukhadukkha,* while the *paṭiccasamuppāda* formula as expressed in it speaks only of the origin (and of course the cessation) of *dukkha* alone.

These two suttas speak explicitly of the *paṭiccasamuppāda* solution as a middle solution that avoids two extremes. Here again the two passages where the middle way solution is proposed do not fit perfectly well into their respective contexts. The introductory dialogues reject not only the origin from self and the origin from another of *dukkha* and *sukhadukkha* respectively, but they reject also, as emphatically, their chance origination. But while giving the middle way solution only the two first are taken into account. Therefore the inadmissibility of chance origination also mentioned in the introductory dialogues is entirely ignored. The Commentary does not fail to remark that by resorting to the *paṭiccasamuppāda* the fortuitous origination of *dukkha* is also excluded, but this is not explicitly stated in the text. If chance origination were taken into account, then the middle way represented by the *paṭiccasamuppāda* would lie between production by an intelligent agent (self or another) and chance origination. In fact, however, the middle way postulated by the *paṭiccasamuppāda* is supposed to go in between causality by self and causality by another, the latter one not referring, as was the case previously, to a creator or god but to the discontinuity of personality with the annihilation of one and the arisal of another in a given samsaric line of existence. Another lack of adaptation of the two passages to their respective contexts is in the fact that the introductory dialogues seem to speak of the causality of self, of another, or of chance origination regarding the fruit of the action, while the two passages to which we are now referring deal with the relation between the doer of the action (*kāraka*) and the experiencer of the fruit of the action (*vedaka*), whether they are identical either in the spirit of the heresy called 'eternalism' (sutta 17) or in the spirit of the *sakkāyadiṭṭhi* that identifies *attā* with the *khandhas* (sutta 18), or whether they are different either in the spirit of the 'annihilationist heresy' (sutta 17) or due to the absolute difference between feeling and experiencer, that the Commentary equates also with 'annihilationism' (sutta 18). The later date of these passages is evinced by the part of the Nikāyas where they are found[20] and the foregoing analysis which has shown these two suttas to be a veritable patch-work.

Besides, the rejection of the so called 'eternalism' and 'annihilationism' has the value of a denial of *attā* precisely as contemplated by those heresies, not of an absolute denial of *attā,* as will become clear in the second part of the book. The middle way of the Nikāyas as regards the metaphysical nature of *attā,* follows rather the line of abstention than the line of commitment, i.e., it prefers to observe in the matter a meaningful silence than to try to express what is inexpressible. The Nikāyas are outspoken in saying what the *attā* is not, but without ever denying the truth of *attā.*

The *anattavāda* proves unsatisfactory on many a count, precisely in this very context. The *anattavādins* find an easy middle way between the *sayaṅkataṁ* and *paraṅkataṁ* of this context by denying altogether any *attā* and admitting only as sufficient explanation for the existence of *dukha* and *sukhadukkha* a stream of phenomena, each of them finding the reason for its existence in the preceding one. But if this solution be considered adequate to explain the rolling on of the *paṭiccasamuppāda,* it does not explain by any means the possibility of its cessation and consequent *nibbāna,* which is expressed in these very texts we are now studying as, *evametassa kevalassa dukkhakkhandhassa nirodho hoti.* Being essentially samsaric and tending therefore of their very nature to keep the round of existences going on, how can possibly the links of the chain ever cease by themselves? *Viññāṇa,* to take one example, cannot be said to cease unless it be previously existing, but at the very moment of its existence, by that very reason, it gives rise to *nāmarūpa,* following the well known principle, *imasmiṁ sati idaṁ hoti, imassuppādā idaṁ uppajjati,* 'when this is that is also, by the production of this that is also produced'.[21] The same applies to *nāmarūpa* in relation to *saḷāyatana,* etc. Therefore, as it has been already stated, intentional absolute cessation (*nirodha*) leading to the destruction 'of this total mass of pain' is to be forcibly imposed by a superior agent who is no part of the *paṭiccasamuppāda* and can exercise its influence over it. We need not turn many pages to find an illustration of the point at issue:

> That ignorance by which the wise man was covered and that craving by which he was possessed, by which [ignorance and craving] this body arose, that very ignorance has been abandoned by the wise man, and that craving has been destroyed. What is the reason for this? The wise man lived the brahma-life for the complete destruction of pain. That is why the wise man after the dissolution of the body is not to come to a body. He, while being one not to come to a body becomes free from birth, old-age, and death, afflictions, lamentations, pain, mental anguish, tribulations. I say, he becomes free from Pain.[22]

This text shows the wise man engaged in the destruction of ignorance and craving (the most important links of the *paṭiccasamuppāda*) by embracing the brahma-life (a term which doubtless has in the context a general meaning comprehending all the items of Buddhist training) 'for the complete destruction of pain'. What is the link of the chain that moves the wise man to act in this way while it leaves the fool unmoved? The cause of this march to freedom is not to be found in the *paṭiccasamuppāda* chain but in the moral agent who is not of necessity bound to *saṁsāra* and can choose to be freed from it.

That in the Buddhism of the Nikāyas we cannot do away with the doer and the experiencer can be proved by means of many other texts. Let us adduce at least one more:

> And what, Puṇṇa, is a dark deed having a dark result? Herein, Puṇṇa, someone performs a harmful bodily activity, a harmful activity of speech, a harmful mental activity. He, having performed a harmful bodily activity, etc., is reborn in a world that is harmful. He thus being born in a world that is harmful is touched by harmful sense-contacts, experiences a harmful feeling which is extremely painful, even as being condemned to hell. In this way there happens a rebirth of a being from a being, by what he does by that he is reborn, and once he is reborn sense-contacts touch him. Thus say I that beings are heirs to their *kamma*.[23]

Therefore a being is reborn from a being depending on a free choice of good or evil. Wrong actions make the doer be reborn in a world that is harmful.

Once he is reborn there he has nothing to do in the production of the suffering that he has to undergo, which is entirely due to natural causes. This is concisely expressed by the words, *yaṁ karoti tena uppajjati, uppannamenaṁ phassā phusanti,* an unambiguous reference both to the doer and the experiencer, and the identity of both.

On the other hand, the *anattavāda* that is accepted as a necessary conclusion of the *paṭiccasamuppāda* doctrine is an one-sided view due to an oversimplification of the matter. Thus we read in the *Visuddhimagga*:

> And because the clause 'Contitioned by ignorance activities come to pass', inhibits the view that there is a doer; and the clause 'Conditioned by activities consciousness comes to pass', inhibits the view of the transmigration of the self; and the clause 'Conditioned by consciousness name-and-form comes to pass', inhibits the idea of density, by showing the break-up of things conceived to be the self; and the clause 'Conditioned by name-and-form sixfold sense comes to pass', inhibits such views as the self sees, etc. knows, touches, feels, craves, grasps, becomes, is born, decays, dies:- therefore, as inhibiting also false views, this wheel of becoming is fittingly to be known.[24]

The first question that comes into the mind after reading those words, 'this wheel of becoming is fittingly to be known', is 'by whom is it to be known? Who can make it the object of his knowledge in order to be saved from it unless he be by nature different from it?

Let us now ponder the first statement, ' "Conditioned by ignorance activities come to pass", inhibits the view that there is a doer'. Now, is *avijjā* a self-subsisting entity or an attribute that somehow or other inheres in a subject? The latter seems to be the case as it is attested by the passage quoted above, 'That ignorance by which the wise man was covered and that craving by which he was possessed...', to which we may add:

> Enmeshed in ignorance, bhikkhus, are people, blinded, enveloped by it,[25]

and:

> Then herein the ignorance of the learned disciple of the Noble One is destroyed and knowledge arises (in him).[26]

The same thing is established by the frequent exhortations to leave aside ignorance. How can anyone be exhorted to leave aside ignorance if the latter does not affect him? But we read:

> Throw away the barrier, leave aside ignorance...,[27]

and:

> What things, bhikkhus, ought to be banished by means of wisdom? Ignorance and the craving for existence... .[28]

Such being the case, do activities 'come to pass' merely as a result of *avijjā* 'being there' all by itself or are they produced by a doer who is affected by ignorance? Further, *avijjā and saṅkhārā,* as they stand in the formula are wholly undetermined. On whom depends the kind and degree of *avijjā* that is there and the kind of activities to be produced? If no influence external to the *paṭiccasamuppāda* chain is forthcoming then every single process will be a monotonous repetition of the previous one. But above all stands the difficulty of getting rid of *avijjā* and obtaining *vijjā.* Will ignorance withdraw all by itself and respectfully make room for wisdom?

Let us now take into consideration the last statement:

> 'Conditioned by name-and-form sixfold sense comes to pass', inhibits such view as the self sees, etc..

But do the senses proceed all by themselves and display their activity without interference? If the answer is in the affirmative, then what is the meaning of so many exhortations found in the Nikāyas to control of the senses? Do the senses control themselves spontaneously or are they controlled by another? See for instance:

> Bhikkhus, there being no control of the senses, the virtue of one fallen from control of the senses is brought to destruction, there being no virtue the right concentration of one fallen from virtue is brought to destruction... .[29]

This subversive chain of successive destructions continues being described having the following links, right knowledge and insight, indifference and dispassion, knowledge and insight of liberation. The opposite is the case when sense-control is found in the adherent. Many are the testimonies that could be adduced. Let us give just one, where the Buddha is referring to the time when he was given to the enjoyment of sensual pleasures and decided to break away from them:

> I myself at other time, knowing as it really is the origin and destruction [impermanence], the satisfaction and danger and outcome of sensual pleasures, getting rid of craving for sensual pleasures, removing the fever of sensual pleasures, dwell devoid of thirst, with a mind inwardly

> calmed. I see other beings not rid of passion for sensual pleasures consumed by craving for sensual pleasures... .[30]

Who is it that falls away or does not fall away from sense-control, who feels or does not feel attachment to sense-pleasures? Can anyone say that he is identified with the senses, that he is not by nature independent form the senses and superior to them?

And as regards the statement, ' "Conditioned by name-and-form sixfold sense come to pass", inhibits such views as the self... feels...', what to think of the following?

> Even so the learned disciple of the Noble One being affected by a painful feeling does not grieve, is not wearied, does not bemoan, does not cry beating his breast, does not fall into confusion.... Being affected by that painful feeling he does not feel repugnance. The obsession of repugnance for a painful feeling does not obsess him who does not feel repugnance for a painful feeling.... If he experiences a pleasant feeling he experiences it with detachment. If he experiences a feeling that is neither pleasant nor painful he experiences it with detachment. This is called "a learned disciple of the Noble One, who is detached from birth, old-age, death... detached from pain.[31]

Here again, who is it that keeps himself detached from all kinds of feeling and independent from them?

If the moral agent is responsible for ignorance, attachment to sensual pleasures, attachment to feelings and thereby bound to transmigration, then he is responsible for transmigration and pays the penalty for his shortcomings by transmigrating; therefore the statement, ' "Conditioned by activities consciousness comes to pass', inhibits the view of the transmigration of the self', is a glaring one-sided statement and oversimplification explicitly contradicted by a number of passages quoted and to be quoted in the following section.

THE SELF AND REBIRTH

The standpoint of later Buddhism in this matter is clear from what we are told in the *Visuddhimagga*:

> Further just as the rehearsing voice from the mouth of the teacher does

> not enter the pupil's mouth, yet it cannot be denied that, because of it, the rehearsal takes place in the latter's mouth; as the charmed water drunk by a [sick man's] messenger does not enter the stomach of the sick man, yet it cannot be denied that, because of it, the disease is cured; as the decoration of the face does not go to the reflection of the face on the surface of a mirror and so on, yet it cannot be denied that, because of it, the decoration appears there; as the flame of a lamp does not go from one wick to the other, yet it cannot be denied that, because of it, the flame appears on the other wick; – even so nothing comes over to this existence from the past, nor does anything pass over to the future from the present, yet it cannot be denied that because of the aggregates, sense-organs, elements of the past existence they are born here, or that, because of them being here, they are born in the future.[32]

According to this, there is nothing that passes over from one existence to another. The existence that ceases becomes merely the reason for another existence to begin, but nothing was relayed from the former existence to the present one nor will it be relayed from this existence to the next. This assertion can readily be admitted in what concerns the phenomenal part of man,[33] but what about the 'spiritual' part of man? Is it not there to give a 'personal continuity' to successive existences in a given transmigrational line? The followers of the *anattā* doctrine deny that there is such permanent principle of 'personal identity'. Let us remark in passing the impression that the whole system went on developing in a chain of extreme views, even though the Buddhism of the Nikāyas shows a definite dislike for extreme views and boasts of being a 'middle way'. First we have the absolute denial of the objective truth of *attā,* this led to the denial of the reality of the moral agent and the consequent denial of any real doer of *kamma* and of the experiencer of the fruit of *kamma,* and now we are told that absolutely nothing passes on from one existence to another.

The Nikāyas do not seem to know any of these metaphysical subtleties, they profess the doctrine of retribution in a straightforward way, taking it for granted and not showing any doubt about there being a 'personal continuity' running through succesive existences. The texts adduced to prove the reality of the doer and the experiencer imply also this very continuity. The number of illustrations that could be adduced is very large. Let us note down a few.

We read in the *Kūṭadantasutta* of the *Dīghanikāya*:

> Does the venerable Gotama admit that one who offers such sacrifice or has it offered is reborn at the dissolution of the body, after death, in a happy heavenly world?
>
> I admit, brāhmaṇa, that one who offers such sacrifice or has it offered is reborn after the dissolution of the body, after death, in a happy heavenly world. At that time, *I* was the brāhmaṇa priest, the one who caused that sacrifice to be offered.[34]

This continuity of personality is implied in the often described recollection of past existences, which present themselves to the mind as previous experiences of one and the same conscious subject.

> In such an existence, I was one who had such a name, who belonged to such a family, who had such a complexion, who took such a food, who experienced such pleasure and pain, who had such span of life. Then having passed away from there I arose somewhere else. There again I was one who had such a name.... Then having passed away from there I arose here... .[35]

In this text the different existential experiences are connected by means of the same 'I', to whom they are related.

As a matter of fact, given the realistic outlook that pervades the Nikāyas, a good number of entire books, like the *Vimānavatthu, Petavatthu, Apadānas, Jātaka, Buddhavaṁsa* and *Caryāpiṭaka* would be rendered meaningless if this perspective of personal continuity through the transmigrational process were removed from them. It may be added that without the ideological background of personal identity through transmigration the Buddhology of the Nikāyas would have never developed for want of a real connection between the different stages through which a certain being has to go on evolving until it reaches the sublime peak of Buddhahood. Thus we have in the *Buddhavaṁsa* an account of the meetings of Gotama in his foregone existences with the previous Buddhas and their prediction that, after a staggering number of years, that very man there present would attain perfect enlightenment.

To give one instance:

> Look at this ascetic, a man of matted hair, a man of severe penance,
> Within countless kalpas, he will become a Buddha in the world.[36]

Such were supposedly the words of the Buddha Dīpaṅkara at the sight of

Gotama, when the latter in one of his previous existences was a brāhmaṇa called Sumedha, who renounced the world becoming an ascetic.

In the *Cariyāpiṭaka,* where the acts conducive to the practice of the *pāramitās* are described, the narration is attributed to Buddha himself who speaks in the first person, although the facts recounted are supposed to have taken place countless kalpas before.

The lateness of these books attests to the fact that even at the end of the Nikayan period their authors wrote as if they knew nothing of the *anattā* doctrine and the consequent discontinuity of 'personality' or better the absolute lack of it in the transmigrational process.

We meet with similar testimonies even in the earlier parts of the canon:

> Face to face with the Lord, your reverence, have I heard, face to face with him have I learnt this, 'Conscious and mindful, Ānanda, was the Bodhisatta reborn in the Tusita group...'. Face to face... 'Conscious and mindful, Ānanda, did the Bodhisatta stay in the Tusita group...'. Face to face... 'Conscious and mindful, Ānanda, did the Bodhisatta enter his mother's womb after passing away from the Tusita group...'.[37]

Finally we find in a sutta the continuity of personality through transmigration projected on the background of the impermanence of worldly things enjoyed during the process:

> It may perhaps, Ānanda, occur to you, 'It might be that the kind Mahāsudassano was at that time another person (*añño*)'. But this should not, Ānanda, be viewed so. *I* was at that time king Mahāsudassano.... *Mine* at that time were the four and eighty thousand cities.... *Mine* at that time were the four and eighty thousand palaces.... *Mine*....

In contrast with this continuity of personality through transmigration we find a great emphasis laid on the impermanence of that worldly glory and prosperity which in times past was the Buddha's own:

> See, Ānanda, how all these component things are now past, vanished, destroyed. Thus impermanent, Ānanda, are component things, thus unstable, Ānanda, are component things, thus untrustworthy, Ānanda, are component things. Insomuch, Ānanda, is meet to feel disgust, to be detached to be set free from all component things.[38]

The *sutta* implies that there is someone to see the impermanence, the transitoriness, the untrustworthiness of worldly things through successive existences and to grow weary of them, to be estranged from them, to be set free from them, because, as we will be told in the second part of the book, they are not his self.

As regards the death of the body we discover in the Nikāyas a way of talking similar to that of the *Bhagavadgītā*[39] that implies a difference between what dies in man and what is immortal in him:

> Even as a snake goes on having let aside its wornout (*jiṇṇaṁ*) slough,
> In the same way your father and mother let aside their bodies here.[40]

Finally we may consider the compound *attabhāva,* which may be translated as 'personal or individual existence', and in this sense is exclusively Buddhist. The compound has clearly a samsaric meaning and in it *attā* seems to stand for the connecting link between the performance of actions and their corresponding results, either in the current existence or in a different one. Thus:

> There are, bhikkhus, these three causes for the origination of actions. What three? Greed, ill-will, and delusion. The action, bhikkhus, that is effected out of greed, that originates from greed, that has greed as its productive cause, that springs out of greed, wherever the individual existence (*attabhāva*) of him [that performs it] is found, there that action produces its fruit, there one experiences the coming to fruition of that action, either in this very life or after having risen in another phase of existence.[41]

8

A Brief General Assessment of the First Part

It will not be out of place to close this first part of the book with a general, though brief, assessment of the main points established by the research undertaken on the usages of the term *attā* in the Nikāyas.

1. A prominent place ought to be given to the fact that the distinction between the *vyāvahārika* and the *pāramārthika* use of the term *attā,* introduced to brand all the usages of *attā* in the Nikāyas as *vyāvahārika,* i.e., as a merely conventional term without any reality behind it, is of later origin. The all-important distinction in the Nikāyas regarding the usage of the term *attā* is the distinction between the usage of the term with a 'heretical' sense, that is to say as identified either theoretically or only practically with the peripheral man and as not identified with man's external adjuncts and having therefore no asmimanic connotation. This is a point of great importance and indicative of the different attitudes taken regarding *attā* by early and later Buddhism. It is to be stressed that the all-pervading 'conventionalism' of some scholars in relation to *attā* is not Nikayan. The term *attā* has at times a merely reflexive sense, but there are lots of cases where *attā* means much more than that.

2. The term *attā* and the concept for which it stands are used in the Nikāyas without any sort of inhibition. This significant phenomenon is not confined to some specific parts of the Nikāyas, but pervades the whole range of them, showing thereby a general acceptance. In this respect, the ideal books of the Nikāyas are the two *Niddesas.* The first commentators who wrote those books, drawing from a complete knowledge of the Nikāyas, strike an ideal balanced attitude between *attā* and *anattā,* accepting both. It is in the *Paṭisambhidāmagga* where the balance begins to tilt in favour of *anattā,* this showing that, at least from the ideological point of view, this voluminous work is the latest of all the books of the Nikāyas.

3. Certain usages of the term *attā* in the Nikāyas reveal an unmistakable intention to refer to the highest existential value in man, to a reality that ranks high above all other things, in comparison with which all other

things fade away, and for the sake of which all other things ought to be disdained and utterly renounced. The *attā* that stands for the wayfarer towards perfection, bent only on achieving liberation, displays the characteristics of a dynamic reality trying to assert itself above everything else and eventually succeeding in doing so. This condemns to failure all later attempts to give it only a merely conventional value.

4. The *attā* doctrine as presented in the Nikāyas is not a negative one, either by the absolute denial of *attā* or by an one-sided insistence on cessation. The *attā* doctrine in the Nikāyas is eminently positive dwelling on inner development and impelling the adherent to bring to realization all his 'spiritual' potentialities. These teachings can be set into a coherent system of thought, which does not differ in its general lines from what other systems which maintain the reality of the self teach on *attā* or its equivalent.

5. After reviewing such an ideological panorama, one finds it impossible to agree with those that maintain that he specific characteristic of Buddhism *vis-à-vis* all other systems and from its very inception was the absolute denial of *attā*. I. B. Horner's remark may be quoted here:

> At M, ii, 223 there is a sudden introduction of the word *attā*, around which controversy has grown with the centuries. Here it appears to be used in no more than the ordinary way in which all speak of 'self'... The *Comy.* fails to explain how the forceful word *attā* figures in these passages. From another angle its appearance must give those who like to say that the Buddha 'denied' *attā* pause to think. *Attā* is not denied here, or anywhere else in the Pāli Canon; it is accepted.[1]

This kind of remark could have been appended to a very great number of passages in the Nikāyas.

Now, if it were true that the originality of the Buddha's message, as presented in the Nikāyas, was an absolute and uncompromising denial of *attā*, in opposition to all other systems, and that from the very first sermon,[2] then the word *attā* would have become taboo as being a positive means to express what may be called the 'spiritual' reality of man as contrasted with his samsaric accidents. In such a case, the use of the term *attā* would have been confined to rare and in no way significant cases. That such is not the case in the Nikāyas os borne out by the fact that *attā* is profusedly used and very often refers to the existential core of man as opposed to the peripheral samsaric adjuncts, and that it is used with a positive import throughout the entire range of the Nikāyas. This can be easily explained if the *anattā* doctrine taught in the Nikāyas does not consist in an absolute denial of *attā* but only in a relative one, referring to the *khandhas,* the senses, the objects of sense, the sense-contacts, the spheres of sense, which neither are the self nor belong to the self or affect it in any ontological way. That such is the *anattā* doctrine taught in the Nikāyas will become clear in the second part of this book. In this way the thesis expounded in the first part will not be contradicted by the antithesis to be explained in the second part, and then a coherent synthesis will be possible, a synthesis that will show the real face of Nikayan Buddhism.

PART TWO

The Metaphysical Self

9

The Doctrine of Anattā Can Coexist With the Reality of Attā

In the first part of the book, we contemplated the moral agent, the self, in action, as the hero of the existential drama, going through the vicissitudes of a moral career, where it showed itself either sunk in the mire of samsaric impurity, or making manly efforts to purify itself ever more and more, till the attainment of the very peak of perfection, and consequent liberation.

Now we stop to reflect. We have seen the self in action, as a victim of his own errors or as the beneficiary of his own victories, the final one, absolute victory, included. But, what is the real nature of the self? What, in the last analysis, am I? These questions bid our attention turn from what we have called 'the existential self' to what now we call 'the metaphysical self'. The latter is going to be the subject of enquiry in the second part of the book. A word of caution seems necessary here. If we expect to get a clear idea of what the self is in itself, of what, in the last analysis, we are, we shall be sorely disappointed. We are not going to be told what the self is in itself, what, in the last analysis we are, but rather what the self is not, what in the last analysis we are not. We are going to be warned that all the dogmas professing speculative theories (*diṭṭhis*) on the self are rooted in what is the basic 'heresy' or 'error' in the Nikāyas, to wit, the *sakkāya-diṭṭhi,* which identifies the self with what is merely empirical and therefore non-self (*anattā*).

We shall in the first place take up and analyse texts which explicitly teach the doctrine of anattā. The main question to be kept in mind is whether such texts teach absolute *anattā,* i.e., whether they deny any reality to the self, or only relative *anattā,* i.e., whether they teach only that the phenomenal factors are not the self. Even though we do not agree with Mrs. Rhys Davids as to the kind of *attā* of which the Nikāyas speak, we fully concur with her when she says, 'The original *anattā* teaching is only a denying of what man might wrongly hold to be the self- surely a very different thing from denying his reality'.[1]

The *anattā* doctrine, as such, is not exclusively Buddhist. A common and relevant characteristic of some important Indian philosophical systems is an irreducible dualism, based on the acceptance of two ultimate principles, which in the last analysis are wholly different and exclusive from each other. Making use of a general apellation we may designate those two principles as 'spirit' and 'matter'. Thus we have in Jainism the two fundamental categories of *jīva* and *ajīva,* and in the Sāṅkhya-Yoga, *puruṣa* and *prakṛti.* We may venture to anticipate that at the root of Nikayan Buddhism there are also two antagonistic principles, *attā* and *anattā,* even though the doctrine may never have been proposed in this way, and might scandalize the votaries of absolute *anattā.* The difference between early Buddhism – of which we are speaking – and the other systems consists first of all in the insistence of the former on teaching *anattā,* an insistence that is more quantitative than qualitative, assuming the form of a frequent repetition of certain stock passages. Secondly, Buddhism differs from the other systems in the kind of ideological development through which it went later on, giving an almost absolute prevalence to texts teaching *anattā,* and ignoring or explaining away those other texts in which *attā* is admitted as a matter of fact, without realizing the inner tension between *attā* and *anattā* that can be detected in the Scriptures.

Hiralal Jain and A. N. Upadhye provide us with the right perspective for the evaluation of early Buddhism. They distinguish between two types of Indian religious leaders: the priest and the ascetic, a division certified by the Nikāyas, where the expression samaṇas and brāhmaṇas, as embracing all religious adherents is of very frequent occurence, and where brahmanic ritualism, founded on caste, is constantly shown to be antagonistic *to* the 'spiritual' or ascetic approach of the samaṇas. The above mentioned authors refer to the thought-ferment in ancient Eastern India, where a succesion of ascetic teachers concentrated on the spirit (*ātman*) in man, having as their aim to separate matter from spirit (both being considered equally real in their own right), so that the latter might achieve a state of liberation. They come to the following conclusion:

> Thus it will be seen that here, in the Eastern stream of religious thought, there is no place either for a Deity who shapes the universe and meddles in its matters, or for a priest invested with mysterious power to propitiate Him. This line of thought is well represented by Jaina Tīrthaṅkaras like Neminātha, Pārsva, and Mahāvīra, by Ājivika Teachers like

Gosāla, by Sāṅkhya philosophers like Kapila and promulgators of Buddhism like Buddha.[2]

This division of beliefs is confirmed in two verses of the *Samayasāra* of Kundakundācārya, a Jain writer of the first century A. D.:

> For the people [it is] Viṣṇu [who] creates celestial, hellish, animal and human beings; and if, according to [some] samaṇas, the *ātman* creates the six kinds of organic bodies (*kāyān*), no difference is there between the professed opinion (*siddhānta*) of the people and that of the samaṇas. For the people it is Viṣṇu that creates, and for the samaṇas it is the *ātman* that creates.[3]

Naturally enough, Kundakunda rejects such opinions saying that in the case of a perpetual creation of worlds, human and divine, no liberation (*mokṣa*) is possible. The commentary on this passage runs as follows, in A. Chakravarti's words, when making the transition between such doctrine and its refutation:

> Next, when the Self and non-Self are so entirely distinct and when there is no chance of association of any kind between the two, much less the causal relation, how does the feeling of doer occur in the Self? The following *gāthās* offer an explanation.[4]

The importance of this testimony rests on the fact that it implies that the samaṇas, as a whole, were all intent on discussing the nature of *ātman,* to whom creative powers were attributed by some of them, in opposition to theistic Hinduism, which admitted the existence of a Creator.

Within the frame of this mental view, which seems to be a legitimate one, early Buddhism should be aligned with the Eastern current of thought, taking it to be akin to other systems, charactriezed by their antagonism with any idea of theistic creationism, by their lack of any ritualistic bias, and radically founded on a irreducible dualism between self and non-self.[5]

That the teaching of the doctrine of *anattā* can coexist with a firm profession of the reality of *attā,* or its equivalent, is proved, for instance, by explicit statements found in the *Sāṅkhyakārikā.* One of the frequent ways of stating the *anattā* doctrine in the Nikāyas consists in the formula, '*netaṁ mama, nesohamasmi, na meso attā* (this is not mine, this I am not, this is not my self)'. There is a parallel expression in *Sāṅkhyakārikā,* 64:

> Thus by the study of the (twenty-five) true principles, one attains a

> knowledge which is complete, pure, due to the absence of error, and absolute, namely, '*I am not, nothing is mine, there is no I*'.

Vācaspati Miśra comments in his *Tattva-Kaumudī*:

> 'I am not', saying this it merely precludes action as regards the self (*ātmani*). And thus, all internal actions, such as apprehension, self-consciousness, volitions, perception, etc., as well as all external actions should be known as denied of the self. And since there is as regards the self no intentness on action, therefore 'there is no I'. *I* is a term that stands for the agent, as in 'I know', 'I offer sacrifice', 'I give', on account of the reference to the agent in all such cases. And due to the absence of action, there is in every case absence of an agent. Therefore, it has been well said, 'there is no I'. Hence precisely follows that 'nothing is mine'. Because it is the agent that obtains possessiveness. Hence wherefrom can there be possessiveness belonging to the very nature [of the self]? Another interpretation might be: 'I am not' means 'I am Spirit (*puruṣa*)' not one endowed with productivity. And because of not being endowed with productivity, lack of action was indicated when saying, 'there is no I'. And due to the lack of action, lack of possessiveness was indicated when saying, 'nothing is mine'.

All this means that the self, as such, is not affected by the activities of *prakṛti,* that it is metaphysically different from phenomenal reality, and therefore untouched by its changes, never qualified by them. The Nikāyas will tell us something very similar, that samsaric phenomena are not the self or something belonging to the self (*attaniya*), that the self, as such, does not exercise any kind of possessiveness, and we have seen it propounded in the last chapter of the first part that the result of *kamma* is not due in any way to any efficient causality on the part of the self. As a matter of fact, the internal and external activities, mental and bodily, to which the above quotation refers, may be said to coincide with the khandhas of the Nikāyas, of which one ought to say, 'this is not mine, this I am not, this is not my self'.[6]

In the *Yoga-sūtras* of Patañjali we meet with a *sūtra* that rings of pure and unadulterated Nikayan Buddhism:

> Ignorance consists in viewing what is permanent, pure, pleasant, and the self (*nityaśucisukhātmakhyātiḥ*) in what is impermanent, impure, painful and non-self (*anityāśuciduḥkhānātmasu*)'. (II, 5).

And in the corresponding *bhāṣya* we read:

> He who having accepted any substance either manifest or unmanifest as being of the nature of self (*ātmatvenābhipratītya*), rejoices at the acquisition of it, taking it to be an acquisition of his self (*ātmasampadaṁ*), grieves at its loss, thinking it to be a loss of his self (*ātmabyāpadaṁ*), [such a one] is an entirely unelightened man.

As regards Jainism, in addition to the testimonies given above, we may adduce:

> Even the mystic Yogīndu clearly says: 'Ātman is never anything but ātman; the non-soul (*para padhārtha*) is always different from the soul; neither the ātman can become the non-soul nor the non-soul can become ātman'.[7]

Also:

> [To say with reference to] any other alien thing (*paradravyaṁ*), be it animate, inanimate, or mixed: 'I am that, that is I, I am its own, that is mine, that was formerly mine, I was formerly its own, that will be mine again, I will moreover be that', such erroneous fancies entertains the bewildered man about the self (*ātmavikalpa*), while the unbewildered man who knows according to truth does not entertain them.[8]

The preceding considerations and the evidence adduced give us an insight into what very likely was the setting of original Buddhism, showing at the same time the possibility of an *anattā* doctrine which does not exclude the reality of *attā,* but emphasizes it all the more. Whether this is true or not of Buddism will be decided after going through the evidence to be examined in this second part of the book.

10

The Doctrine of *Anattā* Taught Through the Denial of Positive Terms

We shall study the *anattā* doctrine in two parts, corresponding to this and the following chapter. In the present chapter we shall catalogue and study texts that teach it through the denial of positive terms such as *mama, ahaṁ, attā, attaniya.* In the following chapter our attention will be directed to those texts that teach the doctrine of *anattā* through the predication of the negative term *anattā.*

THIS IS NOT MY SELF

We begin with the texts that seem to offer the oldest formulation of the doctrine namely those in which we are told regarding something, 'That is not mine, that I am not, that is not my self'. The formula appears to be a more direct, natural and discursive way of propounding the *anattā* doctrine. The presentation of the doctrine by the predication of *anattā* seems to display greater simplicity and precision and a refinement of thought that requires more time to develop.

The first set of texts to be examined are those that refer to the *khandhas.* Let us first dwell on a stock passage that occurs with different kinds of introductions and in combination with other stock passages:

> 'What do you think of this, Soṇa, is material form (or 'body' = *rūpaṁ*) permanent or impermanent?'
> 'Impermanent, Lord.'
> 'And what is impermanent is it painful or pleasant?'
> 'Painful, Lord.'
> 'And as regards what is impermanent, painful, mutable by nature, is it befitting to regard it as "That is mine, that I am, that is my self"?'
> 'Not so, Lord.'

The same reasoning applies to feeling (*vedanā*), perception (*saññā*), coefficients of consciousness or inner complexes (*saṅkhārā*), and consciousness (*viññāṇa*).

> Therefore, Soṇa, whatever material form is there, either past, future or present, either subjective or external, either gross or subtle, either mean or excellent, either near or remote, any kind of material form should be discerned by means of higher wisdom as it really is, as 'That is not mine, that I am not, that is not my self'.

The same is asserted of the other khandhas.

> Thus discerning, Soṇa, the learned ariyan disciple feels disgust for material form... (the same applies to the other khandhas). Feeling disgust he is free from attachment. Through riddance from attachment he is liberated. At being liberated there is knowledge of being liberated. He knows, 'Destroyed is birth, lived is the brahma-life, done is what was to be done, there will be no more living in these conditions'.[1]

Pondering over this text, we come to the following conclusions:

1. What kind of *attā* is the one referred to in the phrase, *na m'eso attā*? Is it a hypothetical or theoretical *attā*? Is it an abstract term unconnected with any personal reality? If the term comes in a series with *n'etaṁ mama* and *n'eso'ham'asmi,* which obviously refer to the concrete reflecting subject, *attā* is bound to be also the concrete *attā* of the same reflecting subject. As it has been pointed out, *attā* has basically a reflexive meaning even when used in the nominative case; therefore when I say, 'this is not my self', I mean to say, 'this not *my own* self'. It will not do to say that this *attā* is the 'empirical self', because it is being opposed to the *khandhas* which constitute the empirical self and are identified with the self by those immersed in the spirit of the *sakkāyadiṭṭhi.*

2. The reason why one should feel disgust for the *khandhas* is that they are impermanent, painful, changeable by nature and therefore cannot be mine, I cannot be the *khandhas* and the *khandhas* cannot be my self. The criterion used here for the utter rejection of the *khandhas* is in the last analysis that they are not my very self. This gives me the motive to feel repulsion at them and to discard them, and nevertheless I am told by the votaries of absolute *anattā* that the self in me is no reality. It is as if I was exhorted in the following way, 'Feel disgust for the khandhas, get detached from them, disown them, because they are not your self, but of course that self of yours is no reality at all'. Would that make any sense? The tenor of the exhortation seems to imply that *attā* (everyone's own self!) metaphysically speaking should be regarded as having nothing in common with the

khandhas, which are impermanent, painful and mutable by nature. Far from denying the realtiy of *attā,* all this establishes it as a superior kind of reality, the only reality that matters for me, the only reality that I really am.

3. Who in the last analysis is the one who feels disgust for the *khandhas,* feeling disgust for them loses all attachment to them, losing all attachment to them is liberated, and being liberated has knowledge of such liberation? Is it not the one who refuses to accept as the innermost core of his personality, as what he really is, what is impermanent, painful, mutable by nature, that is, the *khandhas*? Therefore, unless we say that there is liberation but no one is liberated (a philosophical subtlety that is not Nikayan) we are bound to say that the liberated man is a reality and that the *attā* of the liberated man, that refuses to identify itself with the khandhas is also a reality.

4. It is important to note that already in this first instance the treatment of the subject is not theroretical but practical, discussed in a soteriological context, which leads to liberation from what is impermanent, painful and mutable by nature. And that is usually the case in other contexts and texts as well. This supports the contention that the *attā* of which the texts speak is the concrete *attā* of the man in question.

5. If man were a mere bundle of phenomena called *khandhas* and nothing else, what in him would feel disgust for the *khandhas* to be detached from them, be thus liberated and have the knowledge of such liberation? Would the *khandhas* themselves feel disgust for the *khandhas,* be detached from the *khandhas,* be thus liberated and know that they are liberated? The whole reasoning will be absurd unless we admit that there is in man more than the *khandhas* show there is in him.

Some might be tempted to say that mind, in the form of *citta,* is the one that is liberated and has knowledge of such liberation.[2] But in the *Assutavāsutta* of the *Nidānasaṁyutta* we see the Buddha telling the bhikkhus that the ignorant common man may find it easy to feel disgust for the body, to become detached from it and to wish to be freed from it:

> But this, bhikkhus, which we call intellect (*citta*), and mind (*mano*), and consciousness (*viññāṇa*), regarding it, the unlearned common man is unable to feel disgust from it, to detach himself from it, to liberate himself from it. Why so? For a long time, bhikkhus, this has been for the

unlearned common man the thing cleaved to, the cherished thing, the thing grasped, thinking, 'this is mine, this I am, this is my self'... .[3]

Then the Buddha is reported to have said that it would be better for the unlearned common man to approach the body as the self, instead of the mind, as the body appears endowed with greater permanence than the mind which is in continual change, even as a monkey that goes through the forest swinging from branch to branch. The *sutta* continues with the consideration of the *paṭiccasamuppāda,* and then comes the final paragraph where the learned ariyan disciple feels disgust for the *khandhas* (*viññāṇa* included), gets detached from them, is liberated and has knowledge of his liberation. Therefore those texts that speak of the liberation of *citta* speak of a relative liberation, the absolute one being reserved for the moral agent who ought to leave behind even *citta.*[4]

The passage appears in a shorter form in different parts of the canon. Thus we are told that in order to suppress all proclivity to conceit of 'I' and 'mine' (*ahaṅkāramamaṅkāramānānusayā*) as regards this consciousness-joined body and all external phenomena:

> Whatever material form, Rāhula, is there, either past or present or future, either subjective or external, either gross or subtle, either mean or excellent, either near or remote, any kind of material form is looked upon, as it really is, by means of higher wisdom, as, 'this is not mine, this I am not, this is not my self'. [The same is repeated of all the other *khandhas.*][5]

Ahaṅkāra and *mamaṅkāra* (which are presented in this *sutta* as the result of the erroneous identidication of the self with the *khandhas*) are not concepts that necessarily demand the doctrine of absolute *anattā,* as it is proved by the importance given to *ahaṅkāra* in other systems which admit the reality of the self, like the Sāṅkhya. Cf., for instance, 'The ordinary sense of both the words (*ahaṅkāra* and *abhimāna*) is *pride,* and the technical import is "the pride or conceit of individuality"; "self-sufficiency"; the notion that "I do, I feel, I think, I am", as explained by Vācaspati: "I alone preside and have power over all that is perceived and known, and all these objects of sense are for my use. There is no other supreme except I; I AM. This pride, from its exclusive (selfish) application, is egotism *ahaṅkāra*)".'[6]

The same short form of the text just quoted is found in a context where the problem is how to suppress all proclivity to conceit of 'I' and 'mine', so that the mind may transcend multiplicity, be peaceful and fully liberated.[7] The ideal of unity vs. multiplicity, of integration vs. dispersion is common to all yogic practices accepted by different systems.

The view regarding everyone of the *khandhas* that, 'this is mine, this I am, this is my self', is considered the reason for *saṁsāra* turning round and round, like a dog tied with a leash to a stake or a pillar.[8] This is as it ought to be, for a man cannot be liberated from the round of successive existences until he ceases identifying himself (his self!) with what is phenomenal and samsaric.

This identification of the *khandhas* with the self is at the root of all 'theories' or 'heretical views' about the self and the world. This being a point of great exegetical importance for the interpretation of texts, it will, therefore, be fitting to prove it by quoting several testimonies.

> All these manyfold views, Lord, that arise in the world, either with reference to theories on the self or with reference to theories on the world, will there be riddance from those views, Lord, will there be rejection of those views for the bhikkhu who ponders things at their very source? All these manyfold views, Cunda, that arise in the world either with reference to theories on the self or with reference to theories on the world, wherever these views arise, wherever they become obsessive, wherever thay beset a man, there can be riddance from them, there can be rejection of them for one who regarding them with perfect wisdom as they really are thinks, 'this is not mine, this I am not, this is not my self'.[9]

Also:

> There are bhikkhus, these six tenets of speculative opinions. What six? Herein, bhikkhus, the unlearned common man, disregarding the noble ones, ignorant of the *dhamma* of the noble ones, untrained in the *dhamma* of the noble ones, regards material form as 'this is mine, this I am, this is my self'; he regards feelings...; he regards perception...; he regards inner complexes...; he regards consciousnes.... And whatever is seen, heard, thought, known, obtained, searched for, excogitated by the mind, he also regards that as, 'this is mine, this I am, this is my self'. And even the speculative tenet, 'this is the world, this is the self, I myself after death shall become permanent, stable, unchangeable, thus to remain for ever', he also regards it as 'this is mine, this I am, this is my self'.

The opposite is said of the ariyan disciple who therefore is not troubled about what does not exist.[10]

The householder Anāthapiṇḍika goes to see the wanderers, who ask him about the view of the Exalted One and the view of the bhikkhus. He replies that he does not know them fully. Then he is requested to propound his own view. He answers that it will be easy, but requests then to propound first their own views. Everyone of the 'unexplained questions' is proposed by a different wanderer adding that this is true the rest is false. Anāthapiṇḍika makes the following comment on each one of the views proposed:

> The view of this reverend one arises having as its cause one's own unsytematic mental acitivity or the utterance of someone else. A view like this is something become, mentally compounded, thought out, depending on some condition. And whatever is something become, mentally compounded... is impermanent. Whatever is impermanent is painful. To what is painful this worthy one is clinging, to what is painful this worthy one has reached.

Then Anāthapiṇḍika is requested to make known his own view:

> Sirs, whatever is become, mentally compounded... that is impermanent. Whatever is impermanent is painful. Whatever is painful, 'this is not mine, this I am not, this is not my self'. I am of such view, Sirs.

And later on:

> Whatever, Sirs, is something become, mentally compounded... that is impermanent. Whatever is impermanent is painful. Whatever is painful, 'this is not mine, this I am not, this not my self'. Thus has this been well seen by me by means of higher wisdom. And I know as it really is the further escape from that.

Obviously the Buddha approved of such way of thinking.[11]

The point we wish to make is confirmed in the *Mahāniddesa.* The commentator distinguishes between two kinds of *upayo* (clinging): *taṇhūpayo* and *diṭṭhūpayo,* and after describing both he continues:

> His clinging due to craving has been abandoned, his clinging due to wrong view has been given up. And the man who is unattached, having abandoned craving, having given up wrong view, how could he fall on material form, how could he resort to material form, grasp material form, hold on to material form, be attached to material form, saying, 'this is my self?' [The same applies to the other khandhas].[12]

Since this is a point of great importance, it will be fitting to quote a text that will be discussed later on but proves our contention with great lucidity and explicitness:

> Whatever samaṇas and brāhmaṇas, bhikkhus, insist on regarding the self in different ways, all of them do it with reference to the five factors of clinging to existence, or some of them. What five? Herein, bhikkhus, the unlearned common man, disregarding the noble ones, ignorant of the dhamma of the noble ones... regards the body as the self, or the self as having a body etc. [The same is repeated of the other khandhas].[13]

All these testimonies yield a truth that ought to be established as a principle of universal application in the Nikāyas, to wit, that all heterodox thinkers, be they samaṇas or brāhmaṇas, lean on the same rational basis, to wit, the identification of the self with the *khandhas.* This principle well applied will provide the answer to difficult passages and reveal the latent meaning of the so called 'silences of the Buddha'. It is presumed in the Nikāyas that all the adversaries suffer from this fundamental misconception and the Buddha is presented as knowing that whatever answer he gives to their queries is going to be wrongly interpreted due to this erroneous ideological background. This is also the reason why he never says anything positive about the self, even though he never denies it and in many passages its implicit reality becomes obvious for one not enmesshed in the prejudice of the doctrine of absolute *anattā.* The self denied in the Nikāyas is the self that is identified with what is empirical and phenomenal. This is the great aberration that deludes men and keeps them subject to suffering and *saṁsāra.*

The *Viṇopamasutta* of the *Saḷāyatanasaṁyutta* has two parts. The first part deals with the control of the senses. The second part has as its theme that the phenomenal man, the man of the *khandhas,* is not such as can be said of him, 'I', or 'mine', or 'I am', exactly the triad we found denied in Sāṅkhya-kārikā, 64, *nāsmi, na me, nāhaṁ.*

A rāja or minister is supposed to hear for the first time the sound of the lute and be entranced with it . He asks for the lute that is immediately brought to him. Then he asks for the sound. He is told that the lute is able to produce sound due to its different parts and the effort of the player. Then the rāja breaks up the lute into many pieces, after which he splinters those pieces again and again, till at the end he burns everything in the fire and winnows the ashes in a strong wind or lets them be borne down by the swift stream of a river, and exclaims, 'A miserable thing indeed is this that they call lute. And being like this whatever it is they call a lute, these people become extremely careless and are led astray by it'. The Buddha adds:

> Even so, bhikkhus, a bhikkhu investigates material form as far as material form gives scope for it, investigates feeling..., investigates perception...; investigates the inner complexes...; investigates consciousness. For one who thus investigates... whatever was there for him as 'I' or 'mine' or 'I am', that ceases to be for him.[14]

This passage is worthy to be aligned with the famous verses of Vajirā, alluded to in the first chapter of this book, and a careful analysis of it will lead us to the same conclusion, the denial of selfhood regarding the *khandhas,* not the absolute denial of *attā.* It is obvious that what is decomposed through investigation in the final paragraph is not man as a whole, but the phenomenal man, the man of the *khandhas.* The sound of the *viṇā* seems to stand in the simile for the self, even though this is not explicitly stated. The king may dismember the lute, he may separate its parts, he may splinter them ever more minutely, he may even burn the splinters, he will not be able to find the sound. In the same way a man may dwell on the *khandhas,* he may analyse them with the greatest care, he will not be able to find the self in them. The *khandhas* are not 'I', nor 'mine', nor can I say 'I am' with reference to them.

We may finally take note of a metrical passage where it is also said of the *khandhas,* 'that I am not, that is not mine':

> Material form, feeling, perception, consciousness and whatever is mentally compounded,
> 'That I am not, that is not mine', thus one is freed regarding them.
> Him thus detached, the self in safety (*khemattaṁ*), having transcended all fetters,
> (Even) searching (for him) in every sphere, the host of Māra did not find.[15]

Does this passage contain an absolute denial of *attā*? It seems not.

1. First of all, the composer of these verses did not think it improper to refer to the one who does not consider the *khandhas* as 'that I am, that is mine', and is therefore detached from them (*virajjati*), as *khematta,* 'one whose self is secure', and as 'one who has transcended all fetters', and is

thus liberated or on the point of being liberated.

2. The complete rejection of the *khandhas* does not result in the complete disintegration of 'the man', but into his achieving a condition where Māra cannot approach him. The reality of the man who has rejected the *khandhas* for ever is gone into the realm of the metempirical. The self in him has returned to its own primeval simplicity and aloofness.

3. It is to be noted that the man in question has not yet died. He is still alive, therefore his *khandhas* are not yet ultimately dissolved and can be seen by Māra, but *he* cannot be reached by the arch-enemy, *he* is *khematta,* 'one whose self is secure'.

We pass now to a second set of texts that deny with reference to the senses (the preceding set referred to the *khandhas*), 'this is mine, this I am, this is my self'.

Rāhula approaches the Buddha and asks him to explain the *dhamma* in short, so that having heard it, he may abide, 'alone, secluded, watchful, ardent and resolute as to the self (*pahitatto*)':

'What do you think, Rāhula, is sight permanent or impermanent?'

'Impermanent, Lord.'

'And what is impermanent, what is it, painful or pleasant?'

'Painful, Lord.'

'And what is impermanent, painful, mutable by nature, is it befitting to consider it as, "this is mine, this I am, this is my self"?'

'Not so, Lord.'

[The same applies to the other sense, mind included].

> Thus discerning, Rāhula, the learned ariyan disciple feels disgust for the sense of sight, feels disgust for the sense of hearing.... Feeling disgust he is detached. Through detachment he is liberated. At being liberated he has knowledge of being liberated. He knows, 'Destroyed is birth, lived is the brahma-life, done is what was to be done, there will be no more living in these conditions'.[16]

Special mention deserves the *Rāhulovādasutta* of the *Saḷāyatanasaṁyutta,* where the senses, the sense-objects, sensorial consciousness and sensorial contact are presented as forming a complete system with the *khandhas,* a thing we have also observed in the series of *suttas* enumerated in the last footnote. After having said of everyone of the factors just enumerated that they are impermanent, painful, and therefore it cannot be said of them, 'This is mine, this I am, this is my self', it is concluded:

> Thus discerning, Rāhula, the learned ariyan disciple feels disgust for the eye, feels disgust for material forms, feels disgust for visual consciousness, feels disgust for visual contact, and whatever is there in feeling (*vedanā*), in perception (*saññā*), in inner complexes (*saṅkhārā*), and in consciousness (*viññāṇa*) that originates dependent on visual contact, he also feels disgust for that. [The same is asserted of the other senses]... Feeling disgust he is detached. Through detachment he is liberated..., etc.[17]

It is then evident that *vedanā, saññā, saṅkhārā,* and *viññāṇa* depend for their functioning on sense data. Therefore when the five *khandhas* are enumerated beginning with *rūpa,* the body, this is included in the enumeration as the field of action of the senses.

Sāriputta asks Channa whether or not he regards the senses the different types of sensorial consciousness and sense-objects as, 'This is mine, this I am, this is my self'. Channa replies in the negative. Sāriputta asks Channa what is the reason for that.

> Seing that there is cessation, knowing by higher knowledge that there is cessation regarding the eye, reverend Sāriputta, regarding visual consciousness, regarding things to be known by visual consciousness, I regard the eye, visual consciousness etc. as 'This is not mine, this I am not, this is not my self'.

When this had been said, venerable Cunda the great spoke thus to venerable Channa:

> Therefore, reverend Channa, this teaching of the Blessed One should be unceasingly pondered with the mind, 'There is wavering for one who clings, there is no wavering for one who does not cling; by the absence of wavering there is impassibility, there being impassibility there is no yearning, by the absence of yearning there is no [samsaric] coming and going, by the absence of coming and going there is no passing away and arising, by the absence of passing away and arising there is no here, no yonder, nothing in between the two. That is precisely the end of Pain.'[18]

The reason given by Channa to prove that the senses, their corresponding consciousness and their objects are not such as could be said of them, 'This is mine, this I am, this is my self', is that they are subject to cessation, and therefore impermanent. This argument so often repeated implies that whatever is impermanent cannot be the self. Now can it be said that this self is a merely hypothetical self not the true one? If it were so, we would be able to arrange the argument in the following way, 'If there was a self it would be impossible to identify it with what is impermanent. But of course there is no real self. In spite of that regard what is impermanent as "This is not mine, this I am not, this is not my self", and make of this the driving force to do away with the things most cherished in the world. Thus you will be liberated, but of course there is in you no reality that can be liberated.' All this simply does not make any sense. The words of Cunda the Great describe in a kind of *paṭicca*-reasoning, very frequently found in the canon, man's liberation from the round of existences and consequently the end of *dukkha.* The chain begins with, 'For him who clings not...' to whom whatever comes after should apply including the end of *dukkha.* There is certainly someone who is liberated, even though of his condition as a liberated being we are not told anything positive, because it transcends all our empirical concepts.

The *Chachakkasutta* of the *Majjhima,* after describing the six internal sensorial spheres, the six external sensorial spheres, the six kinds of sensorial consciousness, the six kinds of sensorial contact, the six kinds of corresponding feeling, the six kinds of corresponding craving, continues:

> If anyone were to say, 'the eye is the self (*cakkhu attā*)', that is not fitting. The arisal of the eye as well as its decaying is known. Thus as regards that whose arisal and decaying is known one would equivalently say, 'the self in me arises and disappears (*attā me uppajjati ca veti ca*)'. For this reason it would not be fitting for one to say, 'the eye is the self'. Therefore the eye is non-self.[19]

The same reasoning applies to all the factors mentioned above. Then we are told that to consider those factors as, 'This is mine, this I am, this is my self', is the way leading to the arisal of *sakkāya,* while the contrary is the way leading to the cessation of *sakkāya,* 'samsaric individuality'.

It has been already indicated that the self mentioned in all these passages cannot be a merely hypothetical and unreal self, but the self of the reflecting subject. Here we are told that it would be absurd for anyone to say, 'The self arises in me and passes away'. Will this be absurd because the self is not real or because the self can in no way be impermanent? From all the conclusions we have so far arrived at, it can be affirmed without hesitation that the second alternative is the true one. Besides the expression, 'the self in me' or 'my self' clearly indicates that it refers to the self of the concrete individual who speaks.

The elements come in also for rejection, because regarding them it cannot be said either, 'This is mine, this I am, this is my self'. Let us quote one testimony that occurs at least thrice in the Nikāyas, and all the three times the outcome of this rejection is the cleaning of the mind from passion or attachment.

> That earth-element, Rāhula, which is subjective and that earth-element which is external constitute the earth-element. This should be regarded by means of higher knowledge, as it really is, as, 'This is not mine, this I am not, this is not my self'. Thus seing it by means of higher knowledge, as it really is, one feels disgust for the earth-element and cleanses his mind of attachment (*virājeti*) for the earth-element.

The same reasoning applies to the water-element, the fire-element and the air-element. The sutta ends with a paragraph that contains the expression to be studied later, on, *n'ev'aṭattānaṁ na attaniyaṁ*):

> And because, Rāhula, a bhikkhu does not see in these four elements, either the self or what belongs to the self, it is said, Rāhula, that such a bhikkhu has cut off craving, has destroyed all bonds and by a perfect understanding of conceit has made an end of Pain.[20]

This text is interesting because it shows that the expression to be studied later on, *n'ev'attānaṁ na attaniyaṁ* is equivalent in meaning to 'This is not mine, this I am not, this is not my self'.

The most comprehensive enumeration of things concerning which it is wrong to hold that 'This is mine, this I am, this is my self', is found in the *Paṭisambhidāmagga,* under the heading, *Kathám abhinivesaparāmaso diṭṭhi*? 'of what kind is the wrong view [full of] mental adherence and grasping'? The text proceeds in this away, 'That material form (*rūpaṁ*) is mine, that I am [material form], that [material form] is my self, this is a wrong view [full of] mental adherence and grasping'. The same is asserted regarding the other *khandhas,* the senses, sense-objects, the sixfold sensorial consciousness, the sixfold sensorial contact, the sixfold sensorial consciousness, the sixfold sensorial contact, the sixfold feeling arising out of sensorial contact, the sixfold perception of sense-objects, the sixfold intention concerning sense-objects, the sixfold craving for sense-objects, the six kinds of cogitation (*vitakka*) on sense-objects, the sixfold pondering over (*vicāra*) sense-objects, the six elements (*viññāṇadhātu* and *ākāsadhātu* included), the ten aids to concentration (*kasiṇas*), the different parts of the body (head-hair, body-hair, nails, teeth, etc.), the six internal sensorial spheres, the six external sensorial spheres, the elemental substrata (*dhātu*) of the senses, the sense-objects and sensorial consciousness, the powers (not only *cakkhuindriya,* etc., but also the vital power, the female-power, the virile-power, the power for happiness, the power for pain, the power for mental well-being, the power for mental dejection, the power for equanimity, the power for faith, the power for vigour, the power for wisdom), the material and immaterial *dhātus,* the different kinds of modes of existence, the *jhānas,* the *brahmavihāras,* the *vimokkhas* (*except the last one*), ignorance, composite things, consciousness, name-and-form, the sixfold sphere, contact, craving, grasping, birth, old-age and death.[21]

It is important to note that the last *vimokkha,* which consists in the absolute cessation of sensation and feeling (*saññāvedayitanirodha*) is not included among the things of which one should think, 'This is not mine, this I am not, this is not my self'. The first reason is obviously that one who is able to think in this way is not yet in a condition where all sensation and feeling have been suppressed. Is there no hint also that in this condition and self finds 'itself' entirely aloof from whatever is not self? That this *saññāvedayitanirodha,* which is not liable to the disparagement 'this is not mine, etc.,' is not something purely negative but a positive perfection is clear from the *Nivāpasutta* of the *Majjhima,* where the 'spiritual' progress of the practitioner is described as a riddance of the pleasures of sense, of the evil states of the mind, after which, the practitioner gives himself to the progressive practice of the four *jhānas,* followed by the progressive practice of the *vimokkhas.* When coming to the last one, it is said:

> And there is still something further, bhikkhus, a bhikkhu having entirely transcended the sphere of neither-perception-nor-non-perception, having attained to the cessation of perception and feeling, dwells [in it]. And having seen by means of intuitive wisdom, his *āsavas* are entirely destroyed. This one, bhikkhus, is said to be a bhikkhu who has encircled Māra with darkness, who has suppressed the bearings of Māra's eyes, gone where he cannot be seen by the eyes of the sinful-one, he has crossed over the [samsaric] entanglement in the world.[22]

It is to be noted that escaping from Māra's range of vision applies to all the steps beginning with the first *jhāna,* but only referring to the last one (the last *vimokkha* previously excepted from the refrain, 'This is not mine, etc') it is said that the one who has attained to it 'has crossed over the samsaric entanglement', that is to say is liberated. Putting things together shall we not be able to say that in the cessation of perception and feeling, which is equivalent to liberation, the self has come into its own? It is also worth noticing that all the *vimokkhas* receive the designation of *āyatana,* but not the last one, that is why it has been referred to above as a 'condition'.

This study of the passages that contain the refrain, 'This is not mine, this I am not, this is not my self', cannot be closed without giving due consideration to Venerable Nyānaponika Mahāthera's opposite opinion. We are now interested with the passage where he makes an explicit reference to this saying. He first quotes S III, p. 278, Khandhasaṁyutta, 47:

> Any ascetics or brāhmans who conceive manifold (things or ideas) as the self, all of them conceive the five aggregates (as the self) or any one of them.

Then he continues:

> This textual passage also excludes any misinterpretation of the standard formulation of the *Anattā* doctrine: 'This does not belong to me, this I am not, this is not my self'. Some writers believe that this statement permits the conclusion that the Buddha supposed a self to exist outside, or beyond, the five aggregates to which the above formula usually refers. This wrong deduction is finally disposed of by the words of the Buddha quoted above, which clearly say that all the manifold conceptions of a self can have reference only to the five aggregates or to any one, or several, of them. How else could any idea of a self or a personality be formed, if not from the material of the five aggregates and from a misconception of them? On what else could notions about self be based alternatively?...[23]

We must concur with Ven. Nyānaponika as to the basic importance of the *sakkāyadiṭṭhi* to which the paragraph quoted above refers. But we must disagree in that *all* the references to *attā* found in the canon belong to this category, only those that refer to the 'heretics', as has been proved above. We plead guilty to the accusation levelled against those who believe that the statement, 'This is not mine, etc.' allows the *reality* (the word 'existence' has a samsaric connotation) of a self besides the *khandhas,* and strong reasons have been given to establish this view. A negative argument will be introduced now to confirm it. Ven. Nyānaponika says that there is no other possible conception of the self but that which takes all the *khandhas* or some of them for the self. This will apply even to *attā,* as contained in the saying, 'This is not mine, this I am not, this is not my self'. Then when, as directed by the Buddha, I think and say of *rūpa,* 'this is not my self', such statement will have to be paraphrased as, 'material form is not my self, which as a matter of fact is identified with material form'. That is a contradiction. If all conceptions of the self are to be based on the identification of the aggregates with the self, then whenever I mention the term 'self' I am referring to that identification. But that leads me to the above given paraphrase where I say that *attā* is identified with material form, but that material form is not *attā.* In our view, the saying, 'This is not my self', purports to contradict the position of those for whom material form and the other aggregates are the self. If I say that material form etc. are not my self, my first intention is to assert that I am not of those who fall into the error of identifying the self with material form, etc. Therefore I am referring to an *attā* that is not identified with material form, etc., and opposing it to the *attā* of the heretics which is conceived as identified with material form, etc. Further still, it is indisputable that *ahaṁ* stands for *attā,* and that *mama* refers directly to *ahaṁ* and through it to *attā.* Therefore when I state regarding material form, etc., *n'etaṁ aham'asmi,* in Ven. Nyānaponika's supposition I will be saying that, 'I, identified with material form, etc., am not material form, etc.'. And when I say also regarding material form, etc., 'material form, etc., does not belong to this self of mine which as a matter of fact is identified with material form, etc.'. All becomes logical and crystal clear if we accept two kinds of self or *attā,* the one branded as *diṭṭhigataṁ* in the *Niddesa,* and its opposite, the true self or *attā.* Then when I say regarding material form, etc., *n'eso me attā.* I mean to say that I do not fall into the error of identifying material form, etc., with *attā,* as the heretics do, and that for me material form, etc., is not my self. I thereby give to understand that my idea of the self is different from that of the *diṭṭhi* followers, that I have an idea of the self that is the true one. Let us further keep in mind that, 'This is not mine, this I am not, this is not my self', is expected to afford me an impelling motive to feel disgust for the khandhas, to become detached from them, and be thereby liberated. This will make sense if my reasoning follows a line of thought such as, 'material form is not my (true) self, therefore I am not material form and material form is not mine, and that is why I feel disgust for it, get detached from it, and thereby am liberated'.

'HE DOES NOT REGARD THE KHANDHAS, ETC., EITHER AS THE SELF OR THE SELF AS QUALIFIED BY THEM'

There is another way of showing with greater emphasis and in greater detail the ontological separation, the difference in being, between the self and what later on will be called non-self. We shall quote as typical the following text:

> And how, bhikkhus, is there worry born of grasping? Herein, bhikkhus, the unlearned common man, disregarding the noble ones, ignorant of the *dhamma* of the noble ones... regards the body as the self or the self as having a body, or the body [as being] in the self, or the self [as being] in the body (*rūpaṁ attato samanupassati, rūpavantaṁ vā attānaṁ, attani vā rūpaṁ, rūpasmiṁ vā attānaṁ*). The body of such a man undergoes change, suffers alteration. Owing to the condition of change and alteration in the body, the consciousness (*viññāṇa*) of such a man does not cease to think of the change in his body. From not ceasing to think of the change in his body, worrying thoughts persist in gripping the mind. From the mind being thus gripped he is fearful, and owing to vexation and a sense of longing and clinging he is troubled.[24]

The same applies to the rest of the *khandhas.* The opposite is asserted with reference to every one of the *khandhas* in the case of a man who does not regard the *khandhas* as the self, nor the self as qualified by the *khandhas,* nor the *khandhas* in the self, nor the self in the *khandhas.*

The formula now under study rejects from every possible point of view any ontological relation between *attā* and the *khandhas.* The first kind of relation to be rejected is one of direct and explicit identity, *na rūpaṁ attato samanupassati.* The second kind of relation discarded is the one that would regard the self as substantially modified and qualified by the *khandhas, na rūpavantaṁ vā attānaṁ* (*samanupassati*). The third and fourth kind of relation utterly disapproved is regarding the self as the real substrate of the *khandhas,* or these as the real substrate of the self, *na attani vā rūpaṁ, na rūpasmiṁ vā attānaṁ* (*samanupassati*).

It is to be emphasized here, as it has been done above, that when saying that one regards or does not regard the *khandhas* as the self (*attato*), the *attā* in question is not a hypothetical or theoretical *attā,* but the very self of the person involved. We fail to see how this denies the reality of *attā* in an absolute way, on the contrary, it asserts *attā* as free in reality from any ontological admixture with the peripheral factors of samsaric existence. The man who erroneously thinks the self (his self!) to be the *khandhas* or to be objectively and ontologically involved in them suffers from a very harmful kind of alienation, from which he has to rid himself is he seriously aspires to the liberating integration of his self. The fact that, as we have been told in the passage just quoted, the man who succeeds in regarding the *khandhas* not as the self (his self!), as not having any ontological relation to the self is not affected by the fluctuation of the *khandhas* and stays untroubled, indicates also that he attains to an integration of his self that transcends whatever is mutable, the reality of *attā* being thus clearly implied.

This view that the *khandhas* are the self, or qualify the self, etc., is presented as the cause of being attached to different samsaric conditions:

> Whatever samaṇas and brāmaṇas, bhikkhus, insist on regarding the self in different ways, all of them do it regarding the five factors of clinging to existence, or some of them. What five? Herein, bhikkhus, the unlearned common man, disregarding the noble ones, ignorant of the *dhamma* of the noble ones... regards the body as the self, or the self as having a body, etc. [The same is repeated of the rest of the *khandhas*]. Thus this conviction 'I am' is not done away by him. And such conviction 'I am' not being done away by him there takes place no overcoming of the five senses: sight, hearing, smell, taste and touch. The mind, bhikkhus, is also there, mental objects are also there, the element of ignorance is also there. As regards such, an unlearned common man affected also by feeling born of the contact with ignorance (*avijjā*), there is found in his case [the conviction] 'I am', as well as [the conviction] 'this I am' and 'I shall be' and 'I should not be' and 'I shall become one having a body' or 'I shall become one without a body' or 'I shall be conscious' or

'I shall be without consciousness' or 'I shall be one neither-conscious-nor-unconscious'. It is not so with the learned ariyan disciple.[25]

One who regards the *khandhas* as the self and the self as ontologically related to the *khandhas* is entirely engulfed in the empirical self of the *diṭṭhis,* identifying the *khandhas* with the pure, independent, absolute, metaphysical self. Such a man does not cease to be bound to becoming, and while in that condition cannot be freed from *saṁsāra.*

The senses are also discriminated from what is the self or belongs to the self. Not only the different kinds of sensorial contact, but also other kinds of *phasso,* including the greatest attainments, are excluded from the self or what belongs to the self, but not all....

Commenting on, *vivekadassī phassesu* ('a searcher of discrimination as regards contacts or attainments'), we are given first a comprehensive list of different kinds of *phasso,* beginning with the six sensorial contacts. There follows a list of nineteen different contacts or achievements. Then it is explained that

> He [the *vivekadassī*] regards the sensorial contact of the eyes as excluded from (*vivittaṁ*) the self, from what belongs to the self, from what is permanent, stable, unchangeable.[26]

The same applies to all other kinds of phasso previously enumerated, *excepting*: *suññato phasso* (the attainment of the void), *animitto phasso* (non-phenomenal attainment), *appaṇihito phasso* (desireless or craving-less attainment), and *lokuttaro phasso* (the attainment of what is transcendental).[27]

That it was the commentator's intention not to include these kinds of *phasso* among those that are kept apart from the self or what belongs to the self is evinced from the fact not only that they are not mentioned at all, but further still that their exclusion implies the intentional skipping over *suññato phasso, animitto phasso,* and *appaṇihito phasso,* which in the introductory list are given between *arūpāvacaro phasso* (the attainment that concerns what is formless or immaterial) and *lokiyo phasso* (the attainment of what is worldly), both of which are included among those that are not the self or what belongs to the self. Does this not at least give us a hint that in the commentator's mind these superior kinds of *phasso,* which transcend what is merely empirical, stood in a different kind of relation to the self or what belongs to the self? Of these superior kinds of *phasso* we are told:

> Whatever attainments are there noble, rid of the *āsavas, transcendent (lokuttarā)*, connected with the void [or *nibbāna*], he sees all of them apart from passion (*rāga*), ill-will (*dosa*), infatuation (*moha*), anger, enmity, etc., etc.[28]

This list of imperfections corresponds exactly with the list of shortcomings from which the perfect man, 'one whose self has attained *nibbāna* (*abhinibbutatto*)' is said to be free.[29] Is it not extremely significant that the imperfections from which these superior kinds of attainments are considered free are exactly the same as those from which a bhikkhu who is said to be *abhinibbutatto,* 'one whose self has attained *nibbāna*' is also said to be free? We can further see a very telling affinity between these attainments intentionally excluded from what should not be considered either as the self or what belongs to the self, and the exclusion of the eighth *vimokkha* in a similar context, as indicated above. All these data seem to point at the fact that in the Nikāyas the self, in its very being, is metempirical. This gives us the right perspective to value the insistence with which it is asserted in the Nikāyas that whatever is phenomenal is not the self and does not stand in any sort of ontological relation to the self. On the other hand, the *sakkāyadiṭṭhi,* the fundamental *diṭṭhi* in the Nikāyas, consists precisely in the identification of the self with the empirical man.

We come now to discuss a text that *prima facie* and independently from the context in which is found, might seem to contain an assertion of absolute *anattā.* Ven. Nyānaponika introduces the text with the following considerations,

> If the words 'I', 'ego', 'personality', 'self', etc., should have a meaning at all, any form of an ego-conception, even the most abstract and diluted one, must necessarily be connected with the idea of particularity or separateness, i.e., with a differentiation from what is regarded as *not* 'ego'. But from what could that particularity or differentiation be derived if not from the available data of experience, i.e., the physical and mental phenomena which have been comprised by the Buddha under the classification of the five aggregates?[30]

The fact is that whatever be its origin, 'the idea of particularity or separateness, i.e., with a differentiation from what is regarded as *not* "ego" ' is present everywhere in the canon, and is therefore a datum of revelation if not of experience. The texts quoted in the second part of this book bear witness to it, and there are still more to come, specially a few where 'the differentiation from what is *not* "ego" ' is explicitly expressed with relative terms such as *attā* and *para,* and the aggregates are considered to be not *attā* but *para* ('alien, another').

The illustrious author is right when asserting that all our concepts have their root in experience, to which all can somehow or other be referred in the last analysis. But our knowledge is not a mere factual apprehension of facts, it has also a discerning function, exercising a judgment of values, and in this judgment of values the aggregates or *khandhas* are found deficient, faulty, precisely because they are impermanent, painful, and therefore cannot be the self of man. This requires a perspective whose point of view must be somewhere outside the aggregates and not limited by them.

As a consequence of this judgment of values and as a token of its teleological orientation our knowledge may also be called 'aspirational', tending towards ever higher and higher achievements that are expected to bring man to perfection. Thus in the Pāli canon we are made to find the aggregates to be unsatisfactory for being impermanent, painful and therefore not the self, and are exhorted to do away with, to discard, them. This is not a process of mere elimination for elimination's sake, but of elimination for the sake of fulfilment. If the only available data of experience are the five aggregates, if our inner world is strictly confined to them, and if they are by nature transient and painful, whence the idea and the 'ideal' of what is permanent and griefless is to derive, but from the aspirational character of our knowledge, which by the way is also a datum of experience? This shows that there is in man more than 'meets the eye'. We are told time and again to demur to accept that *we are* what is impermanent and painful ('This is not mine, this I am not, this is not my self'), because from the innermost core of our being, which lies deeper than the aggregates there wells up an irrepressible aspiration to permanence and happiness. Permanence and happiness are not found in the five aggregates, and hence the 'idea of particularity and separateness, i.e., a differentiation from what is regarded as *not* "ego" ', that is to say the five aggregates.

Another name for the 'aspirational' character of our knowledge is 'intuition or insight', which reveals to us what is beyond experience, and is, nevertheless the deepest reality in us. Unhappily, to describe this reality we depend on phenomenal experience, which does not attain to it and cannot therefore provide us with adequate terms to describe it. Hence such description is to be done *via negationis,* by means of denials, which are not intended to be mere denials but negative assertions of a superior kind of reality. Thus when the Pāli canon refers to the metaphysical self, it tells us *what the self is not* (impermanent, painful, mutable, the five aggregates, the senses, etc., etc.). But on the other hand, it also abstains from telling us that the eighth *vimokkha* and the highest kinds of attainments (*phassā*), which cross the line of what is empirical, are not the self. But it cannot tell us, in positive terms, *what the self is.*

Ven. Nyānaponika makes much of a text, of which we said above that *prima facie* and taken out of the context in which it appears, contains what might appear to be an absolute denial of *attā.* The text in question is:

> 'But, bhikkhus, there being self, would there be for me what belongs to self?'
>
> 'Yes, Lord.'
>
> 'Or, bhikkhus, there being what belongs to self would there be for me self?'
>
> 'Yes, Lord.'
>
> 'But there being in truth and in reality neither self nor what belongs to self, is it not so that the speculative opinion that says, "This is the world, this is the self, I myself shall become after death permanent, stable, perennial, immutable by nature, I shall remain like this unto what is eternal", would not this teaching be pure and absolute folly?'
>
> 'How could it not be pure and absolute folly?'[31]

Ven. Nyānaponika, after quoting this passage, hastens to say:

> The first sentence of that text expresses, in a manner as simple as emphatic, the fact pointed out before: that the assumption of a self requires also something 'belonging to a self (*attaniya*)' i.e., properties by which that self receives its distinguishing characteristics. To speak of a self devoid of such differentiating attributes, having therefore nothing to characterise it and to give meaningful contents to the word, will be entirely senseless and in contradiction to the accepted usage of these terms 'self', 'ego', etc.[32]

Let us first of all remark in passing that the *nirguṇa* self, the self without attributes is admitted in Indian philosophy without any fear of senselessness and contradiction. Ven. Nyānaponika's words apply fully to the self of the heretics, the one identified with the empirical man. But they do not apply to the self whose nature transcends what is empirical in man, and whose only distinctive characteristic is not to be in any way characterized by what is empirical, that is to say, by what is impermanent, painful, mutable. To assert that if it is not impermanent, painful, mutable, then it ought to be permanent, happy, immutable, is equivalent strictly speaking to uttering something that in the last analysis has not got much of positive meaning. Nothing that is permanent, entirely happy and immutable falls within our range of experience, but just the opposite, therefore such terms have for us a radically negative meaning. When we speak of something permanent we mean something that is not impermanent, the latter being what we experience, and the same applies to entirely happy and immutable. That is why the Pāli canon tells us what the self is not, never what the self is, and it can never tell us what the self is. Nevertheless what we are told is more than enough to move us to loathe whatever is samsaric, to shun it and to be thereby liberated. Liberation, and nothing else, is the purpose of the teaching of the Nikāyas. Liberation is not attained by means of speculation but by means of realization, which is based on intuition and insight, and intuition and insight transcend experience. All theories on the nature of the self are purely speculative, as they can give us only an empirical notion of the self, which by nature is metempirical. What is purely speculative is useless from the point of view of salvation and becomes harmful when leading to attachment to any pet theory to be defended against all others, fostering thus the identification of the self with what is a mere mental formation, a *diṭṭhi.*

Let us now examine the question whether the text quoted above contains an absolute denial of *attā* or only a relative one. Ven. Nyānaponika obviously thinks that the denial is an absolute one. But the true sense of any given text is to be sought not independently from, but subject to the immediate context in which it is found. The translation of what constitutes the immediate context in question will be as follows:

> 'You ought to take hold of a possession, bhikkhus, the possession of which is permanent, stable, perennial, immutable by nature, that would remain like this unto what is eternal.[33] But do you, bhikkhus, see by any chance such possession, the possession of which would be permanent, stable, etc.?'

'Not so, Lord.'

'Well said, bhikkhus, I too, bhikkhus, do not see such possession.... You ought to cling, bhikkhus, to such a clinging to a theory on self, by clinging to which there would not arise for him who so clings pain, lamentation, grief, mental uneasiness, tribulation.[34] But do you, bhikkhus, see by any chance such clinging to a theory on self, by clinging to which there would not arise for him who so clings pain, lamentation, etc.?'

'Not so, Lord.'

'Well said, bhikkhus. I too, bhikkhus, do not see such clinging to a theory on self, by clinging to which there would not arise.... You ought to rely, bhikkhus, on such reliance on mere theory by relying on which there would not arise for him so relying, pain, lamentation, etc.[35] But do you, bhikkhus, see by any chance any reliance on mere theory, by relying on which there would not arise for him so relying pain, lamentation, etc.?'

'Not so, Lord.'

'Well said, bhikkhus. I too, bhikkhus, do not see any reliance on mere theory, by relying on which there would not arise for him so relying, pain, lamentation, etc. *But bhikkhus, there being self, would there be for me what belongs to self?*'

'*Yes, Lord.*'

'*Or, bhikkhus, there being what belongs to self would there be for me self?*'

'*Yes, Lord.*'

'*But there not being in truth and in reality either self or what belongs to self, is it not so that the speculative opinion that says, "This is the world, this is the self, I myself shall become after death permanent, stable, perennial, immutable by nature, I shall remain like this unto what is eternal", would not this teaching be pure and absolute folly?*'

'*How could it not be pure and absolute folly?*'[36]

'Then what do you think, bhikkhus, is material form permanent or impermanent?'

'Impermanent, Lord.'

'And what is impermanent, is it painful or pleasant?'

'Painful, Lord.'

'And what is impermanent, painful, mutable by nature, is it fit to regard it as "This is mine, this I am, this is my self"?'

'Not so, Lord.'

[The same reasoning is applied to the other *khandhas.*]

'Therefore herein, bhikkhus, whatever material form is there, either past or future or present, either internal or external, either gross or subtle, either mean or excellent, either near or remote, all kinds of material form should be regarded by means of higher knowledge as "This is not mine, this I am not, this is not my self". Thus discerning, bhikkhus, the learned noble disciple feels disgust for material form [the same applies to the rest of the *khandhas*], by feeling disgust he is detached from them, through detachment he is liberated, at being liberated there is knowledge of liberation. He knows, "Destroyed is birth, etc." '[37]

Set in this broad context, the passage in question denies the heretical self that is identified with the *khandhas* or aggregates, but that is not an absolute denial of the reality of *attā.* It should be kept in mind, that:

1. The passage is introduced immediately after having denounced *attavādupādāna,* 'clinging to theory on self', and *diṭṭhinissaya,* 'reliance on mere theory', as the cause of pain, lamentation, grief, mental uneasiness, tribulation.

2. Whatever the passage says refers to a *diṭṭhi,* that of the eternalists, who from the Nikayan point of view held the absurd doctrine that this very self of our daily experience which identifies itself with the aggregates (which thus become *attaniya*) will become after death eternal. A quotation has been given in a footnote of a passage from another part of the sutta where it is said of this very theory, 'This is not mine, this I am not, this is not my self'.

3. The words, 'But bhikkhus, there being self, would there be for me what belongs to self', come immediately after having declared that in the world of experience, transient and painful (not in the metaphysical world) it is impossible to have such a possession, such a clinging to, and reliance on theory on self as would banish all pain. But if in what is empirical and transient (theory on self included) no true self can be found, how can there be such kind of possession or theory on self (*attaniya*)?

4. Immediately after the passage in question and confirming its doctrine we are faced with the well known stock passage where we find explicitly

stated the idea of particularity and separateness of the true self in relation to the aggregates, declared by the formula, 'This is not mine, this I am not, this is not my self', with the consequent 'logical' detachment from the aggregates and subsequent liberation from them.

Summarizing, the text signalled out by Ven. Nyānaponika as teaching absolute *anattā,* firstly refers to the false theory (*diṭṭhi*) of the eternalists, secondly it is sandwiched between two passages, one of which deals with *attavādupādāna,* 'clinging to theory on self,' and *diṭṭhinissaya,* 'reliance on mere theory', while the other is an eloquent rejection of the *khandhas* as being the true self.

All the canons of interpretation persuade us to see in the text in question a reference confined to the *sakkāyadiṭṭhi* in its eternalist form. The idea of *attā* contained in such *diṭṭhi* does not correspond with truth and reality, being a false and disastrous notion, born of ignorance, not merely a harmless conventional idea. Therefore, within the frame of mind reflected in the context, the passage in question could be paraphrased as follows, making explicit between brackets what is implicitly understood:

> 'There being self [in the aggregates] would there be [in them] for me what belongs to self?'
>
> 'Yes, Lord.'
>
> 'There being what belongs to self [in the aggregates] would there be for me [in them] self?'
>
> 'Yes, Lord.'
>
> 'There not being truthfully and really [in the aggregates] either self or what belongs to self, is not so that the speculative opinion which says, "This is the world, this is the self, I myself [identified with the aggregates] shall become, after dying, permanent, etc.", would be pure and absolute folly?'
>
> 'How could it be otherwise...?'

The eternalist theory is found faulty on two counts, first for applying the pronoun 'I' to things where no self is to be found, and secondly for imagining that those things (the aggregates) can become in any way permanent, eternal. In fine, the passage in question cannot be claimed to contain an absolute denial of *attā,* but only of the *attā* of the eternalists, which is basically the *attā* of the *sakkāyadiṭṭhi.* Two final animadversions may be passed on Ven. Nyānaponika's words quoted above.

1. Only the self of the *diṭṭhis* is assumed and receives its distinguishing characteristics from the aggregates, which in their turn are assumed to be identified with the self. The true self is not *assumed,* it is *experienced* as a primary datum in the process of salvation, where according to the testimony of the scriptures, it constitutes at the same time the existential discerning subject which tends towards liberation and the ontological criterion for discernment, as it is clearly shown in the formula, 'This is not mine, this I am not, this is not my self'. Whatever is to be rejected is such because it is impermanent, the cause of pain, and *therefore* cannot be *the self.* The process of salvation is nothing more and nothing less than the process of rejection by the self of what is non-self. The only characteristic of the true self, of which the scriptures speak, is a negative one, that of not being characterized by what is empirical and therefore impermanent and the cause of pain.

2. To speak of 'the accepted usage of these terms "self", "ego", etc.,' with reference to the *attā* of the *diṭṭhis* is a misleading understatement. The *attā* of the *diṭṭhis,* as has been pointed out, is not a harmless conventional idea but an absolutely disastrous misapprehension born of craving and prejudice.

VOID OF THE SELF OR OF WHAT BELONGS TO THE SELF

Another way of proposing the doctrine of the non-self is by asserting that all samsaric factors are 'void' of the self or of what belongs to the self (*suññaṁ attena vā attaniyena vā*).

> The world is void, the world is void, thus, Lord, it is said. In what respect, Lord, is the world said to be void?
> In so far, Ānanda, as the world is void of the self or of what belongs to the self, in so far is the world said to be void. And what is it, Ānanda, that is void of the self or of what belongs to the self? The eye, Ānanda is void of the self or of what belongs to the self; visible forms...; sight-consciousness...; the eye's sensorial contact...; and whatever feeling there arises dependent on the eye's sensorial contact, be it pleasant or unpleasant or neither pleasant nor unpleasant, that, too, is void of the self or of what belongs to the self. [The same is asserted of the other

senses, mind included.][38]

Commenting on *suññato lokaṁ avekkhassu,* regard the world as void,' several explanations are given:

1. First of all we are told that the world is 'void' for two reasons,

(a) 'Due to the discernment of its proceeding under [physical] necessity (*avasiyapavattasallakkhaṇavasena*)', where obviously the action of no self is felt or required. The text quoted to prove it asserts that the aggregates are non-self, because if they were the self they would not be prone to illness or affliction and we would be able to change them at will, a text that will be dealt with in the following section.

(b) 'Due to the consideration of the vanity of samsaric compounds (*tucchasaṅkhārasamanupassanāvasena*)'. This is substantiated by saying that in everyone of the *khandhas* there is no substance, no pith (*sāro*). Of every *khandha* we find asserted what is asserted of *rūpa*:

> Body is essenceless, without essence, deprived of essence, and that regarding either the quintessence of permanence, or the quintessence of happiness, or the quintessence of the self (*attasārasārena*)....[39]

We meet here with a way of speaking that would have no explanation if absolute *anattā* were the established truth in the Nikāyas. The repetition of the word *sāra* in *niccasārasārena, sukhasārasārena,* and *attasārasā rena,* is doubtless intended to give the word an intensive meaning, that is why *sāra* has been translated as 'essense' and *sārāsāra* as 'quintessence'. Now an intensive meaning of this kind is meant to show the greatest possible appreciation for the thing in question and by contrast the supreme inanity of the things that lack the thing so much appreciated. That the Nikāyas show a great appreciation for permanence (*nicca*), and happiness (*sukha*) is a thing that even the votaries of absolute *anattā* will readily concede, but lo and behold *attā* being here mentioned in the most emphatic and appreciatory way in a series with *nicca* and *sukha* and as a matter of fact as the culmination of the series. One who considered *attā* as *sārasāra* (quintessence) cannot be said to consider *attā* as an unreal entity.

2. The text continues saying that there are six reasons more why one should consider the world as 'void', because

> the eye is void either of the self or of what belongs to the self, of what is permanent, perennial, immutable by nature....

The same is repeated of the other senses, their corresponding objects, their corresponding types of sense-consciousness, their corresponding types of sensorial contact, and the consequent types of feelings dependent on them.

3. There are six other reasons why should the world be considered 'void'. Firs it is asserted of each of the *khandhas* that they ought to be considered

> empty, vain, void, non-self, essenceless, as destruction, as annihilation, as the root of suffering, as full of the *āsavas,* as something compound.

Not the khandhas alone, but one should see in that light also: *cutti, upapatti, paṭisandhi, bhava, saṁsāravaṭṭha,* being all nouns having a transmigrational connotation.

4. Twelve more reasons are given to demonstrate the vacuity of the world. In this case we are told of every *khandha,* that

> it is not a being (*satto*), not a soul (*jīvo*), not a man (*naro*), not a human being (*mānavo*), not a woman (*itthī*), not a person (*puriso*) not a self (*attā*), not anything belonging to the self (*attaniya*), not 'I' (*ahaṁ*) not mine (*mama*), not anybody (*koci*), not anything belonging to anybody (*kassaci*),

giving thus altogether twelve different ways of connoting personality. Two things are noteworthy, the presence of *puriso* which reminds us of the *puruṣa* of the Sānkhya, and the absence of *puggalo,* which would become later on the term to connote personality for the *puggalavādins.*

5. At the end of this long comment, the passage already noted, 'The world is void, the world is void, etc.' is quoted.[40]

The passage from the *Cullaniddesa,* just analysed, comments on one *pāda* of the following stanza, which tells us that the world is void of the self, linking together the consideration of the world as void and the uprooting of the wrong view on the self, which consists precisely in the identification of the self with the worldly components:

> Regard the world as void, Mogharāja, ever mindful,
> Uproot the wrong view on the self (*attānudiṭṭhiṁ*), thus you will be one who has crossed over death,
> The Lord of death does not see one who thus regards the world.[41]

'Idaṁ' (this all) which doubtless must be taken as a synonym of *loko* (the world) is also proclaimed to be void of the self or of what belongs to the self. Among the three kinds of *cetovimutti* described in the *Godattasutta* of the *Cittasaṁyutta,* we find the *suññatā cetovimutti:*

> Herein, venerable sir, a bhikkhu gone either to the forest, or to the root of a tree, or to a lonely spot, reflects thus, 'Void is this of the self or what belongs to the self'.[42]

Finally, the special relationship between *suññatā* and *anattā* is brought forward by saying:

> Reflecting on non-self (*anattato*) the establishment of of the void (*suññatupaṭṭhānaṁ*) takes place.[43]

The existential approach to the problem of man and the central position granted to man in Nikayan Buddhism are clear from the little interest they betray in the physical world as such. The physical world deserves attention only in its relation to man. Thus the word *loko* in 'the world is void, the world is void...' does not refer to the physical world, the universe, but to the samsaric environment in which man's existence runs its course. This becomes evident from the texts just adduced which explain the vacuity of the world as the vacuity of the spheres of sensorial contact and of the aggregates. This is confirmed with an explicit definition of the term *loko* given in sutta 84 of the *Saḷāyatanasaṁyutta,* where to a corresponding question of Ānanda, the Buddha says, 'What is transitory by nature (*palokadhammaṁ*) is called *loko* (world) in the discipline of the Noble One'. 'And what, Ānanda, is transitory by nature?' The answer enumerates the senses, their objects, their corresponding consciousness, their corresponding sensorial contacts, and the feelings dependent on those contacts. The spheres of sensorial contacts and the *khandhas* are the world from which men have been saved, are being saved, and will be saved, as we read in the *Dasakanipāto* of the *Aṅguttara* (10, 5).

WHAT IS NOT YOUR OWN...

There are some texts which are equivalent in spirit to the previous ones, and which help us to take the right perspective for the interpretation of all the other texts studied in this chapter. Such are, for instance, those texts which have as their theme that we should put away what is not our own. Thus:

> 'Get rid, bhikkhus, of what is not yours. Once you have got rid of it, it will be for your welfare and happiness. And what, bhikkhus, is not your

> own? Bodily form, bhikkhus, is not yours, get rid of it. Once you have got rid of it it will be for your welfare and happiness.... [The same is asserted of the rest of the *khandhas.*] Just as if, bhikkhus, a man should collect whatever is found in this Jeta grove: grass, sticks, branches, and foliage, and burn it, or do whatever he pleases with it. What then? Would it occur to you that this man is getting hold of us, burning, us, doing whatever he pleases with us?'
>
> 'Not so, Lord.'
>
> 'And why?'
>
> 'Because Lord, that is not [our] self (*attā*) or what belongs to [our] self (*attaniya*).'
>
> 'Even so, bhikkhus, bodily form is not yours, get rid of it. Once you have got rid of it it will be for your welfare and happiness. [The same is asserted of the rest of the *khandhas.*]'[44]

This *sutta* is one of the elements used in the composition of the *Alagaddūpamasutta* of the *Majjhima,* which, as it is mostly the case with the *suttas* of the *Dīgha* and *Majjhima* is an artificial composition achieved by the juxtaposition of divers elements. This *sutta* occurs in No. 17, and comes therefore after the passage discussed above. The Jetavana passage contains clearly what Ven. Nyānaponika expressed as 'the idea of particularity or separateness, i.e.,... a differentation from what is not "ego".' The passage offers a positive statement of *attā* as opposed to the khandhas, which are not *attā.* This part of the *Alagaddūpamasutta* (identical with sutta 33 of the *Khandhasaṁyutta*) confirms the opinion that the passage, 'But bhikkhus, there being self, would there be for me what belongs to self, etc.,' does not propound the doctrine of absolute *anattā,* but only of relative *anattā,* unless one can think of a compiler adhering to the doctrine of absolute *anattā* in the middle of the *sutta* and reverting to the doctrine of relative *anattā* at the end of the same *sutta.*[45]

That the Natumhākasutta of the Khandhasaṁyutta propounds the doctrine of relative *anattā* will become evident from an unprejudiced analysis of it. The key to the interpretation of the sutta lies in the simile of the Jeta grove. The grass, the sticks, the branches, the foliage stand for the aggregates or *khandhas.* If anyone were to burn all the fuel of the Jeta grove the bhikkhus cannot complain that they themselves are being burnt. As they themselves answer, the fuel of the Jeta grove is neither their (physical) self nor anything belonging to it. There is a perfect parallelism in this *sutta* between the physical man and the metaphysical man, that is to say, what man in the last analysis *is*. The phrase, 'Because, Lord, that is not our self or what belongs to our self', means to say in the first place that the fuel of the Jeta grove is not the physical self of the bhikkhus nor belongs to it in any way. But when applying the simile to the inner man, the Buddha announces, '*In the same way,* bhikkhus, bodily form is not yours, get rid of it'. Therefore, the phrase, 'Because that, Lord, is not our self or what belongs to our self', applies also to the *khandhas,* which in the very same way are not the metaphysical self of the bhikkhus. The metaphysical self is shown here as having nothing in common with the aggregates, even as the fuel of the Jeta grove has nothing in common with the physical self of the bhikkhus; the *khandhas* are as alien to the metaphysical self of the bhikkhus as the fuel of the Jeta grove is alien to their physical self. And because the aggregates are not their self or what belongs to their self, the bhikkhus are told that they are not theirs (*na tumhākaṁ*), and therefore that they ought to get rid of them. Two are the main conclusions that follow from this way of reasoning.

1. When it is said of the fuel of the Jeta grove that it is not the physical self of the bhikkhus nor belongs to such self in any way, the reality of the physical self is not thereby denied. In the very same way, and by force of the noted parallelism, when the *khandhas* are said not to be the metaphysical self of the bhikkhus nor anything that belongs to it, the reality of the metaphysical self is not thereby denied, it is implicitly asserted.

2. There is a correlation between *tumhākaṁ* and *vo* in the phrase, *yaṁ na tumhākaṁ taṁ pahajatha; taṁ vo pahīnaṁ dīgharattaṁ sukhāya bhavissati,* 'get rid, bhikkhus, of what is not yours (*tumhākaṁ*). Once you have got rid of it, it will be for your (*vo*) welfare and happiness for a long time'. Here *vo* refers obviously to the same concrete subject of possession (a possession that is denied) as *tumhākaṁ.* That is to say, the *attā,* in the case of the bhikkhu who gets rid of the *khandhas,* becomes both the agent and the beneficiary of the happiness resulting from getting rid of the *khandhas.* Hence, the ultimate identity of *attā* as the metaphysical core of man and as the moral agent that strives for perfection, an identity that covers a reality that is valid on two levels, metaphysical and moral, without thereby being split. Consequently it was only logical that the realtiy of the moral

agent should be denied, once the reality of the metaphysical self was also denied.

3. By getting rid of the *khandhas,* by disentangling themselves (their selves!) from them, the *attā* of the monks would be reinstated in its own pristine ontological independence, an independence shattered on the moral level when they identify themselves (their selves!) in one way or another with the *khandhas.*

The same reasoning, illustrated with the same simile, is applied to sensorial objects and their corresponding sensorial consciousness.[46]

PERMANENCE, HAPPINESS, SELF, VS. IMPERMANENCE, PAIN, NON-SELF

The contrast between these two series of terms can also contribute to make us develop the right perspective for the interpretation of the texts we have adduced.

In the *Sammasasutta* of the *Saṁyutta,* we are told first of all that the grief of old-age and death is due to *upadhi,* 'samsaric adherence', *Upadhi* may be either subjective or objective, and is always the result of craving (*taṇhā*), which in its turn is dependent on attractive and pleasant sensorial objects. The text continues:

> All those who in the past, bhikkhus, whether samaṇas or brāhmaṇas, regarded whatever had an attractive and pleasant form as permanent, regarded it as pleasant, regarded it as self (*attato*), regarded it as health, regarded it as safety, caused craving to grow. Those who caused craving to grow, made also samsaric adherence to grow. Those who made samsaric adherence to grow made also pain to grow. Those who made pain to grow were not liberated from birth, old-age, death, pains, lamentations, griefs, mental uneasiness, tribulation; they were not liberated from Pain.[47]

The same is repeated regarding the future and the present. There follows a beautiful simile where the reality of the moral agent and his power of choice between good and evil show very strikingly. The whole reasoning is then repeated in a negative way.

This *sutta* is interesting because it groups self (*attā*) with permanence, happiness, health, safety (all positive terms) as if it had some sort of affinity with them, while non-self (*anattā*) is grouped with impermanence, grief, sickness and insecurity, and this is as it ought to be, because *anattā* stands for whatever is samsaric and therefore impermanent, painful, unhealthy, insecure. Is it not logical to assert that if one rejects even an attractive and pleasant form just because it is impermanent, it is because he appreciates permanence more than sensual pleasure? Cannot the same reasoning be applied to the other pairs of opposites, grief-happiness, sickness-health, insecurity-safety? And finally, as the pair of opposites self-non-self are found in the middle of the series, is it not logical to say that if one rejects an attractive and pleasant form just because it is not the self, it is because he appreciates the self more than sensual pleasure? On the other hand, one cannot disapprove of impermanence as such, without thereby showing that he contemplates permanence as his ideal. The same applies to other pairs, grief-happiness, sickness-health, insecurity-safety. And in the same way, one does not disapprove, reject, get rid of what is non-self, precisely because it is non-self, without thereby showing that he contemplates the self as his ideal. Such a way of thinking does not certainly run in the direction of the doctrine of absolute *anattā.*

The series, 'permanent, happy, self', occurs in other passages that speak of possibilities and impossibilities:

> Herein, Ānanda, a bhikkhu comprehends, 'This is unlikely, impossible, that a man of [right] view should approach a composite thing as permanent'. And he comprehends, 'This is likely, that a common man should approach a composite thing as permanent'. [The same is asserted and denied substituting 'pleasant' and 'painful' for permanent and impermanent respectively.] He comprehends, 'This is unlikely, impossible, that a man of [right] view should approach any *dhamma* [samaric attribute or thing] as self (*attato*)'. And he comprehends, 'This is likely, that a common man should approach any *dhamma* as self.[48]

An arrangement of terms is observed here that became stereotyped, coupling *anicca* and *dukkha* with *saṅkhārā* and *anattā* with *dhammā.*[49]

AS ALIEN NOT AS THE SELF

We have met with pronouncements that declare regarding the aggregates, the senses, etc., 'This is not mine, this I am not, this is not my self', as well as that they are not 'either the self or anything belonging to the self'. What is non-self is usually designated by the term *anattā,* a negative term, but, as we are going to see presently, it may also be called *para,* a positive term that functions very much like a relative term of *attā. Attā-para* constitute a perfect logical division by dychotomy. Whatever is not *attā* may be called *para,* which means 'alien', i.e., 'not one's own', this being the meaning given to alien by the *Oxford Dictionary.* This division of reality into two positive but opposite terms implies a dividing mentality that takes both the extremes to be *real.*

Vaṅgīsa was feeling discontented with a life of renunciation and went to Ānanda to confess that he was burning with attachment to sensual pleasures and wanted to know how to cool down such attachment and the burning of his mind. He was told among other things:

> Regard all composite things as alien (*parato*), as painful, and not as your self (*mā ca attato*),
> Extinguishing the great attachment, do not be consumed time and again.[50]

In the *Caravagga* of the *Aṅguttara* we meet with a line expressing the same thought:

> Knowing all composite things as alien, as painful, and not as his self... (*no ca attato*).[51]

In the *Theragāthā* regarding the five *khandhas* as alien not as self is praised as a great achievement,

> "They indeed penetrate what is subtle, as a hair tip with an arrow,
> Who regard the five *khandhas* as alien, not as their self (*parato no ca attato*)."[52]

And the *Therīgāthā* affors us the following advice,

> "Setting up your mind, one-pointed, well recollected, Consider composite things as alien, not as your self (*parato no ca attato*)."[53]

In the above texts, it is said that some people either regard (*passanti*) the aggregates or know composite things as alien (*parato*), not as their self (*no attato*) or they are exhorted to do so. Let us reflect over this.

1. Who is supposed to be in each one of those cases the active subject of such regarding or consideration? Will it be one of the aggregates or all of them together? How can anyone of the *khandhas* or all of them together

consider the *khandhas* themselves as alien (*parato*), as 'another thing'? Besides, in order to consider something as *para,* the considering subject should be able to see himself as *attā,* but the *khandhas* can be regarded as *attā,* only in the spirit of the *sakkāyadiṭṭhi,* which contradicts the spirit in which the texts adduced are composed. Consequently, the considering subject has to be a *reality* different from the aggregates. It has to be also a *personal* reality, for it has to be able to refer to himself as *attā,* and to reject the aggregates as *para.*

2. When someone is stated to regard or is exhorted to regard the aggregates or all composite things as something alien (*parato*), not as the self (*attato*), what is the *attā* referred to? Is it a theroretical or hypothetical *attā,* whose reality ought to be denied or is it the core of the adherent's personality? The latter ought to be the case if we wish the exercise to have any practical value, not being limited to a fruitless confrontation of the concrete *khandhas* with something that in the hypothesis of absolute *anattā* is an unreality, when in the perspective in which the vision and comparison of the *khandhas* and the self is proposed primacy is given to *attā,* which is to be accepted above the *khandhas* that should be rejected. *Attā* when referring to a person and being opposed to whatever is not self (*para*), is nothing else but that person's own individuality or personal essence. As a matter of fact, the adherent is exhorted to regard *his khandhas,* which form his empirical 'ego', as 'alien' to *what he really is* (*attā*). Is this equivalent to a denial of *attā,* or is it not rather a clear assertion of its reality, which is *de facto* 'ontologically' independent from the aggregates, and ought to be therefore *de jure* 'morally' independent from them?

3. It has already been indicated that there is between *attā* and *para* a relative opposition, which is equivalent to a contradictory opposition, because whatever is *para* is not *attā,* there being nothing in between. This opposition reflected on the moral level takes the form of a moral incompatibility between the two. To think *attā* and *para* (*non-attā*) compatible in any way is the most harmful of errors, which makes liberation impossible. It may be said that the opposition between *attā* and *para* (*non-attā, anattā*) in this context is like the opposition between *mitra* (friend) and *amitra* (enemy) where the latter does not merely mean mere absence of a friend, but the objective opposition of an enemy.

4. Finally, with reference to Ven. Nyānaponika's words quoted above,

here we have 'the idea of particularity or separateness, i.e.,... a differentiation from what is regarded as *not* "ego" (better as not the self)' given to us by the sacred text itself. And this is done in opposition to the aggregates, which, according to him are the only available data of experience from which such 'particularity, separateness, differentiation' could possibly be derived. *Attā* and its opposite *para* (the khandhas), in these texts, are not something we assume, but data given to us by Scripture itself.

It will be fitting, before we close this chapter, to say something about the fallacy of the *anattā* doctrine, taken in its absolute sense. Those who propound the doctrine of absolute *anattā* and do it on the strength of those texts according to which we ought to say of the *khandhas,* 'This is not mine, this I am not, this is not my self', seem to take for granted that in man there is nothing beyond the *khandhas.* The complete argument would run like this:

> The *khandhas* being impermanent, painful, liable to alteration, are not the self in man,
> But in man there is nothing else but the *khandhas,*
> Therefore there is no self in man.

We would like to see any text in the Nikāyas that teaches either explicitly or implicitly that there is in man nothing else but the *khandhas.* Many texts have been adduced that imply just the opposite and many more could still be adduced.

Let us take at least one text more for our consideration. After asserting of every sense, of the sense-objects, of the different kinds of sensorial consciousness, of the different kinds of sensorial contact, of each one of the *khandhas,* 'This is not mine, this I am not, this is not my self', the text continues:

> Seing thus, Rāhula, the learned ariyan disciple gets disgusted with the eye, with visual forms, with visual consciousness, with visual contact, and whatever is there that arises from visual contact in the form of feeling, in the form of perception, in the form of inner complexes, in the form of consciousness, he also gets disgusted with it. (The same applies to the rest of the senses including the mind and mental states). Feeling disgust, he looses all atachment, due to detachment he is liberated. At being liberated there is knowledge of being liberated. He knows....[54]

Is there anything else in man's phenomenal existence not included in the catalogue of things from which he turns away because they are not the self (his self!) and by turning away from which *he* is liberated? There must needs be a difference between the one who actively rejects whatever is phenomenal in his existence (senses, objects, sensorial activites, the *khandhas*) because that is not his self and the things rejected by him. Therefore the things rejected are not the complete man, the one who actively rejects them remains to be accounted for. What is there in man that is liberated following that rejection? It would be absurd to say that liberation affects the things rejected, when liberation follows precisely their wilful rejection. Therefore, there is in man some reality beyond the things rejected, that is the moral agent of such liberating rejection, who strives to establish on the moral level, the autonomy that is the self's own in the metaphysical level.

The Doctrine of Non-Self Taught Through the Predication of the Negative Term Anattā

To begin with, it is to be noted that the negative predicate *anattā,* used to convey the idea that certain things are not the self, i.e., are the non-self, is used not as an adjective but as a noun. The proof is in the fact that it stays unchanged whatever be the subject's gender and number: *rūpaṁ anattā, vedanā anattā, saṅkhārā anattā, viññāṇaṁ anattā.*[1] The practical consequence of this is important. What is affirmed by means of the predicate *anattā* is not an abstract idea, but a concrete existing reality. Therefore, if I say that material form (*rūpaṁ*) is *anattā,* I do not merely say that material form exhibits the characteristic of non-selfhood, but that material form is part of the totality of things constituting the non-self (*anattā*), a totality of things opposed and contradictory to the self (*attā*). This confirms the polarity existing in the Nikāyas between the self and the non-self, implying the reality of two positive entities, possessed of antithetical natures. In this ideological set up the reality of *anattā,* of which no one doubts, implies the reality of *attā,* there being a continual existential conflict between the two, until *attā* succeeds in asserting its absolute independence from the former.

When the texts speak of *anattā* as embracing the whole of its denotation, the translation of the therm *anattā* will be 'the non-self', referring to the totality of things that constitute the non-self as opposed to the self. But even though *attā* may always be translated as 'the self', inasmuch as it is an homogeneous entity, not allowing any divisions, the same is not the case with *anattā.* There are many disparate things that come in under the category of *anattā.* Therefore when it is asserted of some of those things, not of all, that they are *anattā,* we shall not be able to translate this *anattā* as 'the non-self', but as 'non-self'. Thus if I am told, '*rūpaṁ anattā*', we shall not be able to translate it as, 'bodily form is *the* non-self', there being many other things besides bodily form falling under the denotation of non-self. A case, for instance, where *anattā* will allow itself to be translated as 'the non-self', is the following:

See the world together with its devas full of conceit for *the self* (*attamā-*

> *niṁ*) in what is *the non-self* (*anattani*),
> Established on name-and-form, it thinks 'this is true'.…[2]

CONNECTION WITH THE PRECEDING CHAPTER

This chapter does not introduce a new topic. The wording of the formulas to be examined may be different from those of the preceding chapter, but their purport is substantially the same. This implies that if the *anattā* taught through the denial of positive terms was only a relative one, as it has been shown, the *anattā* taught in the formulas to be analysed in the present chapter will be also a relative one. This will be confirmed after showing that the scope of the formulations studied in this chapter is not broader or narrower than the scope of the formulations investigated in the preceding chapter, but coincident with it.

We find in this connection a series of texts that yield the following statement of equality, viz. *anattā* = *n'etaṁ mama, n'eso'ham'asmi, na me'so attā.*

> The eye, bhikkhus, is impermanent, what is impermanent is painful, what is painful is non-self (*anattā*), what is non-self, 'That is not mine, that I am not, that is not my self'. Thus is how this should be regarded by means of superior knowledge.…

The same is asserted of the other senses and their respective objects, every one of the *suttas* ending with the well known passage:

> Thus discerning, bhikkhus, the learned ariyan disciple feels disgust for the eye,…, etc. Feeling disgust he is detached. Being detached he is liberated, …, etc.[3]

The *Udāyisutta* of the *Saḷāyatanasaṁyutta* yields the statement of equality, *anattā* = neither *attā* nor *attaniya.* Ānanda is questioned by Udāyin, whether just as the body has been presented in many ways by the Blessed One as bein non-self (*anattā*), one can do the same regarding consciousness. Ānanda replies indicating how consciousness depends for its existence on the activity of the senses and ceases with it. The idea behind this is doubtless that consciousness is *anattā,* because it is impermanent and depends for its existence on what is *anattā.* Then the simile is given of a man searching for heart of wood where it is not found, namely in a plantain trunk:

even so, friend, a bhikkhu does not see in the sixfold sphere of sense neither the self (*attā*) nor what belongs to the self (*attaniya*). Thus discerning he is not attached to anything in the world. Not being attached he is not troubled. Not being troubled he attains *nibbāna* as regards the very self (*paccattaññeva*). He knows, 'Destroyed is birth...'.[4]

This is one of the several cases where we see how reluctant some people were to accept the *anattā* of *viññāṇa*.

We find the equivalence between *suññaṁ* and *anattā* in the following:

Regard thoroughly with perfect wisdom what is impermanent as painful. [Regarding] the void (*suññaṁ*) as non-self (*anattā*) people destroy grief....[5]

The equivalence of *suññato* and *anattato* is shown in texts to be studied presently.

In some texts analysed in the preceding chapter, *para* stood as the contradictory of *attā*. There are a number of texts where *parato* and *anatatto* occur in a series of what we may call 'intentional' synonyms. Such texts will yield the statement of equality, *para* = *na attā* = *anattā*, showing again the connection of this chapter with the previous one. Thus we read:

What is the way, Ānanda, what is the method for the rejection of the five lower fetters? Herein Ānanda, a bhikkhu, through detachment from all samsaric adherences, through rejection of evil qualities, through the complete calming down of unchastity, aloof from sensual pleasures, dwells having entered into the first *jhāna*... whatever is found there connected with material form, feeling, perception, inner complexes, or consciousness, he looks at those things as impermanent, painful, a disease, a [festering] boil, a dart, a misfortune, an affliction, as something alien (*parato*), as decay, as empty (*suññato*), as non-self (*anattato*). He turns his mind from such things, and having turned his mind from such things he concentrates his mind on the deathless element, to wit, the calming down of all activities, the expelling of all samsaric adherences, the destruction of craving, detachment, cessation, *nibbāna*....[6]

A simple form of the series of "intentional" synonyms is found in:

Bhikkhus, whatever samaṇas and brāhmaṇas in the past regarded any pleasant and agreable material form as permanent, regarded it as pleasant, regarded it as the self, regarded it as health, regarded it as security,

> all of them caused attachment to increase. Those who caused attachment to increase made samsaric adherences to grow. Those who made samsaric adherences to grow promoted pain. Those who promoted pain were not freed from birth, old-age, death, suffering, etc.[7]

The same applies to samaṇas and brāhmaṇas of the future and to the existing ones. The opposite is asserted of those who regarded (will regard, or regard at present) any pleasant and agreable material form as impermanent, painful, as non-self, as disease, as danger (*aniccato, dukkhato, anattato, rogato, bhayato*), which clearly is an enlargement of the usual triad, *aniccato, dukkhato, anattato,* and of which the longer series quoted above may be the final product even though *rogato* has changed its place and *bhayato* has disappeared altogether.

Finally, *anattādhīno* is used as a synonym of *parādhīno,* 'depending on another ', and *attādhīno* is taken as synonymous with *aparādhīno,* in the *Majjhimanikāya.*[8]

The quotations just given in this section prove that whether the *anattā* doctrine be taught by the denial of positive terms, as was the case with the texts studied in the preceding chapter, or by the predication of the negative term *anattā,* the meaning is substantially the same. Therefore it is only left to show that the scope of the second set of texts coincides exactly with the scope of the first set, the conclusion being that both sets of texts teach only relative *anattā.* Even in the quotations given in this section to show the connection between the present chapter and the preceding one, one can see that the *anattā* doctrine taught in them is also a relative one and that the soteriological aim of the doctrine is never forgotten.

SCOPE OF THE ANATTĀ STATEMENTS

We are now going to see how the scope of the *anattā* statements is the same as the scope of the statements that denied the self through the negation of positive terms, viz., the *khandhas*; the senses, sensorial objects, etc.; the elements...

1. The khandhas are anattā

Suttas 12, 13 an 14 of the *Khandhasaṁyutta* apply to the *khandhas* the same reasoning based, in the first case on their impermanence, in the second case on being painful, in the third case on being non-self:

> Body, bhikkhus, is non-self (*anattā*), feeling is non-self, perception is non-self, the inner complexes are non-self, consciousness is non-self. Discerning thus, a learned ariyan disciple is repelled by the body, is also repelled by feeling, is also repelled by perception, is also repelled by the inner complexes, is also repelled by consciousness. Being repelled he gets rid of all attachment to them; without attachment he is freed. At being freed, he has the knowledge of freedom. He knows, 'Destroyed is birth, lived is the brahma-life, done is what was to be done, there will be no more living in these conditions'.[9]

Let us note once again that the *anattā* doctrine in the Nikāyas is no theoretical mental exercise but an exercise in liberation that ought to be attained by discarding those things that are branded as non-self (*anattā*). Also:

> 'Non-self, non-self', (*anattā, anattā'ti*) thus it is said, Lord. But what precisely is non-self?
>
> Body, Rādha, is non-self, feeling is non-self, perception is non-self, the inner complexes are non-self, consciousness is non-self. Discerning thus, Rādha.... [The same conclusion as in the previous text.][10]

A *sutta* begins by asserting the reality of the self with the term *pahitatto* in a request addressed by a certain bhikkhu to the Buddha that the *dhamma* may be explained to him 'in a nutshell', so that he may abide 'in solitude, diligent, ardent, with a resolute self'. The Buddha says:

> You must put away desire, bhikkhus,
> for whatever is non-self.

The bhikkhu replies that he understands, and directed by the Buddha to explain in full what he has just taught briefly, the bhikkhu continues:

> Body, Lord, is non-self, I must put away desire for it; feeling Lord, is non-self, I must put away desire for it, etc., etc.[11]

There is a text worthy to be noted because one of the sentences contained in it, if taken out of the context might be thought to teach the doctrine of absolute *anattā*:

> How does he regard the body? He regards it as impermanent, not as permanent; as painful, not as pleasant; as non-self, not as self. He is disgusted, not delighted. He detaches himself, not attaches himself. He

> causes it to cease, does not cause it to originate. He renounces it, does not cling to it. Regarding it as impermanent, he abandons the idea of permanence. Regarding it as painful, he abandons the idea of happiness. Regarding it as non-self, he abandons the idea of the self. Feeling disgusted, he abandons delight. Detaching himself, he abandons attachment. Making it to cease, he abandons origination. Renouncing it, he abandons clinging.[12]

We have here the sentence, *anattato anupassanto attasaññaṁ pajahati.* From the context it is evident that the idea of the self that is abandoned here is that which identifies the body with the self or sees any kind of ontological relation between the body and the self. Therefore the sentence will have the following meaning, 'regarding [the body] as non-self, he abandons the idea of the self [regarding the body]'. Nevertheless, I think that such and similar sentences played an important role in establishing as indisputable the doctrine of absolute *anattā,* specially when they were isolated from their context and given an absolute value.

Regarding the *khandhas* as non-self is the way to arahantship and salvation:

> Regarding the *khandhas* as impermanent, as painful, as non-self (*anattato*),
> Casting away all the *āsavas,* I attained arahantship.[13]

We may remind ourselves once more of what we have called 'the fallacy of absolute *anattā*'. If there is nothing else in man but the *khandhas*, who is there to be freed from the body, and from feeling, and from perception, and from the inner complexes, and from consciousness? And if the *khandhas,* which constitute only the empirical man, are called *the non-self* in man, who else can be left there to be freed from them but *the self*?

2. *The senses, sensorial objects, etc., are anattā*

The senses and their objects are non-self and originate from what is non-self:

> The eye, bhikkhus, is non-self. And whatever is the reason, whatever is the condition for the arisal of the eye is also non-self. Being produced from non-self, how can the eye, bhikkhus, be the self? [The same applies to the other senses].[14]

The *sutta* concludes with the stock passage of one who so considering the senses (or their objects) becomes disgusted with them, detaches himself from them and is ultimately liberated.

> Whatever, bhikkhus, is non-self, you ought to get rid of desire, of attachment, of desire and attachment for it. And what, bhikkhus, is non-self? The eye, bhikkhus, is non-self, you ought to get rid of desire, of attachment, of desire and attachment for it, etc.[15]

Finally we have the most comprehensive texts where the senses, their objects, sensorial consciousness, etc., are declared to be *anattā*:

> I shall, bhikkhus, teach you a method conducive to *nibbāna.* Listen to it, reflect upon it in your minds, I am going to speak. And, of what kind, bhikkhus, is the method conducive to *nibbāna*? Herein, bhikkhus, a bhikkhu regards the eye as non-self, regards visual forms as non-self, regards visual consciousness as non-self, regards the eye's sensorial contact as non-self. And whatever feeling, be it either pleasant or unpleasant, or neither pleasant nor unpleasant arising dependent on this sensorial contact of the eye, that also he regards as non-self.... [The same applies to the rest of the senses.][16]

The consideration of the senses, their objects, etc., as non-self is the way to getting rid of the heretical view that identifies the self with the senses, etc. (*sakkāyadiṭṭhi*).

> How knowing, how seing, Lord, is the heretical notion of the self (*attānudiṭṭhi*) cast away?
>
> Knowing and seing the eye, bhikkhus, as non-self, the heretical view of the self (*attānudiṭṭhi*) is cast away. [The same applies to visible forms, to visual consciousness, to visual contact, to feelings arising from such sensorial contact. All this applies, too, to all the other senses.][17]

3. *The elements are anattā*

The elements in this passage are said to be six: earth, water, fire, air, space and *viññāṇa.* This is the most comprehensive list of elements found in the Nikāyas and a proof of its lateness, as it has already been indicated.

> How knowing, how seing, the mind of such a man, being detached from these six elements, is freed from the *āsavas*?

... 'I approached, reverend one, the earth element as non-self, I did not approach the self as founded on the earth element. And whatever obstinacy, prejudice, and bias of mind due to clinging and attachment based on the earth element, by their destruction, by detachment from them, by their cessation, by their abandonment, by their renunciation, I know that my mind is free.' [The same is said of the other five elements.][18]

This passage contains a remarkable detail which should not be allowed to pass unheeded. The usual way of exposing the *anattā* doctrine in the Nikāyas is reflected in the phrase, 'I approached, reverend one, the earth element as non-self' (*pathavīdhātuṁ ahaṁ, āvuso, anattato upagacchiṁ*)'. The phrase immediately following this one is certainly unusual, 'I did not approach the self as founded on the earth element (*na ca pathavīdhātunissitaṁ attānaṁ* [*upagacchiṁ*])'. How can one who speaks in this way be said to be a votary of absolute *anattā*? If it were so he would equivalently be saying, 'and I did not approach the self, *which is not real,* as dependent on the earth element'. To put it in a way that became classical in Indian philosophy, this would be equivalent to saying, 'and I did not approach *the horns of a rabbit* as dependent on the earth element'. What value can have a statement where one emphatically asserts that he does not approach something that is not real as dependent on something real? The correlation established by the contrast of the two phrases demands that if in 'I approached the earth element as non-self', the earth element so approached is something real, so too in, 'And I did not approach the self as dependent on the earth element', the self referred to be also real. Our attention is drawn here not only to the elements which are said to be non-self, but also *to the self,* that ought not be considered in any way dependent on the elements. In short, a man who did not believe in the reality of *attā* could not have spoken as he speaks here.

4. *Most comprehensive passages*

There are a number of passages where *anattā* is predicated of many of the things so far mentioned together. Thus:

The Lord taught me *dhamma,* (He taught me) that the *khandhas,* the spheres of sense, the elements, are disgusting, impermanent, painful, non-self (*anattā*).[19]

The *Āhuneyyavagga* of the *Aṅguttara* classifies as persons worthy of offerings and gifts and as an unsurpassed field of merit in the world, those who see 'impermanence, pain, non-self, destruction, decay, cessation, and renunciation' in:

1. the six senses, their objects, their corresponding consciousness, their corresponding contacts;
2. feelings, perceptions, intentions, craving, reflections (*vitakka*), deliberations (*vicāra*), sprung from every one of the sensorial contacts;
3. the aggregates or *khandhas*.[20]

In the texts so far surveyed we see that the scope of the *anattā* statements coincides with the scope of the texts reviewed in the first chapter where the doctrine of *anattā* was propounded through the denial of positive terms. Here, as there, the *anattā* doctrine is never exposed as a purely mental exercise, as a theory maintained solely on theoretical grounds, but as a necessary condition for detachment and liberation. But (the question keeps recurring to the mind every time one reads about detachment and liberation) '*whose* liberation'? One thing is clear, the liberation showed as an ideal in the Nikāyas is 'liberation from the non-self'. Then who else can be liberated but the self? *Anattā* comes very often in a series with *anicca* and *dukkha.* And the partisans of absolute *anattā* would make us hold that while one can abhor what is impermanent and painful, because he aspires, in the most natural way and without any trace of conceit, to what is permanent and brings happiness, one should abhor the non-self, *precisely because it is the non-self,* without there being in reality a counterpart to the non-self that can be no other but *the self.* It has been remarked more than once that there is a polarity set forth in the Nikāyas between *attā* and *anattā,* and the realtiy of the latter demands the reality of the former, otherwise many of the things we read in the sacred texts will make very little sense, if any. The incompatibility between *attā* and *anattā* in every man is an incompatibility between two realities, the conflict between them is a real conflict, and the solution of the conflict by the return of the self to the isolation from the non-self that is due to it by its own nature is also a real one.

INTIMATE RELATIONSHIP BETWEEN ANATTĀ AND DUKKHA

In many of the passages so far discussed, the reasoning proceeded in the following way. We were told that something was impermanent, that what was impermanent was painful, and that what was painful could not be considered as 'mine, I, or my self', or that it should be considered as non-self. In a number of passages the idea or consideration of non-self is attached in a special manner to what is painful, to *dukkha.* This again continues giving to *anattā* a relative value not an absolute one.

A disciple of the Buddha was very ill. He sent a message to the master with the request that he should come and visit him. The main exhortation given to the sick man is as follows:

> Therefore, Dīghāvu, establishing yourself in these four limbs of stream-winning, you should foster the six states that are constituent parts of wisdom. Herein, Dīghāvu, do you dwell regarding impermanence in all compound things, aware of pain in what is impermanent, aware of non-self (*anattasaññī*) in what is painful, aware of detachment, aware of cessation. Thus, Dīghāvu, you should train yourself.[21]

Dīghāvu confessed that all these conditions were found in him, the result being that, dying not long after, he was reborn as an apparitional being, never to come back to the world, destined to attain *nibbāna.*

There are a number of passages that prescribe the fostering of this awareness of non-self in what is painful:

> Bhikkhus, the awareness of non-self in what is painful (*dukkhe anattasaññā*), when fostered and made to grow is of great fruit and profit. . . .[22]

In a group of *suttas* where a rather complete programme of spiritual training is described, one of the practices recommended after the prescriptions, 'he fosters the awareness of impermanence' and 'he fosters the awareness of what is painful', is:

> He fosters the awareness of non-self in what is painful (*dukkhe anattasaññaṁ*). Of such a one, bhikkhus, it is said, 'This bhikkhu dwells possessing sound knowledge, implementing the teaching of his master, a follower of advice, he does not eat in vain the country food'.[23]

See also:

> Bhikkhus, there are five things, which when fostered and made to grow have as their fruits liberation of mind and liberation through insight,

> and the advantages of the fruits of liberation through insight. What five? The awareness of impermanence, the awareness of pain in what is impermanent, the awareness of non-self in what is painful, etc.[24]

The awareness of impermanence, the awareness of pain in what is impermanent and the awareness of non-self in what is painful occur at the end of seven kinds of awareness to be fostered, which merge into, and conduce to *nibbāna*. Everyone of the seven kinds of awareness is treated separately. When coming to awareness of non-self in what is painful, the text reads:

> The awareness of non-self in what is painful, when fostered and made to grow is of great fruit, of great profit, plunged into the deathless, having the deathless as its ultimate goal. This that has been so said, why has it been so said? The mind of a bhikkhu who dwells with the mind full of the awareness of non-self in what is painful is freed from the conceit expressed by 'I' and 'mine' with relation to this consciousness-informed body and in all external signs; having surpassed all conceit, [his mind is] pacified, freed. [If he does not dwell thus...] then, bhikkhus, he should know this, 'The awareness of non-self in what is painful has not been developed in my case; there is not, regarding me, any difference between the previous and present condition; not attained by me is the power of development. Thus he is mindful of this'. [The opposite case is then explained.][25]

THE AWARENESS OF NON-SELF

We have been able to observe how the *anattā* texts examined so far do not teach absolute *anattā,* but a qualified one, an *anattā* always somehow restricted either to the *khandhas,* or to the senses and their activities, to the elements, to *dukkha.* But we discover a number of places where 'the awareness of non-self' (*anattasaññā*) is used all by itself, without any qualification, and its cultivation is recomended. We may deem these to be transitional texts that by dint of repetition were among the causes why later Buddhism, losing sight of the restrictions imposed on *anattā* by the early texts, came eventually to accept the doctrine of absolute *anattā.* Thus we read:

> For as long, bhikkhus, as the bhikkhus will foster the consciousness of non-self [spiritual] growth is to be expected regarding the bhikkhus, not decline.[26]

This passage is translated in *Dialogues of the Buddha,* II, p. 84, as:

> So long as the brethren exercise themselves in the realization of the idea of the absence of any soul....

Why to give an absolute value to *anattasaññā* translating it as 'the idea of the absence of *any* soul', when as we have seen, the fundamental texts always limit the scope of *anattā,* the absence of self, to certain definite things? This confirms what has been just remarked, that the use of *anattasaññā* all by itself had a great share in the development of the idea of absolute *anattā.* The incongruity of giving to *anattasaññā* an absolute value will be apparent from the following text where the term occurs:

> Therefore, bhikkhus, you should train yourselves in this way, 'Sinful, unprofitable states will not continue overpowering our mind, as it used to be filled (with them) at the time of renunciation. Our mind will be filled with the awareness of impermanence, with the awareness of non-self, with the awareness of the foul, with the awareness of danger; knowing what is straight and crooked in the world, our mind will be filled with awareness of that; knowing becoming and de-becoming in the world, our mind will be filled with awareness of that; knowing arisal and destruction in the world, our mind will be filled with awareness of that; our mind will be filled with the awareness of abandonment;... of detachment;... of cessation. This is how, bhikkhus, you should train yourselves.'[27]

Would one be justified in translating the phrase, *asubhasaññāparicittaṁ ca no cittaṁ bhavissati* as 'and our mind will be filled with the awareness of *absolute* foulness', when we known from other texts which are the *asubha* things on which the bhikkhu should meditate, and that not all things are *asubha*?[28] The obvious answer is 'no'. Then why should anyone translate, in imitation of what was done in the above quoted text, *anattasaññāparicittaṁ ca no cittaṁ bhavissati,* as 'and our mind will be filled with the awareness of *absolute* non-self' (giving the term *anattasaññā* an absolute value), when there are so many texts asserting the reality of *attā* (first part of this book), and so many others which limit the scope of *anattā,* and thereby implicitly denying its absolute value (second part of this book)?

The same reasoning may be applied to the following text:

The awareness of the foul (*asubha*) is to be fostered for the abandoning of attachment, kindness is to be fostered for the abandoning of ill-will, mindfulness in breathing is to be fostered for the interruption of continuous thought, the awareness of impermanence is to be fostered for the complete uprooting of conceit. Because the awareness of non-self (*anattasaññā*) is established in the case of one who is possessed of the idea of impermanence, the one possessed of the awareness of non-self (*anattasaññī*) obtains the complete uprooting of conceit, *nibbāna* in this very life.[29]

Awareness of impermanence leads to awareness of non-self, and this in its turn leads to the complete uprooting of conceit. But even as impermanence has no absolute value in the Nikāyas, the same will apply to non-self. And what is conceit but the erroneous identification of the self with the non-self, implying that the man of right view is not guilty of such identification, but separates the one from the other, confessing thereby implicitly the reality of both?[30]

Even though the term *anattasaññā* is often found without any qualification as to the extent of the *anattā* implied in it, the general tone of the Nikāyas demands that such qualification should be understood. In fact there are several cases where a *sutta* that speaks of *dukkhe anattasaññā* (thus with a qualification) is found in the vicinity of another *sutta* that speaks of *anattasaññā* without any qualification. It would be an exegetical blunder to ignore the former *suttas* when interpreting the latter ones.

This our position is fully confirmed by the *Girimānandasutta* of the *Aṅguttara,* where Ānanda is instructed by the Buddha to visit Girimānanda, who was sick, that he might explain to him the ten kinds of awareness. One of them is precisely *anattasaññā,* thus without any limitation, but when the *sutta* comes to explain such awareness in detail, the text reads:

And of what kind, Ānanda, is the awareness of non-self? Herein, Ānanda, a bhikkhu, gone either to the forest, or to the root of a tree, or to a lonely spot, reflects thus, 'The eye is non-self, visible forms are non-self; the ear is non-self, sounds are non-self; the sense of smell is non-self, odours are non-self; the tongue is non-self, tastes are non-self; the body is non-self, touch is non-self, the mind is non-self, mental objects are non-self.' Thus he dwells contemplating non-self in the sixfold sphere of sense, internal as well as external. This is called, Ānanda, the awareness of non-self.[31]

Keeping in mind the overall teaching of the Nikāyas on the subject no one will be justified in attributing to *anattasaññā* or any other similar term an absolute value.

ANATTĀ PROCLAIMED BY MEANS OF UNIVERSAL STATEMENTS

Numerous are the statements that proclaim the *anattā* doctrine by means of universal propositions, which doubtless had also their share in establishing in the minds of future generations of Buddhists the doctrine of absolute *anattā.* But do those universal propositions really teach absolute *anattā*? They always confine the doctrine within certain limits, broad though they may be. They never declare that *attā* is not a reality, but that a certain totality of things are not the self or are non-self.

1. Sabbe saṅkhārā anattā

'All compound things are non-self', this is a statement whose acceptance does not offer any special difficulty. Impermanence is always the first radical deficiency by which a thing is recognized to be non-self. All compound things are basically unstable, their parts keep together only with the concurrence of the conditions on which they depend. Such concurrence is purely contingent, bound by no degree of necessity. That is why the usual epithet applied to them is *aniccā,* impermanent, and consequently they are said to be also *dukkhā,* painful.

As a rule, the series runs in this way, *sabbe saṅkhārā aniccā, sabbe saṅkhārā dukkhā, sabbe dhammā anattā.* There is only one passage, as far as we know, where the third member of the series is also, *sabbe saṅkhārā anattā,* and even in this case, the Siamese edition offers as v. 1. *dhammā* for *saṅkhārā.*[32]

The term *saṅkhārā,* when it designs one of the *khandhas* stands for the inner activities, complexes, mental and volitional as well as emotional 'fabrications'. It can refer also to external things, as in:

> Bhikkhus, impermanent are compounded things, unstable are compounded things, unsatisfactory are compounded things. How much is this fit to develop repulsion for all compounded things, to develop repulsion for all compounded things, to develop freedom from all compounded things.[33]

In this context, *saṅkhārā* refers to 'compounded things' of the physical world, which is to become extinct by the gradual appearance of more and more suns until, with the appearance of the seventh, the earth, together with mount Sineru, will be burnt without remainder. We have here a piece of cosmology so rare in the Nikāyas, but the Nikayan twist is not lacking in it, since the impermanence of the physical world is turned into a motive for feeling repulsion leading to liberation.

The special connection between *saṅkhārā* and impermanence, evident in so many parts of the Nikāyas, is based on the following fact thus stated:

> Bhikkhus, there are three composition-properties of what is compounded. What three? Its arisal is apparent, its decay is apparent, its mutability while it lasts is apparent.[34]

It is worth noticing that the *vimokkhas,* even the highly perfect ones, are said to be *saṅkhataṁ,* 'something mentally compounded'. This does not apply to the last one, consisting in the cessation of perception and feeling (*saññāvedayitaniroddha*). The position here seems to be parallel to the one we met before, when all the *vimokkhas* were said to be, 'not mine, not I, not my self', excepting also the last one. The text runs as follows:

> If I should focus this equanimity, thus purified, thus cleansed, on the sphere of infinite space... that is something compounded; If I should... on the sphere of infinite consciousness... that is something compounded; if I should... on the sphere of no-thing... that is something compounded; if I should... on the sphere of neither-perception-nor-non-perception and should develop my mind in accordance with that, that is something compounded. He therefore neither constructs nor develops any complexes either for becoming or de-becoming. Not constructing, not developing any complexes either for becoming or de-becoming, he grasps after nothing in the world; not grasping he is not troubled, not being troubled he attains *nibbāna* in his very self (*paccattaṁyeva*). He knows, 'Destroyed is birth..., etc.'[35]

Let us remind ourselves that we are studying a solitary text that says, *sabbe saṅkhārā anattā,* but such a text could have been repeated to satiety, as are *sabbe saṅkhāra aniccā* and *sabbe saṅkhārā dukkhā,* for we well know that whatever is *anicca* is also *dukkha,* and consequently also *anattā.* The point here is that the last *vimokkha* is not said to be *saṅkhāta,* therefore the formula *sabbe saṅkhārā anattā* does not apply to it, its universality being thereby limited.

2. Sabbaṁ anattā

'All is *anattā*', can there be a *prima facie* more comprehensive formula for the proclamation of *anattā*? But the section in which such statement occurs opens with a *sutta* that defines precisely what *sabbaṁ* is. Another proof that no text should be taken in isolation from the immediate or the general context in which it is found:

> Bhikkhus, I shall declare to you 'the all' (*sabbaṁ*). Listen to me. And what, bhikkhus, is 'the all'? It is the eye and visible forms; the ear and sounds; the nose and odours; the tongue and tastes; the body and touches; the mind and mental states. This is called, bhikkhus, 'the all'. Anyone, bhikkhus, who would speak thus, 'Disavowing that all, I shall declare to you another all', that would constitute idle talk. When questioned he would not be able to explain, and further he would get into trouble. And what is the reason for that? Because, bhikkhus, that would be beyond his scope.[36]

The word translated as 'beyond his scope' is *avisayasmiṁ.* Now, *visaya* means either 'object of sense', or 'sphere of the objects of sense'. Any 'all' that is not part of this *visaya* can be the object only of speculative talk, not of direct experience. A reader of the Nikāyas knows very well the little worth assigned in them to purely speculative discussions. From what we are told in the *suttas* that follow, (24, 25, etc.), 'the all' includes also the different kinds os sensorial consciousness, the different sensorial contacts, and the feelings dependent on such contacts. Of all this, it is said:

> The all, bhikkhus, is non-self. And what kind of all is non-self? The eye, bhikkhus, is non-self, visible forms are non-self, visual consciousness is non-self, the eye's contact is non-self, and whatever feeling originates dependent on this eye's contact, be it either pleasant or painful, or neither pleasant nor painful, that also is non-self. [The same applies to the

> rest of the senses.]
> Knowing this, the learned ariyan disciple feels disgust for the eye, for visible forms, for visual consciousness, for the eye's sensorial contact, regarding whatever feeling originates dependent on the eye's sensorial contact, he feels disgust also for this. [The same applies to the other senses.] Feeling disgust he gets rid of attachment, once rid of attachment he is set free, and being free knowledge comes to him that he is free. He knows, 'Destroyed is birth, lived is the brahma-life, etc.'[37]

Definitely, the statement *sabbaṁ anattā* does not propose the *anattā* doctrine with a wider scope than the one already known to us. And once more the thought that has been haunting us all through comes again to our mind. Here, as in many other passages, the senses, the objects of sense, etc., are presented as inspiring us with disgust, just because they are non-self. That is an implicit confession that the self is the ruling criterion to measure the worth of things and the ideal that should guide us, being a reality directly opposed to the one that would fill us with disgust. The existential conflict portrayed here, and in so many other passages, does not make any sense unless one can repudiate the reality that is non-self, precisely because it is non-self, for the sake of the self. A similar reasoning applies to a number of immediately preceding *suttas,* every one of which gives a motive for us to detach ourselves from the world of the senses. The motives are the following, 'the all, bhikkhus, is impermanent', 'the all, bhikkhus, is painful', 'the all, bhikkhus, is to be abandoned', 'the all, bhikkhus, is full of annoyance', 'the all, bhikkhus, is full of oppression'. All these bad qualities *naturally* repel us because the ideal for us is the opposite in every case, that is to say, what is permanent, what is pleasant, what is worthy to be kept, what makes us be at ease, what makes us feel free. And why should not the same apply to non-self when given as a motive to disown the same things, to reject them? The exhortation to disown something, precisely because it is non-self, when self is supposed to be no reality, is an exhortation to cast off an external reality for the sake of a shade, of a figment of our imagination.

3. Sabbe dhammā anattā

This universal statement is of very frequent occurrence. The study of its meaning is not so easy, given the variety of meanings that the term *dhamma* has in the Nikāyas. Let us first of all scrutinize those passages where the sense of the term is fixed by the very context.

> How knowing, Lord, how seing one's own ignorance is set aside and wisdom is attained?
>
> Herein, bhikkhu, a bhikkhu has learnt, 'No *dhamma* is worthy to be adhered to'. That bhikkhu, having learnt that no *dhamma* is worthy to be adhered to, fully knows all *dhammas* (*sabbaṁ dhammaṁ*), and fully knowing all *dhammas,* having comprehended all *dhammas,* he regards all phenomena (*nimittāni*) as alien (*aññato*), he regards the eye as alien, he regards visible forms as alien, he regards visual consciousness as alien, he regards the eye's sensorial contact as alien, and even the feeling arising dependent on that sensorial contact, be it either pleasant or painful or neither pleasant nor painful, he regards it also as alien. [The same applies to all the other senses.][38]

It is evident that in this passage the term *dhamma* is related to *nimitta,* a term applied to whatever is phenomenal. The text specifies what kind of *dhamma* the author had in view, that is, the senses, their objects, etc. That is to say the *anattā* taught in this passage by referring to the term *aññato* is not wider in scope than the *anattā* taught in other passages. Of this kind of *dhammas* it can be truthfully said, all *dhammas* are *anattā,* and *nibbāna* cannot be counted among them. The same will apply to the term *dhamma* as presented in the following text:

> Bhikkhus, if a bhikkhu perceives six [spiritual] advantages, he will be able to establish the awareness of non-self as regards all *dhammas* without exception. What six? I shall not become immerged in any part of the world, all kinds of conceit will be destroyed in me, I shall attain an uncommon knowledge, all conditions (*hetu*) will be well seen by me, and also that [all] *dhammas* are dependent on conditions.[39]

The *dhammas* of this passage are explicitly said to be conditioned and are therefore impermanent and cannot be but *anattā.* As a preparation to see this truth one ought to get rid of conceit which is precisely the false identification of the peripheral phenomena, which are *anattā,* with the self. If regarding these *dhammas* we say, *sabbe dhammā anattā,* it is obvious that *nibbāna* cannot be included in *sabbe dhammā,* as *nibbāna* can in no way be said to be conditioned. We are dealing now with the problem we promised to tackle when we called attention for the first time to the stereotyped formula, *sabbe saṅkhārā aniccā, sabbe saṅkhārā dukkhā, sabbe dhammā anattā,* which occurs in the *Majjhimanikāya* (Vol. III, p. 127 f., *Bahudhātusutta*) and in the *Aṅguttaranikāya* (Vol. I, p. 266, *Tikanipāto,* 14, 4), and is later on repeated to satiety in the *Niddesa.* As we have already noted it, to her translation of the passage in the *Majjhima,* I. B. Horner appends the following footnote:

> ...*Saṅkhāra* and *dhamma* just below go together at Dhp 277-278, the former with *anicca* and *dukkha* (*sabbe saṅkhārā aniccā... dukkhā*) and the latter with *anattā* (*sabbe dhammā anattā*). As a category, *dhamma* is wider than *saṅkhāra,* for it includes the uncompounded *nibbāna.* This is *anattā* but it is neither impermanent nor painful; on the contrary is permanent and blissful. Everything else is impermanent and painful as well as being *anattā.* The force of *dhamma* in this context and this sense is therefore to include *nibbāna.*[40]

It is evident that *nibbāna* could not be included among the *dhammas* to which the two passages already quoted in this section refer. Let us continue giving more evidence for the case in point; there is plenty of it in the Nikāyas.

There is a beautiful passage where the *dhammas* mentioned stand for the empirical attributes of man. The passage speaks explicitly only of the human body, but we gather from the context that such body is alive and active, being the empirical receptacle of all human actions.

> I have seen a beautiful many-coloured
> Doll, made of wood and rags,
> With threads and pins
> Tied together, dancing in a varied way.
> If you were to pull out the threads and pins,
> To loosen them, to separate them, to scatter them,
> There would be no doll left, all broken into parts.
> On what would you set your mind there?
> Similar to that are these bodies for me.
> Without those qualities (*dhammehi*) they are not;
> Regarding that which does not exist without qualities,
> On what would you set your mind?[41]

Doubtless the *dhammas* of this text are the *khandhas* which work within the body. The first text quoted in this section referred to the senses as *dhammas.* And we also have come across another text where the *khandhas* have been designated as *dhammas.*[42]

In the following text, the term *dhamma* stands also for the empirical factors in man,

When all the *dhammas* have been swept away,
All the ways of talking have been removed.[43]

This occurs in a context that speaks of one who has attained *nibbāna,* and whose consciousness has become extinct. To the question whether the sage thus liberated ceases to exist or is for ever happy, the Buddha answers that there is no way of gauging the liberated man and speaking meaningfully of him. All the *dhammas* that are the only points of reference when speaking of an individual have vanished in his case (*sabbesu dhammesu samohatesu...*), he, thereby, having reached a condition of ineffability *samūhatā vādapathā pi sabbe*). Clearly here the *dhammas* are opposed to *nibbāna.*

All the *dhammas* catalogued so far are such that to them the triad of epithets, *anicca, dukkha* and *anattā* can be rightly applied. The same will apply to the *dhammas* mentioned in several passages where they obviously stand for realities dependent on some condition.

Knowing *kamma* as *kamma,* and the result of *kamma* as what it is (*vipākato*),
Regarding the *dhammas* produced dependent on conditions as they should be regarded by means of insight,
One goes toward the great security, calm, blessed with perfection.[44]

Commenting on, *sabbesu dhammesu samūhatesu* the commentator explains *sabbesu dhammesu* as *sabbesu khandhesu* (the *khandhas*), *sabbesu āyatanesu* (the spheres of sense), *sabbesu dhātusu* (the elements), followed by a long series of expressions all implying rebirth, like *sabbāsu gatīsu, sabbāsu upapattīsu,* etc.[45]

The Buddha is supposed to have uttered regarding himself the words:
Unsoiled by no *dhamma,* or untainted in no *dhamma*
(*sabbesu dhammesu anupalitto*).[46]

There is a frequently used phrase, *pāragū sabbadhammānaṁ,* which may mean either, 'gone beyond or having transcended all *dhammas*', or 'well versed in all *dhammas*'. The first translation seems to be preferable, as it is evident from the following texts:

> Having transcended all *dhammas* (*pāragū sabbadhammānaṁ*), free from clinging he has attained *nibbāna.*[47]

Here, transcending all *dhammas* is equivalent to the attainment of *nibbāna.* Also:

> When the brāhmaṇa is one who has gone beyond his own *dhammas* (*yadā sakesu dhammesu, pārāgū hoti*...),
> Then he is beyond (*ativattati*) this goblin and his din.[48]

We have here a meaningful correspondence between *pāragū* in the first line and *ativattati* in the second.

Pāragū is used again in connection with *parinibbuto* in:

> The conqueror (*jino*), Padumuttaro by name, who has gone beyond all *dhammas* (*sabbadhammāna pāragū*),
> Like a mass of fire that has burnt out itself, perfectly enlightened, has attained complete *nibbāna* (*parinibbuto*).[49]

The phrase *pāragū sabbadhammānaṁ* occurs twice in the *Suttanipāta*[50] and both the times E. M. Hare translates it as 'yon-farer of all things', making 'all *dhammas*' equivalent to *samsāra,* which ought to be transcended. But when commenting on *pāragū sabbadhammānaṁ,* the *Cullaniddesa,* attributes to *pāragū* the sense of 'going to the end, reaching perfection' in every sort of achievement.[51]

The samsaric character of the meaning of *dhamma* and its consequent opposition to the achievements that lead immediately to *nibbāna* or to *nibbāna* itself is clearly stated in the following text:

> Surely, bhikkhus, that a bhikkhu who regards any *dhamma* as non-self will come to be endowed with suitable endurance, is quite fitting. That one endowed with suitable endurance will enter into the right way, is quite fitting. That one entered into the right way will realize either the fruit of entering into the stream, or the fruit of an once returner, or the fruit of a non-returner, or arahantship, is quite fitting.[52]

An unbiased reading of this text leaves a firm impression that those *sabbadhamme* that ought to be regarded as non-self and the final result of such view, viz. the attainment of arahantship or *nibbāna,* belong to two different categories in the mind of the author. This is also proved from the larger text in which the *sutta* is found. The two previous *suttas* deal precisely in exactly the same way with the bhikkhu who considers (or does not consider) all *saṅkhārā* as *aniccā* (*sutta* 3), and as *dukkhā* (*sutta* 4). In these *suttas* too the *saṅkhārā* that ought to be regarded as *aniccā* and *dukkhā* belong clearly to a different category than that of the fruit to be expected, which are the same as the ones just quoted. The *sutta* that follows the one just quoted (*sutta* 6) applies the same reasoning to the bhikkhu who regards *nibbāna* as happy (*sukhato*) against the one who regards it as painful (*dukkhato*). This is the authentic Nikayan spirit, the consideration of *nibbāna* as full of happiness, not as *anattā*.[53]

Similar considerations will be valid regarding a group of *suttas* found in the *Sattakanipāto* of the *Aṅguttara,* which written on the same pattern are entitled respectively, *Aniccānupassīsutta, Dukkhānupassīsutta* and *Anattānupassīsutta.* Let us quote the last one, where seven types of men are described, all of whom are 'those who see *anattā* in all *dhammas*' (*sabbesu dhammesu anattānupassino*).

> Herein, bhikkhus, a certain person (*puggalo*) dwells regarding all *dhammas* as non-self, aware of non-self, conscious of non-self, continuously constantly, uninterruptedly applying his mind [to it], fathoming it by means of wisdom. He, after the destruction of the *āsavas,* dwells having obtained, having realized all by himself by means of higher wisdom, in this very life, the freedom of mind which is without *āsavas,* the freedom born of wisdom.

The second type of those who regard all *dhammas* as non-self come to the destruction of the *āsavas* and to the end of their lives at the same time, not to one first and then to the other. The third type is constituted by those who become *antarāparinibbāyino,* 'who will obtain *nibbāna* after an interval, once they have destroyed the five lower fetters. Others are those who reduce the time for entering into *nibbāna* (*upahaccaparinibbāyino*), etc.[54]

A similar association of the trio, *sabbe saṅkhārā aniccā, sabbe saṅkhārā dukkhā, sabbe dhammā anattā* is found in the *Dhammapada.* The wording of the three *ślokas* is exactly the same, except for their beginnings, which are, *sabbe saṅkhārā aniccā ti, sabbe saṅkhārā dukkhā ti,* and *sabbe dhammā anattā ti.* The third one reads:

> All *dhammas* are non-self, when one sees this by means of wisdom,
> Then he feels disgust for pain, that is the way to purity.[55]

Keeping in mind I. B. Horner's opinion that *nibbāna* is included in *sabbe dhammā,* We do not see how seing by means of wisdom that *nibbāna* is *anattā* can develop disgust for *dukkha,* which is absolutely absent from *nibbāna.* Therefore the saying *sabbe dhammā anattā* must refer to those *dhammas* which are *anattā* because they are *dukkhā,* folowing the line of thought so often described in the Nikāyas that because something is *anicca* is also *dukkha* and therefore it must also be *anattā.*

It is from these passages that the trio passed on to the *Niddesa* where it occurs in a stock passage, very often repeated when the term *dhamma* (the doctrine) is to be commented on. Thus we are given a summary of the *dhamma* or 'doctrine' that one should know, when commenting on the phrase *samecca dhammaṁ,* 'knowing the doctrine'. The *dhamma* that the wise man ought to know embraces the following items: *sabbe saṅkhārā aniccā, sabbe saṅkhārā dukkhā, sabbe dhammā anattā*; the doctrine of the *paṭiccasumuppāda* in order of origination and in order of cessation; the four Noble Truths regarding *dukkha*; the four Noble Truths applied to the *āsavas*; the *dhammas* that should be known, abolished, fostered; the origin, cessation, pleasure and danger inherent in the sixfold sphere of sense and the escape from it; the same regarding the *khandhas*; the same regarding the *mahābhūtas*; finally the dictum, 'whatever is of a nature to arise, all that is also of a nature to cease' (*yaṁ kiñci samudayadhammaṁ, sabbaṁ taṁ nirodhadhammaṁ*).[56]

This summary of the teaching (*dhamma*) is not very systematic. The term *dhamma* is used twice in it. When it is used in *sabbe dhammā anattā,* it stands for the samsaric phenomena that man ought to transcend, as has been shown in the preceding texts. When it is used in connection with things that should be known, abolished or fostered, it seems to refer to moral qualites, and here it is that *nibbāna* may be included as a *dhamma.*

The *Cullaniddesa* gives us a recapitulation of the different meanings of *dhamma,* while commenting on 'well versed in all the dhammas' (*kusalo sabbadhammānaṁ*). Several explanations are given:

1. The explanation just analysed, where *nibbāna* would be included among the things to be known and fostered.

2. The second explanation tells us that one is 'well versed in all the *dhammas*' if he regards all *dhammas* as impermanent, painful, as illness, etc., the well known catalogue. *Nibbāna* cannot fall within the scope of these 'all *dhammas*' which are impermanent, painful, non-self.

3. The fourth explanation says that 'all *dhammas* stand for the twelve sensorial spheres', interior as well as exterior, 'the desire for which should be cast away, cut to the very roots, turned into a palm-tree stump, destroyed, never to spring in future'. *Nibbāna* cannot find a place here among these 'all *dhammas*'.

4. Only in the third explanation which has been placed here on purpose, there occurs *nibbāna* at the end of an inventory of *dhammas,* which includes items to be repudiated forthwith, like the *khandhas,* the elements, the spheres of sense, etc., and others to be fostered like the limbs of wisdom (*bojjhaṅgā*), the way (*magga*), and finally *nibbāna.*[57]

Nibbāna is also called an uncompounded *dhamma* in:

> As many compounded and uncompounded *dhammas* are there, freedom from attachment is proclaimed foremost, that is, the crushing of pride, the restraining of craving, the utter removal of attachment, the annihilation of becoming, cessation, *nibbāna.*[58]

In short, among so many texts quoted to fix the meaning of the word *dhamma* in the Nikāyas, and to see whether *nibbāna* is called a *dhamma* and should be included in the dictum 'all *dhammas* are non-self' (*sabbe dhammā anattā*), we managed to find just two texts only where *nibbāna* is called a *dhamma.* To these two texts we might be able to add a third one where liberation and *nibbāna* might be considered to be *dhammas,* although the case seems to be opposite to that:

> Bhikkhus, if wanderers of other views were to ask you, 'What friends, is the root of all *dhammas*? Whence do all *dhammas* proceed? Whence do all *dhammas* arise? Where to do all *dhammas* flow down together? What have all *dhammas* as master? What is beyond all *dhammas*? What is the essence of all *dhammas*?'

The answer according to the Buddha ought to be as follows:

> All *dhammas* have desire (*chanda*) as their root; all *dhammas* proceed from mental actions, all *dhammas* arise from contact; all *dhammas* flow down together into feeling; the master of all *dhammas* is mindfulness; wisdom is beyond all *dhammas*; the essence of all *dhammas is liberation.*[59]

The answer exhibits a typical Nikayan twist to a series of questions that very likely were cosmologically oriented. The *dhammas* which the answer mentions are subjective and those of which we can very well say, *sabbe dhammā anattā.* Mindfulness, which is appointed their master, wisdom which is asserted to transcend them, and liberation which is metaphorically called the essence of the *dhammas,* are obviously no part of them, but lead to their mastery and ultimate repudiation. It must be recognized that calling liberation (*vimutti*) the essence of *dhammas* which to all appearances have a samsaric nature is, to say the least, strange. One is tempted to suppose that the original reading of the text was not *vimuttisārā,* 'which have liberation as their essence,' but *vimuttisarā,* 'those that flow towards *vimutti* or have vimutti as their point of confluence'; something like the rivers flowing into the sea and disappearing. This is confirmed by another part of the *Aṅguttara,* where the text just quoted is literally reproduced with three more questions and their corresponding answers added, viz. 'By what are all *dhammas* presided? Where do all *dhammas* merge? What is the end of all *dhammas*?' The answers to these questions are, 'All *dhammas* are presided by *samādhi*; all *dhammas* merge into the deathless; all *dhammas* have *nibbāna* as their end' (*amatogadhā sabbe dhammā, nibbānapariyosānā sabbe dhammā*).[60] No, *nibbāna* does not seem to be included among these '*all dhammas*' which are the topic of discussion here.

In the *Paṭisambhidāmagga,* the latest of the Nikayan works, *nibbāna* is said to be a *dhamma,* but a *transcendent dhamma, lokuttara dhamma* together with the four *satipaṭṭhānas,* the four *sammappadhānas,* the four *iddhipādas,* etc.[61] While the *dhammas* referred to in *sabbe dhammā anattā* seem to be wholly samsaric in the sense that they form part of the samsaric process from which one has to disentangle himself, that is to say, they are not samsaric merely in a moral sense.

In the *Cullaniddesa* we read, 'by the most excellent *dhamma* is understood the deathless *nibbāna*' (*dhammamuttamaṁ vuccati amataṁ nibbānaṁ*), but a careful scrutiny of the context being explained here will bear out that *dhamma* means here 'teaching'. The previous stanza uttered by the Buddha is:

> I shall declare to you *dhamma* (the teaching), to be verified in this very life, not to be known by mere tradition,
> Knowing which, walking mindful, one may cross the entanglement of the world.

To this Mettagū answers:

And I welcome, O great sage, that most excellent *dhamma* (*dhammaṁ'uttamaṁ*),
Knowing which, walking mindful, one may cross the entanglement of the world.[62]

Thus among the numerous texts reviewed in this section we find just three of them where *nibbāna* is explicitly spoken of as a *dhamma,* and one of them is of a rather late origin; in the rest of them the term *dhamma* exhibits a connotation contradictory to *nibbāna.* In addition to this most of the texts where *dhamma* cannot stand for *nibbāna* speak precisely of '*all dhammas*'. Thus, 'no *dhamma* is worth adhering to' (*sabbaṁ dhammaṁ nālaṁ abhinivesāya*); 'to establish the awareness of non-self regarding all *dhammas*... [all] *dhammas* are dependent on conditions' (*sabbadhammesu... anattasaññaṁ upaṭṭhāpetum... hetusamuppānnā ca dhammā*); 'when all *dhammas* have been swept away' (*sabbesu dhammesu samohatesu* or *samūhatesu*); 'untained by any *dhamma* or in all *dhammas*' (*sabbesu dhammesu anupalitto*); 'one who transcends or leaves behind all *dhammas*' (*pāragū sabbadhammānaṁ*); 'that a bhikkhu who regards all dhammas as non-self...' (*sabbadhammā anattato samanupasanto...*), etc. Textual evidence is certainly against the inclusion of *nibbāna* among the *dhammas* branded as non-self in the dictum, *sabbe dhammā anattā,* and therefore the scope of the *anattā* doctrine is not different here from the scope attributed to it in all the contexts reviewed before.

Nowhere in the Nikāyas are we told that *nibbāna* is *anattā.* We find the statement in the *Parivāra,* which is the latest of the *Vinayapiṭaka* books and probably in the whole *Tipiṭaka*:

All compositions are impermanent, and all compounded things are painful and non-self,
And even *nibbāna* is designated as non-self, this is a fixed opinion (*nibbānaṁ c'eva paññati anattā*).[63]

In the spirit of the Nikāyas, to say that *nibbāna* is *anattā* is a mere piece of speculative doctrine with no apparent soteriological value. The labelling of something as *anattā* in the authentic Nikayan spirit has as its purpose the development of disgust for it, the consequent detachment from it, this detachment leading to liberation. Does it make sense to say in this context, '*nibbāna* is *anattā,* therefore the learned ariyan disciple develops disgust for it, feeling disgust for it he loses all attachment to it, losing all attachment to it he is liberated, he knows, "Destroyed is birth, etc."?' Is it not kind ofblasphemous to say that *nibbāna* should inspire one with disgust as if it were an *asubha* thing?[64] In the consideration of *nibbāna* as *anattā,* such as found in the *Parivāra* we witness the confluence of two oppoiste currents. One of those currents comes from the original source that makes use of impermanence, pain and being non-self, as motives for rejection, for detachment, and ultimate liberation. The other current flows backwards from the ideological environment where the doctrine of absolute *anattā* is considered uncontrovertible and has become the subject of sophisticated philosophizing. It may be said that in the original Nikayan spirit, *anattā* is posited as *a means* for detachment and ultimate liberation, while in the later spirit *anattā,* and that absolute, is posited as an *ideological end* in itself to which everything else should be subservient. For one who has carefully weighed all the evidence collected so far, it will be crystal clear that if we were to say, *sabbe dhammā anattā,* and include there *nibbāna* we ought to make a distinction between the samsaric *dhammas* and *nibbāna* as *dhamma,* the term *anattā* not being applicable to both in the same way. The samsaric *dhammas* are *anattā* (as well as *aniccā, dukkhā,* etc.) and therefore on account of that, they ought to be shunned, discarded, eliminated, so as to attain liberation. But if we were to say that *nibbāna* is *anattā,* this does not impel us to shun, discard, eliminate *nibbāna* and doing so to attain liberation. It is clear that, from the original Nikayan way of looking at things, to say that *nibbāna* is *anattā* (a thing that will be true if *nibbāna* is given an independent *sabhāva,* as it was done with the passing of time) will always be a piece of theorizing devoid of all practical value.

But if *sabbe dhammā anattā* (in contrast with *sabbe saṅkhārā dukkhā* and *sabbe saṅkhārā aniccā*) is not meant to refer to *nibbāna,* then what other reason can be given for this trio to have been fixed in the way it was fixed? The first property that strikes one as belonging to a composite thing, dependent on contingent conditions is its instability, its impermanence. Thus in the most natural way there arises the dictum *sabbe saṅkhārā aniccā.* These composite things may be either subjective or external to man. *Dhammā* in the dictum *sabbe dhammā anattā* seems to apply only to subjective factors like the senses, etc., things that impel man to identify his self with them, and which therefore need in a special way to be labelled as *anattā.* As a matter of fact there is some evidence that the group of dicta, with which we are dealing, had originally only two members, viz. *sabbe saṅkhārā aniccā* and *sabbe dhammā anattā.*

In the *Channasutta* of the *Saṁyutta,* Channa begs the bhikkhus to advise and exhort him. The exhortation offered consist merely in asserting that everyone of the *khandhas* is *anattā,* and the two dicta, *sabbe saṅkhārā aniccā* and *sabbe dhammā anattā.*[65]

In the *Cūḷasaccakasutta* of the *Majjhima,* Aggivesana requests Assaji to tell him how does the Buddha train his disciples and what is the advice mostly imparted to them by him. Again we find the same formula repeated, the assertion of *anattā* regarding everyone of the *khandhas* and the two dicta, *sabbe saṅkhārā aniccā* and *sabbe dhammā anattā.* The teaching is later on confirmed by the Buddha himself.[66]

It was quite natural to add to this pair another member containing the term *dukkhā,* as there are so many passages in the canon where *anicca, dukkha* and *anattā* occur in immediate succession.

REASONS GIVEN TO ASSERT THAT SOMETHING IS ANATTĀ

The reasons most generally given have been impermanence, pain and mutability. The direct conclusion of this way of thinking is that the self has absolutely nothing to do with impermanence and pain, these are characteristics of the non-self. The *anattavādins* will have to draw the conclusion in some way like this, 'The self, if it were a reality, which we deny, would have nothing to do with impermanence, change and pain, therefore whatever is impermanent, liable to change and painful cannot be the self, which is not a reality, therefore we have to do away with whatever is impermanent, liable to change and painful'. As it has been pointed out several times, the *anattavādins* divest the reasoning of all logic.

The same is expressed in a slightly different way when we are told that the eye, whose arisal and destruction are evident, is the self, for that would be equivalent to saying that the self arises and disappears.[67] The implication here seems to be that man cannot stop being what he really is, his very self.

Let us suppose that someone tried to draw a straightforward conclusion from all this in the following way, 'Whatever is impermanent, mutable by nature and painful is not my self, therefore my self is something permanent, immutable by nature and happy'. Let us further suppose that by coming to this conclusion the man in question were convinced that he had gained some 'positive' knowledge of the ontological nature of the self. Such a man would betray a very superficial knowledge of the Nikayan teaching. The Nikāyas do not give us any 'positive' knowledge of what the self is in its very being, they always tell us what the self is not so that we may abhor it and do away with it. As R. C. Zaehner very appropriately has remarked, 'The Buddhists... were so careful not to define what the self was that it has often been maintained that they denied the existence of a self altogether'.[68] According to the Nikāyas we cannot have a positive objective knowledge of the true nature of the self. Consciousness, for all its lofty position in man, is wholly non-self. The objects of consciousness are also non-self. On the other hand, all our concepts are derived from experience, which is the experience of the non-self, and can in no way be adequate to describe what the self really it. Let us take, for instance, the concept of permanence, one of those concepts which our hypothetical man was ready to apply to the self. Even if, at first considering, it may appear to convey a positive meaning, we shall have to confess that in reality it is a negative term. Why? We only experience what is impermanent, even though we are dissatisfied with it. It is also true that we aspire to what is permanent, but as a matter of fact, 'permanent' means for us 'what is not impermanent', the latter being the universal characteristic of whatever falls within the range of our experience. This 'otherness' (*para*) of what is empirical in relation to the self is akin to the relation of ontological independence postulated in Sāṅkhya-Yoga between the self and the non-self, which is called *kaivalya,* a term that may be paraphrased as 'ontological isolation'.[69] The great difference between Sāṅkhya-Yoga and Buddhism in this respect is that, as can be seen from the *sūtra* just quoted, the former ascribes to the self at least the positive attribute of 'pure consciousness',[70] while in early Buddhism all consciousness is considered *para,* non-self, and the last and most perfect *vimokkha* consists in the complete cessation of sensation and feeling, that is to say, in the complete suppression of empirical consciousness. In the Nikāyas we do not meet with the term kaivalya, but there is a token of affinity between Buddhism and Sāṅkhya-Yoga in the use of *kevalī* as an epithet descriptive of the perfect man.[71] The term is used in Jainism, too, which also attributes to the self the positive attribute of knowledge. Herein, Buddhism stands alone, and this is its greatest originality as compared with the other Indian systems of philosophy. A very eloquent testimony of this fact (others have been recorded here and there in this book) is found in the *Poṭṭhapādasutta* of the *Dīghanikāya* (I, p. 155-156). The dialogue on this topic begins with the words:

> Is then, Sir, consciousness identical with man's self or is consciousness one thing and the self another?

The Buddha asks his inquirer to what kind of self is he referring, and Poṭṭhapāda refers to three kinds of *sakkāyadiṭṭhi* selves. Poṭṭhapāda mentions successively: a material self, corporeal, made up of the four elements, nourished by solid food; a mind-made (*manomaya*) self, with all its major and minor limbs, not lacking any powers (*indriya*); finally, an incorporeal self made of consciousness (*saññāmaya*). The Buddha's argument, in every case, runs like this: whatever kind of self you resort to (let us not forget that it will always be a *diṭṭhigata* self), your experience tells you that ideas and mental states arise and fade away, and therefore cannot be identified with the self, which in its turn cannot be identified with what is impermanent, therefore, the self and consciousness cannot be one and the same thing. This part of the dialogue closes with the words:

> Is it possible, Sir, for me to come to know whether consciousness is the self of man or consciousness is one thing and the self another?
>
> Difficult to comprehend is this for you, Poṭṭhapāda, who are of different views, different inclinations, different tastes, who follow different practices, who receive different teaching....

This was an occasion, among others, when the Buddha could have replied quite clearly and more to the point (if he was teaching absolute *anattā,* of course) that Poṭṭhapāda's question was an idle one, since there is absolutely no self in man. Instead he takes trouble to disabuse Poṭṭhapāda of the wrong idea that identifies the self with consciousness (even while recognizing that it will be difficult for him to comprehend the doctrine), using the same reason always used to deny that the *khandhas,* etc., are the self, namely their impermanence. Does this kind of procedure not leave a place for the reality of the self?

Another reason for denying that something is the self is the lack of spontaneous mastery over it:

> Body, bhikkhus, is non-self. If body were the self, then this body would not be prone to sickness, and it would be possible to say [effectively] as regards the body, 'let the body be such for me'. But because, bhikkhus, the body is non-self, that is why it is prone to sickness and it is not possible to say [effectively] as regards the body, 'let the body be such for me'.

To the lack of spontaneous mastery over the body, subjection to pain is added here as a reason for saying that the body is non-self. The same reasons apply to the other *khandhas.* Then comes the stock passage, 'Now, what do you think, bhikkhus, is the body permanent or impermanent, etc.', which concludes denying of every *khandha,* 'This is not mine, this I am not, this is not my self', with the usual final conclusion of becoming disgusted with the *khandhas,* being detached from them and ultimately liberated.[72]

The lack of mastery mentioned in this text cannot be an absolute one, otherwise the mastery of the self, as moral agent, over the senses, etc., and his efforts towards ever a greater purity and final liberation would not exist at all. The text refers to the essential freedom and spontaneous self-possession that the pure self is expected to have. Ontologically, the *khandhas* follow the rule of necessity imposed on them by their previous conditions. The self cannot interfere there. A visual sensation, for instance, arises when all the necessary conditions have been realized, and the self cannot do any thing at that stage to stop the corresponding visual sensation to arise or to make any objective change in the characteristics of such sensation. On the moral level, the self can exercise his mastery, which is not an easy one, over the samsaric factors of individuality and even make them stop altogether, attaining to complete isolation from them in emancipation. To give a practical example, once the conditions required for a lustful sensation have been realized, the self cannot do anything in preventing that lustful sensation from arising, but it could have exercised his mastery by preventing the conditions from materializing and when the sensation takes place the self may maintain himself aloof from, or indifferent to it.

The Buddha argues in a similar way against Aggivesana, who states his opinion in no uncertain terms:

> Yes, friend Gotama, I profess this: the body is my self, feeling is my self, perception is my self, the inner complexes are my self, consciousness is my self.

The Buddha gives then the simile of the king who has got power over his subjects. Then, he continues:

> As regards what you say, Aggivesana, 'the body is my self', what do you think, is there any mastery of you over that body [so as to be able to say effectively] 'let the body be such for me, let not the body be such for me'?

With great reluctance and only under the threat of severe punishment Aggivesana replies:

> It is not so, friend Gotama.

The Buddha applies the same reasoning to the rest of the *khandhas.* There follows the stock passage, 'What do you think, Aggivesana, is the body permanent or impermanent, etc.'. Then the Buddha insists specially on the impossibility of identifying the self with pain (*dukkha*):

> What do you think, Aggivesana, anyone clinging to pain, adhering to pain, cleaving to pain, one who thinks thus of pain, 'this is mine, this I am, this is my self', would such a one comprehend what is pain, or would he ever dwell having thoroughly annihilated Pain?
>
> How could that be so, friend Gotama?[73]

This comprehending of Pain refers to understanding it as the basic misery of *saṁsāra.* This is expressed so often by saying that what is painful cannot be the self. The impossibility to annihilate *dukkha* for one who identifies it with his self, refers at least indirectly to the impossibility of the self annihilating itself.

The ontological incommunicability between the self and the non-self is also taught in the following text,

> Body, bhikkhus, is non-self. That which is the condition (*pacayo*), that which is the cause (*hetu*) of the arising of the body is also non-self. Being produced from what is non-self, bhikkhus, how can the body be the self?

The same reasoning applies to the rest of the *khandhas.* The conclusion is the usual one: feeling of disgust, detachment, liberation and knowledge of liberation.[74]

12

Asmimāna, Sakkāyadiṭṭhi, Sassatavāda and Ucchedavāda

We would not be able to get a complete view of the *anattā* doctrine in the Nikāyas without singling out for special attention the topics to be discussed in this chapter. We have already witnessed how uncompromising is in early Buddhsim the ontological separation between self and non-self. But what are the consequences of not professing such separation or of not attuning one's own conduct to it? One who does not profess the ontological separation between the self and the non-self falls into the heresy called *sakkāyadiṭṭhi,* which is at the root of all other *diṭṭhis,* and will be overpowered by the capital sin of *asmimāna.*

ASMIMĀNA

In the first part of the book we have alluded to *asmimāna* as a moral vice. We are going to examine now the ontological background of this moral depravity. *Asmimāna* is a radical defect and its influence is all-pervading. There is no moral wickedness which, in the last analysis, may not be said to be in some way or other a manifestation of *asmimāna.* All moral deviations consist, to a greater or lesser degree, in a wrong 'self-assertion', the assertion of a self erroneously identified with the samsaric factors, or acting in the spirit of such identification. The reason for the moral deviation of *asmimāna* lies in man's ontological being. This provides us with a typical example of how moral life has as its foundation man's ontological nature. Moral activities will be right when they conform to the ontological nature of man, and will be wrong when the contrary is the case. Early Buddhism points to the ontological separation between self and non-self in man as the criterion of all moral good and wrong.[1]

The word *asmimāna* means etymologically, 'the conceit (*māna*) of I am (*asmi*)'. *Asmimāna* manifests itself primarily as an unhealthy preoccupation with the empirical self, in opposition to the true self, as if the empirical self were the only one that matters.

He who frames conceits, bhikkhus, is a slave of Māra, the man without conceit is free from the Evil One. 'I am', bhikkhus, this is a kind of conceit; 'This I am', bhikkhus, this is a kind of conceit; 'I shall come to be...'; 'I shall not come to be...'; 'I shall become one endowed with consciousness...'; 'I shall become corporeal ...'; 'I shall become incorporeal...'; 'I shall become one not endowed with consciousness...'; 'I shall become one endowed with conciousness...'; 'I shall become one who possesses neither consciousness nor unconsciousness...'; All conceit, bhikkhus, is a disease, a tumour, a dart. Therefore, bhikkhus, you should take this resolution, 'Let us dwell with a mind which does not frame conceits'. Such is the way, bhikkhus, you should train yourselves.[2]

All the conceit-inspired statements of this text have a samsaric character and refer either to the present existence or to some existence to come. This preoccupation with the empirical self, which is or wishes to be, tends to perpetuate its existence within the samsaric process, hence the great affinity between craving and conceit. Craving and conceit interact on each other. The passage from which we are going to quote describes four kinds of craving: craving as regards robes, craving as regards alms-bowls, craving as regards lodging, and craving as regards becoming or not becoming, which is the most harmful of all. Craving for not becoming does not mean here craving for emancipation, but it has an entirely samsaric character like the one of the *ucchedavādins,* of whom we shall speak later on. The passage continues:

Mālukya's son, inasmuch as craving is abandoned by a bhikkhu, destroyed to the very root, made like a stump of palm-tree unable to sprout again, never to arise in the future, this is said to be a bhikkhu who has destroyed craving, has undone his fetters, and by the perfect comprehension of conceit has made an end of Pain.[3]

The same affinity between craving and conceit is discovered in:

These three cravings and these three kinds of conceit ought to be given up.

...The craving for sensual pleasures, the craving for becoming, the craving for de-becoming...

...Preoccupation with self, thinking lowly of self, thinking highly of self...[4]

Given the samsaric character of conceit, it ought to be counteracted by the thought of *nibbāna* and the effort to attain it:

> Lord, could the attainment of concentration of a bhikkhu be of such a kind that there would not be [in him] any tendencies to conceit of ideas of 'I' and 'mine' as regards this consciousness-endowed body and all external objects, and that he should get the freedom of mind and the freedom through insight where there are no tendencies to conceit of ideas of 'I' and 'mine'?
>
> It could be, Ānanda.
>
> By what process?
>
> Herein, Ānanda, a bhikkhu has this idea, 'this is the calm, this is the excellent condition, that is, the cessation of all activities, the abandoning of all samsaric encumbrances, the destruction of craving, detachment, cessation, *nibbāna*'.[5]

A man who has entirely destroyed conceit in himself can sing the paean of victory:

> And how, bhikkhus, is a bhikkhu an ariyan, one who has laid down the flag, one who has put down the burden, entirely unattached? Herein, bhikkhus, the conceit 'I am' has been abandoned by the bhikkhu, destroyed to the very root, made like a stump of palm-tree, unable to sprout again, never to arise in the future.[6]

That the disappearance of conceit in man is equivalent to *nibbāna* is very eloquently expressed in:

> Where there is stability, there different kinds of conceit are not active, and when different kinds of conceit are not active a sage is said to be 'at peace' (*santo*). This saying, in reference to what was it said? 'I am', bhikkhus, is a kind of conceit; 'This I am'... ; 'I shall become'... ; 'I shall not become'... ; 'I shall become corporeal'... ; 'I shall become incorporeal'... ; 'I shall become endowed with consciousness'... ; 'I shall become without consciousness'... ; 'I shall become neither endowed with consciousness nor without it'.... Conceit, bhikkhus, is a disease, a tumour, a dart. The sage who has left behind all conceits is said to be at peace (*santo*). The sage who is at peace, bhikkhus, is not born, does not grow old, does not die, is not troubled, has no longings. Because in his case there is nothing, due to which he should be born; not being born, how could he grow old?; not growing old, how could he die?; not having to die, how should he be troubled?; not being troubled, why should he

have any longings?'[7]

The text illustrates very effectively the relation between *asmimāna* and continuous becoming. *Asmimāna,* as we shall soon see, by causing a man to identify himself (his self!) with the factors of transmigration is responsible for keeping him within the cycle of births and deaths, undergoing all the concomittant misery. To come to a condition of not being born, not growing old, and not dying is equivalent to having attained *nibbāna,*[8] and the epithet *santo* ('at peace') used with such emphasis applies also to one who has attained *nibbāna.*[9]

The entire uprooting of conceit and consequent *nibbāna* are also explicitly linked in:

Above, below, entirely free in every way,
Not giving heed to 'such I am',
Thus completely free, he has crossed the flood,
Uncrossed before, for not becoming again.[10]

But what is the reason of the connection between the uprooting of conceit and the attainment of *nibbāna*? The reason is precisely the very nature of *asmimāna.* What is the fundamental constituent of *asmimāna*? It is none other than the identification of the self with the non-self in man. This is a further confirmation of our opinion that all hinges in the Nikāyas on the opposition between the self and the non-self, which has been designated several times as the polarity between the self and the non-self.

> Puṇṇa, friends, the venerable son of Mantāṇi, was very helpful to us when we were newcomers. He used to instruct us with this instruction, 'Depending on something, friend Ānanda, there exists [the conceit] 'I am', not without such dependence.... Depending on the body...; depending on feeling...; depending on perception...; depending on the inner complexes...; depending on consciousness there exists [the conceit] 'I am', not without such dependence.[11]

There follows the stock passage, 'What do you think, friend Ānanda, is body permanent, or impermanent...', asserting of everyone of the *khandhas,* 'This is not mine, this I am not, this is not my self', proving unmistakably that the ultimate constituent of conceit is the wrong identification of the *khandhas* with the self, or what is the same, the identification of the self with the non-self in man. Conceit has got as its final root not only the identification of the self with the aggregates but also with the senses their objects, etc., this being another group of things singled out as *anattā* in the previous chapters:

> Bhikkhus, whatever samaṇas and brāmaṇas go on regarding the self in divers ways, all of them regard [as the self] the five grasping-aggregates or any one of them. What five? Herein, bhikkhus, the unlearned common man... regards the body as the self, or the self as having a body, or the body in the self, or the self in the body. [The same is asserted of the rest of the *khandhas*.] Thus this consideration 'I am' has not been discarded by him, and since this consideration 'I am' has not been discarded by him there takes place in his case an overpowering by the five senses – the sense of sight, of hearing, of smell, of taste, of touch. The mind, bhikkhus, is there also and the mental objects, and the element of ignorance. And there takes place the consideration 'I am' for the unlearned common man affected by feelings arisen from ignorance, and also the consideration 'This I am', and 'I shall become', and 'I shall not become', and 'I shall become corporeal', and 'I shall become incorporeal', and 'I shall become endowed with consciousness', and 'I shall become without consciousness', and 'I shall become neither conscious nor unconscious'. And there, bhikkhus, the five senses hold their ground. But in the case of a learned ariyan disciple ignorance is dispelled, wisdom arises. And, on account of the fading away of ignorance and the arisal of wisdom, it does not occur to him, 'I am', or 'This I am, etc.'[12]

As stated elsewhere, the first lines of this long passage, quoted by some to prove that the Nikāyas teach the doctrine of absolute *anattā,* do not refer in any way to the true self, but to the self as conceived by those who do not belong to the fold, all of whom, as we shall see in the next section, are presumed to be steeped in the mentality of the *sakkāyadiṭṭhi,* which identifies the non-self with the self.

We get still two more testimonies where conceit is explicitly said to depend on the identification of the self with the senses:

> Because the venerable Upasena had for a very long time abolished all tendencies to conceit of 'I' and 'mine', that is why it did not occur to him, 'I am the eye, the eye is mine, etc.'. [The same is asserted of all other senses.][13]

And:

> What there being, on what depending, to what clinging, does it occur to

one, 'Better am I', 'Equal am I', 'Inferior am I?'
...
There being eye, depending on the eye, clinging to the eye, there occurs to one, 'Better am I, etc.'. [The same applies to the rest of the senses. Then comes the stock passage:] What do you think, bhikkhus, is the eye permanent or impermanent, etc.? [The conclusion is the usual one of feeling disgust, etc.][14]

Imagination and wishful thinking are part and parcel of conceit and are upshots of the wrong identification of the non-self with the self:

And how, bhikkhus, does one turn to the past? He thinks, 'In the past, I was one who had such bodily from', and derives pleasure from it; he thinks, 'In the past, I was one who had such feelings', and derives pleasure form it; etc. [The same is said of the rest of the *khandhas.* Then the opposite case is described of one who does not turn to the past.] And how, bhikkhus, does one long for the future? He thinks, 'May I be of such bodily form in the future', and derives pleasure from it; he thinks, 'May I be of such feelings in the future', and derives pleasure from it; etc. [The same applies to the rest of the *khandhas.* Then the opposite case is described of one who does not long after the future.] And how, bhikkhus, is one involved in the *dhammas* now existing? Herein, bhikkhus, an unlearned common man... regards the body as the self, or the self as having a body, or the body in the self, or the self in the body... [The same repeated of the rest of the *khandhas.* Then the opposite case is described of one who does not get involved in the *dhammas* now existing.][15]

The *dhammas* mentioned in the just quoted passages, in which unlearned people allow themselves to be involved are doubtless of a samsaric character and subjective to man's empirical individuality. These are the *dhammas* to which the saying *sabbe dhammā anattā* applies, not to *nibbāna,* a topic that was discussed in the previous chapter.

If the radical constituent of conceit is the wrong identification of the self with the non-self, it will follow that the best way to counteract conceit and destroy it will be the consideration of the *khandhas,* the senses etc. as non-self.

How knowing, Lord, how seing, is the mind free from the conceit of 'I' and 'mine' regarding this consciousness-endowed body and all external objects?

> Whatever material form, Rāhula, be it either past or future or now existing, either gross or subtle, either low or excellent, either distant or close, seing all material form by means of perfect wisdom as it really is, as, 'This is not mine, this I am not, this is not my self', one is liberated without any samsaric substrate being left.[16]

The same applies to the rest of the *khandhas.* The consideration of the ontological aloofness of the self regarding the senses is also conducive to the uprooting of conceit:

> I will show you, bhikkhus, a way conducive to the uprooting of all conceit...
>
> ...Herein, bhikkhus, a bhikkhu does not fancy [himself to be] the eye; does not fancy [himself to be] in the eye; does not fancy [himself] as the eye; does not fancy 'the eye is mine'.

The same is repeated of visible forms, of visual consciousness, of visual contact, of the feelings proceeding from such contact. All this is applied to all the other senses. The same is asserted of 'the all' (*sabbaṁ*), which according to *sutta* 23 of the same section stands for the senses and their objects. The *sutta* ends with the stock passage:

> He, in this way, not framing conceits is not attached to anything in the world; not being attached, he is not troubled, not being troubled, he attains *nibbāna* in his very self. He knows, 'Destroyed is birth, lived is the brahma life, etc.'[17]

The following *sutta* (31) is almost a literal repetition of the previous one. There is, however, an addition. After every series of different kinds of conceit about the senses, their objects, etc., we read:

> And that which he fancies he is, that about what he fancies he is, that like what he fancies he is, that of which he fancies 'it is mine', that is entirely different from what he fancies. Fond of change is the world, attached to becoming, it delights only in becoming.

The end of the *sutta* reads:

> As regards the aggregates, the elements, the spheres of sense, because he does not fancy himself to be that, he does not fancy himself to be in that, he does not fancy himself as that, he does not fancy 'this is mine', he, in this way, not building conceits... etc.[18]

See also:

> I will show you, bhikkhus, a way conducive to the uprooting of all conceit. Listen to it. And what is the way, bhikkhus, conducive to the uprooting of all conceit?
> What do you think, bhikkhus, is the eye permanent or impermanent?
> Impermanent, Lord.
> And what is impermanent, what is it, painful or pleasant?
> Painful, Lord.
> And what is impermanent, painful, mutable by nature, is it fitting to say of it, 'This is mine, this I am, this is my self?'
> Not so, Lord.

The same applies to visible forms and to the other senses together with their respective objects. The *sutta* ends with the stock passage of feeling disgust, becoming detached, being liberated and having knowledge of such liberation.[19]

And finally:

> ...the awareness of impermanence ought to be developed for the utter destruction of the conceit 'I am'.[20] The awareness of non-self is established in the case of one possesssed of the awareness of impermanence. One possessed of the awareness of non-self achieves the utter destruction of the conceit 'I am', that is *nibbāna* in this very life.[21]

What precedes, therefore, proves, without leaving any place for doubt, that conceit has got an ontological root, the wrong identification of the empirical factors with the self, and that the best remedy against conceit is the knowledge of the empirical factors as what they really are, non-self.

It will be of interest now to note the relation of the *vimokkhas* to any kind of conceit. We may focus our attention in the first place on the *Sappurisasutta* of the *Majjhima,* where we see the unworthy man boasting of his material and spiritual advantages and despising others for not obtaining them. The worthy man, on the contrary dismisses all conceit about the same advantages and achievements. When, for instance, a bhikkhu has renounced the world coming from a noble and lofty family he does not boast of it, but tries to keep things in their proper place by reflecting that having renounced the world, leaving a noble and lofty family, does not, of itself, destroy the three vices: covetousness, ill-will and infatuation, and that one who did not come to the Order from a noble and lofty family can very well be an observant bhikkhu deserving respect on that account. In the case of some 'spiritual' achievements like the four *jhānas* and the *vimokkhas,* the unworthy man boasts of his success in every case and despises others who have not reached so far. The worthy man, conscious of some 'spiritual' achievement, looks at things in the right perspective by reflecting, for instance, in the following way:

> The non identification of the ego with the attainment of the first *jhāna* has been spoken of by the Blessed One. Because by whatever thing men become conceited, that thing is otherwise from that, [from what they think it is, i.e., it is not genuine].[22]

The same is repeated of the rest of the *jhānas* and the *vimokkhas.* But when we come to the last *vimokkha,* the only one who is said to achieve it is the worthy man, the result of such achievement being:

> Seing by means of higher wisdom, the *āsavas* of such a man are destroyed. And, bhikkhus, this bhikkhu is not conceited about anything, is not conceited anywhere, is not conceited under the influence of anything.[23]

This coincides with what has already been pointed out, that the last *vimokkha* stands on a very special kind of relation to the self. Here we are told that it is impossible to associate any kind of conceit with the last *vimokkha.* Conceit is based on the wrong identification of the non-self with the self, which becomes an impossibility in the case of the last *vimokkha.* Is this not due to the fact that in the last *vimokkha* the self comes into its own, staying pure and unmixed with whatever is non-self?

The impossibility to associate any conceit with the attainment of the last *vimokkha* is taught again in another context:

> Friend Visākha, it does not occur to a bhikkhu who is entering into the stopping of perception and feeling: 'I will enter into the stopping of perception and feeling', or 'I am entering into the stopping of perception and feeling', or 'I have entered into the stopping of perception and feeling'. For his mind has been previously so developed that it leads him [spontaneously] to *nibbāna.*[24]

There is in the last *vimokkha* no room for the conceit of 'I' or 'mine', therefore there can be no consciousness of the empirical 'ego', neither before entering, nor while entering, nor while staying in it.

One of the *vimokkhas* is the sphere of no-thing (*ākiñcaññāyatana*).

As a preparation for its attainment the text prescribes either a reflection in solitude bearing on 'void is this of self or of what belongs to the self', or the reflection,

> In this I am nothing of anything anywhere, and there is nothing in anything anywhere [that belongs to me =*mama*].[25]

We have finally the *suttas* where Sariputta describes his own attainment of the *jhānas* and the *vimokkhas*. Ānanda sees Sāriputta coming along and exclaims:

> Serene are your senses, friend Sāriputta, clean and very pure is your complexion; how are you faring today, friend Sāriputta?

Sāriputta answers:

> Herein, friend, aloof from sensual pleasures, aloof from noxious qualities, I (*ahaṁ*) dwell having attained the first *jhāna,* which is born of solitude, full of zest and happiness, accompanied by discursive thoughts. But as regards this (*tassa*) it never occurs to me (*mayhaṁ*) – 'I (*ahaṁ*) am attaining the first *jhāna*', or 'I have attained the first *jhāna*', or 'I have emerged from the first *jhāna*'.

There follows the comment:

> In such a way all tendencies to conceit of 'I' and 'mine' have been extirpated for a long time regarding venerable Sāriputta, that it does not occur to him – 'I am attaining the first *jhāna*', or 'I have attained the first *jhāna*', or 'I have emerged from the first *jhāna*'.[26]

The following *suttas* apply the same reasoning to: the attainment of the second *jhāna* (*sutta* 2), of the third *jhāna* (*sutta* 3), of the fourth *jhāna* (*sutta* 4), of the sphere of infinity of space (*sutta* 5), of the sphere of infinity of consciousness (*sutta* 6), of the sphere of no-thing (*sutta* 7), of the sphere of neither-perception-nor-non-perception (*sutta* 8), of cessation of perception and feeling (this is never called 'sphere', *āyatana*) (*sutta* 9).

Analysing carefully the text, we can find two kinds of 'I' in it. One is the asmimanic 'I' contained in expressions like, '*I* am attaining the first *jhāna, I* have attained the first *jhāna, I* have emerged from the first *jhāna*'. These, we are told, are expressions that Sāriputta could not utter, because all conceit had been extirpated in him already for a long time. There the emphasis is obviously on the '*I*', on which the attention is focussed as it were through a magnifying lens. This is the bloated '*I*' of the selfishly satisfied man, who considers himself superior to others. There is another 'I' in the text represented by *ahaṁ* as subject of the verb *viharāmi* (*Idh'ahaṁ... pathamaṁ jhānaṁ upasampajja viharāmi*) and *mayhaṁ* (*tassa mayhaṁ, āvuso, na evaṁ hoti...*) where the implicit 'I' is opposed to and shown to be incompatible with the asmimanic 'I' contained in the expressions that follow. The former 'I' stands for the moral agent that strives after perfection and benefits by its acquisition. Since moral perfection includes the annihilation of the asmimanic self, the self that strives after perfection and is responsible for such annihilation ought to be by its very nature not only different from, but antagonistic to, and incompatible with, the asmimanic self. Now, in the case of the last *vimokkha* which consists in the cessation of all empirical awareness and feeling (*saññāvedayitanirodha*) all empirical notion of self, be it the asmimanic self or the genuine moral agent disappear altogether. Nevertheless, even in this case, Sāriputta is able to say, '*I* dwell having attained the cessation of awareness and feeling'. If the 'I' of this sentence cannot stand either for the asmimanic self or for the genuine empirical moral agent, what kind of self does it stand for? Nothing is left but to say that it stands for the true self who, in that condition attains to a complete aloofness from the empirical factors in the isolation that is his very being.[27]

SAKKĀYADIṬṬI

When the erroneous identification of the self with the peripheral samsaric factors in man is not just a passing moral weakness but a deep-rooted conviction, such deviation becomes a 'heresy', which is called *sakkāyadiṭṭhi*. As we shall presently see this is a radical 'heresy' or *diṭṭhi* in the Nikāyas, this being consonant with, and confirming once more the central position occupied in early Buddhism by the doctrine of the absolute incompatibility (ontological as well as moral), or unmitigated polarity between the self and the non-self. The right view in early Buddhism is the one that sees between the self and the non-self an ontologically unbridgeable chasm.

The description of *sakkāyadiṭṭhi* is clearly stated in the texts. We get, first of all, a description of *sakkāyo* in a dialogue between the lay follower Visākha and the bhikkunī Dhammadinnā:

'*Sakkāyo, sakkāyo',* thus my lady, it is said. But what, my lady, has been said to be *sakkāyo* by the Blessed One?

These factors of the fivefold clinging to existence have been said to be *sakkāyo* by the Blessed One: the clinging factor of body, the clinging factor of feeling, the clinging factor of perception, the clinging factor of the inner complexes, the clinging factor of consciousness.[28]

The idea conveyed by the term *sakkāyo* may be rendered in English as 'the existential (*sat*) aggregate (*kāyo*)', the word 'existential' having here a transmigrational connotation. That *sakkāyo* has an eminently transmigrational connotation is borne out by the passage that follows in the text that has just been quoted. The passage explains consecutively: the arisal of *sakkāyo,* the cessation of *sakkāyo,* and the way conducive to the cessation of *sakkāyo.*

Craving (*taṇhā*) which is the cause of further becoming, accompanied by pleasure and attachment, finding pleasure in this or that, as- craving for sensual pleasures, craving for becoming, craving for de-becoming. This, friend Visākha, has been said by the Exalted One to be the arisal of *sakkāyo.*[29]

...

Detachment, friend Visākha, and cessation without remnant, renunciation, rejection of craving, liberation from it, this, friend Visākha, has been said by the Blessed One to be the cessation of *sakkāyo.*

The way conducive to the cessation of *sakkāyo* is none other than the Eightfold Noble Path.[30] Later on in the text comes the description of *sakkāyadiṭṭhi,* 'the heresy of the existential aggregate':

How, my lady, there comes to be *sakkāyadiṭṭhi*?

Herein, firend Visākha, the unlearned common man, disregarding the ariyans... regards the body as the self, or the self as having a body, or the body in the self, or the self in the body. Regards feeling.... Regards perception.... Regards the inner complexes.... Regards consciousness as the self, or the self as having consciousness, or consciousness in the self, or the self in consciousness. Thus, friend Visākha, there comes to be *sakkāyadiṭṭhi.*

But how, my lady, there comes to be no *sakkāyadiṭṭhi*?

Herein, friend Visākha, the learned ariyan disciple... does not regard the body as the self, or the self as having a body, or the self in the body, or the body in the self. [The same is repeated regarding the other *khan-*

dhas.] Thus, friend Visākha, there comes to be no *sakkāyadiṭṭhi.*[31]

The same question recurs here that came to the mind in other passages where similar references to the self were found. It is evident that in the description of the *sakkāyadiṭṭhi* the speaker refers to the asmimanic self, when saying that the self is identified with the aggregates. But to what self is the speaker referring when describing the conditions where no *sakkāyadiṭṭhi* arises, saying that the ariyan disciple does not regard the body as *the self* or *the self* as having a body. Obviously the *attā* mentioned here is not an abstract notion, or the *attā* of the heretics, but the true, concrete *attā* of the speaker, 'his own very self', as we would say it in English. This comes out more clearly when we are told that there is no *sakkāyadiṭṭhi* when one does not regard the self (his own very self!) as having body, feelings, etc. How can one direct his attention to an unreal thing (in this case the self) and strive by means of superior wisdom not to regard it as having something else which is real (in this case, the body, feelings, etc.) and be all the better for it?

It is therefore clear that *sakkāyadiṭṭhi* consists in the identification of the *khandhas* with the self and consequently of the self with the *khandhas.* We have a confirmation of this in:

> What there being, bhikkhus, depending on what, clinging to what, there arises the wrong view of the existential aggregate?
>
> ...
>
> There being a body, bhikkhus, depending on body, clinging to body, there arises the wrong view of the existential aggregate. There being feeling, depending on feeling, clinging to feeling, there arises the wrong view of the existential aggregate... [This is applied to the rest of the khandhas. The text continues:]
>
> What do you think of this, bhikkhus, is the body permanent or impermanent?
>
> Impermanent, Lord.
>
> ...
>
> And what is impermanent, painful, mutable by nature, would there by any chance arise the wrong view of the existential aggregate independently from it?
>
> Not so, Lord.
>
> [The same reasoning applies to the other *khandhas.* The *sutta* ends with

the stock passage:]

Thus seing, bhikkhus, the learned ariyan disciple gets disgusted with the body, with feeling, with perception... Being disgusted he becomes detached. Through detachment he is freed, etc.[32]

Finally, as was to be expected, *sakkāyo* may arise also out of the identification of the self with the senses, their objects, etc.

And this, bhikkhus, is the way leading to the arisal of *sakkāyo.* One regards the eye as, 'This is mine, this I am, this is my self'.

[The same is asserted of visible forms, of visual consciousness, of visual contact, and of the feelings and craving resulting from such contact. The same applies to all the other senses, their objects, their corresponding consciousness, their corresponding contacts, and the feelings and craving resulting from them. Then the text continues:]

And this, bhikkhus, is the way leading to the cessation of *sakkāyo.* One considers the eye as, 'This is not mine, this I am not, this is not my self'.

The topic is worked out in detail in the same way as above, but everything being stated in the negative.[33]

Sakkāyadiṭṭhi and *attānudiṭṭhi* are equivalent in meaning. The term *attānudiṭṭhi* occurs in the following passage, which is commented on in the *Cullaniddesa.*

Look at the world as void, Mogharāja, ever mindful, rejecting the wrong view regarding the self (*attānudiṭṭhi*).
In this way you will be one who has crossed beyond death.
The king of death does not see one who thus looks at the world.[34]

Commenting on the words, 'rejecting the wrong view regarding the self (*attānudiṭṭhiṁ*)', the *Cullaniddessa* says, 'the wrong view regarding the self (*attānudiṭṭhi*)' means the twentyfold wrong view of the existential aggregate (*sakkāyadiṭṭhi*), thus proving that in the mind of the commentator *attānudiṭṭhi* and *sakkāyadiṭṭhi* meant one and the same thing.[35]

In the *Paṭisambhidāmagga* we meet with the following question, 'In what twenty different forms is there adherence to wrong view regarding the self (*attānudiṭṭhiyā*)'? The answer covers exactly the same ground as the one covered by the *sakkāyadiṭṭhi,* establishing thus the perfect correspondence between both the *diṭṭhis.* The treatment of the subject is original in so far as it tries to illustrate the different kinds of imagined relation between the self and the *khandhas* by means of similes. Thus:

1. To illustrate the pretended relation of identity between the *khandhas* and the self, the following simile is given:

> As if one were to think regarding an oil-lamp: 'What is the flame, that is the colour; what is the colour that is the flame', thus looking at the flame and the colour as one single thing.

2. To illustrate how the self can be conceived as possessed of the *khandhas,* the simile given is:

> It is as if there was a tree casting a shade, and regarding it a man would speak thus, 'This is the tree, this is the shade. The tree is one thing, the shade is another thing. And this tree here is a shade-casting-tree by means of this shade'.

3. The relation that regards the *khandhas* in the self is illustrated thus:

> It is as if there was a flower endowed with scent, and regarding it a man would speak thus, 'This is the flower, this is the scent. The flower is one thing, the scent is another thing. But this scent is in the flower'.

4. The illustration of the view that regards the self in the *khandhas* is as follows:

> It is as if there was a precious stone consigned to a casket, and regarding it a man would speak, 'This is the precious stone, this is the casket. The precious stone is one thing, the casket is another thing. And this precious stone is in the casket'.[36]

Another term considered equivalent to *sakkāyadiṭṭhi* (and therefore to *attānudiṭṭhi* also) is *attavāda.* This emerges from the fact that to the question, 'In what twenty forms is there adherence to the wrong view connected with wrong theory on self (*attānuvāda*)?', which is similar to the previous questions, the answer given coinciding in every detail with that given to the previous questions.[37]

The originality of the absolute separation between the self and the non-self, which is the central point in early Buddhism (and this explains also the central position given to *sakkāyadiṭṭhi* among all wrong views) is emphasized in a passage where we are told that the doctrine of *sakkāyo* is like the roaring of a lion that comes out of his lair at eventide and roars thrice making all the beasts, even the strongest, tremble. In the same way, at the appearance of a Tathāgata and at his preaching on the impermanence of the *khandhas,* even the gods tremble when they begin to realize that they are not permanent, as they thought, but impermanent, not stable but unstable, not lasting but perishable. Their discouraging conclusion put into words is:

It seems (*kira*) that we too are impermanent, unstable, not lasting, [merely] confined into our existential aggregate (*sakkāyo*).

And the sutta ends with the following verses attributed to the Buddha, even though he speaks in them in the third person:

When the Buddha set the wheel of the Law rolling by his wisdom,
He, the master of the world together with the gods, without a rival,
[Preaching on] the existential aggregate (*sakkhāyo*) and its cessation, as well as its coming to be,
And the Noble Eightfold Path, that leads to the calming down of Pain,
Even the gods, full of beauty and glory, who live for ages on end,
Fearful, were perturbed, as the other beasts [hearing] the lion,
'Not having escaped the existential aggregate (*sakkāyo*)', they said, 'it seems that we too are impermanent',
After having heard the word of the Arahant, entirely free.[38]

The essentially transmigrational character of *sakkāyo* is evinced from the opposition that exists between *sakkāyo* and *nibbāna*:

Bhikkhus, a bhikkhu possessed of six bad qualities cannot realize the unsurpassed conditon of coolness. What six? Herein, bhikkhus, a bhikkhu does not check his mind when he ought to do it, he does not exert his mind when he ought to do it, he does not gladden his mind when he ought to do it, he does not take care of his mind when it ought to be cared for, he is bent on low things and addicted to the existential aggregate. [The opposite case is then described, ending with the words:]... he is intent on excellent things and finds delight on *nibbāna.*[39]

There is in this text a striking opposition between *sakkāyābhirato* and *nibbānābhirato.*[40]

Five factors of deliverance (*nissāraṇīyā dhātuyo*) are enumerated elsewhere. One of them is:

And again, bhikkhus, while reflecting on the existential aggregate the mind of a bhikkhu does not jump at the existential aggregate, does not find satisfaction with it, does not settle on it, does not give himself up to it. But while reflecting on the cessation of the existential aggregate, his mind jumps at it, finds satisfaction with it, settles on it, gives itself up to it. That mind of his is happy, well developed, well lifted up, well liberated regarding the existential aggregate; and as for the *āsavas,* burning and destructive, that arise depending on the existential aggregate, he is free from them and does not feel that feeling. This is declared to be the deliverance from the existential aggregate.[41]

There is a text where *sakkāyo* is said to be involved in the *vimokkhas,* but not in the last one, following on the line of thought already recorded that the last *vimokkha* is related to the self in a very special way, being as it is entirely disconnected with the non-self:

Herein, Ānanda, an ariyan disciple reflects, 'Those sensual pleasures enjoyed in this existence and those to be enjoyed in another existence; those perceptions of sensual pleasures enjoyed in this existence and those to be enjoyed in another existence; those visible forms enjoyed in this existence and those to be enjoyed in another existence; those perceptions of visible forms enjoyed in this existence and those to be enjoyed in another existence, and the perception of imperturbability, and the perception of the sphere of no-thing, and the perception of the sphere of neither-perception-nor-non-perception- this is *sakkāya* as far as it is *sakkāya*'.

Then, in contrast with all this, it is said:

But this is the deathless, that is, the deliverance of mind without any grasping.[42]

Inasmuch as Nikayan Buddhism professes as its central tenet the ontological separation of the self from the non-self, no step towards perfection is possible without getting rid first of all of the *sakkāyadiṭṭhi,* which identifies the factors of existence with the self and the self with the factors of existence. That is why the *sakkāyadiṭṭhi* is the first fetter to be discarded by the *sotāpanno,* 'the converted man'.[43]

We come now to a point of great importance not only for the evaluation of Nikayan Buddhism, but also for the right understanding of some difficult passages that might otherwise be misunderstood. We are referring to the basic position attributed to the *sakkāyadiṭṭhi* in relation to all other *diṭṭhis.* The *sakkāyadiṭṭhi*, or the erroneous identification of the self with the peripheral existential adjuncts, is assumed to be implicitly contained in all other *diṭṭhis* and to give them its peculiar colouring.

The *Diṭṭhisaṁyutta* provides us with a veritable mine of information regarding this point. It is true that in it the underlying condition for all *diṭṭhis* is not precisely the *sakkāyadiṭṭhi,* but what has been called *sakkāyo.* But since *sakkāyo* represents the ideological contents of the *sakkāyadiṭṭhi* both may be taken as equivalent for our purpose. Let us give in full the first *sutta* of the above mentioned *Diṭṭhisaṁyutta,* for it is on the same pattern that all other *suttas* of the section are composed.

> ... The Blessed One spoke thus, 'What there being, bhikkhus, depending on what, clinging to what, there arises the following *diṭṭhi*: Winds do not blow, rivers do not flow, pregnant women do not give birth, moon and sun do not rise and set, there is [only] the staying immovable [of all] like a pillar.'?
>
> ...
>
> There being body, bhikkhus, depending on body, clinging to body, there arises the following *diṭṭhi,* 'Winds do not blow etc.' There being feeling.... There being perception.... There being inner complexes.... There being consciousness....
>
> What do you think of this, bhikkhus, is body permanent or impermanent?
>
> Impermanent, Lord.
>
> And what is impermanent, is it painful or pleasant?
>
> Painful, Lord.
>
> And what is impermanent, painful, mutable by nature, would there arise without dependence on that the following *diṭṭhi,* 'Winds do not blow, etc.'?
>
> Not so, Lord.

[The same applies to *vedanā, saññā, saṅkhārā, viññāṇa.* Then the text continues:]

> And what is seen, heard, felt, thought, obtained, sought after, cogitated by the mind, is all this permanent or impermanent?
>
> Impermanent, Lord.
>
> And what is impermanent, is it painful or pleasant?
>
> Painful, Lord.
>
> And what is impermanent, painful, mutable by nature, would there arise without dependence on that the following *diṭṭhi,* 'Winds do not blow, etc.'?
>
> Not so, Lord.
>
> And just because, bhikkhus, the ariyan disciple has left aside all doubts

in this matter, has left aside also all doubts concerning pain, and the origin of pain, and the cessation of pain, and the way leading to the cessation of pain, he is said to be, bhikkhus, the ariyan disciple who has entered the current of salvation (*sotāpanno*), never to be doomed, certain to attain the goal of illumination.[44]

That the *sakkāyadiṭṭhi* is basically involved here is proved not only because, as we have indicated, the *diṭṭhi* in question is based on what has been called *sakkāyo* at the beginning of this section, but also because we are told at the end of the *sutta* that one who puts aside all doubts in this matter and has no doubts left regarding the Four Noble Truths, is a *sotāpanno,* and we have just seen above that by *sotāpatti* one gets rid first of all of the *sakkāyadiṭṭhi.*

The same reasoning as the one exhibited in this *sutta* is applied to the wrong view, 'This is mine, this I am, this is my self', (*sutta* 2); to the eternalist view, 'This is the world, this is the self, after death, I myself, shall become permanent, stable, eternal, immutable by nature' (*sutta* 3); to the annihilationist theory 'If I were not it would not be mine, if I were not to become it will not be mine' (*sutta* 4); to the *n'atthi*-theory of Ajita (*sutta* 5); to the heresy of Pūraṇa Kassapa (*sutta* 6); to the heresy of Makkhali Gosāla (*sutta* 7); to the heresy of Pakuddha Kaccāyana (*sutta* 8); to the theory that the world is eternal (*sutta* 9); to the theory that the world is not eternal (*sutta* 10); and so on to the theories: that the world is limited (*sutta* 11); that the world is unlimited (*sutta* 12), that body and soul are one and the same thing (*sutta* 13), that body and soul are different things (*sutta* 14), that the Tathāgata exists after death (*sutta* 15), that the Tathā gata does not exist after death (*sutta* 16), that the Tathāgata both exists and does not exist after death (*sutta* 17), that the Tathāgata both neither exists nor does not exist after death (*sutta* 18). The whole preceding series of *suttas* is repeated from *sutta* 19 to *sutta* 36, but with a different conclusion, namely, 'Thus, bhikkhus, there being pain, depending on pain, clinging to pain, there arises the following *diṭṭhi*...'. This very conclusion is appended to the *suttas* that follow and deal with the following theories: 'that the self, after death, exists unimparied and corporeal' (*sutta* 37); 'that the self, after death, exists unimpaired and incorporeal' (*sutta* 38); 'that the self, after death, exists unimparied and both corporeal and incorporeal' (*sutta* 39); 'that the self, after death exists unimpaired and both neither corporeal nor incorporeal' (*sutta* 40); 'that the self, after death, exists unimpaired and absolutely happy' (*sutta* 41); 'that the self, after death, exists unimparied and absolutely unhappy' (*sutta* 42); 'that the self, after death, exists unimpaired and both happy and unhappy' (*sutta* 43); 'that the self, after death, exists unimpaired an neither happy nor unhappy' (*sutta* 44). The whole series of 'heresies' is dealth with again in *suttas* 45-70 with the conclusion, 'Thus, bhikkhus, what is impermanent is painful. That existing, depending on that there arises the following *diṭṭhi*...'. Again the whole series of 'heresies' are taken up in *suttas* 71-96. In them, after saying that the 'heresy' in question arises dependent on the *khandhas*, and after adding of every *khanda* that, being impermanent and painful, it is not proper to say of it, 'This is mine, this I am, this is my self', the conclusion in every case is that everyone of the *khandhas*, whether past or future or present, whether interior or exterior, gross or subtle, low or excellent, near or distant, should be regarded with perfect wisdom as it really is, as 'This is not mine, this I am not, this is not my self'. The final conclusion of these last series of *suttas* is that the ariyan disciple develops disgust for the *khandhas*, becomes detached from them, is liberated and at being liberated there is knoweldge of such liberation, coming to know, 'Destroyed is birth, lived is the brahma-life, etc.'. It is then apparent that all the 'heresies' or 'theoretical views' have as common ground the mentality that identifies the self with the empirical factors in man.

The teaching of the *Vacchagottasaṁyutta* is similar to that of the *Diṭṭhisaṁyutta*, which has been just analysed. Let us propose as a pattern for all the other suttas the first one:

> What is, master Gotama, the reason, what is the cause for speculative theories of all sorts to arise in the world, such as – 'the world is eternal', 'the world is not eternal', 'the world is limited', 'the world is unlimited', 'what is the soul that is the body', 'the soul is one thing, the body is another thing', 'the Tathāgata exists after death', etc.
>
> Due to ignorance as regards the body, Vaccha, due to ignorance as regards the origin of the body, due to ignorance as regards the cessation of the body, due to ignorance as regards the way that leads to the cessation of the body, speculative opinions of all sorts arise in the world, such as-...[45]

The *suttas* that follow are composed on the same pattern and attribute the arisal of the manifold speculative theories to: ignorance regarding feeling, the origin of feeling, etc. (*sutta* 2); ignorance regarding perception... (*sutta* 3); ignorance regarding the inner complexes... (*sutta* 4); ignorance regarding consciousness... (*sutta* 5).[46]

There is a passage that attributes the arisal of the manifold speculative theories explicitly to *sakkāyadiṭṭhi.* Citta the householder, questions the venerable eldermost among the elder bhikkhus:

> My lord Thera, all these manifold speculative theories which arise in the world, like, 'the world is eternal, ... not eternal, ... finite, ... infinite...'; 'the soul and the body are one and the same thing', 'are different ...'; 'the Tathāgata exists after death, etc.', and *the sixty two speculative theories enumerated in the Brahmajāla,* my lord Thera, owing to the existence of what do these speculative theories exist, and owing to the non-existence of what they do not exist?

[Even though questioned three times, the eldermost bhikkhu was not ready to answer. Then the venerable Isidatta happened to come there, and after asking for leave from the eldermost thera, gave the answer to Citta's query:]

> All these manifold speculative theories, householder, which arise in the world, like... there being *sakkāyadiṭṭhi* they exist, and there not being *sakkāyadiṭṭhi* they do not exist.
>
> And how, lord, there comes to be *sakkāyadiṭṭhi*?
>
> Herein, householder, an unlearned common man... regards the body as the self, or the self as having the body, or the body in the self, or the self in the body... [The same is applicable to the other *khandhas.*] Thus householder there comes to be *sakkāyadiṭṭhi.*

The opposite is then answered to the question, 'And how, lord, there comes to be no *sakkāyadiṭṭhi*?'[47]

Another passage teaches the same doctrine in a different way. The wanderer Vacchagotta asks Mogallāna whether the world is eternal or not, finite or infinite, whether the soul and the body are one and the same thing or not, and the usual questions about the existence or non-existence of the Tathāgata after death. To everyone of the questions Mogallāna answers in the same way, 'This Vaccha, has not been explained by the Blessed One'. Then Vacchagota asks for the reason why the wanderers of other faiths give definite answers to those questions. Mogallāna gives the following reason:

> The wanderers of other faiths, Vaccha, regard the eye as, 'This is mine, this I am, this is my self'. [The same being asserted of the other senses.]

Vacchagotta accosts the Buddha himself with the same questions and gets identical answers.[48]

In the following *sutta* Vacchagotta goes straight to the Buddha, and after the same dialogue as the one described before, the Buddha gives as reason why the wanderers of other faiths give definite answers to those questions:

> The wanderers of other faiths regard the body as the self, or the self as having a body, or the body in the self, or the self in the body.... [The same applies to the rest of the *khandhas.*]

Since all the *diṭṭhis* are ultimately based on the *sakkāyadiṭṭhi* and the latter coincides with *asmimāna* in identifying the self with the samsaric factors, we may say also that *asmimāna* is at the root of all the *diṭṭhis.* This fact is made explicit in the *Mahāniddesa.* Commenting on the word *mamattā,* the commentator distinguishes between two kinds of selfish possessiveness, the selfish possessiveness connected with craving (*taṇhāmamattā*) and the selfish possessiveness connected with views and theories (*diṭṭhimamattā*). When describing the second kind of selfish possessiveness, the commentary begins its catalogue of views and theories with the twentyfold *sakkāyadiṭṭhi* and winds it up with a reference to the sixty-two *diṭṭhis* of the *Brahmajāla.*[49]

Since *sakkāyadiṭṭhi* is the common factor of all *diṭṭhis,* it is manifest that the best remedy against the *diṭṭhi* tendency will be the consideration of the non-selfhood of the *khandhas,* the senses, etc.

The capital importance of the *sakkāyadiṭṭhi* among all *diṭṭhis* and the fact of its being the root-element in all of them, leads us to enunciate *an exegetical principle of great importance.* The principle is the following, 'In the Nikāyas, all non-Buddhists are presumed to labour under the total influence of the *sakkāyadiṭṭhi,* and therefore all of them are thought to identify the self with the peripheral existential factors'.

This principle has to be taken into account as an exegetical tool whenever there is a confrontation between Buddhist and non-Buddhist ideologies. It has also to be applied where, even though the teaching is addressed to the bhikkhus, one can see either an explicit or a merely implicit reference to a view that is non-Buddhist. It is with this frame of mind, for instance, that the reader will understand how we were justified in paraphrasing (in Chapter 10) the text that begins with '*Attani vā, bhikkhave, sati attaniyaṁ me ti assā'ti*?, etc. by making explicit what is implicit in the text and thus showing that the true self is not called in question.

Now we intend taking up some particular texts and applying to them the exegetical principle just enunciated and see how it can shed light on them for being correctly understood.

Channa is introduced in the *Saṁyutta* asking his fellow bhikkhus for some religious exhortation. They just confine themselves to tell him of everyone of the *khandhas* that they are impermanent, that they are non-self, winding up with the two sayings, *sabbe saṅkhārā aniccā* and *sabbe dhammā anattā.* On hearing this, Channa thought:

> Yes, for me also this is so: the body is impermanent, feeling is impermanent, etc., the body is non-self, feeling is non-self, etc., 'all compounded things are impermanent', 'all *dhammas* are non-self'. But even so, when it is question of the complete annihilation of the activities, the complete rejection of samsaric encumbrances, the destruction of craving, detachment, cessation, *nibbāna,* my mind does not jump at it, does not find satisfaction with it, does not settle on it, does not give itself up to it. Out of mental trouble grasping arises [and] the following thought keeps coming back to my mind, 'Then, in this case, is there any self for me (*atha kho carahi me attā'ti*?)'? This does not occur to one who sees the *dhamma.* Who would be there to teach me the *dhamma* so that I might see it?[50]

The reader can plainly see that Channa may have accepted the truth of the non-selfhood of the *khandhas,* but his acceptance was not the result of having seen it by means of higher wisdom. He may have professed this truth but this profession of faith was not a wholehearted one, the spirit of the *sakkāyadiṭṭhi* was still lurking in his heart of hearts, and he felt himself at a loss as to whether he had a self at all. He himself confesses that this attitude of his was entirely asmimanic, as he felt no attraction, and felt no enthusiasm stirring him towards 'the complete annihilation of activities, the complete rejection of samsaric encumbrances, the destruction of craving, detachment, cessation, *nibbāna*'. It is then clear that the self of which Channa speaks is not the true self, but the asmimanic self of the *sakkāyadiṭṭhi.* If absolute *anattā* had been the indisputable teaching of the Buddha, when Channa came to Ānanda and exposed to him the drift of his thoughts, to those words of his, 'Then in that case is there a self for me?' Ānanda should have answered that in reality there was no self at all and that Channa, to become a genuine Buddhist, had to give up the idea of *any* self. But the answer was not as simple as that, this showing that the doctrine of absolute *anattā* is an erroneous oversimplification. Channa had not the right attitude of mind to distinguish between the empirical asmimanic self and the metaphysical self of which nothing positive had ever been said by the Buddha. As an answer to Channa's query, 'Then in that case is there a self for me?', Ānanda recounts the words uttered by the Buddha himself and addressed to Kaccānagotta. The words are directed to the correction of Channa's mental attitude.

> As a general rule, Kaccāna, the world is bent on the pair of opposites, 'being and non-being'. For one who sees by means of perfect wisdom, as it really is, the origin of the world, the 'non-being' in vogue in the world is not valid. For one who sees by means of perfect wisdom as it really is, the cessation of the world, the 'being' in vogue in the world is not valid. The world, Kaccāna, is for the most part bound by prejudice and in the grip of attachment. And the one who does not fall into the grip of attachment, into the obstinacy, prejudice an bias of the mind, who does not grasp at them, who does not fix his attention on them saying, 'This my self' (*attā me ti*), but professes that only pain goes on arising, only pain goes on being destroyed, that one has no doubt, suffers no perplexity, and in this matter his knowledge is not dependent on another. In this way, Kaccāna, there is right view.[51]

Here again, 'This is the self for me', refers to the asmimanic self of the *sakkāyadiṭṭhi* and has nothing to do with the true self. 'Being' and 'non-being' mentioned at the beginning of this instruction ought to be evaluated as an expression of an ideology entirely immersed in the *sakkāyadiṭṭhi.* 'Being' and 'non-being' here do not transcend the empirical world so often declared to be the non-self. Therefore the true self is not involved in them. But even on the empirical level, these 'being' and 'non-being' are two extremes that overstep the limits of what empirical reality is according to early Buddhism. If the world has an origin, it means that absolute 'non-being' does not apply to it. If the world ceases it means that absolute 'being' does not apply to it. In between those extremes runs the dogma of dependent origination which makes the existence of the world real but contingent, that is to say devoid of absolute value. This is expressed in the lines that come immediately in the original:

> 'Everything is', this, Kaccāna, is one extreme. 'Nothing is', this is another extreme. Without falling into either extreme, the Tathāgata, following the middle way, teaches *dhamma*: dependent on ignorance there arise the activities, etc., etc. ... by the cessation of ignorance there takes place the cessation of the activities, etc., etc. ...

Early Buddhism forbids us to think that any true self is involved in the world process, and hence it frowns upon the saying, 'This is the self for me', professing that 'only pain arises, only pain goes on being destroyed', without the cooperation of any self. The true self is not denied here. The only thing asserted here is that the empirical world is a process that goes on without any ontological dependence on a self, that any connection of such a process with any self implies that such a self is entirely asmimanic, a harmful illusion, a disastrous error.

The *Sabbāsavasutta* of the *Majjhima* has as its topic, 'the complete stopping of the *āsavas*'. Its teaching centres on right reflection. The passage that interests us now is the following:

> By fixing one's own attention on things to which no attention should be paid, and by not fixing one's own attention on things to which attention should be paid, for him who so does, the *āsavas* that had not arisen arise, and those that had arisen grow stronger.
>
> He does not reflect fittingly [who reflects] thus: 'Was I in the past?', 'Was I not in the past?', 'What was I in the past?', 'How was I in the past?', 'Having been what, what did I become in the past?', 'Shall I come to be in the future?', 'What shall I come to be in the future?', 'How shall I come to be in the future?', 'Having been what, what shall I come to be in the future?'. Or now he is inwardly doubtful as regards the present: 'Am I?', 'Am I not?', 'What am I?', 'How am I?', 'This being of mine (*satto*) whence it came?', 'Whither going, [this being of mine] shall come to be?'.[52] In one who in this way does not reflect as he ought, there arise one or other of six views (*diṭṭhi*): 'My self exists' (*atthi me attā*), this opinion arises in him as though it were true, as though it were real; 'My self does not exist' (*n'atthi me attā*), this opinion arises in him as though...; 'By my very self am I aware of my self' (*attanā va attānaṁ sañjānāmi*),

this opinion...; 'By my very self am I aware of the non-self' (*attanā va anattānaṁ sañjānāmi*), this opinion...; 'Just by the non-self am I aware of my self' (*anattanā va attānaṁ sañjānāmi*), this opinion...; or rather he holds the view that, 'This very self of mine that speaks and experiences and knows, that experiences here and there the fruit of good and bad works, this very self of mine, permanent, constant, eternal, immutable, will stand for ever and ever'. This is called, bhikkhus, going to wrong views, holding of wrong views, the wilds of wrong views, the wriggling of wrong views, the fetter of wrong views. Caught in the fetter of wrong views, the uninstructed common man is not freed from birht, old-age, death, grief, lamentations, pain, mental anguish, tribulations, 'he is not freed from Pain', that is what I say.[53]

The asmimanic self-centredness of one who reflects asking in his mind all those questions of the first half of the passage is manifest. All of them have as the object of inquiry the empirical asmimanic self, that is to say the self of the *sakkāyadiṭṭhi.* To a man speaking with this mentality of *satto, ayaṁ nu kho satto kuto āgato*?, one could very well object the famous words of the bhikkhunī Vajirā.[54] There is no permanent essence in what is merely a congeries of conditioned phenomena. The true self is not empirical, the true self is not found in the congeries of conditioned phenomena so often called non-self. The same asmimanic spirit is reflected in the catalogue of *diṭṭhis* enumerated in the second part of the passage. The self mentioned in anyone of those statements is the self of the *sakkāyadiṭṭhi* and the disapproval of those views does not affect in the least the reality of the metaphysical self. And now a simple but meaningful question, 'Is it not significant that the only time when the dogma of *anattā* is stated in so many words in the sacred text (*n'atthi me attā*) it turns out to be a *diṭṭhi* and nothing else but a *diṭṭhi*? We meet here with a statement like, 'by the self I am aware of the self', whose disapproval seems to jeopardize the acceptability of a similar text registered in the first part of the book, *attanā attānaṁ samanupassati.* The similarity of the two statements is only apparent. The statement found in the passage we are now discussing refers to the asmimanic self, while the statement recorded before refers to the true self in its capacity of moral agent struggling for liberation, and as such contradicting the asmimanic self and trying to destroy it. The same asmimanic nature applies to *attā* and *anattā* as contained in, *attanā va anat-*

tānaṁ sañjānāmi and *anattanā va attānaṁ sañjānāmi.* In the last case, if *attānaṁ* is taken to refer intentionally to the metaphysical self, the saying will contain the greatest absurdity, for, as it has been often noted, in Nikayan Buddhism, consciousness is non-self an can never reach the self in its metaphysical being, there is an unbridgeable chasm between the two.

In the paragraphs previous to the passage we want to discuss now, the Buddha has taught about the *sakkāyadiṭṭhi* and how can one be freed from *asmimāna* by seing the *khandhas,* as they really are, not as the self or what belongs to the self:

> 'Then a reasoning arose in the mind of a certain bhikkhu in such wise, 'Thus it is said, sir, that the body is non-self, feeling is non-self, perception is non-self, the inner complexes are non-self, consciousness is non-self; [then] what self do the works done by the non-self affect? (*anattakatāni kammāni kaṁ attānaṁ phusantī'ti*?)'. Then the Blessed One knowing the mental reasoning of that bhikkhu, addressed the bhikkhus thus, 'This case, bhikkhus, occurs that here a certain foolish man, unwise, affected by ignorance, with a mind overwhelmed by craving, should think of going beyond the teaching of the master, thinking: thus it is said, sir, that the body is non-self...'.[55]

A little reflection becomes imperative here. We have taken notice, in the first part of the book, of the manifold ways in which good and bad actions affect the moral self. But the aim of the question with which we are now confronted is evidently different. The question here is directed to the dilucidation of the *nature* of the self affected by moral actions and to the *nature* of the effect caused by moral actions on the self. These are metaphysical questions that the Buddha systematically avoided as having no soteriological value. The question that arose in the mind of the bhikkhu in question clearly implies one thing, that he was full of the *sakkāyadiṭṭhi* spirit. He assumed that the deeds wrought *by means* of the *khandhas* could only affect a self identified with them or ontologically related to them. But such kind of self was being constantly denied by the Buddha; hence the tantalizing effect of such teaching on the bhikkhu. The bhikkhu's mentality is perfectly reflected in the choice of the verb *phusati,* which bespeaks of an influence that would affect the self's very being. The bhikkhu may have had an inkling of the complete separation and incommunicability between the self and the non-self as preached by the Buddha, but this fundamental position of the Buddha's teaching precluded any direct ontological influence of moral deeds on that self that dimly appeared as entirely unconnected with the *khandhas*. Now, if absolute *anattā* was the pivotal truth in early Buddhism, as so many scholars would have us accept, this was an opportunity for the Buddha to make it unmistakably clear. To the question, 'then what self do the works done by the non-self affect?', he should have answered simply and unequivocally that there was no self at all, and that it was high time they realized it and made it part of their religious life. He was not talking here to ignorant lay-men or prejudiced wanderers belonging to other faiths, but to his bhikkhus. But he did not do so. Keeping in mind the absolute ontological incommunicability between the metaphysical self and the non-self, the Buddha could have answered something like what we read in the *Sāṅkhya-kārikā,* 62:

> Therefore no one is bound, no one is liberated or transmigrates either; *Prakṛti* connected with a variety of beings transmigrates, is bound, and liberated.

But this is a metaphysical subtlety, entirely out of touch with our *existential* experience (we all feel and know ourselves bound and aspire to liberation), and hence of no soteriological value. If the Buddha had given such an answer, he would have emptied of all meaning, for the bhikkhu in question and for those who thought like him, all those forceful expressions systematically discussed in the first part of the book,[56] where we studied the effect of good and bad deeds on the self, the only self such people knew of was the asmimanic self of the *sakkāyadiṭṭhi.* We thought it necessary to distinguish, regarding the self, between two levels: the moral level and the metaphysical level, both reflecting their own kind of reality regarding the same true self. This is not a philosophical solution to the problem with which we are confronted here, but a systematic answer to the conflict existing between texts that speak of the true self as reflected on the empirical level (the agent of purification and liberation, which therefore cannot be the asmimanic self) and the texts that refer to the self as isolated from what is empirical. The Buddha himself declares in the text just quoted that one who tries to philosophize on this point tries to go ahead of the master, meaning to say that he never tried to elucidate this point. One who tries to philosophize on this matter, betrays a mind entirely beset by *asmimāna,* and that on two counts. First of all because he shows an unhealthy preoccupation with the self. In the second place, because he has the presumption to go ahead of his master, as if the master's doctrine were incomplete or as if he knew better, he shows himself, 'unwise, affected by ignorance, with a mind overwhelmed by craving'. It is then evident that the bhikkhu in question is under the influence of the *sakkāyadiṭṭhi,* and therefore his speculation is not about the true self, that is above all speculation, but about the asmimanic self.

In what comes of the passage, the preservation of the text is not unanimously uniform. The Nālandā Edition chooses the reading *paṭivinītā,* and gives as other possible readings, *paṭiccavinītā* (Roman and Sinhalese editions), and *paṭipucchāmi vinītā* (Siamese edition). The last variant is ungrammatical, as *vinītā* is nominative when it should be accusative, *vinīte,* agreeing with *tumhe,* which in this case would be the object of *paṭipucchāmi.* The most likely reading seems to be *paṭiccavinītā,* which will mean, 'trained to look for dependent origination'. The whole phrase will then be, *paṭiccavinītā kho me tumhe, bhikkhave, tatra tatra (v. 1. tesu tesu) dhammesu.* Therefore the exhortation of the Buddha will continue in this way:

> You have been trained by me, bhikkhus, to look for dependent origination in *dhammas* everywhere...[57]

This doubtless refers to the *paṭiccasamuppāda,* which is the pivotal teaching of the Buddha regarding the empirical process. The only thing that one needs to know is the conditioned evolution of the samsaric process, which is based on *avijjā, and how to stop it.* But this, as has been often indicated, postulates a moral agent that refuses to be driven by *avijjā* and whatever originates from it. The rest is mere speculation with no practical value and always betraying the presence of *asmimāna.* Then the Buddha concludes with the stock passage where the bhikkhus are compelled to confess that the *khandhas* are not the self, and that they should be regarded as the non-self by means of perfect wisdom. Therefore, they should develop disgust for them, detach themselves from them, and thereby be liberated and know that they are liberated.[58] No one will deny that in the final passage, so often reiterated in the Nikāyas, there occurs a direct and explicit reference to the self, like 'This is not mine, this I am not, this is not my *self*'. This reference differs from the one found in the question criticised by the Buddha ('What self do the works done by the non-self affect?') in that the former is a spontaneous simple, natural reference to the self, while the second betrays an unhealthy sophisticated mentality bent on speculation, and therefore soaked in the spirit of the *sakkāyadiṭṭhi.*

The same problem gets a passing reference in the *Cūḷasaccakasutta* of the *Majjhima,* in a dialogue between the Buddha and Aggivessana, the Jain. The latter puts a question about how the Buddha trains his disciples. The Buddha proposes the doctrine of the impermanence and non-selfhood of everyone of other *khandhas,* adding the two sayings, *sabbe saṅkhārā aniccā* and *sabbe dhammā anattā.* With permission from the Buddha, Aggivessana objects with the following similes:

> Even as, friend Gotama, all the individuals of the vegetable kingdom and the animal kingdom (*bījagāmabhūtagāma*), which attain growth, increase, abundance, all of them do so depending on the earth, finding support on the earth, and that is how they attain growth, increase, abundance. Even as, friend Gotama, whatever strenuous professions men exercise, all of them are accomplished depending on the earth, finding support on the earth, and that is how they are accomplished. In the same way, a human being on account of having the body as self (*rūpattāyaṁ* which it seems should be read *rūpattatāya*) begets merit and demerit with the support of the body; on account of feelings being his self (again *vedanāttāyaṁ* likely to be corrected into *vedanāttatāya,* and the same applies to the rest) begets merit and demerit with the support of his feelings; on account of perception being his self...; on account of the inner complexes being his self...; on account of his consciousness being the self begets merit and demerit with the support of his consciousness.[59]

Aggivessana is touching here the crux of the problem. We may paraphrase his objection in the following way, 'Without a self there is no moral agent or a subject of moral responsibility; without what you call the non-self, viz. the *khandhas,* there is no possibility of moral action. Thus your doctrine that denies the identity of the self with the *khandhas* precludes all possibility of the self assuming responsibility for the actions of the *khandhas,* therefore you are not a *kiriyavādin'.*[60] Unhappily for us, the Buddha does not give any direct answer to this objection, he only tackles Aggivessana on his position that the *khandhas* are the self by making him confess that he has no absolute mastery over them, a mastery that should be there if the *khandhas* and the self were one and the same thing. This last point has already been dealt with.

We come now to discuss one of the most interesting passages found regarding the reality or unreality of the self. This time the wanderer Vacchagotta comes up to the Buddha and initiates a dialogue in which the silence of one of the parties plays a very important role.

> 'Now, what, friend Gotama, does the self exist?' (*atth'attā'ti*). When this was said, the Blessed One remained silent. 'Then what, friend Gotama, does the self not exist?' (*n'atth'attā'ti*). For the second time, the Blessed one remained silent. Then the wanderer Vacchagotta got up from his seat and left. Not long after the wanderer Vacchagotta had left, Ānanda said this to the Blessed One, 'But why, Lord, on being put a question by the wanderer Vacchagotta you did not answer his question?'
>
> If I, Ānanda, on being questioned by the wanderer Vacchagotta whether the self exists, would have answered that the self exists, this would have coincided with what is professed by those samaṇas and brāhmaṇas who are eternalists. And if I, Ānanda, on being questioned by the wanderer Vacchagotta whether the self does not exist, would have answered that the self does not exist, this would have coincided with what is professed by those samaṇas and brāhmaṇas who are annihilationists. And if I, Ā nanda, on being questioned by the wanderer Vacchagotta whether the self exists, would have answered that the self exists, would have this been suitable for the arisal of the knowledge that 'all *dhammas* are non-self'?[61]
>
> Not so, Lord.
>
> And if I, Ānanda, on being questioned by the wanderer Vacchagotta whether the self does not exist would have answered that the self does not exist, this would have resulted in a greater bewilderment for the already bewildered Vacchagotta, the wanderer, who would have thought, 'Formerly there was a self for me, which now does not exist' (*ahu vā me nūna pubbe attā, so etarahi n'atthī'ti*).[62]

For a balanced evaluation of this passage, we have to remind ourselves of the principle established above. Vacchagotta did not profess the Buddhist faith, therefore he suscribed single-mindedly to the belief that the self is identified with the *khandhas*. The Buddha, on the other hand, wholeheartedly rejected such identification, and as we have often said this was a pivotal point in his teaching. In these circumstances, the dialogue between

Vacchagotta and the Buddha was impossible, the term 'self' had an entirely different meaning for both of the parties concerned. This gives us the meaning of the Buddha's silence. If the Buddha had answered in the affirmative, Vacchagotta would have wrongly interpreted the answer as conforming to the doctrine of the eternalists, who attribute perpetuity to the self of the *sakkāyadiṭṭhi,* the only one of which Vacchagotta had any knowledge. If the Buddha had answered in the negative, Vacchagotta would have been misled to think that the Buddha was siding with the annihilationists, or better, perhaps, nihilists. If, again, the Buddha had answered in the affirmative, he would have appeared to favour Vacchagotta's idea of the self as identified with the *khandhas.* This would have made impossible the arisal in Vacchagotta's mind of the knowledge that all those empirical factors are non-self, *sabbe dhammā anattā.* Finally, if the Buddha had answered in the negative, then, Vacchagotta's confusion, a result of his adherence to the *sakkāyadiṭṭhi,* would have increased enormously. He would have thought, 'First I was sure I had a self, and now I have to think I have none'. Therefore, all the conclusions to which Vacchagotta would have arrived would have been false because of his adherence to the *sakkāyadiṭṭhi* and his inability to transcend it. All this shows that in this dialogue the reality of the true self is not brought into question, on the contrary, it is asserted as it constitutes the implicit solution to all the difficulties emanating from Vacchagotta's belief in the self of the *sakkāyadiṭṭhi.* And now, even at the risk of being told that we carry exegetical subtlety a bit too far we cannot refrain from making the following remark. If the teaching of the Buddha had as its central dogma the doctrine of absolute *anattā,* the only answer available to him would have been the negative one, *n'atth'attā.* This answer would have been true either in the empirical, heretical sense or in the metaphysical sense. The very fact that the possibility of giving an affirmative answer, *atth'attā* is somehow contemplated belies the opinion that the Buddha's conviction and preaching was in favour of absolute *anattā.* If absolute *anattā* was *the* truth, then the affirmative answer, *atth'attā* would have proved false in any way from the Buddha's point of view. It would have been false from the empirical point of view, as he denies so often the identity of the empirical factors with the self. This he himself confesses when he confesses that an affirmative answer would have contradicted his oft-recurring saying, *sabbe dhammā anattā.*

It would have proved false also from the empirical point of view in those cases where according to us there is a reference to the reality of the moral agent. It would have proved false, finally from the metaphysical point of view, for an *anattā* doctrine that has an absolute value will apply to all levels of being. On the other hand, if the *anattā* doctrine had only a relative value, both the answers would have been possible, provided they were correctly understood, a thing that could not be expected from Vacchagotta. 'Yes, there is a self', would have applied to the self as distinct from the empirical factors, while, 'No, there is no self', would have applied to the self identified by other people with the empirical factors, that is to say, the self of the *sakkāyadiṭṭhi.* Another reason for Buddha's repeated silence was his conviction that the true metaphysical self is transcendent, and therefore above the empirical concepts of existence and non-existence. We have hinted at this before and will insist on it in the coming chapter.[63]

SASSATAVĀDA AND UCCHEDAVĀDA

These two *diṭṭhis* deserve special attention, considering the importance given to them in the canon and how Buddhism contends to be a middle way between them. This is taken by the anattavādins as a confirmation of their position. We are going to see whether they are or not justified in doing so.

The direct connection between these two *diṭṭhis* is stated in the *Paṭisambhidāmagga.*

When elaborating on the eternalist view, the latter is called *sakkāyavatthukā sassatadiṭṭhi,* and it is asserted that it contains fifteen different kinds of adherence to wrong view, three for every *khandha.* Thus:

> Herein, the unlearned common man... (regards) either the self as having a body, or the body in the self, or the self in the body...
> How does one regard the self as having a body? Herein, someone regards feeling..., perception..., the inner complexes..., consciousness as the self. [There follows the simile of the tree and its shade.][64]

According to this explanation the four last *khandhas* are regarded as identical with the self, while *rūpa,* the body is distinct from the self but qualifies it as belonging to it.

The annihilationist theory is introduced as, *sakkāyavatthukā diṭṭhi.* In this case, the unlearned common man regards everyone of the *khandhas* as identical with the self. [65]

The root of the *sassatavāda* consists in the attachment to existence, while the root of the *ucchedavāda* consists in the loathing that some men feel for the body. Both, attachment and disgust, produce the same effect, the perpetuation of the cycle of samsaric existences. Loathing and disgust are a kind of inverted attachment. Both attachment and disgust, presuppose an involvement of the ego in what is empirical, while liberation consists in the suppression of any such kind of involvement.

> On the one hand, bhikkhus, there are those samaṇas and brāhmaṇas who propound the breaking up, the destruction, the annihilation of the existing being. On the other hand, those samaṇas and brāhmaṇas who propound the self to be conscious and unimpaired after death revile them; also, those samaṇas and brāhmaṇas who propound the self to be unconscious and unimpaired after death revile them; also, those samaṇas and brāhmaṇas who propound the self to be neither conscious nor unconscious and unimpaired after death revile them. What is the reason for this? All these venerable samaṇas and brāhmaṇas give expression to a high sounding attachment- 'Thus shall we come to be after death, thus shall we come to be after death'. In the same way as it occurs to a merchant going to trade, 'In future that will be mine, by means of this I shall get that', in this very way, these venerable samaṇas and brāhmaṇas appear to be like merchants, I think, when they imagine, 'Thus shall we come to be after death, thus shall we come to be after death'. This, bhikkhus, the Tathāgata knows. And those venerable samaṇas and brāhmaṇas who propound the breaking up, the destruction, the annihilation of the existing being, afraid of their own bodies, disgusted with their own bodies, keep running and running around their bodies. [There follows the simile of the dog tied with a lash to a strong pillar or pole who keeps turning around the pillar or pole.] Knowing that this is compounded and material, and that there is this, which is the cessation of compounded things, the Tathāgata, showing the escape from it, has gone beyond it.[66]

The particular importance of this text lies in that it shows a genuine positive panorama of eschatological optimism, flashing a perspective of hope between the two extremes of eternalism and annihilationism. It is no question here of the samsaric perspective of the *paṭiccasamuppāda,* which is presented at times as the middle way between the two extremes, but a perspective of liberation through transcendence. The positive attachment of the eternalists and the negative attachment of the annihilationists are something compounded (*saṅkhataṁ*), that is to say samsaric. The Buddha has transcended all this showing the escape from it all. Is this not another case where the true self, even though not explicitly mentioned as *attā,* is opposed to the heretical self of the *sakkāyadiṭṭhi,* which thrives in what is 'compounded' and is therefore involved in eternalism and annihilationism?

We can see in two other *suttas* that clinging is the decisive factor behind eternalism and annihilationism. Both the suttas follow the same pattern,

> What there being, bhikkhus, depending on what, clinging to what, there arises a *diṭṭhi* like this, 'This is the self, this is the world, I myself shall become after death permanent, immovable, eternal, unchangeable by nature?'
>
> ...
>
> There being body, bhikkhus, depending on body, clinging to body, there arises a *diṭṭhi* like this, 'This is the self, this is the world, etc.'. There being feeling, depending on feeling, clinging to feeling... There being perception, depending on perception... There being inner complexes... There being consciousness, depending on consciousness, clinging to consciousness, there arises a *diṭṭhi* like this...[67]

The following sutta (153) speaks of the annihilationist theory, 'And if I were not, it would not be mine; if it were not, it will not be mine' (*no c'assaṁ, no ca me siyā, n'ābhavissa na me bhavissati*), and attributes its arisal among other things to clinging to body, as in the text just quoted, while we were told above that the annihilationist is such because he loathes his own body. As it has been indicated, loathing is a negative kind of clinging, both being manifestations of *asmimāna* or undue preoccupation with self.

In a passage of the *Alagaddūpamasutta,* after having said that one who regards the *khandhas* as 'This is not mine, this I am not, this is not my self', will not be troubled by things non-existent, or lost, or taken away, then the bhikkhus ask the Buddha whether it is possible for one to be anxious about things that do not exist.

Can there be, Lord, anxiety for a thing inwardly non-existing?
There can be, bhikkhus,... Herein, bhikkhus, a certain man professes this view, 'This is the world, this is the self; I myself shall become after death permanent, immovable, eternal, unchangeable by nature'. He hears the Tathāgata or a disciple of the Tathāgata preaching the dhamma for the complete uprooting of all bias and prejudice, prepossession and obstinacy regarding speculative dogmas, for the calming down of all activities, for the discharge of all samsaric encumbrances, for the destruction of craving, for detachment, for cessation, *nibbāna.* It occurs to him, 'Surely I shall be annihilated, surely I am going to perish, surely I shall become no more'. He grieves, feels miserable, laments, cries beating his breast, falls into confusion. This is how, bhikkhus, there can be anxiety for a thing inwardly non-existing.
Can there be, Lord, no anxiety for a thing inwardly non-existing?
There can be, bhikkhus,... [The opposite case is described of one not professing the eternalist view, who on hearing the dhamma does not draw the conclusion that he is going to be annihilated and does not lament and feel miserable about it.][68]

The non-existing thing that causes anxiety in the first case is doubtless the eternalist view of the self, whose annihilation is apprehended as a necessary conclusion flowing from the teaching exposed in the *dhamma.* What does not exist cannot be annihilated. The eternalist self exists only in the holder's mind, being in itself entirely false and therefore non-existing. As a matter of fact, the annihilationist view of the self that, in this case, is thought to be the gist of the Buddha's teaching is as false as the eternalist view. Both views are excluded by the *dhamma,* as both views are based on the *sakkāyadiṭṭhi,* the fundamental heresy rejected by the *dhamma.* In the second case the non-existing thing is again the eternalist view of the self that the hearer of *dhamma* does not harbour in his mind and therefore he is not led to think that the teaching of the *dhamma* countenances its annihilation. Here again the reality or unreality of the true self remains outside the scope of the text in question. And by the way, through the converted application of the exegetical principle stated above we conclude that the person spoken of in the first case is a non-Buddhist, as he is thoroughly enmeshed in the spirit of the *sakkāyadiṭṭhi,* which is the basis both of eternalism and annihilationism. The person involved in the second case has a genuine Buddhist mentality, for he is absolutely free from the clutches of the *sakkāyadiṭṭhi.*

The second quotation given in this section has shown us early Buddhism as a middle way between eternalism and annihilationism. This middle way consists in leaving aside both the extremes and transcending them, 'Knowing that this is compounded and material, and that there is this, which is the cessation of compounded things, the Tathāgata, showing the escape from it, has gone beyond it'.[69] Let us scrutinize now other parts of the canon that propound this same middle way.

> Prepossessed by two speculative views, bhikkhus, both god and men, some stick fast, some go too far; and those who have eyes see.
>
> And how, bhikkhus, do some stick fast? Gods and men, bhikkhus, are fond of becoming, in love with becoming, utterly pleased with becoming; when the *dhamma* is explained for the stopping of becoming their mind does not jump at it, does not find satisfaction in it, does not settle on it, does not give itself up to it. Thus, bhikkhus, some people stick fast.
>
> And how, bhikkhus, some go too far? Some, afflicted by becoming, vexed by becoming, disgusted with becoming, welcome non-becoming, saying, 'Since, friend, after the dissolution of the body, after death, this self (*ayaṁ attā*) is annihilated, is destroyed, does not exist after death, this is what is real, this is what is excellent, this is the true view. Thus, bhikkhus, some go to far.
>
> And how, bhikkhus, does one who has got eyes see? Herein, bhikkhus, one regards what has become as having become, regarding what has become as something that has become he attains to revulsion, to deatchment, to cessation of what has become. Thus, bhikkhus, one who has got eyes sees.

The *sutta* ends with the following verses:

> Those who regard what has become as having become, and go beyond what has become,
>
> They are released in what really is, by the destruction of craving for becoming.
>
> One who truly knows what has become, free from craving for becoming or non-becoming,
>
> That bhikkhu, by the cessation of what has become, does not proceed

to any further existence.[70]

The *sutta* introduces first those who stick fast to becoming, wishing to perpetuate their empirical, asmimanic self. Then it introduces by contrast those who go too fast by wishing the annihilation of their empirical asmimanic self. The verb used for sticking fast is *olīyanti,* and the verb for going too far is *atidhavanti.* The very contrast tells us that if *olīyanti* is the opposite of *atidhavanti,* and the latter means to go too far, then the former has the meaning of 'being unable to go any further'. And if in the second case those who go too far do it by thinking that the self is annihilated after death, then those who are unable to go any further are those who wish to keep the self (the asmimanic self) for ever in the round of existences. One who has got eyes to see is not unable to go any further as those of the first extreme position are, but, as expressed in the verses, he transcends becoming (*bhūtassa ca atikkamaṁ*) and by destroying all craving for becoming (*bhāvataṇhā parikkhayā*) he is released in what is real (*yathābhūte*). Can any one deny that in saying that one is released in what is real the reality of the true self is implicitly asserted? Otherwise what is the connection between the one that is released and that reality into which he is released? The Siamese edition has it *yathābhūtaṁ* in place of *yathābhūte,* but the meaning is not substantially changed, as *yathābhūtaṁ* will mean 'in truth, in realtiy'. As regards the other extreme, the annihilationist loathes becoming and sees liberation in death where the self that is identified with empirical existence is annihilated together with it. In contrast with him, the one who has got eyes sees things as they really are, as things become, not as the self, and in that he disagrees both with the eternalist and the annihilationist. Besides, even though he seems to agree to a certain degree with the annihilationist (the motives of both are entirely different) in feeling disgust for becoming he does not go too far in thinking that the self ends up with death, but contemplates the possibility to attain liberation by detaching himself (his self!) from becoming and non-becoming. The eternalist is wrong due to his attachment to becoming, the annihilationist is wrong due to his attachment to non-becoming, the one who has got eyes to see steers a middle way by detaching himself from becoming and non-becoming and thereby transcending both and attaining liberation. To say, in this context, that early Buddhism occupies a middle position between eternalism and annihilationism, because the former wishes to perpetuated the empirical asmimanic self, and the latter wishes the annihilation of the asmimanic self, while Buddhism denies absolutely the reality of any self, leaves without explanation the fact of transcendence over both becoming and non-becoming and consequent liberation. Who transcends becoming and non-becoming and thus attains liberation? Both transcendence and liberation are asserted in the verses just translated.

This middle position of early Buddhism between eternalism and annihilationism finds expression in another part of the canon in a text already quoted on a previous occasion. To Kaccāna's question, about what is right view, the Buddha answers,

> The world, for the most part, Kaccāna, is bent on the dyad, 'being and non-being'. What is termed 'non-being' in the world is proved not to be so for one who by means of perfect wisdom sees as it really is the origin of the world. What in the world is termed 'being', is proved not to be so for one who by means of perfect wisdom sees as it really is the cessation of the world. The world, Kaccāna, is for the most part bound by bias and in the grip of attachment. And one who does not fall into the grip of attachment, the obstinacy, prejudice and bias of the mind, who does not grasp at them, who does not fix his attention on them by saying, 'This is my self (*attā me*), but professes that 'only pain goes on arising, only pain goes on being destroyed', has no doubt, suffers no perplexity, and in this matter his knowledge is not dependent on another. In this way, Kaccāna, there is right view.
>
> 'Everything is', this, Kaccāna, is one extreme; 'Nothing is', this is the other extreme. Without falling into any of both extremes, the Tathāgata, going the middle way teaches the *dhamma,* 'Dependent on ignorance there arise the activities, dependent on the activities there arises consciousness etc., etc.'. [There follows the formula of the *paṭiccasamuppāda* both in order of origination and in order of cessation.][71]

Buddhism contends here to occupy a middle position between eternalism and annihilationism, which in this case can be better termed nihilism. The two extremes contemplated here are given an absolute value. Thus '*sabbaṁ atthi*' seems to represent the world as an essentially immutable reality, possessing absolute being, where changes will have to be considered not real but merely apparent. This eternalist position has been expressed in another context as, 'Winds do not blow, rivers do not flow, etc.'. The nihilism represented by the formula '*sabbam n'atthi*' may be explained as an extreme into which some people fell, as an ultimate logical conclusion of the impermanence of things, a truth that was by no means restricted to Buddhism. The *sutta* opposes against the absolute being of the world the truth of its cessation, and against the absolute non-being of the world the *sutta* opposes the fact of its origination, which presupposes it to be real, but not with an absolute reality.[72] The Buddhist position finds expression in two formulae, which in the last analysis are equivalent. The first formula reads, 'only pain goes on arising, only pain goes on being destroyed', which is directly opposed to the identity of the self with the samsaric process, '*attā me*'. The second formula consists in the *paṭiccasamuppāda,* both in its *anuloma* and *paṭiloma* enunciations. The *paṭiccasamuppāda* doctrine contradicts the absolute being and non-being of the world by attributing to it a relative being founded on dependent origination. The true self stays all the time out of this discussion. The *paṭiccasamuppāda* doctrine posits an intermediate position between the absolute being and non-being of the world on the samsaric level of successive conditioned phenomena. The '*attā me*' which is rejected is not the true self but the self of the *sakkāyadiṭṭhi,* the asmimanic self, as it is spelled out by the words that introduce the formula, '*attā me*' into the context, 'and one who does not fall into the grip of attachment, the obstinacy, prejudice and bias of the mind, who does not grasp at them, who does not fix his attention on them by saying, "This is my self", etc.'. On the other hand let us not forget what we have been told above, that there is another solution to the conflict between the two extremes, viz. the solution of transcending both of them and winning liberation, a solution that presupposes the reality of the self.

Finally we may resume here another passage also discussed before. The wanderer Timbaruka comes to the Buddha and asks whether pain and pleasure are made by self (*sayaṁkataṁ*), or are made by another (*paraṅkataṁ*), or are due to chance (*adhiccasamuppannaṁ*). To everyone of the questions the Buddha answers with a 'No'. Applying our exegetical principle, we shall notice that the fundamental difference between the wanderer Timbaruka and the Buddha was that the former was referring to the self of the *sakkāyadiṭṭhi,* a self entirely committed to, and identified with, the samsaric process of pleasure and pain; while for the Buddha the self had no ontological relation with the empirical phenomena. After that, the

Buddha explains how his position is a middle one. One of the extremes is expressed as '*sā vedanā so vedayati*', which comes to say that feeling and the one who experiences the feeling are one and the same thing. This is equivalent to saying that pleasure and pain are made by self, and in the commentary this is taken to be an expression of eternalism. The second extreme is expressed as, '*aññā vedanā añño vedayati*', that is to say, the feeling and the experiencer are different. This is equivalent to saying that pleasure and pain are made by another, and this the commentary takes as equivalent to annihilationism. In both the cases, the self is identified with *vedanā,* therefore we are confronted here with the self of the *sakkāyadiṭṭhi.* The Buddha avoids these two extremes by attributing the production of pleasure and pain to the *paṭiccasamuppāda* process. Here again the true self is left outside the sphere of discussion.[73]

13

Self and Non-self After Liberation

The crucial test for upholding or denying the reality of the true self is in the four so-called *abyākatā pañhā,* or unexplained questions, viz. 'Does the Tathāgata exist after death?', 'Does not the Tathāgata exist after death?', 'Does the Tathāgata both exist and not exist after death?', 'Does not the Taṭhāgata both exist and not exist after death?' The Tathāgata is a perfect man who both has transcended all samsaric conditions and broken all the bonds of rebirth. What happens to him after death? As A. B. Keith says,

> ... when the bodily apparatus ceases to operate, what is the condition of the enlightened one? Are we to believe that at this stage the existence of the enlightened one ceases, as is the view that appeals to modern rationalism? Or does the Parinirvāna mean the final severance of connexion with the world of experience, and the enjoyment of another sphere of existence which is true reality, and accordingly exempt from possibility of explanations by empirical descriptions? The problem of the continued existence of the Tathāgata after death is in the ultimate issue the same as the existence of a true self; if such exists, then the enlightened one must necessarily, as the highest product of the world, be the possessor of such a self.[1]

We are ready to agree with what A. B. Keith wishes to convey, although we do not approve of expressions such as, 'at this stage of existence', 'the enjoyment of another sphere of existence', 'the problem of continued existence', which are redolent of transmigrational significance and seem to overlook the absolute discontinuity between samsaric existence and *parinibbāna.* As a matter of fact, the unexplained questions are given in the Commentary a universal value, by applying them not only to the Buddha but to all liberated beings.[2]

BUDDHA WAS NOT A NIHILIST

No wonder if strangers to the faith accused the Buddha of nihilism, when the Nikāyas bear testimony to the fact that even some of his disciples could become the victims of such an aberrant interpretation of his teaching. Thus we read in the *Yamakasutta* of the *Saṁyutta:*

> At that time there occurred to a certain bhikkhu called Yamaka the following evil heretical thought (*pāpakaṁ diṭṭhigataṁ*), 'Thus do I understand the *dhamma* taught by the Blessed One, that a bhikkhu whose *āsavas* have been destroyed, at the dissolution of the body, is annihilated, is destroyed, is no more after death'.[3]

In spite of being recriminated for that by his fellow bhikkhus, Yamaka persisted in his heretical opinion. It took such a great master as Sāriputta to convince him of the untenability of his opinion. According to F. L. Woodward, the Commentary says:

> If his view were this: 'the aggregates rise and cease; there is ceasing of the round of existence' – it would be no heresy, but expert knowledge of the teaching. But in so far as he thought: 'a being is broken up and perishes', herein arises a heretical view.[4]

The words of the Commentary can be accepted as they stand, but not their implication that there is no true self at all. It is correct to say that one who thinks, 'the aggregates rise and cease, there is ceasing of existence', thinks no heresy but shows expert knowledge of the teaching. It is also correct to say that at the death of a liberated man 'there is ceasing of the round of existence', but that is not all there is to it, there is also the attainment of *nibbāna.* Applying the principle stated above we will have to say that Yamaka, even though a bhikkhu, while speaking in such a manner, was being influenced by the *sakkāyadiṭṭhi* and ought to be condemned for it. But it is obvious, on the other hand, that one who identifies man's self with the *khandhas* does not allow for any realtiy of man to be accounted for after the latter's death, and we can see that this was the point at issue judging from the trend of thought of the *sutta* as a whole. The question here (if we are allowed to put it in our own words) is not so much whether at death a self or being is annihilated or destroyed, but rather whether after the Tathāgata's death there remains any self or no self at all. Yamaka's words imply that no self remains and he was therefore expressing himself as a nihilist would do. Sāriputta submits Yamaka to a kind of cross examination that constitutes a résumé of many of the important topics so far discussed in the book. Sāriputta begins by asking Yamaka:

What do you think of this, friend Yamaka, is body permanent or impermanent?

Impermanent, friend.

The same question and the same answer occur after that regarding everyone of the *khandhas,* followed by the stock passage of becoming disgusted at them, detached from them, and thereby liberated, with the usual knowledge of such liberation.[5]

Yamaka's cross examination by Sāriputta continues:

What do you think of this, Yamaka, do you regard the body as the Tathāgata?

Not so, friend.

Do your regard feeling as the Tathāgata?

Not so, friend.

[The same is applied to the rest of the *khandhas.*]

If Yamaka had been an out and out heretic he would have answered in the affirmative all the five questions. His answering them in the negative shows that he was a man basically of sound doctrine but in whose mind there still lay dormant a propension to the spirit of the *sakkāyadiṭṭhi.* Yamaka's negative answers to these five questions was a necessary sequel to the *khandhas* being *anattā,* and to the *khandhas* being within the scope of the saying, 'This is not mine, this I am not, this is not my self.' The dialogue continues:

What do you think of this, friend Yamaka, do you regard the Tathāgata as being in the body?

Not so, friend.

The negative answer in this case was required as a sequel to those passages where we are taught that the self is not in the *khandhas.* Now comes a question meant to be antithetical to the previous one:

Do you, friend Yamaka, regard the Tathāgata as separated from the body? (*aññatra rūpā*)

Not so, friend.

[This pair of questions are applied to everyone of the *khandhas.*]

We take *aññatra* as corresponding not to the Sanskrit word *anyatara,* which may mean, 'either of the two, other, different', but as corresponding to the Sanskrit word *anyatra,* which means, 'elsewhere, in another place'. F. L. Woodward seems to favour the first rendering when he translates, 'Do you regard a Tathāgata as distinct from the body?.' If the question is given this sense, the answer should have been affirmative, because if the *khandhas* are not the self, it is obvious that the self or person is distinct from the *khandhas.* If we take into consideration the teaching frequently found in the Nikāyas that the self is not in the *khandhas,* even if *aññatra* is translated as 'seperated from', the answer ought to have been also affirmative. But since all along Yamaka's answers are orthodox we are bound to look for an orthodox sense of the question to which a negative answer will aptly be applied. Even if the *khandhas* are not in the self, and the self is not in the *khandhas* (all this ontologically speaking), there is some kind of extrinsic relationship, between the *khandhas* and the self. We may express this in another more suggestive way, if the relation between the *khandhas* and the self is not an *essential* one, it may be qualified at least as an intimate *existential* relationship. After all the *khandhas* of the Buddha were the *khandhas* of the Buddha and of no one else, and there was no possibility to know the existence of the Buddha and to communicate with him, but through the *khandhas.*[6] It is only from this point of view that a negative answer appears acceptable. After all we shall see soon that the Tathāgata without the *khandhas,* after liberation, turns out to be for us an unconceivable and ineffable realtiy. Then Sāriputta refers to all the *khandhas* together:

> What do you think of this, friend Yamaka, do you regard body, feeling, perception, the inner complexes, consciousness as the Tathāgata?
> Not so, friend.
> What do you think of this, do you regard the Tathāgata as incorporeal, without feeling, without perception, without the inner complexes, without consciousness?
> Not so, friend.

The same considerations ought to be borne in mind regarding this pair of questions as those made in the case of the previous pair. As a conclusion of the foregoing antinomies Sāriputta tells Yamaka,

> Then, friend Yamaka, if the Tathāgata is not comprehended by you in this very life as he truly and really is; is it fitting for you to explain things

in this way, 'Thus do I understand the *dhamma* explained by the Blessed One, that a bhikkhu whose *āsavas* have been destroyed, at the dissolution of the body, is annihilated, is destroyed, is no more after death?

F. L. Woodward gives this paragraph quite a different sense if we are to abide by the literal sense of the expressions he chooses, 'Then, friend Yamaka, since in this very life a Tathāgata is not to be regarded as existing in truth, in realtiy, is it proper for you to assert, "As I understand the doctrine taught by the Exalted One, etc."'. From his way of rendering the passage it is apparent that Woodward understands it as denying that the Tathāgata *is* in truth and reality, which would deny all ultimate truth and reality to the Tathāgata. The crux of the problem is in the participle *anupalabbhiyamāno*. How should this participle be translated? Before this question is decided, there are some preliminary remarks to be made.

1. *Anupalabbhiyamāno* is a hybrid formation. The original root is *upalabhati,* whose passive voice is *upalabbhati,* and therefore the present participle passive ought to be *upalabbhamāno,* but in our case, the suffix *-mano* has been added to *upallabbhiya,* which seems to be the potential passive participle which in its negative form will be *anupalabbhiya* and could be translated as 'incomprehensible'. Was this perhaps the original form?

2. As regards the meaning of the word, two translations are possible. In the active voice the root *upalabhati* has the meaning of 'obtaining, comprehending, finding, etc.'. It is in the passive voice where two meanings are possible. Thus *anupalabbhati* may mean either 'not to be obtained, found, *comprehended',* or in a derivative sense, 'not to be, not to exist'.[7]

3. Since the form is not *anupalabbhiyamāne,* in what is called an absolute construction, then the verb *atthi* is to be understood after *anupalabbhiyamāno.* This seems to preclude the advisability of giving the latter the meaning of 'being or existing', as if it were a synonym of *atthi.*

4. The Tathāgata has been mentioned in the preceding dialogue as a really existing person, even though endowed with antithetical attributes. Therefore the conclusion of the dialogue cannot be that he is not existing in truth and reality. This would be equivalent to saying that the Buddha was merely an appearance, not a realtiy, a doctrine that may be a product of later philosophizing, but does not fit in with the original doctrine of the Nikāyas. The point that the dialogue conveys is that the Tathāgata, even

though being a reality in his own being, cannot be conceived by our mind being either way between two antithetical predicates. Therefore the meaning is that the Tathāgata, even though real, is in this very life 'inconceivable or incomprehensible'. How then can anyone lay claim to any knowledge of him after death?[8]

Now Sāriputta wants to make sure that Yamaka has learnt the lesson and says,

> If they were to ask you, friend Yamaka, like this, 'The bhikkhu who is an arahant, whose *āsavas* have been destroyed, what will be of him at the dissolution of the body, after death?'
>
> ... Questioned thus, friend, I would answer in the following way, 'The body, friend, is impermanent, whatever is impermanent is painful, what was painful has been suppressed, had disappeared...' [The same applies to the rest of the *khandhas*.][9]

Yamaka has learnt the lesson. The only thing of which we have adequate knowledge when a Tathāgata dies is that what was impermanent and painful in him vanishes for ever. We know nothing positive of the Tathāgata's condition after death.

Sāriputta congratulates Yamaka for having learnt the lesson and continues with what he considers basically the main issue, the irreconcilable opposition between the *khandhas* and the self. The simile given to illustrate this point shows a rich man having a treacherous and murderous man as his servant and knowing him not as what he really is but as a friend and companion (*mittato, suhajjato*). The simile obviously applies not to the unreality of the self but to the danger of thinking that the *khandhas* are in league with the self, identified with it, when in realtiy they are the non-self, the irreconcilable enemies of the self. If the conclusion to be drawn is that the self is not real at all, then what is the sense of expressions such as those that occur later on in the same *sutta*, while speaking of the learned ariyan disciple, '*He* (*so*) does not approach the body, does not get hold of the body, does not settle on the body, thinking, "this is my self".' The same is said of the rest of the aggregates. Who is that "he" (*so*) who stubbornly refuses to identify *his self* (*attā*) with the *khandhas*? The same is the case with, 'Those five grasping-aggregates when not approached, not got hold of by him, are conducive to *his* (*tassa*) benefit and welfare for a long time to come'. For whom does that *tassa* stand, but for the one who disowns the *khandhas* as being his self and is the beneficiary of such an action, for the only one who is different from the *khanhdas,* the very self?[10]

The Buddha himself very vehemently repudiates the accusation of being a nihilist in:

> The devas, bhikkhus, together with Indra, Brahmā and Prajāpati, when looking for him, do not find a bhikkhu so liberated in mind [being able to say], 'Here has settled the mind of the Tathāgata'. Why so? I say, bhikkhus that a Tathāgata is untraceable in this very life. Some samaṇas and brāhmaṇas untruly, falsely, mendaciously, baselessly, calumniate me who say that and teach that, saying, 'Gotama the samaṇa is a nihilist (*venayiko*), he teaches the annihilation, destruction, perishing, of the existing (better perhaps, *essential*) being (*sato satassa*)'. When I do not teach so, when I do not say so, those reverend samaṇas and brāhmaṇas untruly, falsely, mendaciously, baselessly, calumniate me saying, 'Gotama the samaṇa is a nihilist, he teaches the annihilation, destruction, perishing of the existing (essential or true) being'. Both previously and at present, I teach pain and the cessation of pain.[11]

We have here a very significant testimony. The repudiation of the calumny that he is a 'nihilist' is very vehemently gainsaid by the Buddha. This means that the calumny was touching the Buddha's system in a very sensitive point. What precisely is this point? The ouset of the conflict, according to this passage, was in the Buddha's teaching of the utter separation of consciousness from the self, a position that, as has already been indicated, is found exclusively in early Buddhism as compared with other systems. This position was hard to swallow not only for his adversaries but also for his followers. The facts to be borne in mind for a right assessment of this passage are the following.

1. The accusation could not be based on the fact that the Buddha did not subscribe to the tenet, 'The Tathāgata exists after death', since he did not subscribe either to the opposite tenet, 'The Tathāgata does not exist after death'.

2. The calumny is here worded as, *sato sattassa ucchedaṁ vināsaṁ vibhavaṁ paññāpeti.* Now, the annihilationist theory was at times worded in a similar way, *santi, bhikkhave, eke samaṇabrāhmaṇā ucchedavādā, sato sattassa ucchedaṁ vināsaṁ vibhavaṁ paññāpenti.*[12] Can we conceive that the Buddha would make such a display of indignation as the one we

have witnessed at the mere allegation that he was an annihilationist from the heretical point of view, that is to say, that he regarded first of all the *khandhas* as the self and that he was consequently saying that the self perished with them? No one could certainly accuse him of identifying the self with the *khandhas,* as he was constantly hammering on the utter difference between the two, even between consciousness and the self, a fact that baffled everyone. Therefore the only possibility left is that he was accused of obliterating the self in man altogether.

3. Yes, we think that from the Buddha's preaching and his insistence on the *anattā* of the *khandhas,* especially of consciousness, his adversaries concluded that he was a *venayiko,* that is to say 'a remover (from *vi-nī*) or obliterator of the self in man'. It may be a subtlety, but one can attribute two different meanings to the words, *sato sattassa ucchedaṁ.* In the annihilationist theory they meant 'the annihilation of the *existing* being', but the Buddha seems to react here as if they meant, 'the suppression of the *true* being'. This Buddha never preached. He only preached the suppression and extermination of the asmimanic self, or what is equivalent the suppression of Pain. It is true that he never proclaimed directly and explicitly the reality of the true self (we shall give the reasons for this below), but obviously he never denied it. He was all against considering the samsaric factors as the self.

4. The *ucchedavāda* supposes that the annihilation of the self takes place at the same time as death, while in the text we are discussing we read, *diṭṭh'ev'āhaṁ, bhikkhave, dhamme ananuvijjo ti vadāmi.* It is therefore evident that the individual in question is not dead, but is proclaimed incomprehensible (*ananuvijjo*) in this very life.

In conclusion, we have to hold that the accusation levelled against the Buddha, as he understood and rejected it, was not precisely that his teaching coincided with the annihilationist theory, but that he emptied man of all his existential value and of all his metaphysical truth. This is what stirred him up to such an emphatic self-defence.

We are provided with two other testimonies which confirm the fact that the Buddha was accused of absolute negativism or nihilism.

We read in the *Dasakanipāto* of the *Aṅguttara:*

This having been said, a certain wanderer said to the householder Vajjiyamāhita, 'Come now, householder, Gotama the samaṇa whose

> praises you utter is a nihilist (*venayiko*), one who does not define anything for certain.
> Here, too, sirs, I speak to your reverences according to truth, 'This is good', has been defined with certainty by the Blessed One; 'This is bad', has been defined with certainty by the Blessed One. The Blessed One who thus defines with certainty what is good and what is bad is not one who does not define anything for certain. No, the Blessed One is not a nihilist or one who does not define anything for certain.[13]

The accusation contained in this text must have been due to the Buddha's attitude of uncompromising refusal to answer the *abyākatā pañhā.* This could very well give his opponent the impression that he was a sceptic, a nihilist, an agnostic, this and his denial of the *khandhas* being the self, as they could not think of any self but the one identified with the *khandhas.* Very fittingly, the householder Vajjiyamāhita, who, we may well suppose, was not conversant with the philosophical subtleties of the sophists, speaks doubtless from experience and asserts that the Buddha who clearly knows and proclaims what is good and what is bad cannot be said to be a nihilist or one who does not define anything for certain.

In the *Aṭṭhakanip*āto of the *Aṅguttara* the Buddha is introduced referring indirectly to the accusation that he was a nihilist. He says that this is true in the moral order where he advocates the annihilation of bad qualities. Is he not telling us in this way that he could in no way be accused of being a nihilist in so far as man's person was concerned? His words are:

> There is, brāhmaṇa, this way, by following which one who were to say, 'Gotama the samaṇa is a nihilist', would be speaking truthfully. Because, I, brāhmaṇa, teach the annihilation of passion. ill-will and confusion; I teach *dhamma* for the annihilation of all sinful and depraved qualities...[14]

TRANSCENDENCE OF THE SELF

We shall introduce this topic by means of a passage, which, if well analysed, will teach us that the condition of emancipation defies description inasmuch as the liberated man has transcended or gone beyond the range of all the ways of desciption at our disposal. The passage contains a dialogue between Sāriputta and Koṭṭhika the Great, the latter being the questioner:

> Friend, after the complete cessation, through detachment, of the six spheres of sensorial contact is there anything else [left]?
> Do not speak like that, friend.
> After the complete cessation... is there nothing else [left]?
> Do not speak like that, friend.
> ...is there and is not there anything else [left]?
> ... neither is there nor is not there anything else [left]?
> Do not speak like that, friend.

Koṭṭhika complains that to all his different questions Sāriputta has given one and the same answer, and he continues:

> Then, friend, how should one see the meaning of this your saying?
> Asking, friend, whether anything is left after the cessation, through detachment, of the six spheres of sensorial contact, one betrays a samsaric obsession where none should be (*appapañcaṁ papañceti*). [The same is asserted of the three other questions.] As long, friend, as the six spheres of sensorial contact run their course, samsaric obsession will be active. As long as the samsaric obsession is active, the course of the six spheres of sensorial contact will continue running. By the complete cessation, through detachment, of the six spheres of sensorial contact, there comes to be cessation of samsaric obsession, the calming down of samsaric obsession.[15]

The meaning of the passage seems to be the following. By the complete cessation, through detachment, of the six spheres of sensorial contact whatever is samsaric ceases to be. But if one wants to know the condition consequent to such cessation, he nullifies, at least mentally, the cessation of whatever is samsaric by projecting his samsaric preoccupations or obsessions on a stage where they have ceased to be once and for all. Whatever he may imagine as a remnant will always be a creation of that sensorial activity that he presupposes to have ceased. Therefore there is an inherent contradiction in his position. The six spheres of sensorial contact and all samsaric obsessions are mutually dependent on each other; there is samsaric obsession only while the six spheres of sensorial contact run their course, and inversely the six spheres of sensorial contact run their course only while samsaric obsessions persist. Therefore, whatever we may try to say of a man after he has brought to an end his samsaric course will be of samsaric origin and exhibit a samsaric character which will contradict the condition where supposedly whatever was samsaric has entirely ceased, never to start again.

MORAL TRANSCENDENCE OF THE SELF

We are told in a number of passages that Māra, the archenemy, is unable to approach those who are perfect or find themselves on the last stages of the way to perfection. This moral unapproachability reflects on the moral level the transcendence that belongs to the self on the metaphysical level.

We have first of all a set of passages where the perfect man is said to become invisible to Māra.

We have already quoted elsewhere the passage where the Buddha tells Mogharāja:

Regard the world as void, Mogharāja, ever mindful,
Uproot the wrong view of the self, thus will you be one who has crossed over death,
The Lord of Death does not see one who thus regards the world.[16]

Other similar passages:

1. Body, feeling, perception, consciousness, whatever is compounded,
   'That I am not, that is not mine', thus he detaches himself therein.
   Looking for him in all places, the hosts of Māra did not find him,
   Who thus detached, secure as to self, has gone beyond all bonds.[17]
2. Knowing this body to be like a bubble of foam,
   Perfectly understanding its mirage-like nature,
   Breaking the flower-tipped arrows of Māra,
   He will go where the King of Death cannot see him.[18]

Other texts tell us that Māra cannot find the way of the perfect ones and cannot approach them:

1. Of those perfect in virtue, abiding in earnestness,
   Freed through perfect wisdom, Māra does not find the way.[19]
2. The whole world is on fire, the whole world is blowing forth flames,
   The whole world is blazing up, the whole world is quaking.
   The unquaking, uninflammable state, not attained by the common

[unlearned] man,
Where there is no approach for Māra, there dwells my passionless mind.[20]

In the *Nivāpasutta of the Majjhima* the following question occurs, 'And how, bhikkhus, is there stoppage on march for Māra and Māra's hosts?'. We are given a complete enumeration of the most perfect practices undertaken by a bhikkhu, namely, the four *jhānas* in succession, followed by the practice of the *vimokkhas,* beginning with the sphere of infinite space, which is beyond all perception of material form. After everyone of those practices it is said:

This is said to be, bhikkhus, a bhikkhu who has made Māra blind, striking the trackless eye of Māra, he has gone where he cannot be seen by the sinful One.

But when it comes to the last *vimokkha,* which as we have remarked several times, is always placed on a different level from the rest, the text adds, to the words quoted, the phrase, *tiṇṇo loke visattikaṁ,* i.e. 'he has crossed over all attachment in the world'.[21]

We have entitled this section, where we have described Māra's bewilderment, and how he is at a loss to discover the perfect man, 'moral transcendence of the self'. We have seen how when a man advances on the way to perfection Māra loses sight of him and is not able to find the way he has gone. Māra is the personification of whatever is samsaric and therefore contrary to *nibbāna.* Māra's harmful activity ca be exercised only through what is empirical and samsaric in man. As soon as a man disengages himself (his self!) from the *khandhas* and the spheres of sensorial contact, Māra finds it impossible to make contact with him. We have another instance of the metaphysical transcendence of the self regarding the *khandhas,* the spheres of sensorial contact, etc., being reflected on the moral level and becoming the determinant factor of the moral order. Whatever tends to assert the absolute independence of the self from the empirical factors is morally good, and whatever moves in the opposite direction is morally wrong.

It is important to note that those people who become invisible to Māra, and whose path Māra is unable to find are people still alive, whose peripheral adjuncts, the *khandhas,* Māra is able to see. This proves that there is in man more than meets the eye. When a man has reached emancipation and is still alive, Māra can see whatever is empirical and samsaric in him, but the liberated man, as liberated, cannot be seen by Māra. Where is man's personality? Is it in what Māra can see or in what Māra cannot see in the perfect man? And if what can be seen by Māra is the non-self, what else will that be that Māra cannot see in the perfect man but the self?

We find at least two passages where Māra is described, not without a certain touch of humour, being all puzzled, running in all directions in search of the consciousness (*viññāṇa*) of a bhikkhu who had attained *nibbāna* after having taken his own life. In both the passages, one referring to Godhika and the other to Vakkhali, the dialogue is the same. The Buddha and his accompanying bhikkhus see a smoky cloud moving here and there. The Buddha makes the following disclosure:

> Do you see, bhikkhus, that smoky cloud going to the east, going to the west, going to the north, going to the south, going upwards, going downwards, going in the intemediate directions?
>
> Yes, Lord.
>
> It is Māra the Evil One; he is looking for the *viññāṇa* of Godhika the clansman, thinking, 'Where has the consciousness of Godhika the clansman established itself? But, bhikkhus with consciousness established nowhere, Godhika the clansman has attained complete *nibbāna*'.[22]

This confirms what has been said above that Māra can see only what is empirical in man, and it is only through what is empirical that his bad influence on man can be exerted. Mark also the positive statement made by the Buddha regarding Godhika *the man*. 'With consciousness established nowhere Godhika the clansman has attained complete *nibbāna.*' Consciousness (*viññāṇa*) is reputed here, as in other passages of the Nikāyas, to be the highest resort of the non-self. Only when consciousness has been entirely eliminated can we be sure that the non-self has been eliminated. But with his former consciousness eliminated, and being therefore impossible for it to establish itself anywhere, Godhika, *the person,* has attained complete *nibbāna.* What is that regarding which the individual Godhika has attained complete *nibbāna,* once the non-self in him has been eliminated?

METAPHYSICAL TRANSCENDENCE OF THE SELF

The metaphysical transcendence of the self has already been hinted at in the previous section through the statement of its moral transcendent, specially in the last passage of those quoted there. Now we shall apply ourselves to those passages where the metaphysical transcendence of the self is taught by positing the fact of the ineffability and incomprehensibility of the liberated man as such.

As an introduction to this topic we shall produce a testimony, according to which, as soon as an individual enters into the path that leads out of the empirical world his person begins to be surrounded by a halo of mystery,

> The course of those whose range of activity is the deliverance of the void and the signless,
> Is as difficult to follow as the course of the birds in the sky.
> The path of him whose range of activity is the deliverance of the void and the signless,
> Is as difficult to follow as the path of the birds in the sky.[23]

While flying in the sky, the birds leave no track, following which one may spot them or overtake them. In a similar way, the man who follows the way that leads out of what is empirical becomes untraceable by all samsaric standards.

Independently from the conditions that lead to existence and reincarnation there can be no way of talking of the individual or defining him. In the *Mahānidānasutta* of the *Dīgha* we are told first that:

> This is the reason, this is the root-cause, this is the origin, this is the condition of name-and-form, to wit this consciousness.

And a little below:

> Therefore, Ānanda, this is the reason, this is the root-cause, this is the origin, this is the condition of consciousness, to wit this name-and-form. In so far, Ānanda, can one be born, or grow old, or die, or fall from one existence, or arise again, in so far arc there ways of verbal explanation, in so far are there ways of verbal expression, in so far are there ways of verbal designation, in so far is there a realm of knowledge, in so far the round of existence runs its course for the manifestation [of an individual] in these conditions, in as far as name-and-form together with consciousness are active in reciprocally being the condition for becoming of one another.

The text proceeds to give illustrations of how one can go on defining the self, (a thing that according to the words just quoted is possible only when the individual forms part of the samsaric process), and the examples given are: to define the self as corporeal and limited, as corporeal and unlimited, as incorporeal and limited, as incorporeal and unlimited, definitions or delimitations that can apply to the present or to the future. Then the text gives instances of how one can regard the self as feeling or as unperceiving. The opinion that the self can be identified with feeling is refuted by saying that there are three kinds of feeling: pleasant, unpleasant and neither pleasant nor unpleasant. While the self is identified with one of them it cannot at the same time be the other two. Besides, feelings are impermanent, compounded, arising in dependence on some conditions of a nature to be destroyed and fade away, of a nature to inspire one with detachment, of a nature to cease. Nothing that has got those qualities can be the self, as it has been repeated to satiety in the sacred texts, those are qualities that apply to the non-self. If the self is identified with some feeling, when that feeling vanishes, one will be obliged to say, '*byagā me attā*', 'my self has vanished'. If the reasoning here has to make any sense, the underlying supposition is the absurdity of conceiving the self as apt to disappear or discontinue being the self. There remains the opinion of one who might say: 'My self is not feeling, my self is unperceiving'. The inconsistency of such assertion is shown by pointing out that the very saying: 'My self is not feeling, my self is unperceiving', is a feeling and perception in itself, therefore the assertion nullifies itself, since the supposition here is that feeling and perception are entirely absent. There occurs again a passage teaching that it would not be proper to attribute the assertions contained in the unanswered questions to one who refuses to regard the self either as feeling or unperceiving and is therefore emancipated. One who is emancipated is free from those expressions that require for their genesis a samsaric condition in the one who utters them and in the one to whom they apply. All the same, the fact that a liberated bhikkhu does not answer the unanswered questions does not prove him to be an ignorant individual, for he has been freed from such samsaric illusions through insight.

> Now when a bhikkhu, Ānanda, does not regard feeling as the self, does not regard the self as unperceiving, does not hold the opinion that, 'My self perceives, because my self is perceiving by nature'. He, abstaining from such opinions, is not attached to anything in the world. Being detached he is not troubled. Being untroubled, he attains *nibbāna* as re-

gards his very self. He knows, 'Destroyed is birth, lived is the brahmalife, done is what was to be done, there will be no more living in such conditions'. And regarding the bhikkhu, Ānanda, whose mind is thus released, if anyone should say, 'The Tathāgata exists after death, such is his view', that is not proper; 'The Tathāgata does not exist after death, such is his view', that is not proper; 'The Tathāgata both exists and does not exist after death, such is his view', that is not proper; 'The Tathāgata both neither exists nor does not exist after death, such is his view', that is not proper. What is the reason for that? Whatever expression or ways of verbal expression are there, whatever explanation or ways of verbal explanation are there, whatever designation or ways of verbal designation are there, whatever knowledge or sphere of knowledge are there, whatever round of existence goes on, from all that the bhikkhu is set free by insight. To say of the bhikkhu who is set free from all that by insight, 'He does not know, he does not see', is not proper.[24]

Coming to passages that deal explicitly with the indefinable character of the self, we begin with:

Knowing thoroughly health, by the destruction of the *āsavas,*
A deliberate practitioner staunch in *dhamma,* a sage, is no more a subject of designation.[25]

We meet in the *Itivuttaka* with a very clear and explicit exposition of this truth in a group of *ślokas* that end with the same last line of the previous passage,

Beings who are obsessed by what can be named, taking their stand in what can be named,
Ignorant of what can be named, they enter into contact with the Lord of Death.
One who having perfectly known what can be named, does not build conceits regarding the name-giver,
Has with his mind attained deliverance, the unsurpassed abode of peace.
He, in mastery of what can be named, calm, addicted to the abode of peace,
A deliberate practioner, staunch in *dhamma,* he, a sage, is no more a subject of designation.[26]

In this text, *akkheyya,* 'what can be named', stands for whatever is samsaric and can therefore be expressed by a name.

Twice at least, the simile of the flame is used to illustrate this point.

Even as the fire that burns in a mass of iron being hammered,
When gradually subsiding, its destiny is not known,
Even so the destiny cannot be explained,
Of those who have crossed the flood of sensual fetters, of those who have attained to happiness immovable.[27]

The *Suttanipāta* provides us with a rather detailed exposition of the subject in hand. Words are being exchanged between Upasīva and the Buddha. The dialogue proceeds in the following way:

If he were to stay thus, entirely unattached,
For many years, O seer of all,
If thus precisely he were to stay cooled, emancipated,
Would the consciousness of such be reborn?

The Buddha's answer does not apply directly to *viññāṇa* but to the *muni* himself:

As a flame scattered at the onset of the wind,
Goes to extinction and is no more a subject of designation,
Even so, the wise, freed from body and name,
Goes to extinction and is no more a subject of designation (*na upeti saṅkhaṁ*).[28]

We should not forget that, according to the mentality of the time, fire was not annihilated at the extinction of the flame, it merely became invisible by being reincorporated into the original cosmic element called fire.[29] The words *atthaṁ paleti,* 'goes into extinction'; are explained in the *Culla-niddesa* in two ways:

1. When they apply to the flame they are said to mean, 'it goes to concealment, it disapperas, it ceases, it subsides, it is allayed'.
2. When they apply to the *muni,* they are explained as, 'he entirely free from samsaric encumbrances attains *nibbāna* by means of the element of *nibbāna*'.

The words *na upeti saṅkhaṁ* are interpreted:

1. In the case of the flame as, 'there is no reason, no condition, no cause, by which it could be designated as: gone in the eastern direction, or gone in the western direction, or gone in the northern direction, or gone in the southern direction, or gone upwards, or gone downwards, or gone horizontally, or gone in an intermediate direction.'

2. In the case of the *muni* as, 'there is no reason, no condition, no cause, by which he should be designated a kṣatriya, or a brāhmaṇa, or a vaiśya, or a śūdra, or a householder, or one who has renounced the world, or god, or man, or corporeal, or incorporeal, or conscious, or unconscious, or neither conscious nor unconscious.[30]

One who has attained *nibbāna* is beyond description, since the samsaric factors that would condition him, qualify him, give him a name or a designation, have been annulled. But such a way of speaking implicitly accepts that there is *someone* who is beyond description or beyond our present categories of thought. Upasīva does not yet see things clearly, so he asks:

He thus gone into extinction, does he not exist,
Or is he for ever rid of disease?
Explain that well to me, O sage,
For thus is this *dhamma* seen by you.

From the wording of the question we can deduce that the phrase 'gone into extinction' (*atthaṅgato*) does not necessarily mean annihilated, since in Upasīva's mind it stands either for the self of the annihilationists or for the self of the eternalists. Since Upasīva is not a Buddhist we must apply to him the exegetical principle established in the previous chapter, according to which, he will be wholly subject to the influence of the *sakkāyadiṭṭhi.* Thus the two alternatives given by him in his question are reduced to the annihilationist and the eternalist views.[31]

The Buddha replies:

There is no way to measure (*na pamānam 'atthi*) one who has gone into extinction,
That, by which they would speak of him, does not exist in his case,
When all the *dhammas* have been swept away,
All the ways of talking have been removed.[32]

The annihilationist and eternalist views apply to the liberated self, after death, concepts drawn from our empirical life. The Buddha is of opinion that it is impossible to say anything truthful and meaningful of one who has attained *nibbāna,* for the only points of reference we ever have to speak of a person, which are the *kilesas,* the *khandhas* and all composite attributes (*abhisaṅkhārā*) have been deleted in his case.[33] This confirms what was pointed out above that the real middle way between eternalism and annihilationism is not 'absolute *anattā*' but 'absolute transcendence'. The stanza has been worded in such a way as to suggest that we are dealing here with a higher and indefinable reality *in man,* which being free from all samsaric qualities can in no way become the subject of discussion as to what its nature is. That highest and undefinable reality is expressed in the most general way by *naṁ* and *tassa* in the second line of the stanza last quoted: 'That by which they would speak of him (*naṁ vajjuṁ*), does not exist in his case (*tassa*)'. One thing is clearly indicated by *naṁ* and *tassa,* that the highest and indefinable reality in man is a person, not a thing. We do not see how the doctrine of absolute *anattā* can account for such personal reality, which appears in the context as the nirvanic continuity of the *muni,* a continuity that persists even after the discontinuity of the samsaric line of existence of the *muni.* Therefore we shall have to distinguish between 'absolute extinction' that would apply to man as a whole, and 'relative extinction' that will apply to whatever is samsaric in man. If that extinction were an absolute one, then there would be emancipation without anyone being emancipated, a way of thinking alien to the Nikāyas, as anyone can see from the passage of the *Suttanipāta* just analysed. And we ask again, 'If what is extinguished in an absolute way is only what the sacred texts call the non-self, what else can the nirvanic reality of man be but the self of the individual in question?'

The wanderer Vacchagotta goes to visit the venerable Sabhiya of the Kaccānas. He questions Sabhiya about the four alternatives of existence or non-existence of the Tathāgata after death. To everyone of the four questions Sabhiya gives the same answer, 'This has not been answered or revealed by the Blessed One'. Then Vacchagotta asks:

What is the reason, friend Kaccāna, what is the cause, why this has not been revealed by Gotama the samaṇa?

That which would be the reason to describe him as corporeal or incorporeal, as conscious or unconscious, or neither conscious nor unconscious, that reason and that cause have been entirely obliterated in every respect and without remnant. How then would one keep on defining him as corporeal or incorporeal, as conscious or unconscious, or as neither conscious nor unconscious?

How long is it since you renounced the world, friend Kaccāna?

Not long, friend, three years.

> That much of knowledge should be considered great in the case of one who got it in such short time. What kind of talk can there be as regards one who has thus transcended (*evaṁ abhikkante*) [all ways of expression][34]

The question cannot be more clearly exposed than it is in this passage. The reality, in its own order, of the emanicipated man is never brought into question. We are told that we cannot state such a person to be existent or non-existent, because existence or non-existence have to be of a definite kind, we cannot speak of an abstract existence or non-existence. This is like saying that existence and non-existence are empirical concepts which ought to be qualified by some modes of existence or non-existence. But those factors by which the existence or non-existence of the Tathāgata after death could be made definite and concrete have been utterly destroyed for ever. The passage assumes that we would have to conceive the existing Tathāgata, after death, either as corporeal or incorporeal, either as conscious or unconscious, but those factors which make it possible for us to make such qualifications regarding the existence of an individual are nowhere found in the case of the Tathāgata, after his death. The Tathāgata after death is thus beyond description, and that is what the last question really means, '*ko pana vādo evaṁ abhikkante*?'

The ineffability of the self is asserted also by expressions that apply to the Tathāgata the attribute of immeasurability. The most significant passage to this effect is the following one, where king Pasenadi comes to the bikkhunī Khemā and asks her the four standard questions about the existence or non-existence of the Tathāgata after death. The answer is in every case the customary one. Tired of hearing the same answer to his different questions, king Pasenadi asks:

> And what is the reason, lady, what is the cause, why this has not been revealed by the Blessed One?

Khemā replies with two counter-questions to which the king is bound to give a negative answer. She asks the king whether he has got an accountant capable to count the grains of sand in the Ganges or the water contained in the ocean. When the king has replied negatively to the second question, Khemā, in her turn, asks:

> And what is the reason for that?
>
> The ocean, lady, is great, deep, immeasurable, unfathomable.

> Even so, mahārāja, that bodily form by which one wanting to define the Tathāgata, would define him, has been abandoned by the Tathāgata, destroyed from the root, made like unto a stump of palm-tree never to arise again in future. Emancipated from designation as body, mahārāja, the Tathāgata is great, deep, immeasurable, unfathomable, even as the ocean. [Therefore] 'the Tathāgata exists after death', does not apply here; 'the Tathāgata does not exist after death', does not apply here; etc.

The king approaches then the Buddha with the same questions, and the Buddha imparts to him the same teaching as the one imparted by Khemā.[35]

The Tathāgata is contemplated here as someone whose reality, even after death, is never denied, but who is all the same beyond our categories of thought. And as we have indicated at the beginning of this chapter, the incomprehensibility of the Tathāgata in these texts is equivalent to the incomprehensibility of the emancipated self or the self in its metaphysical reality.[36]

Several other texts speak also of the immeasurability of the emancipated self:

2. Bow your heads to these and other Paccekabuddhas,
   Of great majesty, with the roots of becoming extirpated,
   Those great sages, who gone beyond all attachment,
   Have attained nibbāna and are *immeasurable* (*appameyye*).[37]
2. Salutation to those great sages, the wise ones, who have crossed the thicket [of *saṁsāra*],
   Who in a greedy world dwell free from longing,
   Those who tearing death's net, the strong net spread out by the deceitful one,
   Proceed, having destroyed all clinging. Who would measure their destiny? (*ko tesaṁ gati māpaye*?)[38]

3. Finally, in a passage of the *Vimānavatthu,* Upatissa is called, '*nibbutaṁ appameyyaṁ*'[39] and in another passage of the same book, where a meritorious deed is descibed, which consists in paying homage to the Buddha's remains, the Buddha is called '*parinibbuto appameyyo*'.[40]

Another way of expressing the same idea is to emphasize that not even the gods can see one who has attained *nibbāna.*

He whose destiny (*gati*) is unknown to devas, *gandhabbas* and men,

One who has destroyed the *āsavas,* an arahant, him do I call a brāmaṇa.[41]

Even the Buddha himself is denied the faculty to see of what nature is the destiny of one who has attained *nibbāna*:

The woman who brought up with care the last body of the sage,
The renowned Gotamī, attained to peace, like a star at the rising of the sun.
Having acquired the title of 'mother of the Buddha', she went to utter calmness,
Where not even the 'Five-eyed-One', the Leader, sees the outcome (*gatiṁ dakkhati*).[42]

Even the Buddha with his multiple and miraculous power of vision could not see the individual who had entered into *nibbāna.* The Buddha, with all his matchless qualities, while still on earth, was 'this side' of reality, where there was nothing hidden from him, but the mysterious reality that is beyond was not the object of his vision. He could come to know when a person had entered *nibbāna* after death and the texts abound in announcements of this type, but from the moment a person was fully emancipated from samsāra, and went into *nibbāna,* that person was beyond the power of vision of the Buddha. This does not mean that the reality of such a person had come to an end, even as the star that becomes invisible at the rising of the sun (using the metaphor provided to us by the very text we are commenting), does not thereby lose its reality. If the person was real before entering *nibbāna,* it continues being real after that, only in an absolute way, with a reality that has escaped all conditions of existence and becoming, and is therefore incomprehensible for us.

After the discussion of the preceding texts, where we are told that the perfect man ascends to a transcendent order of reality, we ought to reflcct that his holds not only of people that enter into *parinibbāna* after death, but also of those who are still alive, but have suppressed all reasons for a new becoming. In the latter case, the ineffability of which we have so often spoken applies obviously to some reality of the individual involved, but since it does not apply to the empirical reality, there must be in the individual in question a mysterious, hidden reality which is the one that is ineffable. What reality can there be in an individual besides the non-self, which as we know comprehends whatever is empirical in man, but *the self,* which by nature is metempirical and thus indescribable? We have met in this book with a number of facts that were pointing in this direction and now we find ourselves face to face with the fact itself that the self, being the innermost reality in man, is something that exceeds our own power of comprehension while we peregrinate through *samsāra*. Man is thus, while he is in this world, an existential paradox, a metaphysical mystery that cannot be gauged by man himself. Such is the original view of man transmitted to us by the earliest Buddhist records.

It cannot be denied that other systems also recognize the ineffability of the individual who has attained to his or her highest destiny,[43] but not with the same radicality as that of early Buddhism. This radicality derives from the fact that early Buddhism places consciousness, all types of consciousness, in the category of non-self. This means to say that whatever kind of denomination we may try to apply to the metaphysical self carries with it the taint of empiricality which makes it absolutely antagonistic to the true nature of the self and therefore, not applicable to it. Hence, all the descriptions of the self found in the Nikāyas are negative, telling us what the self is not, never what the self is. This goes to an extreme, where concepts as general as existence and non-existence are excluded from predication about the self in the *abyākatā pañhā*. The concept of existence and its negation are considered inbued with a samsaric overtone that is out of place when the self is considered in the state of emancipation. In the same way, to say that the emancipated self is conscious is as inadmissible as to say that it is unconscious. Consciousness and unconsciousness are empirical ideas which do not apply to the metempirical self.[44] This is not negative agnosticism, but positive transcendentalism. It is not negative agnosticism, because it is not of a nature to exercise a paralysing influence in man. It is positive transcendentalism, because all the dynamics of early Buddhism are directed towards the arduous task of doing away with what is not the self, precisely because it is not the self, in order to achieve a transcendental emancipation which brings the self to its own, beyond the realm of all samsaric experiences.

THE *abyākatā pañhā* AND THE *sakkāyadiṭṭhi*

There is another aspect of the topic under discussion that cannot be neglected, the intimate relationship between the *abyākatā pañhā* and the *sakkāyadiṭṭhi,* and therefore the ultimate presupposition inherent in them that the self is identified with the peripheral factors in man. We find here recurring again the polarity existing between the self and the non-self, which is the constant theme of the Nikāyas. This was to be expected, for, as it has been pointed out more than once, the *sakkāyadiṭṭhi* is a fundamental *diṭṭhi* found at the root of all other *diṭṭhis*. Hence the view that trying to answer the *abyākatā pañhā* is not only an idle effort, but also spiritually harmful, as it is an upshot of *asmimāna* and fosters it.

The affinity between the *abyākatā pañhā* and the *sakkāyadiṭṭhi* is made explicit in several scriptural texts.

Koṭṭhika the Great approaches Sāriputta with the four standard unanswered questions, to which Sāriputta gives the customary answers. Koṭṭhika asks further:

> What is the cause, friend, what is the reason why this has not been explained by the Blessed One?
>
> To say that the Tathāgata exists after death is to depend on body. [The same applies to the other three alternatives.] To say that the Tathāgata exists after death is to depend on feeling,... is to depend on perception,... is to depend on the inner complexes,... is to depend on consciousness. [All this applies to the other alternatives also.] This is the cause this is the reason why this has not been explained by the Blessed One.[45]

'To depend on body, feeling, etc.', has a double meaning. Firstly that one who proposes the questions or tries to answer them will do it moved by the spirit of the *sakkāyadiṭṭhi.* Secondly that one who speaks in that way supposes the Tathāgata to be essentially identified with the *khandhas.*

In the next *sutta,* to the same question of Koṭṭhika, Sāriputta answers:

> By not knowing, friend, by not seing body as it really is; by not knowing... the arisal of body as it really is;... the cessation of body...; ... the way that leads to the cessation of body as it really is, one holds the view, 'the Tathāgata exists after death', or 'the Tathāgata does not exist after death', etc. [The same reasoning applies to the other *khandhas.* Then the opposite case is explained 'By knowing, friend, by seing body as it really is..., this view does not occur...'][46]

The *suttas* that follow are composed on a similar pattern and refer the holding of the fourfold view about the Tathāgata after death to the influence of the *khandhas,* expressed in several ways:

> When one has not got rid of attachment for the body, of desire for the body, of affection for the body, of the fever of passion for the body, of craving for the body, then he holds the view, 'the Tathāgata exists after death', etc. [The same reasoning is applied to the rest of the *khandhas.*][47]

The opposite case is also described of one who has got rid of attachment, etc., for the body, etc., and does not hold those views.

> When one rejoices in the body, is in love with the body, takes delight in the body, does not know, does not see as it really is the cessation of the body, one holds the view, 'the Tathāgata exists after death', etc. [The same reasoning applies to the other *khandhas.*]

The opposite case is described in a similar way as before.[48] The 'spiritual' harm caused by any willful attention paid to the unanswered questions is clearly expounded in this *sutta.* The *sutta* begins with a reference to the full hearted acceptance of the *khandhas,* found in the man who busies himself with the *abyākatā pañhā,* it goes on describing such a man as one who takes delight and rejoices in *bhava* (samsaric becoming) and is therefore unable even to dream of emancipation. After that, such a man is said to rejoice in grasping (*upādāna*), which constitutes the fuel on which the flame of becoming is being fed; not for nothing the *khanhdas* are often called *pañcupādānakhandhā.* Finally such a man is shown as delighting in *taṇhā* (existential craving), the most glaring manifestation of the asmimanic spirit. One who mentally busies himself with the unanswered questions, not only projects his samsaric mentality beyond the proper limits to no useful purpose, but also, all at once, betrays in the first place a wholehearted attachment to becoming (*bhava*), which binds him within the existential cycle of births and deaths, ever under the influence of samsaric grasping (*upādāna*) and craving (*taṇhā*).

We arrive at the same conclusion through the analysis of a passage in the *Paṭisambhidāmagga.*

1. As regards, 'the Tathāgata exists after death', we are told, 'the body in this case is considered mortal by nature. The Tathāgata after the dissolution of the body exists and endures, arises and is reborn'. The same applies to the rest of the *khandhas,* for instance, 'Consciousness in this case is mortal by nature. The Tathāgata after the dissolution of the body exists

and endures, arises and is reborn'. The author presumes that those who try to answer the *abyākatā pañhā* describe the destiny of the perfect man in terms of samsaric existence and rebirth. Here the wrong assumption does not consist so much in the identification of the Tathāgata with the *khandhas* as in the impossibility of conceiving the Tathāgata without them. The *khandhas* in this case are considered mortal by nature, but after death, the Tathāgata continues a kind of rebirth existence, which will not come to pass without the assumption of a new set of *khandhas.*

2. As regards, 'the Tathāgata does not exist after death', we are told, 'the body in this case is considered mortal by nature. The Tathāgata after the dissolution of the body is annihilated, perishes, does not exist after death'. (The same is applicable to the rest of the *khandhas.*)

3. As regards 'the Tathāgata both exists and does not exist after death', we are told, 'the body in this case is mortal by nature. The Tathāgata after the dissolution of the body exists and does not exist...' (The same applies to the rest of the *khandhas.*)

4. The elaboration of the fourth alternative is similar to that of the third one.[49]

The wording of the passage clearly indicates that the body is taken to be the substratum of all other *khandhas.* Thus although we are told 'feeling is considered here mortal by nature', we are not immediately told, 'the Tathāgata after the dissolution of feeling...', but 'the Tathāgata after the dissolution of the body...'. Such is the case also with the rest of the *khanhdas.*

From what precedes we conclude that the answer given to the *abyākatā pañhā* rests ultimately against the assumption of the identity between the self and the *khandhas.* This is explicitly stated in *sutta* 7 of the *Abyākatasaṁyutta.* Vacchagotta comes to Moggallāna the Great and after the customary questions about the *abyākatā pañhā* and the customary answer to all of them, Vacchagotta asks Moggallāna for the reason why the wanderers of other faiths give a definite answer to those queries. He is told that it is because the wanderers of other faiths regard the senses as 'This is mine, this I am, this is my self', while the Tathāgata does not think so. Vacchagotta then goes to the Buddha, who confirms word by word the answer given him by Moggallāna.[50]

In the following *sutta* the reason given for the difference between the wanderers of other views and the Buddha is given as:

> They regard the body as the self, regard the self as having a body, regard the body in the self, or the self as being in the body. [The same applies to the rest of the *khandhas*.][51]

Let us close this section by the remark already so often made, due to its importance, that we are faced here again by what we have termed 'the central theme in Nikayan Buddhism', viz. the ontological separation, and the clear discernment of such separation that the skilful practitioner should exercise, between the self and the empirical factors, i.e. the non-self.

REASONS FOR KEEPING THE *abyākatā pañhā* UNANSWERED

The general and fundamental reason why the *abyākatā pañhā* are left unanswered is that they constitute a series of speculative and 'spiritually' harmful opinions, called *diṭṭhis*.

> On account of the cessation of all views (*diṭṭhinirodhā*), bhikkhu, there arises no doubt concerning the unanswered questions for the instructed ariyan disciple. 'The Tathāgata exists after death', this is a matter of view (*diṭṭhigataṁ*). [The same is asserted of the other three alternatives.] The unlearned common man has no discernment as regards view, the arising of view, the cessation of view, the way leading to the cessation of view. For him view thrives, he is not freed from birth, old-age, death, sorrow, lamentations, etc., he is not freed from Pain, so I declare. But the instructed ariyan disciple has discernment as regards view, the arising of view, etc. For him view is destroyed, he is freed from birth, old-age, etc., he is freed from Pain, so I declare. Knowing thus, bhikkhu, the instructed ariyan disciple does not declare, 'the Tathāgata exists after death', does not declare, 'the Tathāgata does not exist after death', etc. Knowing thus, bhikkhu, seing thus, the instructed ariyan disciple is by character one who does not answer anything to the unanswered questions. Knowing thus, seing thus, bhikkhus, the instructed ariyan disciple is not afraid, is not shaken, does not quiver, is not a prey to fear regarding the unanswered questions.[52]

Then as regards everyone of the unanswered questions it is declared that they are *taṇhāgataṁ* ('a matter of craving'), *saññāgataṁ* ('a matter of perception'), *maññitagataṁ* ('a matter of conceit'), *papañcitagataṁ* ('a matter of samsaric illusion'), *upādānagātaṁ* ('a matter of existential grasping'), *vippaṭisāragataṁ* ('a matter of remorse'). The idleness of these views and their capacity to do 'spiritual' harm are intertwined.

The most interesting text in this respect in the *Cūḷamālukyasutta* of the *Majjhima.* The bhikkhu Mālukya calls the unanswered questions: *ṭhapitāni* ('set aside'), *paṭikkhitāni* ('rejected'). Mālukya is not satisified with such reticence on Buddha's part and decides that either he will obtain a definite answer to those questions from the Buddha or he will leave the Order. He approaches the Buddha with this grievance and rather bluntly opens his mind to him.

> If the Blessed One knows that the world is eternal let him tell me that it is eternal; if the Blessed One knows that the world is not eternal let him tell me that it is not eternal; if the Blessed One does not know whether the world is eternal or not eternal, then, since he does not know, since he does not see, the honest thing to do will be to say, 'I don't know, I don't see'.

The same is repeated of all and everyone of the unanswered questions. The Buddha makes Mālukya confess that he did not seek admittance to the Order on condition that he should be given an answer to those questions, nor did the Buddha promise him such a thing if he joined the Order. Then comes the parable of the man pierced with an arrow smeared with poison. His relatives and friends would be for calling a physician and surgeon, while the sick man would ask not for one but for many items of information difficult to obtain and quite irrelevant to the case, saying that he would not have the arrow extracted until all that information was given him. The protractedness of the simile is doubtless meant to be a literary contrast with the urgency of the case. It reminds one of the unending discussions held on these points by other wanderers, who thereby neglected what was more urgent and of primary importance, the application of the practical remedies that would cause man to be emancipated from existential Pain. The simile ends with the words, '(since) that would remain assuredly unknown to him, therefore that man would die'. The application of the simile reads:

> In this very way, Mālukhyaputta, if anyone were to express himself thus, 'I shall not undertake to live the brahma-life under the Blessed One,

> unless the Blessed One were to explain to me whether the world is eternal or not, etc., etc., [since] that would remain assuredly unknown to him, therefore that man would die.

Note the contrast between physical and moral harm, so often singled out in the first part of the book. One thing is clear, Buddha was absolutely determined never to answer any of those questions. The text continues saying that it is absurd that anyone should condition the undertaking of the brahma-life to any *diṭṭhi* offered him as acceptable to the Buddha, when he would react in the same way even if the opposite view were offered him as acceptable to the Blessed One. And whether one *diṭṭhi* or another is accepted as true, the incontrovertible fact in every case will be that:

> There is birth, there is old-age, there is death, there are: sorrow, lamentations, pain, mental uneasiness, tribulations, the destruction of which in this very life I announce.

This reasoning is applied to all the *abyākatā pañhā.* The final conclusion is:

> Therefore, Mālukyaputta, hold as unexplained what has been left unexplained by me, and hold as explained what has been explained by me. And what, Mālukyaputta, has been left unexplained by me? 'That the world is eternal' has been left unexplained by me; 'That the world is not eternal' has been left unexplained by me, etc., etc. And why, Mālukyaputta, has this been left unexplained by me? This, Mālukyaputta, is not connected with the goal, it does not belong to the beginning of the brahma-life, it is not conducive to disgust, to detachment, to cessation, to appeasement, to higher knowledge, to illumination, to *nibbāna.*
> And what, Mālukyaputta, has been explained by me? 'This is pain' has been explained by me; 'This is the arisal of pain' has been explained by me; 'This is the cessation of pain' has been explained by me; 'This is the way conducive to the cessation of pain' has been explained by me. And why, Mālukyaputta, this has been explained by me? This, Mālukyaputta, is connected with the goal, this belongs to the beginning of the brahma-life, etc., etc.[53]

The points made clear in this sutta are: (1) The urgency of, and the priority given to, the problem of existential Pain, which the Buddha teaches man to solve in this very life. (2) The irrelevance of any theoretical question as contrasted with this existential problem or the search for its solution. (3)

To indulge in the discussion of those questions or *diṭṭhis* is not only useless, because it distracts the mind from the most important and pressing problem, but also spritually harmful. The negative way of talking in, 'This is not connected with the goal..., it is not conducive to... *nibbāna*', so typical of the Nikāyas, does not convey the mere absence of 'spiritual' profit, but the presence of positive 'spiritual' harm. 'Not being conducive to *nibbāna*' is equivalent to 'leading away from *nibbāna*'.

In the *Aggivacchagottasutta* of the *Majjhima* the same reasons are given for withholding the answer to the *abyākatā pañhā,* but they are given in the broader context of the danger inherent in all *diṭṭhis.* Vacchagotta comes to the Buddha and asks of him whether he is of opinion (*evaṅdiṭṭhi*) that the world is eternal, etc. To everyone of the questions, the Buddha answers, 'No Vaccha, I am not of this opinion'. Then the wanderer asks:

> What danger does your reverence see so as not to accept any of these views?

The Buddha replies:

> 'The world is eternal', this, Vaccha, is a matter of speculative view, the thicket of views, the wilderness of views, the restlessness of views, the turbulence of views, the fetter of views, accompanied by pain, vexation, unrest, the fever of attachment; it is not conducive to disgust, to detachment, to cessation, to higher wisdom, to illumination, to *nibbāna.*

The same thing is repeated regarding every question. The dialogue continues:

> But has the good Gotama any speculative view?
>
> Speculative view has been cast off by the Tathāgata. This is what has been seen[54] by the Tathāgata, 'Such is the body, such is the rising, of the body, such is the destruction of the body; such is feeling...; such is perception...; such are the inner complexes...; such is consciousness, such is the rising of consciousness, such is the destruction of consciousness'. That is why the Tathāgata, by the destruction of all conceits, of all vain imaginings, of all proclivity to the conceit of 'I' and 'mine', by detachment, by cessation, by renunciation, by rejection, is emancipated without any grasping, so I say.[55]

It is then evident that any effort to hold any of the *abyākatā pañhā* is, in the opinion of early Buddhism, an exercise not only in futility but also in *asmimāna,* the vice more emphatically condemned in the Nikāyas.

The refusal to answer the *abyākatā pañhā* is no sign of agnosticism but of higher wisdom. This is asserted in a passage of the *Aṅguttara,* where the wanderer Kokanuda happened to meet Ānanda when both were going for the morning bath. After ascertaining that Ānanda was a follower of the Buddha, Kokanuda asked him whether he held any of the unanswered questions. Ānanda's answer to everyone of them was the same, 'Friend, I do not hold this opinion'. From that the wanderer jumps to the conclusion that Ānanda does not know anything, does not see anything. Ānanda replies that it is not so, that he knows and sees. Asked to explain how can this be, Ānanda replies stating of everyone of the questions that it belongs to the realm of opinion or wrong view (*diṭṭhigataṁ*). Then he proceeds:

> In what concerns the realm of opinion, in what concerns the condition of opinion, the obstinacy of opinion, the bias of opinion, the arisal of opinion, the rooting up of opinion, that I know, that I see. Knowing that, seing that, how can I say, 'I don't know, I don't see'? I know, friend, I see.[56]

That early Buddhism was no agnostic system is borne out by such emphatic assertions as:

> Truth is one, without a second,[57] and
> There are not many divers truths.[58]

The real sage is one who has transcended all discussions and dwells in perfect possession of *the truth.* He has been liberated by that truth and has therefore established himself high above the plane where different opinions, spring, differ and contend.

> A bhikkhu whose mind is thus liberated, Aggivesana, does not agree or disagree with anyone (*na kenaci saṁvadati, na kenaci vivadati*), he makes use of expressions common in the world but without being attached to them.[59]

A final and important remark before we close this chapter. We came to the conclusion that the Buddha's attitude regarding the self was not one of absolute negativism, but one of positve transcendentalism. In the course of the book we have often faced the fact that any positive assertion of the existence of the self, and even its explicit denial, are considered *diṭṭhigataṁ,* that is to say, a way of thinking entirely un-Buddhistic, motivated by the natural tendency to identify the self with the empirical factors, liable to foster *asmimāna* with an undue preoccupation with self and attachment to existence, sure to divert man's attention from the most pressing task, all these being necessary concomitants of the *diṭṭhi* spirit. In the present chapter we have concerned ourselves with the problem of the Tathāgata after death, agreeing with the commentators that Tathāgata in this context stands for the ultimate reality in man, for the self. We have been told that to say of him he exists or does not exist[60] after death is a *diṭṭhi,* and therefore the result of a mentality that identifies the self with the samsaric factors, constituting besides a meaningless attempt, as it would have a merely speculative value. The Tathāgata after death has crossed the utmost limit of what is empirical, therefore he cannot be the object of perception, it cannot be conceived in any way by our mind which is nothing more than a *khandha* an external adjunct without any ontological relation to the true self.

All this gives us the fundamental reason why the Buddha could never say anything positive on the metaphysical self as such and could never make it an object of apperception or reflective awareness. In all texts where the metaphysical self is referred to we get only a spontaneous, direct, not reflected upon awareness of the self. When an individual says of something, 'This is not mine, this I am not, this is not my self', it is clear that *mama, ahaṁ,* and *attā* of the utterance refer to the concrete self of the person involved, which is denied to be 'that thing'. The same is the case with other forms of exhortation as not to see in the empirical factors either the self or something belonging to the self, something which is in the self or something in which the self is, or when we are told, 'such a thing is not *yours,* therefore leave it aside'. Finally the same happens when it is asserted of some object that it is *anattā,* which is a noun, not an adjective, and therefore means properly speaking 'the non-self', in obvious opposition to 'the self'. Buddha never speaks of the self as something whose nature is to be described but always in a soteriological context. Thus the self will be proposed either in action (the moral self), or as the final aim of an action (purification of the moral self and the assertion of the ontological independence of the metaphysical self). In the Nikāyas, the true self is the subject of emancipation, never the object of speculation or philosophical discussion. In the Nikāyas the true self is ever silently present and its reality is never brought into question, but the attention of the disciple is never focussed on it as the object of philosophical speculation. Since the metaphysical self is transcendent by nature and our consciousness is merely empirical, any exclusive attention riveted on the self runs the risk of being of the *sakkāyadiṭṭhi* type. That this was not a mere possibility but an ever present danger is made clear by the reactions not only of non-Buddhist people, but also of the bhikkhus themselves, as registered in many testimonies adduced in this book. Any philosophizing on the self would be a sort of philosophical narcissism, inspired by *asmimāna* or inevitably leading to it. And this applies as well to the assertive attention paid to it in the *attavāda* of the eternalists and annihilationists, as to the negative attention which it attracts in the *anattavāda.* The obsession about the inexistence of the self displayed by the *anattavādins,* their persistent negativism regarding the self, their contentious opposition to those who assert the reality of the self, all these seem to be characteristics belonging to a *diṭṭhi,* and therefore betray the presence of *asmimāna,* which is precisely the implicit assertion of the heretical self, which the *anattavādins* would oppose with all their might. But above the brawl of arguments and counterarguments, one ought to hear the serene utterance, 'A bhikkhu whose mind is thus free does not agree or disagree with anyone'. One who has attained the uttermost peace and absolute quiescence avoids all discussions, nothing will disturb him or push his mind into the turmoil of argumentation or aggressive criticism.

14

Recapitulation

Our research has come to an end. We have examined the evidence found in the Nikāyas for the *attā* as well as for the *anattā.* We have as far as possible let the texts speak for themselves and we have taken into account, if not 'all' the available evidence, at least the greatest part of it. We are not conscious of having eluded any piece of evidence because it did not fit into our preconceived scheme of ideas. We must however confess in all sincerity that the result of our research was from the very beginning present in our minds as a 'hypothesis', as an instrument of work. The idea of this hypothesis had presented itself to us in our previous partial readings of the Nikāyas. But to have a hypothesis as the backbone of one's own research is not only legitimate but advisable. We think that the accusation levelled by T. R. V. Murti against Mrs. Rhys Davids and others that 'it will not do to pick up only those passages that are favourable to our theory and ignore the rest, or call them interpolations or later accretions,' does not apply to us.[1] If we have done anything of that sort we have done it after giving reasons which to us seemed convincing.

Let us remind ourselves of what we said in the Introduction. We said that we could consider the texts that teach *attā* as the thesis, while the texts that teach *anattā,* would provide us with the antithesis, and that after due consideration of both we would see whether the thesis and antithesis nullified each other or whether a synthesis of both would be feasible. I. B. Horner seems to admit the simultaneous and contradictory coexistence of the *attā* and *anattā* doctrine in the canon, classifying the latter as a later development, 'the discrepancy of running the *anattā* doctrine alongside a theory which depends for its rational working out on the belief in the reality of self, suggests that the arahant concept was brought over from ealier days, and that, whatever revision the concept received, it yet did not become completely harmonious with every changed value that was evolved by Monastic Buddhism'.[2] On the other hand, the Theravādins gave prominence to the doctrine of *anattā* and tried to explain away the texts where the reality of the self seems to be asserted. When we make a distinction between moral and metaphysical self (by the way, distinction does not necessarily mean division and separation of entities, it may only be indicative of different aspects of the same reality), when on top of that, we can prove that the *anattā* doctrine taught in the Nikāyas has no absolute value, that is to say, it does not deny the reality of the self in an absolute way but limits itself to the denial of selfhood regarding the empirical factors as a motive for their rejection, then the synthesis of both the doctrines becomes possible, even necessary. This synthesis has the advantage that it stands in no need to distinguish between primary and secondary texts, between earlier and later doctrine. It stands in no need to assert one side of the teaching and to explain away the other, but gives equal prominence to both, as complementary aspects of the same system. The doctrine of *anattā,* when given a relative value, not only does not annul the reality of the self, but reaffirms it by denying the nature of self to things that are by nature opposed to it. Dr. Murti tells us, 'according to Nāgārjuna, Buddha has affirmed the existence of the ātman against the materialists, for there is a continuity of karma and its result, he has denied it against the eternalist who takes it as an immutable identical essence, he has also said that there is neither self nor non-self'.[3] This seems to make of the Buddha, not 'a skilful physician' who 'always graduated his teaching according to the need and the capacity of the taught', but a master who could teach contradictory truths according to convenience. We have a better idea of him. Is it not far better to say that what he affirmed and what he denied were not one and the same thing? When he affirmed the existence of *attā* against the materialists, he affirmed the reality of something objectively true. When he denied the *attā* against the eternalists, he did not deny the true *attā,* but the *attā* of the eternslists that is wrongly identified with the *khandhas.* As for the Buddha saying that there is neither self nor non-self, either it refers to 'heretical' teachings that spoke of the self as identified with the empirical factors, or the assertion presupposes some philosophical subtleties that are post-Nikayan.

Dr. Murti puts a very pertinent question: 'If the *ātman* had been a cardinal doctrine with Buddhism why was it so securely hidden under a bushel that even the immediate followers of the master had no inkling of it?'[4] First of all, this question does not affect us, as we admit that the cardinal doctrine of early Buddhism was not precisely the *attā*, but the utter heterogenity and complete ontological separation between the self and the non-self, both being realities between which there is an essential irreducible polarity, which we who are imperfect either deny with our thoughts by holding that they are identical or by our deeds when acting as if that identity were a fact, being swayed by *asmimāna.* This is *avijjā* and the cause of craving (*taṇhā*) that keeps man bound to samsaric becoming. But even if we grant validity to the question for the sake of clarity, we may answer first of all that the 'immediate' followers of the master were those who composed the *suttas* of the Nikāyas, and in the *suttas* both the reality of *attā* and the doctrine of *anattā* are clearly taught. The 'scholastic' commentators were by no means the 'immediate' followers of the master. In the second place, it cannot be said of all the earlier schools of Buddhism that they had no inkling of the *attā* doctrine, as the Puggalavādins certainly had some inkling of it.

To that question we may answer also with a counterquestion. If absolute *anattā* was from the very beginning the doctrine of the Buddha how can we explain the existence of so many texts where the reality of *attā* is taken for granted and given such a prominence? How can we explain an uninhibited use of the term *attā* such as has been shown to exist in the first part of the book? If the self was no reality what sense did it make to establish the fact that something was not the self as the impelling motive to discard it, to get rid of it, to work for its utter cessation? A possible answer may be that both the doctrines, contradicting each other, are contained in the *suttas,* a fact that *a priori* may not be deemed absurd, as the *suttas* were sayings 'attributed' to the Buddha and collected from different places, where contradictory traditions might have been running at the same time. But we can appeal to some witnesses much closer to original Buddhism than the 'scholastic' commentators and who did not see any conflict of views between the doctrine of *attā* and the doctrine of *anattā* when they composed what is the oldest available synthesis of the doctrine of the *suttas.* We are speaking of the authors and compilers of the *Niddesa,* who do not refrain from asserting the implicit reality of *attā,* even waxing eloquent about it, and nevertheless give due prominence also to texts which teach *anattā* with the same commentarial fervour. As we had occasion to note in the course of the book, the *Niddesa* is a model of balanced attitude between the doctrine of *attā* and the doctrine of *anattā,* a balance that begins to be broken in the *Paṭisambhidāmagga* in favour of the latter, a fact that shows unmistakably that an evolution of thought in this matter was possible.

Therefore our final conclusions run as follows:

1. Nowhere is the reality of the self absolutely and explicitly denied. A convincing and explicit denial of the self would have been, for instance, '*puriso, bhikkhave, anattā...*', but such denial is not found anywhere. The only time when the *anattā* doctrine is literally asserted is taken to be a *diṭṭhi* among other *diṭṭhis,* as we saw in its corresponding place.

2. The *anattā* doctrine taught in the Nikāyas has a relative value, not an absolute one. It does not say simply that the self has no reality at all, but that certain things, with which the unlearned man identifies himself, are not the self and that is why one should grow disgusted with them, become detached from them and be liberated. Since this kind of *anattā* does not negative the self as such but denies selfhood to the things that constitute the non-self, showing thereby them to be empty of any ultimate value and to be repudiated, instead of nullifying the *attā* doctrine complements it. A lot of confusion would be avoided if our distinction between absolute and relative *anattā* were accepted.

3. A lot of confusion has been created also by not distinguishing between the moral and the metaphysical self and by not realizing that what is radically rejected in the Nikāyas is the self of the *sakkāyadiṭṭhi,* that is to say, the self that is wrongly identified with the *khandhas.* This wrong notion of self is supposed to prevail in all non-Buddhist systems, and even to exert its malignant influence to a greater or lesser degree on the bhikkhus themselves, if they are not perfect. Therefore all the passages where any sort of controversy with non-Buddhists is the point at issue, or passages where the bhikkhus themselves are warned of the dangers of any doctrine on self (*attavāda*), become clear if they are taken to refer to the wrong self of the *sakkāyadiṭṭhi.* The true self is never brought into question. This is an exegetical principle apt to clarify many an otherwise obscure passage.

4. As we have pointed out the nature of the true self is never made the subject of discussion. We are only told what is not the self and consequently what the self is not. Beyond that the only thing we are told is that the self is transcendent and therefore ineffable, beyond our powers of compre-

hension. Hence, if anyone, at any time, concentrates his attention on the existence or non-existence of the self after liberation and how or what is it, it is not the true self of what he is thinking but of the *sakkāyadiṭṭhi* self, being thereby a victim of *asmimāna*. Any exercise in proving by means of logic or dialectics that the self exists or does not exist after liberation and any obsession regarding such existence or non-existence of the self are upshots of *asmimāna*.

We wish finally to touch upon a question that has often assailed our minds during the writing of this book. Is not the question of the reality of the self, a question more of words than entities? We speak naturally within the scope of the Nikāyas. T. R. V. Murti confesses that 'the Real is transcendent to thought', but what exactly is that 'Real'? It is evident that in the Nikāyas, that 'Real' is the perfect man himself, the Tathāgata, once he has entered *parinibbāna*. Now in the Nikāyas there is no place for a vedantic type of Tathāgata, as was the case with the Tathāgata of the Madhyamikas. Original Buddhsim belonged by right of birth to the non-Brahmanic world, where the plurality of selves was accepted as a matter of fact. If then the ultimate reality in each man is said to be transcendent what else can that reality in every man be but man's true self? This transcendent self was the one asserted whenever one was made to say of the empirical factors, 'This is not mine, this I am not, this is not my self', a formula that equivalently says, 'I am beyond all this, my self transcends all this'. This is corroborated by the fact that the empirical factors are always said to be not 'that which has no self' (adjective), but simply 'the non-self' (noun), placing thus the empirical factors in clear opposition to the self, which transcends them, and accepting both the extremes of the opposition as real in their own right.

Within such vision of things, the title of the book, 'Self and Non-self in Early Buddhism', is very appropriate as both the doctrine of self and the doctrine of non-self are taught in early Buddhism, both forming part of the totality of the system.

Notes

NOTES TO 'INTRODUCTION'

1. We do not agree with Th. Stcherbatsky when he writes: 'Whether the *anātmadharma* theory was the personal creation of Sakyamuni Buddha himself, or not, is a quite irrelevant question. In any case we do not know of any form of Buddhism without this doctrine...' (*The Central Conception of Buddhism,* Delhi, 1970, p. 56). We deem it important for the history of religious and philosophical ideas to know for certain, if it were at all possible, whether the *anattā* doctrine comes from the Buddha himself or he merely prepared the ground for it.
2. Cf. 'Another unfortunate fact has been the habit of speaking of the passages of the Scriptures as the *ipsissima verba* of Buddha without testing the assumption, in spite of the emphatic words of Franke that "it is given as yet to no mortal man to demonstrate that any one Buddhist sentence was spoken during the lifetime of the Founder"' (E. J. Thomas, *The History of Buddhist Thought,* London, 1953, p. 123). Even so, we shall make use of expressions such as 'the Buddha said', 'the Buddha answered', etc., without thereby implying that we believe the words that follow to have been uttered by the Buddha himself and in that very form.
3. *The Buddha's Ancient Path* (London, 1964), p. 101.
4. Vishwanath Prasad Varma, *Early Buddhism and Its Origins* (New Delhi, 1973), p. 148. Italics ours.

NOTES TO CHAPTER 1: 'PRELIMANARY REMARKS'

1. Mrs. Rhys Davids, *What was the Original Gospel in Buddhism?* (London, 1938), pp. 39–40.
2. M III, p. 351, *Anāthapiṇḍikovādasutta,* 7 and 8.
3. K VII, p. 407, Cpṭ 2, 9, 80.
4. M II, p. 18, *Aṭṭhakanāgarasutta,* 5.
5. *Op. cit.,* p. 40.
6. S V, p. 299, *Sotāpattisaṁyutta,* 6.
7. *Early Buddhism and the Bhagavadgītā* (Delhi, 1971), p. 317 f.
8. *Designation of Human Types* (London, 1969), Intr., p. vii.
9. K IV, pt. II, p. 215, Cln 3, 0, 24. Also, K IV, pt. II, p. 185, Cln 2, 15, 85. Repeated at K V, p. 456, Pṭs 3, 1, 8, 25.

10. K IV, pt. II, p. 312, Cln 3, 0, 34. Cf. also K V, p. 460 f., Pṭs 3, 1, 8, 18–21 and 31.
11. K V, p. 444–445, Pṭs 2, 10, 2, 30.
12. *The Central Conception of Buddhism* (Delhi, 1970), p. 22.
13. Pe Maung Tin, *The Path of Purity* (London, 1971), p. 609. To the last line quoted, the translator appends the following footnote: 'Contradicted in *Expositor',* p. 218, 1, 12.
14. 'A methaphysical theory developed out of one fundamental principle, *viz.,* the idea that existence is an interplay of a plurality of subtle, ultimate, not further analysable elements of Matter, Mind, and Forces', *Op. cit.,* p. 62.
15. D II, p. 80, *Mahāparinibbānasutta,* 35.
16. See *Khettūpamasutta,* S IV, pp. 278–280, *Gamaṇisaṁyutta,* 7. See also A II, p. 376, *Pañcakanipāto,* 10, 9, 2.
17. *Op. cit.,* p. 318. The quotation is from D I, p. 167, *Poṭṭhapādasutta,* 36.
18. *Oḷariko, manomayo* and *arūpo* were taken by other systems to be three different kinds of self. Such was the case with Poṭṭhapāda himself, as it is declared in the same *sutta,* D I, p. 155, *Poṭṭhapādasutta,* 12. The same is asserted in the *Taittiriya Up.,* in the *Brahmānanda Vallī.* This the Buddhists reject, even though it is not explicitly stated in this *sutta.*
19. *Dīghanikāyapāli,* 1. *Sīlakkhanda Vagga,* Nālandā Edition, Intr., p. xviii.
20. *Studies in the Origin of Buddhism* (Allahabad, 1957), p. 90.
21. S I, p. 15, *Devatāsaṁyutta,* 25. Similar is the situation contemplated in: 'A bhikkhu, Aggivessana, thus freed in mind does not agree with anyone, does not disagree with anyone, he makes use of the language spoken in the world, without any sense of grasping', M II, p. 196, *Dīghanakhasutta,* 5.
22. This absolute freedom from asmimanic feelings cannot be used as an argument for absolute *anattā,* since it is demanded by all systems which admit the existence of *attā* in one way of another. See for instance, *Bhagavadgītā,* III, 26.
23. S I, p. 135, *Bhikkhunīsaṁyutta,* 10.
24. A proof of this is afforded by the oft recurring passages where Māra is said to be unable to see the man who has left aside the empirical adjuncts. Cf. Ch. 13, par. 'Moral transcendence of the self'.
25. K IV, Pt. I, p. 61, Mnd 1, 3, 19.
26. K IV, pt. I, p. 87, Mnd, 1, 5, 32.
27. K IV, pt. I, p. 69, Mnd 1, 3, 22. Also, K IV, pt. I, p. 208, Mnd 1, 10, 93, and K IV, pt. I, p. 299, Mnd 1, 14, 154.
28. K IV, Pt. I, p. 75, Mnd 1, 4, 25.
29. K IV, pt. I, p. 90, Mnd 1, 5, 35.
30. Cf. *Attānudiṭṭhi vuccati vīsativatthukā sakkāyadiṭṭhi.* K IV, pt. II, p. 196, Cln

2, 15, 88.

31. D II, p. 94, *Mahāparinibbānasutta,* 56.
32. Prj, p. 353 (4, 22, 159).

NOTES TO CHAPTER 2: 'ATTĀ AS MAN'S HIGHEST VALUE'

1. *Tasmātihānanda, attadīpā viharatha attasaraṇā anaññasaraṇā, dhammadīpā dhammasaraṇā anaññasaraṇā.*
   D II, p. 80, *Mahāparinibbānasutta,* 35.
2. G. C. Pande, *Studies in the Origins of Buddhism* (Allahabad, 1957, p. 487) mentions this passage as a confirmation that the passage of the *Mahāvagga, attānaṁ gaveseyyātha,* may have 'more than merely a reflexive sense'. Ananda K. Coomaraswami and I. B. Horner, *The Living Thoughts of Gotama the Buddha* (Bombay, 1958, p. 177 f.) include this passage of the *Mahāparinibbānasutta,* and the three passages of the *Saṁyutta* among the texts collected under the heading, 'The Greater Self'. Mrs. Rhys Davids takes up these expressions and endeavours to draw from them all the rich meaning they contain in, *A Manual of Buddhism for Advanced Students* (London, 1932), pp. 158–159 and pp. 166–167. She does the same in *What was the Original Gospel of Buddhism?* (London, 1938), pp. 38–40.
3. For this sense of the word *dīpa* see K I, pp. 433–434, Stn 5, 11, 117–119 and K I, p. 540, Stn 5, 11, 170, where *dīpa* is opposed to *ogha.* While commenting on the first of these two passages, the *Cullaniddesa* gives as synonyms of *dīpa* several words, among which the word *saraṇa* is also found (*dīpaṁ, tāṇaṁ, leṇaṁ, saraṇaṁ),* K IV, pt. II, p. 145, Cln 2, 10, 61 and *Ibid.* p. 147 (2, 10, 63). The Jainas who belonged to the same cultural circle as the Buddhists give also prominence to *dīvo* (=*dīpa*) as meaning 'island', and in the verses we are going to quote, *dīvo* and *saraṇaṁ* occur together precisely with reference to *dhamma:*
   Jarāmaraṇavegeṇaṁ bujjhamāṇāṇa pāṇiṇaṁ,
   dhammo dīvo paiṭṭhā ya gaī saraṇamuttamaṁ.
   Pandit Dhirajlal Shah, *The Teachings of Lord Mahāvīra* (Bombay, 1964), p. 70.
4. *Ete hi, Gāmaṇi, maṁdīpā maṁleṇā maṁtāṇā maṁsaraṇā viharanti,* S IV, p. 279, *Gāmaṇisaṁyutta,* 7.
5. The passage as a whole is found again in the *Gilānasutta* S V, p. 132, *Satipaṭṭhānasaṁyutta,* 9. The same advice (*attasaraṇā viharatha,* etc.) including the practice of the four *satipatthānas* is given when Ānanda comes disconso-

late to the Buddha, because with the demise of Sāriputta he has lost a spiritual support, S V, pp. 139–140, *Satipaṭṭhānasaṁyutta,* 13. The same advice, including the practice of the *satipaṭṭhānas,* is again given soon after when Sāriputta and Mogallāna had attained complete *nibbāna,* so that with their passing away the Order gave an impression of emptiness, S V, pp. 140, 141, *Satipaṭṭhnāsaṁyutta,* 14. The same exhortation, in a shorter form, but still containing the description of the *satipaṭṭhānas* is used as an introduction to D III, p. 46, *Cakkavattisutta,* 1, and in what might have been the original conclusion of the *sutta (Ibid.* p. 61, *Cakkavattisutta,* 32). But the connexion of the passage with the main topic of the *sutta* is rather loose and artificial.

6. *Attadīpā tato hotha... dukkhassantaṁ karissatha,* K VII, Apd 2, p. 215 (2, 7, 288).
7. S II-III, p. 274, *Khandhasaṁyutta,* 43.
8. K. II, p. 304, Tha 6, 7, 412.
9. D II, p. 94, *Mahāparinibbānasutta,* 56. An exact repetition of the stanza found at K. VII, p. 260, Apd 2 (3, 8, 322), where Therī Yasodharā speaks also of her impending *parinibbāna.*
10. S II-III, p. 360, *Khandhasaṁyutta,* 95. We take *saraṇattano* to be a contraction of *saraṇamattano.*
11. K I, p. 39, Dhp 18, 236.
12. K I, p. 39, Dhp 18, 238.
13. K II, p. 462, Thi 16, 1, 478. The original reads, *devesu pi attāṇaṁ, nibbānasukhā paraṁ natthi.* The texts reads *attāṇaṁ* with v. l. *attānaṁ.* This variance in readings suggests that the passage has not been well preserved. Taking into consideration the context of the passage, one would expect the reading *attatāṇaṁ,* even though such a reading is not given as a variant in any of the editions. The word *attāṇaṁ,* which would mean 'without a refuge', does not make sense. The same happens with *attānaṁ.* The *pāda,* as it stands is metrically defective, requiring one syllable more. This deficiency is made up by accepting *attatāṇaṁ,* which makes perfect sense. The contraction of *attatāṇaṁ* into *attāṇaṁ* is very likely to have happened in a mechanical recitation.
14. K I, p. 413, Stn 4, 15, 172. That the world is essenceless (*asāro*) is a theme often recurring in the Nikāyas. We saw above the *khandhas* being likened to foam, to a bubble, to a mirage, to a juggler's creation. Do we have here the seed of what developed in later systems as the conviction of the illusory nature of transient phenomena?
15. K IV, pt. I, p. 353, Mnd 1, 15, 172.
16. K I, p. 343, Stn 3, 5, 100.
17. *The Book of the Kindred Sayings,* Vol. I, pp. 101–102.

18. S I, pp. 73–74, *Kosalasaṁyutta,* 8. Repeated at K I, p. 118–119, Ud 5, 1.
19. S I, p. 8, *Devatāsaṁyutta,* 13. The whole passage reads as follows:
    The deity, *Natthi puttasamaṁ pemaṁ, natthi gosamitaṁ dhanaṁ,*
    natthi suriyasamā ābhā, samuddaparamā sarā.
    The Buddha, *Natthi attasamaṁ pemaṁ, natthi dhaññasamaṁ dhanaṁ,*
    natthi paññāsama ābhā, vuṭṭhi ve paramā sarā.
    The Buddha's reply falls somewhat short of what one would expect. One would expect the Buddha to twist every statement of the deity from a common sense assertion to a spiritual truth. Such is the case with the first and third, and even with the fourth if *vuṭṭhi* is taken to mean not 'rain' but 'the arisal in *saṁsāra.* One feels that the Buddha's second statement should read, *natthi dhammasamaṁ dhanaṁ.*
20. See specially, A III, p. 242, *Sattakanipāto,* 7, 4, 14, and A II, p. 190, *Catukkanipāto,* 19, 6, 8, which is repeated and applied to the Buddha himself at M II, p. 388, *Brahmāyusutta,* 5. See also, A I, p. 145, *Tikanipāto,* 6, 4, repeated at A I, p. 200, *Tikanipāto,* 8, 1; K III, p. 154, J, *Sattakanipāto,* 404, 66; K II, p. 307, Tha 6, 12, 443; S V, p. 107, *Bojjhaṅgasaṁyutta,* 55, found also at A II, p. 473, *Pañcakanipāto,* 20, 3, 3, etc.
21. K I, p. 33, Dhp 12, 166:
    Attadatthaṁ paratthena, bahunā pi na hāpaye,
    attadatthaṁ abhiññāya, sadatthapasuto siyā.
22. K IV, pt. II, p. 309, Cln 3, 0, 31. On the other hand, the Thera Samaṅgalo is supposed to have addressed the Buddha Atthadassī as follows, *Attānaṁ tosayitvāna, pare tosesi tvaṁ muni,* K VI, p. 172, Apd 12, 2, 16.
23. K I, p. 32, Dhp 12, 157.
24. S I, pp. 71–72, *Kosalasaṁyutta,* 5.
25. *The Book of the Kindred Sayings,* Vol. V, pp. 305–306. Original found at S V, p. 299, *Sotāpattisaṁyutta,* 6.
26. S V, pp. 144–145, *Satipaṭṭhānasaṁyutta,* 19. The social projection of the self, to which we have just referred, is expressly stated at A III, p. 85, *Chakkanipāto,* 5, 12, *Yo ca rakkhati attānaṁ,* etc.
27. A II, p. 426, *Pañcakanipāto,* 16, 2, 2. *Attānaṁ na paribhoti* occurs again in the next *sutta.*
28. S I, p. 41, *Devatāsaṁyutta,* 78.
29. K III, pt. I, p. 380, J, *Tiṁsanipāto,* 515, 175. Note the parallelism between *attānaṁ nātivatteya* and *adhammaṁ na samācare.* This parallelism is confirmed by the use of the verb *ativattati* in connection with dhamma in:
    Chandā dosā bhayā mohā, yo dhammaṁ ativattati,

āpūrati tassa yaso, sukkkapakkheva candimā.
Prv p. 298, (15, 3, 18).

30. K III, pt. I, p. 114, J, *Pañcakanipāto,* 355, 33.
31. K II, p. 457, Thi 15, 1, 427.
32. K I, p. 23, Dhp 5, 62.
33. K III, pt. I, pp. 137–138, J. *Chakkanipāto,* 386, 81. Repeated at K III, pt. II, p. 151, *Asītinipāto,* 537, 451, changing *niraṁkatvā* for *niraṁkacca.* A slightly different version at K III, pt. II, p. 151, *Asītinipāto,* 537, 453.
34. S I, p. 150, *Brahmasaṁyutta,* 9. But the metrical structure of the stanza seems to indicate that the line *sabbasā pi sahā attanā* was interpolated. The passage is repeated at A II, p. 5, *Catukkanipāto,* 1, 3, 2; also at K I, p. 371, Stn 3, 10 258.
35. S I, pp. 70–71, *Kosalasaṁyutta,* 4. The words are first attributed to king Pasenadi and the Buddha makes them his own by repeating them approvingly. This is also an idea common to other systems that admit the reality of the self. The Jainas have the saying:
    Appā mittamamittaṁ ca duppaṭṭhiyasupaṭṭhiyo.
    Pandit Dhirajlal Shah, *Op. cit.,* p. 55. Also:
    Na taṁ arī kaṇṭhachettā karei, jaṁ se kare appaṇiyā durappā.
    Riṣabhdās Rāṅkā. *Bhagavān Mahāvīr Updeś ane Ācār Mārg* (Bombay, 1973), p. 88. See also *Bhagavadgītā,* VI, 5.
36. S I, p. 55, *Devatāsaṁyutta,* 22.
37. ... *karoti so tathattānaṁ, yathā naṁ icchati diso,* K I, p. 32, Dhp 12, 162.
38. See, for instance, S I, p. 74, *Kosalasaṁyutta,* 8; repeated at K I, pp. 118–119, Ud 5, 1, *evaṁ piyo puthu attā paresaṁ*; A III, p. 228, *Sattakanipāto,* 6, 11, 7, *attūpamā te sattā, attā hi paramo piyo*; K I, p. 29, Dhp 10, 129–132, *attānaṁ upamaṁ katvā, na haneyya na ghātaye*; K I, p. 322, Stn 2, 13, 148, *sāruppaṁ attano viditvā, no ca bhikkhu hiṁseyya kañci loke.*
39. The Dictionary continues saying that *kāma* is the first of the *nīvaraṇas,* of the three *esanās,* of the four *upādānas,* of the four *oghas,* of the four *āsavas,* of the four *taṇhās,* of the four *yogas,* and of the six fetters of existence.
40. This is suggested by the fact that at S I, p. 141, *Brahmasaṁyutta,* 2, 4, the Sinhalese and Roman Editions have *atthakāmena* instead of *attakāmena.* The same occurs with the Siamese edition in the repetition of the verses at A III, p. 222, *Sattakanipāto,* 6, 9, 2. On the other hand we find, *attakāmapāricariyā,* 'ministering to selfish sensual pleasures', Prj pp. 191–193 (2, 4, 57–60).
41. *Muṇḍaka Up.* III, 1, 4.
42. *Bṛhad-āraṇ. Up.* IV, 4, 6.
43. S I, p. 141, *Brahmasaṁyutta,* 2; repeated at A III, p. 222, *Sattakanipāto,* 6,

9, 9. Here the Siamese edition offers *mahattharh* instead of *mahattarh.*

44. A II, p. 24, *Catukkanipāto,* 3, 1, 5.
45. A II, p. 24, *Catukkanipāto,* 3, 1, 6.
46. A III, p. 330, *Aṭṭhakanipāto,* 3, 9, 9. The difficulty to be born as a man in such conditions as to be able to hear the best doctrine (*uttamadhamma*) being preached, and profit by it is also stressed in the Jaina scriptures. See Pandit Dhirajlal Shah, *Op. cit.,* p. 166 f. The *Critical Pāli Dictionary (Copenhagen, 1924 ff., s. v.)* translates *attakāma* as, 'who wishes himself well (sometimes confounded with *attha-kāma,* pursuing the (highest) good'. Following the parallelism of the two terms, it seems preferable to translate *attakāma* as 'pursuing the self', or as we have translated it, 'in love with the self'. Cf. *marh kāmena,* 'through loving me', which occurs in the *Atharvaveda.* William Dwight Whitney, *Sanskrit Grammar* (London, 1950), p. 272.
47. M III, pp. 223–224, *Anuruddhasutta,* 3.
48. D II, p. 84, *Mahāparinibbānasutta,* 39. The composer of the *sutta* did not realize that these statements, being redacted in the third person could have not been uttered by the Buddha, who would have spoken in the first person singular. The original would be more intelligible if instead of *tulamatularh* we had *thūlamathūlarh,* referring to the division of existenses into *oḷarika, arūpa* and *manomaya.*
49. Mvg p. 25, *Mahākkhandhaka,* 36.
50. K VII, Apd 2, p. 233, *Therīapadāna,* 2, 10, 500–501.
51. K II, p. 411, Thi 3, 5, 51.
52. *Op. cit.,* p. 486. What Mrs. Rhys Davids has to say about *paccattarh* reads as follows, 'The next: *paccattarh,* often occurs (alternatively with *svayarh*: this very man) in refrains describing the grasping of something in the most inward way, and not superficially only; as something which had gone to stimulate manhood, and not the memory only… *paccattarh veditabbo viññūhi*: to be understood by the wise *each for himself* is one instance. We have the commentator paraphrasing it as *attano attano abhantare*: of each (man) in the inmost (man). Now it is among us maintained that, in such idiom, merely a reflexive sense is intended, which does not go beyond our idiom in self-prefixed compounds. This is assuming much…', *Sakya or Buddhist Origins* (London, 1931), pp. 189–190.
53. Pct p. 377, *Bhikkhunīvibhaṅga,* 4, 19, 83–84. Later on, p. 388, *Ibid.,* 88, we find the rule, 'whatever *bhikkhunī* should weep striking herself (*attānarh*) again and again, incurs an offence of expiation'. Again we read in the corresponding *vibhaṅga, attānarh ti paccattarh.*
54. S II-III, p. 98 f., *Nidānasarhyutta,* 68. The question is reiterated regarding

everyone of the links of the chain, both in the direction of their dependent origination and of their dependent cessation.

55. This text is found in many places. For instance, A III, p. 8, *Chakkanipāto,* 1, 10, 4; *Ibid.* p. 31, *Chak.,* 3, 5, 2; *Ibid.,* p. 33, *Chak.,* 3, 6, 3; *Ibid.,* p. 70 f., *Chak.,* 5, 5, 1 and 5, 6, 1; S II-III. p. 167, *Kassapasaṁyutta,* 3; S IV, p. 37, *Saḷāyatanasaṁyutta,* 70; K IV, pt. II, p. 80, Cln 2, 4, 22 and p. 104 (2, 5, 35). The same asserted of *nibbāna* at A I, p. 147, *Tikanipāto,* 6, 5, and of the harmful effects for the self and for others caused by *rāga, dosa,* and *moha,* at S IV, p. 298, *Gāmaṇisaṁyutta,* 12.
56. A II, p. 292. *Pañcakanipāto,* 3, 7, 1. Another instance of the same expression is found in, 'As long as the bhikkhus will have established mindfulness in their very self (*paccattaññeva*), to wit, "How the affable companions in the holy life who have not yet come would be made to come, and those who have come would fare in comfort?" [As long as this mindfulness is there] growth only is to be expected, not decline'. A III, p. 169, *Sattakanipāto,* 3, 3, 8, and D II, p. 62, *Mahāparinibbānasutta,* 5. See also, A I, p. 174, *Tikanipāto,* 7, 5; A I, p. 179, *Tik.,* 7, 6; A II, p. 204 f., *Catukkanipāto,* 20, 3, where *attanā va jāneyyātha* could be changed into *paccataññeva jāneyyātha.*
57. K IV, pt. I, pp. 197–198, Mnd 1, 10, 88; *Ibid.* p. 307 (1, 14, 156); K IV, pt. II, p. 80, Cln 2, 4, 22; *Ibid.* pp. 104–105 (2, 5, 35). See also, K IV, pt. I, p. 344, Mnd 1, 14, 169; *Ibid.,* p. 422 (1, 16, 198).
58. *A III, p. 220–221, Sattakanipāto,* 6, 8, 12. Repeated at M I, p. 310, *Cūḷataṇhāsaṅkhayasutta,* 1.
59. Other similar texts: 'Thus, he, not building conceits, is not attached to anything in the world. Not being attached, he is not perturbed. Not being perturbed, he attains utter *nibbāna* in his very self (*paccattaññeva parinibbāyati*). He knows: "...there will be no more of a thus-conditioned existence"'. S IV, p. 21, *Saḷāyatanasaṁyutta,* 30; and, 'Not performing [any act, either meritorious or sinful, or neither], not having any intention, he is not attached to anything in the world.... Not being perturbed he attains utter *nibbāna* in his very self (*paccattaññeva parinibbāyati*), etc.'. S II-III, p. 70, *Nidānasaṁyutta,* 51. See also, *Ibid.,* p. 284. *Khandhasaṁyutta,* 53, where, strange enough, *paccattaññeva parinibbāyati* refers directly to *viññāṇa.* See also, *Ibid. suttas* 54 and 55.
60. S IV, p. 152, *Saḷāyatanasaṁyutta,* 234.
61. *Op. cit.,* pp. 485–486.
62. D II, p. 84, *Mahāparinibbānasutta,* 39. Repeated at S V, p. 225, *Iddhipādasaṁyutta,* 10, and K I, p. 140, Ud 6, 1, 3.
63. K I, p. 52, Dhp 25, 362. There is another definition of *bhikkhu* in the *Ther-*

agāthā, wherein the two last lines coincide exactly with those of this stanza of the *Dhammapada,* K II, p. 365, Tha 17, 2, 981.

64. K IV, pt. I, p. 447, Mnd 1, 16, 210.
65. K I, p. 326, Stn 2, 14, 168.
66. K I, p. 294, Stn 1, 9, 176.
67. S I, pp. 168–169, *Brāhmaṇasaṁyutta,* 9. Mrs. Rhys Davids remarks on this text, 'The commentary has: *"niyakajjatte, attano santānasmiṁ",* that is "in one's own very self, in the self's continuity". There is here no sign of depreciation. And why? Buddhaghosa has lost sight, after centuries, of the original meaning of *ajjhatta* when Sakya began. The term has become for him just what "subjective" now means for us; a term of mind-import, not *of the man who is minding.* And a quaint point about this is, that he unaware uses *niyaka* (one's own), a word which was first used for self-reference as meaning the "permanent". For *niya-ka* is a lingual slide from *nija,* and that from *nicca* (*nitya*). But the Sakyan argument was based on the man being *a-nicca!* Such are the ironies of language.' *Sakya or Buddhist Origins,* pp. 374–375.
68. S V, p. 333, *Sotāpattisaṁyutta,* 30.
69. A II, p. 353, *Pañcakanipāto,* 8, 5, 10; A IV, p. 267, *Dasakanipāto,* 10, 9, 13.
70. A III, p. 178, *Sattakanipāto,* 4, 7–8.
71. K IV, pt. II, p. 315, Cln 3, 0, 35. Cf. also, K IV, pt. I, p. 440, Mnd 1, 16, 207.
72. *The Book of the Gradual Sayings,* Vol. II, p. 163. See for original text, A II, p. 167, *Catukkanipāto,* 17, 10, 6, and K V, p. 339, Pṭs 2, 1, 0, 5.
73. F. L. Woodward, *The Book of the Gradual Sayings,* Vol. I, p. 249. See for original, A II, p. 258–259, *Catukkanipāto,* 25, 3, 5. Also, 'Herein, bhikkhus, the mindfulness of the bhikkhu is well established on the very self (*ajjhattaññeva*)', A II, p. 397, *Pañcakanipāto,* 13, 2; and, 'By the abandonment of these, the mind is fixed, is established, is concentrated, is focussed on the very self (*ajjhattameva*)', M I, p. 159, *Vitakkasaṇṭhānasutta,* 1.
74. K I, p. 411, Stn 4, 14, 154. Two interpretations are given in the *Mahāniddesa* regarding *attaṁ* and *nirattaṁ.* The first interpretation gives those terms the meanings of *attadiṭṭhi* and *ucchedadiṭṭhi.* The second interpretation explains those terms as *gahitaṁ* and *muñcitabbaṁ,* in the sense that the *arahant* is above all growth and loss, but it would be more consonant with the spirit of the *Suttanipāta* to say that the *arahant* is above all disputes, because he is not attached to, or repelled by anything.
75. See for instance, A III, p. 70–71, *Chakkanipāto,* 5, 5, 3; A I, p. 253–254, *Tikanipāto,* 12, 9; Clv p. 368 (9, 7, 17); *ibid.,* p. 368–369 (9, 8, 18–19); etc.
76. K II, p. 417, Thi 5, 4, 86.

NOTES TO CHAPTER 3: 'THE SELF AS THE MORAL AGENT'

1. Pe Maung Thin, *The Path of Purity* (London, 1971), p. 609. The translator appends to the last line the following footnote, 'Contradicted in the "Expositor", p. 218, 1, 12'.
2. S I, p. 64, *Devaputtasaṁyutta,* 30.
3. K III, pt. II, p. 55, J. *Paṇṇāsanipāto,* 528, 162–163.
4. M II, p. 212 f., *Sandakasutta,* 3 f.
5. K I, p. 33, Dhp 12, 165.
6. A I, p. 160 f., *Tikanipāto,* 7, 1.
7. K III, pt. II, p. 53 f., *Paṇṇāsanipāto,* 528, 139 f. No. 5 seems to refer in an unfavourable light to the belief reflected in the *Bhagavadgītā* that a kṣatriya who died in battle went to heaven, II, 2.
8. A III, p. 53, *Chakkanipāto,* 4, 8, 1 and 4.
9. *Ibid.* To note that *sayaṁ* and *attanā* are interchangeable, as it is clear from this commentary of the *Vibhaṅga, nevattanā paṭicodeyyā ti na sayaṁ codeyya,* Pct p. 291, *Bhikkhunīvibhaṅga,* 1, 2, 11.
10. E. M. Hare, *The Book of the Gradual Sayings,* Vol. III (London, 1934), Intr., pp. xii–xiii. Mrs. Rhys Davids is not ready to accept that a brāhmaṇa could hold the opinion that the self is not a doer. Such teaching occurs in the *Bhagavadgītā,* V, 13–14. The truth of the matter seems to be that the Nikāyas abhor all one-sided expressions of truths that cannot be ascertained from experience. A dogmatic absolute expression stating that the self is not a doer goes directly against the spirit of the Nikāyas (which do not admit the monistic self of *Vedānta*), because it contradicts the evidence of experience.
11. M II, p. 251, *Samaṇamuṇḍikasutta,* 6. It is a well known fact that in later Buddhism the mind was substituted for what was considered an 'unreal self'. But the subservience of the mind to the moral agent is clearly brought out in this *sutta,* when after having stated that all sinful behaviour originates in a mind possessed of sensuality, ill-will and confusion, it is said, in the passage we have quoted, that the moral agent, working for the suppression of wrong behaviour should 'force the mind' to the task. The truth of the subservience of the mind to the moral agent is of frequent occurrence in the Nikāyas.
12. A I, p. 136, *Tikanipāto,* 4, 10. The *Critical Pāli Dict., s. v.,* translates *attādhipateyya* as 'having one's own self as master, controlled by one's own conscience'. The affinity between the self and dhamma, already pointed out by us, may be also expressed by saying that the self as inspirer and censor is equivalent to what we call conscience. But the term *attādhipateyya* seems to refer in this context to the rôle performed by the self as moral agent and supreme

master.

13. See for the whole passage, K II, p. 378 f., Tha 19, 1, 1110 f.
14. K I, p. 47, Dhp 23, 327.
15. K VI, p. 87, Apd 1, (3, 3, 109). *Sakkā uddharituṁ attā* occurs also at K VII, p. 7, Apd 2 (43, 3, 46).
16. K I, p. 317, Stn 2, 10, 114. Also, K II, p. 303, Tha 6, 5, 404.
17. K II, p. 345, Tha 16, 3, 767.
18. K I, p. 361, Stn 3, 8, 191. This is a concept that Buddhism has in common with Jainism. Thus we find worldly pleasures being called a dart and poison, *Sallaṁ kāmā visaṁ kāmā...*, Pandit Dhirajlal Shah, *Op. cit.*, p. 153. In another context, *sallaṁ* seems to stand for all the miseries of man:
    davvie bandhaṇummukke savvao chinnabandhaṇe,
    paṇolla pāvakaṁ kammaṁ sallaṁ kantai antaso,
    Ibid., p. 185.
19. K I, p. 43, Dhp 20, 282. Strange enough, *bhava* seems to be used here in the sense not of samsaric becoming but of spiritual progress. With reference to this verse, Mrs. Rhys Davids remarks, 'Here again is a verse warring with the later doctrine of *anattā*: non-self, and finding no emphasis in the Piṭakas', *The Minor Anthologies of the Pāli Canon,* Vol. I (London, 1931), Intr., p. xiii. But this remark seems to be out of place in what concerns the emphasis given to *attā* in the Nikāyas. The whole first part of this book bears witness to it.
20. K I, p. 32, Dhp 12, 158.
21. The simile of the chariot is not confined to the Buddhist texts. We find it also in the *Katha Up.* (III, 3–9) in the usual form of an allegory. We discover clearly stated there the following pictorial details: the self (*ātman*) is the rider and master of the chariot (*rathin*), the body is the chariot, intellect (*buddhi*) is the charioteer (*sārathi*), the senses are the horses, and the objects of sense are the road. The wise know how to control the horses, not so the fools. The allegory obviously refers to a chariot with two persons on board, the travelling master and the charioteer. The latter's immediate responsibility is to lead the horses on the right way under his master's orders. Thus the concluding stanza tells us: 'The man whose charioteer is wise and keeping control of the reins of the mind, reaches to the end of the road, the highest step of Viṣṇu'. There is a passing reference to the allegory in the *Śvetāśvatara Up.* (II, 9) and a more elaborate treatment of the metaphor in the *Maitrāyaṇīya Up.* (II, 6). It is quite natural for the Upaniṣads to attribute the mastery of the chariot to the *ātman.* Does the same apply to the simile as found in the Nikāyas or has the *anattā* doctrine had any influence in the presentation of the simile? The Jainas provide us with a parallel simile of the boat and the boatman. They too very naturally attribute

the controlling power to the soul, saying that the body is the boat, the soul is the sailor and the *saṁsāra* is the ocean crossed by great sages:

Sarīramāhu nāva tti, jīvo vuccai nāvio,
saṁsāro aṇṇavo vutto, jaṁ taranti mahesiṇo,

Pandit Dhirajlal Shah, *Op. cit.*, p. 53.

22. K I, p. 47, Dhp 23, 323.
23. *Agatā disā vuccati amataṁ nibbānaṁ,* K IV, pt. I. p. 412, Mnd 1, 16. 195.
24. K II, pp. 296–297, Tha 5, 9, 355–359.
25. S I, p. 31, *Devatāsaṁyutta,* 46.
26. S V, p. 7, *Maggasaṁyutta,* 4. This translation differs in several points from that of F. L. Woodward, *The Book of the Kindred Sayings,* Vol. V, p. 5. *Dhammā* in the first line is the instrumental case of *dhamma.* Cf. V. Perniola, *A Grammar of the Pāli Language* (Colombo, 1958), p. 20, 'Sometimes the instrumental singular is formed with the ending *-ā* added to the stem either directly or by means of the consonant *-s*: *sahatthā* for *sahatthena* – "with the hand", *pādā* for *pādena* – "with the foot", *vegasā* for *vegena* – "quickly".' *Dhurasamādhi* in the fourth line is translated freely by Woodward as 'yoke-fellow of the balanced mind'. *Dhura* as 'yoke' has been mentioned in the first line, and also who are those yoked, *saddhā* and *paññā,* followed by the pole (*īsā*) and the yoke-straps (*yottaṁ*). In the second *śloka* we have first the chariot, the axle, the wheels, and finally what is called *dhurasamādhi.* In such a context the term should stand for something related to the axle and the wheels. Among the meanings for *dhura* given in Monier-Williams, *A Sanskrit-English Dictionary,* we find: yoke, pole, *peg of the axle.* 'Peg of the axle' fits admirably in the context as the translation for *dhura* in *dhurasamādhi. Samādhi* will have to be taken in the etymological meaning of 'putting together, joining, adjustment'.
27. See for the whole passage, K III, pt. II, pp. 286–287, J, *Mahānipāto,* 545, 1333–1341.
28. K I, p. 395, Stn 4, 7, 51.
29. K IV, pt. I, p. 122, Mnd 1, 7, 51.
30. *The Book of the Kindred Sayings,* Vol. IV, pp. 110–111. Original text at S IV, pp. 159–160, *Saḷāyatanasaṁyutta,* 239. Akin to this is the passage from the *Dīghanikāya*:

    There the bhikkhus have plunged into concentration,
    they have set upright their own minds (*cittamattano ujukaṁ akaṁsu*),
    Having grasped the reins like a skilful charioteer, they, wise, guard their senses,

    D II, p. 189, *Mahāsamayasutta,* 2. Text found also at S I, p. 25, *Devatāsaṁ-*

yutta, 37. The latter seems to contain the original text, found in a *sutta* entitled *Samayasutta.* The phrase *cittam'attano ujukaṁ akaṁsu* begs for some commentary. It is true that, in this phrase, *attano* does not refer to the self as such. This way of speaking is similar to the one found in the *Cullavagga* that reads *attano nakhehi* (Clv p. 223, 5, 13, 32), where clearly *attano* has a merely reflexive sense. *Attano* here does not refer to the spiritual part of man and its usage should never be ranked on a par with those cases where the use of *attā* refer to the inner man. These latter cases will 'also' have a reflexive sense, always inherent in *attā* and its oblique cases, but their final point of reference is entirely different.

31. S I, p. 55, *Devaputtasaṁyutta,* 22.
32. A I, pp. 52–53, *Dukanipāto,* 2, 5.
33. M I, p. 134, *Anumānasutta,* 4.
34. *Anumānasutta,* 5.
35. *Ibid.,* 6.
36. A IV, pp. 182–183, *Dasakanipāto,* 6, 5, 8–10.
37. A III, p. 240, *Sattakanipāto,* 7, 4, 4. To see the difference between early Buddhism and the doctrine of the *Upaniṣads,* one may compare this *attaññu* with the *ātmajña* of the *Upaniṣads* and *attānaṁ jānāti* with *ātmānaṁ jānāti.*
38. M II. p. 29, *Potaliyasutta,* 3. The same is repeated with reference to taking what is not given, lying speech, slanderous talk, covetise and greed, angry fault-finding, wrathful rage, arrogance.
39. M II, p. 123, *Bhaddālisutta,* 3. The whole speech is found in the negative form in the same *sutta,* 4. The condition of the bhikkhu so upraided is described soon after as *attanā pi attānaṁ upavadito* with a v. 1. *attanā pi attā upavadito,* which seems to be the original one, *attānaṁ* having been substituted for *attā* under the influence of the previous *attānaṁ.*
40. S II-III, p. 341, *Khandhasaṁyutta,* 87. Also, *Ibid.,* p. 345, *sutta* 88.
41. K II, p. 314, Tha 8, 1, 496–498. Parallel to this passage is the following:

    If others praise him, when the self (*attā*) is not well composed,
    In vain do others praise him, the self (*attā*) not being well composed.
    If others blame him, when the self is well composed,
    In vain do others blame him, the self being well composed.

    K II, pp. 268–269, Tha 2, 20, 159–160.
42. A I, p. 137, *Tikanipāto,* 4, 10. These verses come at the end of the *Ādhipateyyasutta.* Mrs. Rhys Davids comments on this *sutta*: 'One more proof from the Suttas, that early teaching never saw, in 'self', 'spirit', a fiction of speech I must adduce. It is the Sutta of the three Mandates. The religious man anxious to get better results in his self-training, is shown as helped by three mandates:

(1) that of the self: "Stirred up for me shall unsluggish effort become; called unmuddled mindfulness, serene shall body become, one-pointed the mind..." and having made just the self his mandate he "perseveres in effort and cherishes a pure self." ...', *What was the Original Gospel of Buddhism?* (London, 1938), p. 40. But it seems that, in what follows, the illustrious author goes too far. After indicating the other 'two Mandates', she asks, 'Is it not astonishing that a teaching with these sayings in its scriptures should be said to deny God and the soul?' The denial of the self might be astonishing, not so the denial of God. Several of the texts quoted in this very chapter contain a denial of *Issara,* the creator. But this denial of God is common to another non-brahmanic systems like Jainism and to Sāṅkhya and Yoga, which might have been also non-brahmanic in origin.

43. A II, pp. 127–129, *Catukkanipāto,* 13, 1. Another passage speaks of five disadvantages and five opposite advantages, the first ones being respectively, *attā pi attānaṁ upavadati,* and *attā pi attānaṁ na upavadati,* where the ambivalence of the self is manifest. A II, pp. 493–494, *Pañcakanipāto,* 22, 7. Repeated at Prv p. 236 (7, 5, 25). The *Critical Pāli Dict.* translates *attānuvāda* as 'reproach of oneself', but 'reproach of the self or from the self' seems to be a better translation, as it becomes clear from the quotations just given in this note. Even in the text a distinction is made between *attā* and *maṁ*, giving *attā* a personal and quasi-autonomous character, bringing out clearly, at the same time, the ambivalence of the self, since the self is also implicitly stated in *maṁ.*

44. S I, p. 23, *Devatāsaṁyutta,* 35. Repeated at Prj p. 112 (1, 4, 172). Such hypocrisy was found in Devadatta. Mogallāna's attendant, Kakudha, who had been reborn as a *devaputta* with a mind-made body revealed to his former master Devadatta's intention to win supremacy over the Order of bhikkhus. Mogallāna went to inform the Buddha about it, and the latter replied: 'Keep, Mogallāna, such matter to yourself, keep such matter to yourself. Soon the foolish man will manifest the self by the self', Clv p. 284 (7, 2, 4). The incident of the *Cullavagga* seems to be an elaborate version of the simpler one found at A II, p. 379 f., *Pañcakanipāto,* 10. In both instances there follows a disquisition about five kinds of teachers found in the world, who pretend purity either in their morals, or in their way of maintaining themselves, their teaching of *dhamma,* etc. The disciples know the truth to be otherwise, but they do not dare tell others thinking that, 'What the self will do even by that will the self be known' (*taṁ tumo karissati tumo va yena paññayissati*). We read in the *Jātaka* (K III, pt. I, p. 102, J, 335, 138), 'One who being no lion, but who with the conceit of a lion misrepresents the self (*attānaṁ vikubbati*), like the jackal who attacked an elephant, lies on the ground bemoaning'. These words apply

directly to a jackal who pretending to be a lion attacked an elephant to his own discomfiture. They apply indirectly to Devadatta trying to supersede the Buddha as head of the *Saṅgha.* The opposite disposition is mentioned a little after this, 'Whoever here undertakes a proportionate work, well knowing the vigour and strength of self (*thāmabalaṁ attani saṁviditvā*), circumspect in his muttering, recitation, and things well said, obtains great victories', K III, pt. I, p. 103, *Catukkanipāto,* 335, 140.

45. A II, p. 329, *Pañcakanipāto,* 6, 3. Repeated at A IV, p. 110, *Dasakanipāto,* 2, 1, 2.
46. I. B. Horner, *The Collection of Middle Length Sayings,* Vol. II, p. 335. See for original text, M II, p. 399, *Selasutta,* 3.
47. The whole *Selasutta* is found again at K I, p. 353 f., Stn 3, 7.
48. K VII, p. 303, Bhv 1, 63.
49. D I, p. 148, *Mahāsīhanādasutta,* 22. Similar statements are attributed to the Buddha regarding *tapojigucchā, paññā, vimutti.*
50. Mhv p. 204, *Cammakkhandhaka,* 7.
51. *The Book of Discipline,* Vol. IV (London, 1942), p. 254.
52. A I, p. 202, *Tikanipāto,* 8, 2.
53. A III, p. 72–73, *Chakkanipāto,* 5, 7, 4. The *sutta* ends with:

    Na ussesu na omesu, samatte nopanīyare,
    khīnā jāti vusitaṁ brahmacariyaṁ, caranti saṁyojanavippamuttā,

    where obviously *upanīyare* is used rather like a technical term for any asmimanic activity tending to compare one's own self with superiors, inferiors, or equals. We read in the *Suttanipāta*:

    Samo ti attānamanūpaneyya,
    hīno na maññetha visesī vā pi,

    K I, p. 393, Stn 4, 5, 34. In the commentary to these words found in the *Mahāniddesa,* the verb *na upaneyya* is used in all three cases:

    sadisohamasmī ti attānaṁ na upaneyya, hīnohamasmī ti attānaṁ na upaneyya, seyyohamasmī ti attānaṁ na upaneyya,

    K IV, pt. I, pp. 89–90, Mnd 1, 5, 34.
54. S II-III, p. 58, *Nidānasaṁyutta,* 41, The whole *sutta* occurs again at A IV, p. 246, *Dasakanipāto,* 10. It occurs also, in a shorter form at A IV, p. 46, *Navakanipāto,* 7 and 8.
55. S V, p. 300 f., *Sotāpatisaṁyutta,* 7. In the introduction (*Nidānagāthā*) to the *Theragāthā* we meet with *attūpanāyikā* as a variant to *atthūpanāyikā.* They are epithets qualifying *gāthā,* the metrical compositions of the book. It seems, against the Editors of the Nālandā Edition, that *attūpanāyikā* is the reading most fitting here, since the *śloka* that follows reads:

Yathānāmā yathāgottā, yathādhammaviharino,
yathādhimuttā sappaññā, vihariṁsu atanditā,

which evidently refers to the descriptions contained in the *gāthā* of the names, families, virtues and liberation of the authors, which they themselves are supposed to have made speaking in the first person. There is a rule in the *Pārājika* to the effect that, 'Whatever bhikkhu should boast attributing to his self (*attūpanāyikaṁ*) a state of further men... though not knowing it...', Prj p. 113 (1, 4, 173). In the corresponding *vibhaṅga* the word *attūpanāyikaṁ* is explained as, *te vā kusale dhamme attani upaneti, attānaṁ vā tesu kusalesu dhammesu upaneti.*

56. A III, p. 317, *Aṭṭhakanipāto* 3, 1, 10. This means to say that Ugga was an *anāgamī.*
57. S V, pp. 304–305, *Sotāpattisaṁyutta,* 7–10.
58. K II, p. 270, Tha 2, 26, 171–172.
59. K I, p. 390, Stn 4, 3, 17. Commented upon at K IV, pt. I, p. 55 f., Mnd 1, 3, 17. But as regards *attano* it is not said, as one could expect, *attā vuccati diṭṭhigataṁ.*
60. *The Book of the Kindred Sayings,* Vol. II, p. 40. Original text found at S II-III, p. 46, *Nidānasaṁyutta,* 32.
61. K I, p. 332, Stn 3, 2, 34.
62. Cf. above, *na attānaṁ paribhoti,* Chapter 2, par. 'The self is the best'.
63. K I, p. 338, Stn 3, 4, 75.
64. *Woven Cadences of Early Buddhists* (London, 1947), p. 70.
65. See *ujju* in its form *uju* used in a passage that speaks of concentration, *cittamattano ujukaṁ akaṁsu,* at D II, p. 189, *Mahāsamayasutta,* 2, and S I, p. 25, *Devatāsaṁyutta,* 37.
66. If not an open contradiction to the *vedānta* view, we might see in this line a borrowing of a brahmanic way of speaking with an intentional twist of meaning, as it is the case with other parts of the canon. The closest parallel to this line are found in the *Bhagavadgītā,* VI, 20 and XIII, 24. But there is a difference in terminology that may be significant. The verb used in the *Bhagavadgītā* is *paśyati,* while in our Nikayan text the verb used is *anupassati,* which may be considered a technical term occurring whenever the *satipaṭṭhānas* are described. See, for instance, M I, p. 77 f., *Satipaṭṭhānasutta.*

NOTES TO CHAPTER 4: 'THE SELF AND MORAL EVIL'

1. K I, p. 391, Stn 4, 4, 25.

2. M III, p. 81, *Mahāpuṇṇamasutta,* 5; M I, p. 283, *Cūḷasaccakasutta,* 6.
3. K I, p. 56, Dhp 26, 412, Repeated at K I, p. 366, Stn 3, 9, 235.
4. K I, p. 42, Dhp 19, 267.
5. K I, p. 310, Stn 6, 55.
6. K I, p. 33, Dhp 12, 163.
7. S I, p. 69, *Kosalasaṁyutta,* 20. Repeated at S I, p. 97, *Kosalasaṁyutta,* 23; K I, p. 213, Itv 3, 1. Quoted at K IV, pt. I, p. 310, Mnd 1, 14, 156; *Ibid.* p. 411 (1, 16, 195); K IV, pt. II, p. 268, Cln 3, 0, 8.
8. K I, p. 32, Dhp 12, 161.
9. K II, p. 345, Tha 16, 3, 765–767.
10. A IV, p. 182, *Dasakanipāto,* 6, 5, 8.
11. M I, p. 135, *Mahāassapurasutta,* 17. The whole passage occurs again at D I, p. 63 ff., *Sāmaññaphalasutta,* 67 f. See also M I, p. 135, *Anumānasutta,* 6: *Bhikkhu... sabbepime pāpake akusale dhamme appahine attani samanupassati.* See also, A II, p. 152, *Catukkanipāto,* 16, 8, 2: 'Whoever... beholds in self (*attani samanupassati*) four conditions, ought to come to this conclusion, "I am declining in good conditions. This has been declared by the Blessed One to be decay",' etc.
12. A I, p. 261, Tikanipāto, 13, 6.
13. K I, p. 37, Dhp 16, 209. The first *pāda* occurs also in a *śloka* of the *Theragāthā,* K II, p. 292 (5, 2, 320). The *Critical Pāli Dictionary* translates *attānuyogi*(*n*) as 'meditating upon one's self'. We prefer to give it a more general sense in consonance with the context.
14. A I, p. 273, *Tikanipāto,* 15, 5. The opposite, *akkhataṁ anupahataṁ attānaṁ pariharati,* is asserted of the man possessed of the corresponding virtues, where, *akkhataṁ anupahataṁ,* although negative in form suggests a flourishing spiritual health, as it is the case with similar negative statements often occurring in the Canon. *Khataṁ anupahataṁ,* etc., occurs also in the immediately following *suttas: Ibid.* 15, 6; 15, 7; 15, 8. The same expression appears in the following passages: A II, p. 4–5, *Catukkanipāto,* 1, 3, 1; *Ibid.* pp. 5–6, *Catuk.,* 1, 4, 1; *Ibid.* pp. 242–243, *Catuk.,* 23, 2, 1; *Ibid.* p. 267, *Catuk.,* 26, 10, 1; *Ibid.* pp. 385–386, *Pañcakanipāto,* 11, 3, 7 and 12; repeated at *Ibid.* p. 513, *Pañcak.,* 27, 14; A IV, p. 355, *Dasakanipāto,* 22, 5–8; Prv pp. 295–296 (15, 2, 12–15). In all the preceding passages, *khataṁ upahataṁ attānaṁ pariharati* is opposed to *akkhataṁ anupahataṁ attānaṁ pariharati,* excepting A II, pp. 385–386, *Pañcakanipāto,* 11, 3, 7 and 12. *Attānaṁ upahantvāna* occurs at A III, p. 85, *Catukkanipāto,* 5, 12, 16.
15. A I, p. 148, *Tikanipāto,* 6, 7.
16. M I, pp. 176–177, *Alagaddūpamāsutta,* 4–5. The same incident is recounted

at Clv p. 57 (1, 7, 65), and Pct p. 182 (5, 68, 417). In the latter texts some manuscripts add *diṭṭhigatena* to *duggahitena.* This seems to indicate that the original text is found in the *Majjhimanikāya.*

17. K I, p. 40, Dhp 18, 247. *Māttānaṁ khaṇi brāhmaṇa,* occurs at K II, p. 387, Tha 20. 1, 1182.
18. S I, p. 150, *Brahmasaṁyutta,* 9. Repeated at *Ibid.* p. 152, *Brahmasaṁyutta,* 10. Also at A IV, p. 237 and 238, *Dasakanipāto,* 9, 9, 7 and 11. The *Kokālikasutta* of the *Aṅguttara* is a composition that combines into one both, the *Tudubrahmasutta* and the *Kokālikasutta* of the *Saṁyutta,* placing in between the description of Kokālika's punishment. This shows that the *Kokālikasutta* of the *Aṅguttara* belongs to a later date.
19. Prv pp. 286–288 (13, 3, 6); *jhāpeti* means also 'to kill, to destroy',
20. K II, p. 447, Thi 13, 5, 357.
21. S II-III, p. 200, *Lābhasakkārasaṁyutta,* 35. Similes are given of several plants for which the yielding of fruit means death for the plant itself, as the plantain, the bamboo, the rush, as well as the simile of an animal of alike predicament, the mule. Also at Clv p. 287 (7, 3, 6). In the *Cullavagga suttas* 35 and 36 of the said *Lābhasakkārasaṁyutta* are combined together, indicating that the passage of the *Cullavagga* is a later composition. The *Crit. Pāli Dict.* translates *attavadha* as 'suicide, destruction of oneself', but such translation does not bring out the 'spiritual' connotation of the term in our context.
22. K I, p. 51, Dhp 24, 355.
23. K II, p. 265, Tha 2, 10, 139.
24. K I, p. 33, Dhp 12, 164. The *Crit. Pāli Dict.* translates *attaghāta* as 'one's own destruction', where again due prominence is not given to *attā.*
25. A II, p. 262, *Catukkanipāto,* 26, 2. The ariyan and unariyan quests are treated also at M I, p. 210 f., *Pāsarāsisutta,* 4 f. This *sutta* of the *Majjhima* is an elaborate composition and as such belongs to a later date than its constituent elements. The ariyan and anariyan quests are used by the composer of this *sutta* as an introduction to a biographical account of the conversion and illumination of the Buddha. Here six ariyan and anariyan quests are found in place of the four described in the *Aṅguttara.* If the *Aṅguttara* had copied from the *Majjhima* there is no apparent reason why two of the quests should have been suppressed, to wit, those about what is *jātidhamma* and what is *sokadhamma,* when the six give a more complete picture of the subject matter. There are two more reasons to assert that in this case the *Majjhima* is copying from, and enlarging on, what is found in the *Aṅguttara.* The question that introduces in the *Majjhima* the treatment of the quests mentions in the first place the ariyan quests, while the anariyan quests are mentioned in the second place. It is not

so in the treatment itself, that follows the order of the *Aṅguttara*. The second reason is that the *Majjhima* enlarges upon the treatment of the quests by giving a separate explanation of every one of them.

26. M I, p. 185, *Alagaddūpamāsutta,* 15.
27. D III, p. 210, *Dasuttarasutta,* 2. The abandonment of conceit is a necessary qualification for the crossing to the other bank of the realm of death at S I, p. 6, *Devatāsaṁyutta,* 9. Also, *Ibid.,* p. 28, *sutta* 38.
28. K I, p. 25, Dhp 6, 84.
29. K I, p. 392, Stn 4, 5, 32. See also, K I, p. 390, Stn 4, 3, 19.
30. K IV, pt. I, p. 87, Mnd 1, 5, 32.
31. K VII, pp. 62–63, Apd 2 (49, 7, 122–123). Sāriputta describes the moral excellence of the twenty-four thousand disciples he had in a previous existence saying that 'none was given to self-glorification (*anattukkaṁsakā*), nor despised any other', K VI, p. 22, Apd 1, (1, 3, 196). As a qualification of the good bhikkhu we find it stated four times that 'he neither praises self (*nevattānukaṁseti*), nor despises others', A II, p. 30, *Catukkanipāto,* 3, 8. Repeated at K IV, pt. I, p. 436, Mnd 1, 16, 206. Conceit is divided into two kinds, 'the conceit of self-glorification (*attukaṁsamāno*) and the conceit of despising others', K IV, pt. I, p. 66, Mnd 1, 3, 21; also, *Ibid.* p. 368, (1, 15, 178). With what doubtless is a hasty generalization, the Nigaṇṭhas are said to be, *attukaṁsakaparavambhakā,* given to self-glorification and to the contempt of others', A IV, p. 218, *Dasakanipāto,* 8, 8.
32. K II, p. 305, Tha 6, 9, 423–428.
33. K IV, pt. I, p. 66, Mnd 1, 3, 21.
34. K I, pp. 410–411, Stn 4, 14, 153. That this is also a cause of disputes, so often condemned in the Canon, is testified in K I, p. 392, Stn 4, 5, 31, *tasmā vivadāni avītivatto.* This disputatious spirit goes along with attachment to any *diṭṭhi.*
35. K I, p. 393, Stn 4, 5, 34.
36. K I, pp. 405–406, Stn 4, 12, 123–124. See the description of this 'coronation ceremony' at K IV, pt. I, p. 252, Mnd 1, 12, 124.

NOTES TO CHAPTER 5: 'TOWARDS PERFECTION'

1. A IV, pp. 182–183, *Dasakanipāto,* 5, 9–10. Also, 'if, your reverences, the bhikkhu, while reflecting beholds all these evil and sinful states eliminated in the self (*attani*), he should dwell with joy and gladness, training himself day and night in rightful states', M I, p. 135, *Anumānasutta,* 6.

2. A II, p. 152, *Catukkanipāto,* 16, 8, 3. The opposite case stated at *Ibid.* 16, 8, 2. It will not be out of place here to note that lust, ill-will, and infatuation are given also a basic importance in Jainism, where they are called the root-cause and origin of *kamma,* in a stanza that clearly rings of Buddhism, *Rāgo ya doso vi ya kammabīyaṁ, kammaṁ ca mohappabhavaṁ vayanti, kammaṁ ca jāimaraṇassa mūlaṁ, dukkhaṁ ca jāimaraṇaṁ vayanti.* Pandit Dhirajlal Shah, *Op. cit.,* p. 43.
3. M I, p. 338, *Mahāassapurasutta,* 17.
4. A II, p. 6, *Catukkanipāto,* 14, etc. See n. 14 of the foregoing chapter.
5. A III, p. 9, *Chakkanipāto,* 1, 10, 6–7. Repeated at *Ibid.* pp. 34–35, *Chakkanipāto,* 3, 6, 5–6, where Mahākaccāna is the speaker, not the Buddha. The original text which all the others seems to imitate is A III, p. 32 and 35, *Chakkanipāto,* 3, 5, 5–6 and 3, 6, 5–6, which has been expanded in the *Uposathasutta* (A I, p. 190 f., *Tikanipāto,* 7, 10) with the passage relating to the arahants and their imitation.
6. K III, pt. II, p. 104, J, *Asītinipāto,* 534, 177.
7. K III, pt. I, p. 154, J, *Sattakanipāto,* 404, 66. Also,

   Indeed all those virtues and qualities, O glorious princess,
   Are found in thee (*tayi*), O auspicious one, which thou proclaimest [as found] in the self (*attani*).

   K III, pt. I, p. 284, J, *Pakiṇṇakanipāto,* 489, 117.
8. A II, p. 343, *Pañcakanipāto,* 7, 6. Repeated at A II, pp. 438–439, *Pañcakanipāto,* 17, 3, and A II, p. 439, *Pañcakanipāto,* 17, 4, where the speaker is not the Buddha, but Sāriputta.
9. A IV, p. 203, *Dasakanipāto,* 7, 10, 2–11.
10. K IV, pt. II, p. 295, Cln 3, 0, 24, etc.
11. K IV, pt. II, p. 312, Cln 3, 0, 34; K V, pp. 460–461. Pṭs 3, 1, 8, 31–33.
12. S I, p. 32, *Devatāsaṁyutta,* 48.
13. K III, pt. I, p. 154, J, *Sattakanipāto,* 404, 66.
14. S I, p. 240, *Sakkasaṁyutta,* 22. *Sampassaṁ atthaṁ attano* occurs also at Clv p. 240 (6, 1, 2); repeated at *Ibid.* p. 259 (6, 5, 22). The text, as it stands, betrays a borrowing by the composer of a text already in existence. He attributes the utterance to the Buddha. If it were so, the Buddha would have said *mayā* (by me) or something similar, not *Buddhena.*
15. K V, p. 201, Pṭs 1, 3,3, 28.
16. A few eloquent testimonies follow:

   (1) In the *Dīghanikāya* four kinds of exertions are listed, to wit, exertion for restraint (the most general one), *saṁvarapadhāna*; exertion for elimination (of what is bad), *pahānapadhāna*; exertion for developing (what is good), *bhāvanā-*

padh*āna*; exertion for safeguarding (whatever good has been achieved) *anurakkhaṇapadhāna,* D III, p. 176, *Saṅgītisutta,* 3, 15.

(2) 'For the faithful disciple, bhikkhus, who fares having fully penetrated into the master's teaching, there holds this principle, "Willingly would I be reduced to skin, sinews, and bones, willingly would I let my muscles and blood dry up in my body, but there will be no rest for my energy, while I have not attained what is to be attained by manly effort, by manly strength, by manly vigour",' M II, p. 171, *Kīṭāgirisutta,* 11.

(3) 'I am satisfied, bhikkhus, with this course, I am satisfied in mind, bhikkhus, with this course. Therefore, bhikkhus, display an ever increasing energy for the attainment of what has not yet been attained, for winning what has not yet been won, for the realization of what has not yet been realized', M III, pp. 142–143, *Ānāpānasatisutta,* 2.

(4) 'And besides, Udāyin, a method has been explained by me to my disciples, following which, these disciples of mine develop the four right strivings. Herein, Udāyin, a bhikkhu engenders desire, exerts himself, displays energy, forces his mind, strives towards the non arising of wrong sinful states that have not yet arisen; ... for the obliteration of wrong sinful states that have arisen; ... for the arising of beneficial states that have not yet arisen; ... for the preservation, maintenance, increase, expansion, furtherance, completion of right states of mind which have arisen', M II, p. 234, *Mahāsakuludāyisutta,* 13.

17. D I, p. 47, *Sāmaññaphalasutta,* 19. The final simile presents the question very graphically, 'just as a ball of string thrown along runs unwinding itself, in the same way the fools as well as the wise, after transmigrating and going through the cycle of *saṁsāra* will make an end of Pain'.
18. K I, p. 5, *Khuddakapātha,* 5, 3. *Attasammāpaṇidhi* occurs again in the *Aṅguttara* (A II, p. 35, *Catukkanipāto,* 4, 1). The peculiarity of the passage is in that the term does not occur in the metrical section of the *sutta,* which seems to contain a half moral, half practical advice for the obtention of riches and happiness. The striking fact is that when trying to explain the verses, the composer of the prose section used exactly the terms of the *Kuddakapātha* just quoted. This proves the fact that the *Kuddakapātha* passage was earlier than this prose part of the *Aṅguttara.*
19. *The Book of the Gradual Sayings,* Vol. V, p. 220. 'With self established' would be the translation of *ṭhitatto* not of *pahitatto.*
20. *The Minor Anthologies of the Pāli Canon,* Vol. I, Intr., p. xiii. The philologically improbable exegesis to which Mrs. Rhys Davids refers is given in the P. T. S.'s *Pāli-English Dictionary* as, 'explained by Buddhaghosa with wrong derivation from *peseti* as *pesitatta* thus identifying *pahita 1* (p. p. of *padahati*)

and *pahita 2* (p. p. of *pahiṇati,* 'sent').' A philological exegesis that is not so improbable as we shall soon see.

21. For the whole passage, see K IV, pt. I, p. 417, Mnd 1, 16, 198.
22. A II, pp. 16–17, *Catukkanipāto,* 2, 2.
23. A II, p. 121, *Catukkanipāto,* 12, 3, 5 f. Repeated several times in the *sutta.*
24. K II, p. 366, Tha 17, 2, 983–985. A similar text speaks of a mountain jungle being enough for a self-exerting bhikkhu as a residence:

    Enough for me, a self-exerting bhikkhu (*pahitattassa bhikkhuno*), who am fain to meditate,
    Enough for me, a self-exerting bhikkhu, desirous of my [spiritual] good,
    Enough for me, a self-exerting bhikkhu, desirous of living at ease,
    Enough for me, a self-exerting bhikkhu, desirous of practicing yoga.

    K II, p. 373, Tha 18, 1, 1069–1070.
25. K I, p. 331, Stn 3, 2 (*Padhānasutta*), 28–30. At S I, p. 187, *Vaṅgīsasaṁyutta,* 3, in the line *dhammadaso ti tamāhu pahitattaṁ,* the preferable reading seems to be, with the Sinhalese, Siamese, and Roman editions, *dhammaso ti tamāhu tathattaṁ.* To confirm the point that *pahitatto* means 'self-exerting' and not 'one who has banished the self', let us list other usages of *pahitatto* only with the immediate context, making allowances for possible variations of number and case:

    (1) *āraddhaviriyo pahitatto* ('energetic, self-exerting'), S I, p. 51, *Devaputtasaṁyutta,* 15; A II, p. 466, *Pañcakanipāto,* 17, 7, 11; K II, p. 294, Tha 5, 5, 335; K VI, p. 39, Apd 1 (1, 3, 389); K VI, p. 75, Apd 1 (2, 9, 120); K VI p. 113, Apd 1 (5, 2, 48); K VI, p. 123, Apd 1 (6, 1, 5); K VI, p. 446, Apd 1 (41, 8, 249); K I, pp. 260–261, Itv 4, 11.

    (2) *āraddhaviriyo pahitatto, niccaṁ daḷhaparakkamo* ('energetic, self-exerting, ever exceedingly strenuous'), S I, p. 165, *Brāhmaṇasaṁyutta,* 7; S I, p. 199, *Vanasaṁyutta,* 2; K II, p. 268, Tha 2, 18, 156; K II, p. 296, Tha 5, 8, 353; K II, p. 365, Tha 17, 1, 979; K II, p. 425, Thi 6, 6, 161; K VII, p. 206, Apd 2 (2, 7, 171).

    (3) *appamattā pahitattā* ('diligent, self-exerting'), K I, p. 332, Stn 3, 2, 41.

    (4) *ātāpī pahitattehi* ('being ardent, you shine among the self-exerting'), K VI, p. 99, Apd 1 (4, 1, 22).

    (5) *appamattā ātāpino pahitattā viharatha* ('dwell ever diligent, ardent, self-exerting'), Mvg p. 382, *Kosambakakkhandhaka,* 4, 16; M I, p. 153 f., *Dvedhāvitakkasutta,* several times; M II, p. 15, *Aṭṭhakanāgarasutta,* twice; M II, p. 66, *Kukkuravatikasutta,* 7; A I, pp. 151–152, *Tikanipāto,* 6, 8, several times; A II, p. 290, *Pañcakanipāto,* 2, 1, 13–15, several times; A II, p. 360, *Ibid.,* 8, 7, several times; A II, p. 362, *Ibid.,* 8, 8, several times; A III, pp.

291–292, *Aṭṭhakanipāto,* 2, 1, several times; A III, p. 391 f., *Ibid.,* 7, 4, several times; A IV, p. 166, *Dasakanipāto,* 5, 6, several times; A IV, p. 384, *Ekādasanipāto,* 2, 6, several times; S II-III, p. 199, *Lābhasakkārasaṁyutta,* 31; K I, p. 380, Stn 3, 12.

(6) *eko vūpakaṭṭho appamatto ātāpī pahitatto viharanto* ('dwelling alone, secluded, diligent, ardent, self-exerting'), Mvg p. 202, *Camakkhandhaka,* 2, 5; Clv p. 379 (10, 4, 5); Clv, p. 414 (11, 8, 13); S I, p. 163, *Brāhmaṇasaṁyutta,* 2; S II-III, p. 301 f., *Khandhasaṁyutta, suttas* 63–70; S V, p. 161, *Satipaṭṭhānasaṁyutta,* 46; M III, p. 357, *Puṇṇovādasutta,* 1; A II, p. 333, *Pañcakanipāto,* 6, 6, 4; A III, p. 87, *Chakkanipāto,* 6, 1, 3; A III, p. 388, *Aṭṭhakanipāto,* 7, 3, 1 and 11, where these words constitute the theme of the *sutta,* at the end of which it is said that the bhikkhu so dwelling attains arahantship; K I, p. 359, Stn 3, 7.

(7) *eko adutiyo appamatto ātāpī pahitatto viharanto* (dwelling alone, without company, diligent, ardent, self-exerting'), K IV, pt. I, p. 396, Mnd 1, 16, 191; K IV, pt. II, p. 245, Cln 3, 0, 1.

(8) *padhānapahitatto* ('strenuously self-exerting'), Mvg p. 11, *Mahākkhandhaka,* 10; K I, p. 330, Stn 3, 2, 21; K II, p. 431, Thi 9, 1, 212 (where the gender seems to be wrong, as the speaker is a Therī, due perhaps to the fact that the transmission was done by monks); K VI, Apd 1, p. 60 (1, 3, 625); *Ibid.* p. 63 (1, 3, 656); *Ibid.* p. 74 (2, 8, 108); *Ibid.* p. 102 (4, 4, 60); *Ibid.* p. 110 (5, 1, 10); *Ibid.* p. 129 (6, 8, 64); *Ibid.* p. 131 (6, 10, 86); *Ibid.* p. 346 (35, 5, 37); *Ibid.* p. 433 (41, 4, 96), where the reading is *padhānaṁ pahitattomhi*; K VII, p. 23, Apd 2 (44, 9, 76); *Ibid.* p. 99 (53, 4, 25) where the reading is *padhānaṁ pahitattaṁ taṁ,* with the *varia lectio: ātāpinaṁ pahitattaṁ; Ibid.* p. 178 (56, 11, 190).

26. S II-III, p. 135, *Dhātusaṁyutta,* 14, 18. Repeated at K I, p. 230, Itv 3, 29; K II, p. 267, Tha 2, 14, 248; and K II, p. 284, Tha 3, 16, 266, where instead of *jhāyīhi* we read *jhāyībhi.*

27. K I, p. 53, Dhp 25, 379. The *Crit. Pāli Dict.* translates *attagutto* as 'self-protected, guarding oneself', where *the* self is not given the prominence required by the previous line. There are two more readings for *paṭisaṁsettha attanā,* which convey the point more clearly. The Sinhalese edition reads, *paṭimaṁse attamattanā,* while the Siamese edition reads, *paṭimaṁse tamattanā.* The joy experienced by the integration of personality consequent on self-control, occurs also in:

Sitting alone, resting alone, faring alone, resolute,
In solitude mastering the self (*eko damayamattānaṁ*),
let him stay joyful in the confines of the forest.

K I, p. 45, Dhp 21, 305. And:

When having kept the thoughts of self in check (*vitakke uparundhiyattano*),
Having sought for refuge in a mountain cleft, in the bosom of a mountain,
Rid of sorrow and mental obstructions, he muses,
There is no enjoyment to be found surpassing this.

K II, p. 318, Tha 9, 1, 525.

28. Mhv p. 16, *Mahākkhandhaka,* 8, 20.
29. K I, p. 27, Dhp 8, 103–104. The first *śloka* is found almost literally in the Jaina literature:

Jo sahassaṁ sahassānaṁ, saṅgāme dujjae jie,
egaṁ jiṇejja appāṇaṁ, esa se paramo jao.

Pandit Dhirajlal Shah, *Op. cit.,* p. 55. See also:

They lead a tamed elephant to battle, the king mounts a tamed elephant,
The tamed is best among men, he who endures abuse,
Excellent are the tamed mules, the thoroughbred horses of Sindh,
And great elephants, but one whose self is tamed (*attadanto*) is better still.
For with such riding-animals one would not be able to go to the unexplored region,
As with a self that is well tamed (*attanā sudantena*), the tamed man goes by reason of his taming.

K I, p. 47, Dhp 23, 321–323. Quoted at K IV, pt. I, p. 204, Mnd 1, 10, 90, and K IV, pt. II, p. 71, Cln 2, 4, 18. We find here a testimony of the relation between *attā* and *nibbāna* to be studied later on. It is by means of a well tamed self that one goes to the unexplored region (*agataṁ disaṁ*), that is *nibbāna.* Let us not forget that the rider of the well tamed self is here the self itself.

30. K I, p. 24, Dhp 6, 80; *Ibid.* p. 31, Dhp 10, 143; K II, p. 238, Tha 1, 19; *Ibid.* p. 356, Tha 16, 8, 877; M II, p. 351, *Aṅgulimālasutta,* 9; with the difference that at K I, p. 31 and K II, p. 238 the last line reads *attānaṁ damayanti subbatā.*
31. K II, p. 240, Tha 1, 29.
32. This instrumentality of *citta,* the mind, as regards the moral agent, the self, is strikingly stated in, *Bhikkhu cittaṁ vasaṁ vatteti* (causative), *no ca bhikkhu cittassa vasena vattati,* 'The bhikkhu brings the mind under subjection, and he does not fare under subjection of the mind', M I, p. 266, *Cuḷagosiṅgasutta,* 8.
33. A II, p. 126, *Catukkanipāto,* 12. 7. The Commentary has it *attharūpena,* 'for one's own benefit', Cf. F. L. Woodward, *The Book of the Kindred Sayings,* Vol. II, p. 214, n. 1. Forcible control of the mind should be exercised only in so far as it is necessary for making it a pliable instrument for the moral agent. The Buddha was not in favour of extremes. Thus at S I, p. 14, *Devatāsaṁyutta,*

24, to the utterance of a *devatā* the Buddha adds the following corrective, 'One should not check the mind in every way, Not the mind that has attained to perfect control, In so far as there is sinfulness, is the mind to be checked'.

34. K I, pp. 325–326, Stn 2, 14, 168.
35. K II, p. 342, Tha 16, 2, 727–729. For the control of the senses and the mind, see also, M I, p. 333 f., *Mahāassapurasutta.*
36. K I, p. 32, Dhp 12, 159, *Attā hi kira duddamo* has a parallel expression in Jaina literature, *appā hu khalu duddamo.* Pandit Dhirajlal Shah, *Op. cit.,* p. 54.
37. K II, p. 334, Tha 14, 1, 653. The same *śloka* recurs at K I, p. 46, Dhp 22, 315, but with a third line added to it, showing that the original version is that of the *Theragāthā.* Also:

    Whoever guards the self (*rakkhati attānaṁ*) is also externally guarded,
    Therefore, he should guard the self (*rakkheyya attānaṁ*) the wise, who will always stay unhurt.

    A III, p. 85, *Chakkanipāto,* 5, 12, 16. We find also *attagutto,* 'guarded as to self', applied to a monk who having attained spiritual maturity, is in no need of being guarded by the Buddha. The Buddha will not have to be solicitous for his moral welfare. A II, p. 277–278, *Pañcakanipāto,* 1, 7.
38. K II, p. 266, Tha 1, 11, 142.
39. K I, p. 32, Stn 12, 160.
40. Alone, having attained mastery over the self (*attavasī*),
    I shall presently enter into the forest,
    A delightful place, giving joy to the yogis, the resort of elephants in rut.

    K II, p. 320, Tha 10, 2, 439. K R. Norman translates *attavasī* as 'pursuing my aim'. Mrs. Rhys Davids translates it as 'bound to my quest', and gives a footnote, '*Attavasī,* "in submission to the business of a recluse" (Cmy.)'. The reading of the Nālandā Edition is *attavasī,* without any *v. l.* (such as *atthavasī*). It is a case of misprint or another case of later commentators trying to do away or to explain away *attā* as far as possible? *Attavasī* could also be translated as 'one who is under the spell of the self, or in subjection to the self', and then the self becomes the driving force and the motive for the yogi to go in search of solitude in the forest. This last interpretation of *attavasī* may be confirmed by an analogical use of *cittavasī* in a passage where it clearly means 'being under the spell of the mind, or subject to the mind':

    Yadi cittavasī hessaṁ, parihāyissāmi sīlato,
    sīlena parihīnassa, uttamattho na sijjhati.

    K VII, p. 402, Cpṭ 2, 3, 24.
41. The term is applied to the Buddha, when Udāyin sings his praises, proclaiming that gods and men salute him who is,

The Perfectly Awaken One, born as a man, tamed as to self (*attadanto*), well composed,
advancing on the brahma-path, fond of tranquility of mind.

A III, p. 60, *Chakkanipāto,* 5, 1, 4. The metrical part of this *sutta,* where *attadanto* occurs, is repeated in its entirety at K II, p. 338–339, Tha 5, 2. The original in this case seems to be the *Theragāthā* poem. The *Aṅguttara* verse contains one *śloka* not found in the *Theragāthā* poem, and there is no reason to account for its suppression if the latter was copying from the former. Besides, *sayaṁ* in the *Theragāthā* (697), is changed into *seyyaṁ* in the *Aṅguttara,* under the influence, perhaps of *nisinno* in the second *pāda* of the line. Finally, the introduction in prose in the *Aṅguttara* lacks originality and inspriation, as if it had been artificially added to an original poem. The *śloka* just quoted is applied to the Buddha Paduma, but substituting *manobhāvaniyaṁ* for *manussabhūtaṁ,* at K VII, Apd 2, p. 15 (43, 10, 157). Again we find *attadantaṁ* coupled with *samāhitaṁ,* applied to the sage Senetta, in K II, p. 223, Ptv 1, 42, 755. Once more we find *attadantaṁ* coupled with *samāhitaṁ,* in K VI, p. 54, Apd 1 (1, 3, 562). All this shows that self-control is a necessary condition for recollectedness or integration of mind.

42. 'Steadfastness of mind, firmness, stability, imperturbability, recollectedness, intellectual balance, calm, concentration, right concentration and power of concentration; having obtained the equanimity of the fourth *jhāna,* being with one-pointed mind, with a well balanced mind, that means to be with a self well composed (*samāhitatto*), having obtained equanimity', K IV, pt. I, pp. 440–441, Mnd 1, 16, 207. The sense of *samāhitatto* is also explained in a definition of the ideal bhikkhu, attributed to the Buddha and given at the request of Sāriputta:

With eyes always lowered, never a loafer,
given to the musing of the constantly watchful,
practising equanimity, with a self well composed (*samāhitatto*).

K I, p. 417, Stn 4, 16, 207. See also, *eko santusito samāhitatto,* said of a bhikkhu who resorts to the forest, at K II, p. 235, Tha 1, 6. And:

When shall I, mindful, with a self well composed (*samāhitatto*),
Attain to that which was known by the great sage, the four truths difficult to comprehend?

K II, p. 377, Tha 19, 1, 1101. Finally, we see *samāhitatto* used in combination with *ajjhattaratī* ('in love with the self or with the things of the self'), in a description of a true bhikkhu:

Who fares rightly, saintly, mindful, a muser with fancies controlled, earnest,
In love with the things of the self (*ajjhattaratī*), with a self well composed

(*samāhitatto*), alone, satisfied; such, they say, is a [true] bhikkhu. K II, p. 365, Tha 17, 2, 981.

43. Applied to anchorites in *saññatattā tapassino,* in K II, p. 92, Vmv 2, 13, 141; repeated at *Ibid.,* p. 158, Ptv 1, 18, 220. The first line of the *śloka* is found interpolated at K III, pt. I, p. 358, J, *Tiṁsanipāto,* 511, 18. *Saññatattā tapassino* is also found at K I, p. 311, Stn 2, 7, 64. *Sasaññatattā* is given as a qualification of those worthy to receive the offering of a brāhmaṇa desirous of merit at K I, p. 342, Stn 3, 5, 96.
44. In a description of a muni, at K I, p. 342, Stn 3, 11, 322.
45. Found in a beautiful dialogue where the moral agent addresses the mind, complaining of the latter's inconstancy; K II, p. 380, Tha 19, 1, 1122.
46. K I, p. 66, Ud 1, 4, 8. The whole *sutta* is incorporated into the *Ajapālakathā* of the *Mahāvagga* (p. 4, *Mahākkhandhaka,* 4).
47. K I, p. 299, Stn 3, 12, 218. See also, *vedagū samito yatatto*; K II, p. 236, Tha 1, 10; and *yatattā,* referring to those who are worthy to receive oblations on the part of a brāhmaṇa intent on gaining merit, K I, p. 341, Stn 3, 5, 88.
48. M III, p. 11, *Devadahasutta,* 10. I. B. Horner, *The Collection of Middle Length Sayings,* Vol. III, pp. 10–11, translates, 'a monk does not let the unmastered self be mastered by anguish'. But the P. T. S.'s *Pāli-English Dictionary,* s. v. Addha 2 (which is said to be connected with the Sanskrit word *ārdra,* 'wet') quotes this phrase and translates it as 'he dirties the impure self with ill'. There is a *na* at the beginning of the phrase that seems to be left untranslated. The proper translation seems to be the one just given.
49. See for instance:

    evaṁ tu sañjayassāvi pāvakammanirāsave,
    bhavakoḍīsañciyaṁ kammaṁ tavasā nijjarijjai.

    Pandit Dhirajlal Shah, *Op. cit.,* p. 42. And:

    cariteṇa nigiṇhāi taveṇa parisujjhaī.

    This doctrine is reflected in the Pāli Canon. In the *Cūḷadukkhakkhandhasutta* (6 f.) of the *Majjhima* (M I, p. 128 f.) we meet a Jaina telling the Buddha that, according to Nāṭhaputta, evil deeds previously done should be annuled by means of severe penance. The Buddha argues that such position is absurd, as the Jainas do not know how many evil deeds are actually imputed to them, and how much penance is required to get rid of them, with the consequence that they are bound to practise penance without measure, i.e., in a blind manner. The principle that the Buddhist Canon attributes to the Jainas reads, 'Happiness is not to be obtained by happiness, happiness is to be obtained by pain'.
50. M III, pp. 13–14, *Devadahasutta,* 12.

51. Pe Maung Tin, *The Path of Purity* (London, 1971), p. 2.
52. K I, p. 43, Dhp 20, 277. The two following stanzas are repetitions of this one, changing the first pāda respectively into, *sabbe saṅkhārā dukkhā,* and *sabbe saṅkhārā anattā.*
53. In the *Majjhima* we are told that *anupādāparinibbāna* is not *sīlavisuddhi,* nor *cittavisuddhi,* nor *diṭṭhivisuddhi,* nor *kaṅkāvitaraṇavisuddhi,* nor *maggāmaggañāṇadassanavisuddhi,* nor *ñāṇadassanavisuddhi,* because there is some kind or other of rebirth-basis in every one of them. These types of *visuddhi* are compared to relay chariots. Every one of them conduces only to the immediately following one, until one comes to *ñāṇadassanavisuddhi,* 'purity arising from knowledge and insight'. This last one takes one finally to *nibbāna* without any rebirth-basis. M I, p. 194 f., *Rathavinītasutta,* 7 f.
54. K I, p. 33, Dhp 12, 165. But the 'immediate' source of purity and impurity cannot be one and the same. Purity is an attribute of the true self, that goes on asserting its absolute independence from the non-self. Impurity is generated by the active influence of the asmimanic or *diṭṭhigata* self. The things that make the self impure are listed in the *Cullaniddesa*: any misconduct in body, mind, and word, wrong views, wrong intention, wrong purpose, wrong resolve, which are listed after a clear reference to the asmimanic or *diṭṭhigata* self. K IV, pt. II, p. 323, Cln 3, 0, 41.
55. K I, p. 39, Dhp 18, 239. Also:

    What training undertaking, he, concentrated, prudent, mindful,
    May cleanse the impurity of the self, as the silver-smith cleanses the impurity of the silver?

    K I, p. 415, Stn 4, 16, 197.
56. K IV, pt. I, p. 419, Mnd 1, 16, 197.
57. S V, p. 22, *Maggasaṁyutta,* 34; *Ibid.,* p. 77, *Bhojjhaṅgasaṁyutta,* 17; A IV, pp. 289–290, *Dasakanipāto,* 12, 5 and 6 (twice); A IV, pp. 307–308, *Dasakanipāto,* 17, 3 and 4 (twice); K I, p. 25, Dhp 6, 87. All these passages have something in common. All of them have the same group of *ślokas* repeated together in a context where those just quoted are found. Except for the passage of the *Dhammapada,* all the other passages have a prose section that speaks of the hither and yonder shores, an idea that connects with the first *śloka.* For the rest, the only other specific connection between the respective prose of the *suttas* and their metrical part is found at *Bojjhaṅgasaṁyutta,* 17, where the prose part speaks not only of crossing to the yonder shore, but also of the limbs of wisdom (*bhojjhaṅgā*), which are mentioned in the last *śloka* of the group (where the intervening line seems to be a later addition). It seems, therefore that this was the original place from where all the other passages borrowed the

group of *ślokas.*

58. M I, p. 346, *Cūḷaassapurasutta,* 5.
59. A III, pp. 236–238, *Sattakanipāto,* 7, 3, 14 f. The phrase occurs also at A I, p. 47, *Dukanipāto,* 2, 1.
60. 'Leaving aside the taking of what is not given, abstaining from taking what is not given, Gotama the samaṇa, is a recipient of what is given, one who expects what is given, therefore, on account of this, he dwells with a self made pure', D I, p. 6, *Brahmajālasutta,* 8; *Ibid.,* p. 55, *Sāmaññaphalasutta,* 45. The rest of the passages are found mostly in the *Aṅguttara.* See A I, p. 195, *Tikanipāto,* 7, 10; A III, p. 347, *Aṭṭhakanipāto,* 5, 1, 3; A IV, p. 33, *Navakanipāto,* 2, 8, 1; A IV, p. 265, *Dasakanipāto,* 10, 9, 8. A comparative study of these passages tells us that the last one belongs to the oldest tradition. The reason is that the precept to abstain from intoxicants has not yet been included in the list, while it is found in all the other passages quoted, except those of the *Dīghanikāya,* which are a faithful adaptation of the last one. The last passage quoted from the *Aṅguttara* is not the only one in which the precept to abstain from the intoxicants is lacking. See for instance, A I, p. 179, *Tikanipāto,* 7, 6, where the list is given several times without mentioning the intoxicants, and A II, p. 233, *Catukkanipāto,* 21, 3, 3, where the list occurs twice without any mention of intoxicants. The phrase *sucibhūtena attanā viharati* is found in the Mahānidesa, while commenting upon *theyyaṁ na kare.* K IV, pt. I, p. 427 (1, 16, 202).
61. S I, pp. 168–169, *Brāhmaṇasaṁyutta,* 9.

NOTES TO CHAPTER 6: 'THE SELF AND PERFECTION'

1. A III, pp. 87–88, *Chakkanipāto,* 6, 1, 3. The whole passage is also found in the *Mahāvagga* (pp. 202–203, *Cammakkhandhaka,* 6), as a part of a complete account of Soṇa's conversion and obtention of arahantship. The latter seems to be original setting of the passage, which, taken from the fuller account, was included in the *Chakkanipāto* of the *Aṅguttara,* doubtless because *cha ṭhānāni,* 'six respects', are mentioned in it. If we divide the passage of the *Aṅguttara* into three parts, the first part, dealing with the simile of the *viṇā,* has nothing to do with the number six; the second part is where the *cha ṭhānāni* are enumerated; the third part refers to the senses with the mind, which are again six. A discrepancy in the texts is to be noted. In the *Aṅguttara* we read, *karaṇīyaṁ attano samanupassati* (repeated three times), while in the *Mahāvagga* the reading is, *karaṇīyaṁ attānaṁ samanupassati.* If the *Aṅguttara* reading is a correction made on the *Mahāvagga* reading (both might be

dependent on a third source) it is an acceptable correction. In the first place, the reading of the *Aṅguttara* fits perfectly in the context. In the second place, the reading of the *Mahāvagga* is unusual and the only door open for its acceptance is to consider *karaṇīyaṁ* equivalent to *bhāvetabbaṁ*. But there is no parallel expression as regards this reading, while there are some in the case of *karaṇīyaṁ attano,* one soon to be adduced from the *Dhammapada,* and the other, *attano kiccakārīssa,* 'he would be a doer of what is to be done for the self', K II, p. 342, Tha 16, 2, 727.

2. K I, p. 37, Dhp 16, 217.
3. The *Aṅguttara* speaks of four types of men: one who drifts with the current, one who goes against the current, one whose self is well established (*ṭhitatto*), and one who has crossed, and stands on dry land. *Ṭhitatto* stands here for one due to arise by a spontaneous rebirth, there to attain *nibbāna,* never to return to the world because he has destroyed the five lower fetters. A II, p. 7, *Catukkanipāto,* 1, 5, 1 and 3. This division into four seems to be a later elaboration of a simpler one preserved in the Jaina literature, where, 'going with the current', means *saṁsāra,* and going against the current means 'crossing it', (*aṇusoo saṁsāro paḍisoo tassa uttāro*). Pandit Dhirajlal Shah, *Op. cit.,* p. 132. In the metrical part of the *sutta* the term is explained as follows:

   Whoever, having left aside the five impurities,
   a perfect disciple, not liable to give up,
   has attained to the mastery of the mind, recollected as to the senses,
   Such is called a man whose self is perfectly established (*ṭhitatto*).

   A II, p. 6, *Catukkanipāto,* 1, 5, 4.
4. K I, p. 321, Stn 2, 13, 139.
5. K I, p. 322, Stn 2, 13, 150. The same bhikkhu is called, *saṅkhārānirodhañāṇakusalo, sabbāyatanehi vippamutto, sabbupadhīnaṁ parikkhayāno,* all terms indicative of the highest perfection.
6. K II, p. 235, Tha, 1, 5. See also, so *parinibbuto ṭhitatto* at K II, p. 235, Tha 1, 7 and 8.
7. K I, p. 348, Stn 3, 6, 118. Quoted at K IV, pt. II, p. 90, Cln 2, 4, 28. Other contexts where the term *ṭhitatto* is found:

   (a) In a definition of a true samaṇa:

   One who knowing them well, entirely abandons
   all grasping and all avarice,
   People say he is a true samaṇa, self-controlled,
   of self perfectly established (*ṭhitatto*), unselfish, unattached.

   K III, pt. I, pp. 195–196, J, *Dasakanipāto,* 441, 27.

   (b)K I, p. 299, Stn 1, 12, 217:

Whoever is perfectly established as to self (*ṭhitatto*),
straight like a shuttle,
Loathes sinful deeds....

(c) K I, p. 316, Stn 2, 9, 108:

Leaving aside laughter, chatter, lamentations, ill-will,
Hypocrisy, deceit, greed and conceit,
Anger, harsh speech, impurity, infatuation,
He should fare unelated, with a self perfectly established (*ṭhitatto*).

8. K IV, pt. I, p. 300, Mnd 1, 14, 155.
9. *Khandhapariyante ṭhito, dhātupariyante ṭhito, etc.* K IV, pt. II, p. 91, Cln 2, 4, 28.
10. K V, p. 503 f., Pṭs 3, 9, 2, 12 f.
11. A III, p. 89, *Chakkanipāto,* 6, 1, 11.
12. K IV, pt. I, p. 383, Mnd 1, 15, 187.
13. D III, p. 103, *Pāsādikasutta,* 23. The first five, which possibly might have constituted the original list, are given under the title *abhabbaṭṭhānāni* at D III, p. 182–183, *Saṅgītisutta,* 21.
14. As A. B. Keith very well says, 'Things are impermanent (*anicca*); in early Buddhism they are not literally momentary, a refinement of later thought' (*Buddhist Philosophy,* Varanasi, 1963, p. 92). Strictly speaking, momentariness precludes any sort of duration (*ṭhiti*). But duration in the midst of change is implied in the scheme: *uppādo, vayo,* and *ṭhitassa aññathattaṁ,* that is to say, 'origination, decay, and change of the compound thing (*saṅkhata*), while it lasts (*ṭhitassa*)', A I, pp. 139–140, *Tikanipāto,* 5, 7. And even in the *Mahā niddesa,* while commenting on *appañhidaṁ jīvitamāhu dhīrā,* we read of the insignificance of life's duration (*ṭhitiparittatā*), and the paucity of life's substance (*sarasaparittatā*). In the first verse of those that illustrate the insignificance of life's duration the word *khaṇo* does occur, but not with the later metaphysical meaning, inasfar as it applies not only to pleasure and pain but also to life and individual samsaric existence (*attabhāvo*). See K IV, pt. I, p. 36, Mnd 1, 2, 10; *Ibid.* p. 98 (1, 6, 39). On the other hand, the individual's identity through the changes of life is asserted in:

    Old age befalls like an accursed thing,
    Bodily form, though being the same, appears as if it were different,
    And even though conscious of it, and having never gone away from it,
    I remember my self (*attānaṁ*) as if it were that of another.

    K II, p. 261, Tha 1, 118. This same consciousness of identity through life is implied in the oft-recurring line:

    Ever since I remember my self (*attānaṁ*), since I attained the years of discretion....

K III, pt. I, p. 169, J, *Aṭṭhakanipāto,* 419, 20; *Ibid.,* p. 232, J, *Ekādasanipāto,* 463, 120; K III, pt. II, p. 183, J, *Mahānipāto,* 540, 307; K VI, p. 394, Apd 1 (40, 1, 179); *Ibid.,* p. 427 (41, 1, 24); K VII, p. 58, Apd 2 (49, 4, 68); *Ibid.,* p. 65 (49, 8, 152); *Ibid.,* p. 237, *Therīapadāna* (3, 1, 29).

15. V, 24. The other two passages where the compound *brahmabhūto* occurs are, VI, 27, and XVIII, 54.
16. See *sucibhūtena* above in *sucibhūtena attanā viharati,* D I, p. 6, *Brahmajāla-sutta,* 8, etc., and *tuṇhībhūtaṁ,* A II, p. 195, *Catukkanipāto,* 19, 10, 1.
17. A II, p. 195, *Catukkanipāto,* 19, 10, 3–5.
18. A II, pp. 468–469, *Pañcakanipāto,* 20, 2, 3.
19. M I, p. 148, *Madhupiṇḍikasutta,* 6. This passage is often repeated. See M III, p. 270, *Mahākaccānabhaddekarattasutta,* 4; M III, pp. 306–307, *Uddesavi-bhaṅgasutta,* 3; S IV, p. 88, *Saḷāyatanasaṁyutta,* 116; A IV, p. 284, *Dasaka-nipāto,* 12, 3, etc. A similar semblance of lateness can be discovered in D III, p. 66, *Aggaññasutta,* 8, where the Buddha is called, *dhammakāyo, brahma-kāyo, dhammabhūto, brahmabhūto.* And the same should be said by analogy of a passage where the Buddha calls himself *brahmabhūto.* K I, p. 358, Stn 3, 7, 160.
20. S II-III, pp. 309–310, *Khandhasaṁyutta,* 76.
21. A I, p. 182, *Tikanipāto,* 7, 6.
22. M II, p. 6 and 7, *Kandarakasutta,* 4 and 5. A shorter formula, which may be older, at A II, p. 219, *Catukkanipāto,* 20, 8, and D III, p. 181, *Saṅgītisutta,* 19.
23. M II, p. 14, *Kandarakasutta,* 16. This extensive description of the four types is repeated at M II, p. 89 f., *Apaṇṇakasutta,* 14 f.; *Ibid.,* p. 415 f., *Ghoṭamūkhasutta,* 2 f.; A II, p. 219, *Catukkanipāto,* 20, 8.
24. K IV, pt. I, p. 383, Mnd 1, 15, 187. Similar is the passage that comments on *kāmesu nabhigijjeyya,* 'he should not crave for sensual pleasures', at K IV, pt. II, pp. 39–40, Cln 2, 1, 8. There are other commentarial amplifications wound up in the same way with, 'satisfied, quenched (*nibbuto*), cooled, experiencing happiness, he dwells with a self brahma-become (*brahmabhūtena attanā vi-harati*)'. Thus:

    (a) 'Before the breaking up of the body, before the dissolution of the sam-saric individuality, before the setting aside of the body, before the cutting off of the vital principle, free from craving, having foregone craving... satisfied, quenched, cooled, experiencing happiness, he dwells with a self brahma-be-come', while commenting on *vītataṇho purā bhedā,* at K IV, pt. I, p. 176, Mnd 1, 10, 84. See also K IV, pt. II, p. 14, Cln 2, 4, 29.

(b) 'In a village, he should not make acquisitions, he should not take possession of anything, he should not be bound to anything, he should not be attached to anything, he should be without greed, not enslaved... cooled, experiencing happiness, he dwells with a self brahma-become', while commenting on *gāme nabhisajjeyya,* at K IV, pt. I, p. 331, Mnd 1, 14, 164.

25. *Ñāṇagginā daḍḍhaṁ* with the corresponding variations in number and gender, recurs often in the *Niddesa.* For instance, K IV, pt. I, p. 60, Mnd 1, 3, 18; *Ibid.,* p. 69 (1, 3, 22); *Ibid.,* p. 300 (1, 14, 155); K IV, pt. II, p. 14, Cln 2, 4, 29; *Ibid.,* p. 139 (2, 9, 58); *Ibid.,* p. 156 (2, 11, 69).
26. K IV, pt. II, p. 150, Cln 2, 11, 65.
27. See, for instance, the following passages of the *Mahāniddesa: cakkhusamphussaṁ vivittaṁ passati attena vā attaniyena vā...,* K IV, pt. I, p. 186, Mnd 1, 10, 86; *sabbe saṅkhārā aniccā... sabbe saṅkhārā dukkhā... sabbe dhammā anattā, Ibid.,* p. 206 (1, 10, 91); repeated at *Ibid.,* p. 227 (1, 11, 103); p. 397, (1, 16, 191), etc.; *kathaṁ diṭṭhivinicchayaṁ karoti..., Ibid.,* p. 224 (1, 11, 102); *rūpaṁ... aniccato, dukkhato... parato... anattato... tīreti, Ibid.* p. 233 (1, 11, 107); *yaṁ bhikkhave na tumhākaṁ taṁ pajahatha, Ibid.,* p. 380 (1, 15, 186); *suññaṁ attena vā attaniyena vā, Ibid.,* p. 381 (1, 15, 186), etc.
28. On the history of the translation of *bhāvitatto,* Mrs. Rhys Davids observes, 'Fausböll saw this (that *bhāvanā, bhāvita* is the causative of "becoming" = make become) and renders the term *bhāvitattānaṁ* by *semet ipsum colit*: "cultivates the very self", as were It the man's garden. Max-Müller with his "him whose soul is well grounded", is less accurate, but he is better than many more recent translators, with "meditates on the self", "self-subdued", and the like. The commentator of the *Dhammapada* ((who was certainly *not* Buddhaghosa) has been too much ignored with his "*vaḍḍhitattānaṁ", "*the self made to grow", So, too, has Buddhaghosa's vigorous definition in the Commentary on Dhammasaṅgaṇi – "bhāveti means beget, causes to arise, causes to grow" – been overlooked' (*The Minor Anthologies of the Pāli Canon,* Intr., pp. xx–xxi).
29. K I, p. 426, Stn 5, 5, 74.
30. The explanation of *bhāvitatto* seems to be completed after the last *bhāvita* compound (*bhāvitamaggo*), or at most after the compound *sacchikatanirodho.* Whatever follows becomes simply repetitious. Thus, *tassa maggo bhāvito* repeats *bhāvitamaggo; nirodho sacchikato* repeats *sacchikatanirodho; abhiññeyyaṁ pariññātaṁ* and *paññeyyaṁ pariññātaṁ* repeat *bhāvitapañño,* and *bhāvetabbaṁ bhāvitaṁ* repeats the whole preceding passage where all the particulars to be developed have been listed and reckoned as developed. The lengthy passage that follows, beginning with *cakkhunā rūpaṃ disvā neva sumano,* etc., deals in different ways not precisely with self-development but

with control of the senses and consequent equanimity. The reason for the addition of this lengthy passage is the last stanza quoted at the end of it, where the word *bhāvita* occurs twice.

31. K IV, p. II, p. 68 f., Cln 2, 4, 18.
32. K I, p. 221, Itv 3, 19. See also:

(a) 'of the Noble One, whose self is fully developed (*bhāvitattassa*)... of this Blessed One am I a disciple', M II, pp. 59–60, *Upālisutta,* 21.

(b) *Buddhassa bhāvitattassa* is said of a former Buddha at K VI, p. 249, Apd 1 (22, 2, 6).

(c) 'Both with selves fully developed, both bearing bodies for the last time', said of Ghaṭikāra, who had been a friend of Gotama in a previous existence, and of the Buddha himself. S I, p. 34, *Devatāsaṁyutta,* 50. Also, *Ibid.,* p. 58, *Devaputtasaṁyutta,* 24.

(d) 'Impelled by him, whose self was fully developed (*bhāvitattena*), who was bearing a body for the last time...', said of the Buddha, at K II, p. 387, Tha 20, 1, 1173. The same line found at K II, p. 27, Vmv 1, 21, 197, and K II, p. 168, Ptv 1, 21, 323.

33. K I, p. 229, Itv 3, 28. Other instances:

(a) S I, p. 50, *Devaputtasaṁyutta,* 14:

He who is virtuous, wise, with a self fully developed (*bhāvitatto*),
Inwardly recollected, fond of musing, mindful,
With all grief abandoned, suppressed,
Who has destroyed all the *āsavas,* bearing the last body....

(b) K I, p. 255, Itv 4, 5:

Leading to delight, such is the state of those who know,
That is, of those whose self is fully developed (*bhāvitattānaṁ*), of those who live the life of the Noble Ones....

It is immediately said that they do not come to new existence (*nāgacchanti punabbhavaṁ*).

34. K II, p. 92, Vmv 2, 13, 142. Repeated at K II, p. 158, Ptv 1, 18, 221. Other testimonies:

(a) The *Itivuttaka* gives us the following classification of those who either are already perfect or on their way to perfection, the second class being constituted by the arahants, who are *bhāvitattā*:

First in the world is the Teacher, the great sage,
He is followed by the disciple who has developed the self (*bhāvittato*),
Then comes the learner, who follows the way,
Who has heard much and is endowed with virtues and practice.

K I, p. 236, Itv 3, 35.

(b) In the *Isigilisutta* one of the *paccekasaṁbuddhas* is called *bhāvitatto.* M III, p. 133, *Isigilisutta,* 4.

(c) In the *Nidānagāthā* of the *Theragāthā,* those whose verses follow are called *bhāvitattā.* They were perfect men, as it is clear from the verses that follow, like, 'having atained the unfailing state (*nibbāna*)...', K II, p. 233, Tha, *Nidānagāthā.*

(d) The Theragāthā draws a contrast between the bhikkhus who at that time were around Phussa, men of moral perfection (*bhāvitatte susaṁvute*), and the bhikkhus who in future times will fall short of the ideal set before them and whose miserable condition is described in the poem. Mrs. Rhys Davids, in her translation, *Psalms of the Brethren,* p. xviii, says it is a later poem. It may well describe, under the garb of a prophetic utterance, conditions prevailing at the time of its composition. See K II, p. 363, Tha 17, 1, 949.

35. K I, p. 27, Dhp 8, 106. The immediately following verse provides us with the same teaching. See also:

 Worthy of offerings is the possessor of knowledge (*vedagū*), whose self is fully developed (*bhāvitatto*),
 He is worthy of offerings from men and gods,
 Who having expelled all sin, untainted,
 Goes in search of food, entirely cooled.

 S I, p. 142, *Brahmasaṁyutta,* 3. Other texts warn of the danger of doing harm to such perfect beings or showing them disrespect. K I, p. 310, Stn 2, 6, 57; A III, pp. 172–173, *Sattakanipāto,* 3, 10 and 11.

36. K I, p. 315, Stn 2, 8, 102. The term *bhāvitatto* is applied sometimes to people who were considered to be spiritually perfect, but who, in reality, were not so. It is said of Devadatta, *paṇḍito ti samaññato, bhāvitatto ti sammato,* at Clv p. 304, (7, 10, 21). All the stanzas of this passage are repeated in the *Itivuttaka,* together with the prose part that precedes them, but the prose part is more elaborately redacted in the *Itivuttaka* (3, 40).

37. *Maggaṁ Buddho ācikkhati. Attanā paṭipajjamānā muñceyyuṁ.* K IV, pt. I, p. 28, Mnd 1, 2, 8. And *Ibid.* on the previous page we find, *natthañño mocetā.*

38. K II, p. 257, Tha 1, 101.

39. K II, p. 347, Tha 16, 4, 784. According to the *Crit. Pāli Dict., avyositattā* is here the ablative case of the abstract noun *avyositatta.* A look at the *variae lectiones* shows both interpretations to be possible.

40. M II, p. 234, *Mahāsakuludāyisutta,* 13. Note the subsidiarity of the mind as regards the moral agent. The moral agent, by means of the mind, and not the mind of itself and for itself, is the one 'that contemplates the mind in the mind', The moral agent is the one that 'undertakes effort, exerts the mind', etc.

41. For some other passages of many that could be quoted, see: S IV, p. 316 f., *Asaṅkhatasaṁyutta,* 12; S V, p. 61 f., Bojjhaṅgasaṁyutta (*passim*); A III, p. 388 f., Aṭṭhakanipāto, 7, 3; K IV, pt. I, pp. 7–8. Mnd 1, 1, 3.
42. K II, p. 332, Tha 13, 1, 637.
43. *Na tatra sūryo bhāti, na candratārakaṁ,*
    nemā vidyuto bhānti, kuto'yamagniḥ.

    Kaṭha Up. V, 15; *Muṇḍ. Up.* II, 2, 10; *Śvetāśvatara Up.* III, 2. The triple repetition of the stanza warrants its popularity, and makes its influence even in non-upanishadic circles more likely.
44. K I, p. 72, Ud 1, 10, 22. Repeated at K VII, Apd 2, p. 125 (54, 6, 210–220). Here, too, the verses are attributed to the Buddha, but they are found in a part of the poem that is an obvious addition to Bāhiya's original *Apadāna.* The original passage of the Pāli Canon, of which the present passage is apparently a further elaboration, is the following one:
    Yattha āpo ca pathavī, tejo vāyo na gādhati,
    Ato sarā nivattanti, ettha vaṭṭhaṁ na vattati,
    ettha nāmaṁ ca rūpaṁ ca, asesaṁ uparujjhati.

    S I, p. 16, *Devatāsaṁyutta,* 27.
45. The *Udāna* contains a passage that bears similar marks, but is more Buddhist in character, 'There is, bhikkhus, that sphere, were there is no earth, no water, no fire, no air, no sphere of infinite space, no sphere of infinite consciousness, no sphere of no-thing, no sphere of neither-perception-nor-non-perception, no this world, no other-world, neither both the moon or the sun. There, besides, there is no coming, no going, no staying, no arising, so I declare. It is not something fixed, not something that moves on, it is just something unconceivable (*anārammaṇaṁ*). That is precisely the end of Pain'. K I, p. 162, Ud 8, 1, 2. It will not be out of place to note that these texts are found in the later parts of the *Nikāyas,* and that the objectifying process of what originally was just a subjective condition (*nibbāna*) is already advanced.
46. K I, p. 347, Stn 3, 6, 113. Quoted at K IV, pt. I, p. 59, Mnd 1, 3, 18; K IV, pt. II, p. 42, Cln 2, 1, 8. The word *attanā,* 'as regards the self or by means of the self', occurs ten times in a passage of the *Aṅguttara,* with reference to various points of perfection, the last ones being: *attanā samādhisampanno, attanā paññāsampanno, attanā vimuttisampanno, attanā vimuttiñāṇadassana-sampanno.* A man endowed with these, is one who, either has attained *nibbāna,* or is about to attain it, and all these points of perfection are related to *attā.* A IV, p. 203–204, *Dasakanipāto,* 7, 10.
47. K IV, pt. II, pp. 100–101, Cln 2, 5, 33. Repeated at K IV, pt I, p. 28, Mnd 1, 2, 8, commenting upon *na hi aññamokkhā.* A little below it is stated that:

The Tathāgata is one who shows the way. They are to be saved following it by their [very] self (*attanā*).

K IV, pt. II, p. 101, Cln 2, 5, 33. Also, K IV, pt. I, p. 28, Mnd 1, 2, 8. In the same context we are told:

That whoever, Cunda, is untamed, untrained, has not attained *nibbāna* as regards the self [or by his self, *attanā*], should cause another to be tamed, to be trained, or to attain *nibbāna,* this is not possible.

K IV, pt. I, p. 27, Mnd 1, 2, 8. Also, K IV, pt. II, p. 101, Cln 2, 5, 33.

48. M II, p. 18, *Aṭṭhakanāgarasutta,* 5. Repeated at A IV, p. 387, *Ekādasanipāto,* 2, 6. See also:

Death is very near you, [to take place] within five months,
O prince, know this, cause the self to be freed (*attānaṁ parimocaya*).

K II, p. 92, Vmv 2, 13, 134. And:

I shall cause the self to attain *nibbāna* (*sannibbāpemi attānaṁ*), having obliterated all [samsaric] existences.

K VI, p. 168, Apd 1 (11, 8, 49).

49. K VII, p. 215, *Therīapadāna,* 2, 7, 286–288.
50. A II, pp. 320–321, *Pañcakanipāto,* 5, 8, 4–5. The same is asserted regarding *byādhidhammaṁ, maraṇadhammaṁ, khayadhammaṁ,* and *nassanadhammaṁ.*
51. Cf. above, Chapter 3, par. 'Salvation in general and the self'.
52. S II-III, p. 70, *Nidānasaṁyutta,* 51. There is also a text that applies to *nibbāna* what in other parts of the Canon is said of *dhamma,* '*Nibbāna* is to be attained in this very life, not subject to time, inviting to come and see, leading to the highest good, to be experienced by wise men in their very self (*paccattaṁ veditabbaṁ viññūhi*)', A I, p. 147, *Tikanipāto,* 6, 5.
53. A III, pp. 238–239, *Sattakanipāto,* 7, 3, 21–22. The formula is repeated in connexion with every one of the *jhānas.*
54. K I, p. 94, Ud 3, 5, 13. We are provided with an indirect confirmation of the same in, 'Even as, Nandiya, a bhikkhu, who is absolutely free, does not see anything to be done for the self (*karaṇīyaṁ attano*) or to be added to what has been done', A IV, p. 379, *Ekādasanipāto,* 2, 3, 9. If absolute freedom (*nibbāna*) implies a state of perfection where nothing more is left to be done for the self, this means that absolute freedom is the most that can be done for the self, which therefore becomes the beneficiary of absolute freedom. A similar reasoning may be applied to texts that speak of the destruction of the pain of the self (*dukkhaṁ attano*), where *dukkha* epitomizes the entire misery of *saṁsāra,* and in the contex stands clearly for salvation. See, M II, p. 465, *Vāseṭṭhasutta,* 5, *Yo dukkhassa pajānāti... tamahaṁ brūmi brāhmaṇaṁ.* Re-

peated at K I, p. 55, Dhp 26, 402, and *Ibid.,* p. 366, Stn 3, 9, 225.

55. K I, p. 43, Dhp 20, 285.
56. K IV, pt. I, p. 291, Mnd 1, 14, 150.
57. K I, p. 414, Stn 4, 15, 175. *Sikkhe nibbānamattano* occurs again at K I, p. 428, Stn 5, 6, 86.
58. K IV, pt. I, p. 363, Mnd 1, 15, 175. Repeated at K IV, pt. II, p. 96, Cln 2, 5, 30; and *Ibid.* p. 97 (2, 5, 31).
59. K I, p. 95, Ud 3, 6, 15. See also, K I, p. 335, Stn 3, 4, 52, where the Buddha speaks of himself; K I, p. 337, Stn 3, 4, 67; K I, p. 318, Stn 2, 12, 123; repeated at K II, p. 396, Tha 21, 1, 1272; K I, p. 390, Stn 4, 3, 18; K VI, Apd 1, p. 161 (10, 7, 38); K III, pt. I, p. 87, J, *Catukkanipāto,* 303, 12.
60. K IV, pt. I, p. 59, Mnd 1, 3, 18. We read in the *Apadāna,* 'The triple fire has been extinguished for me (*tiyaggī nibbutā mayhaṁ*)'; where *mayhaṁ* represents the moral agent as the beneficiary of the threefold extinction of the *āsavas,* not as the entity to be extinguished. K VII, p. 33, Apd 2 (46, 2, 12).
61. K IV, pt. I, p. 200, Mnd 1, 10, 89, where we are told of a bhikkhu who learns thoroughly the *suttanta,* the *vinaya* and the *abhidhamma,* not for the sake of some temporal advantage, but for the purpose of the mastery of the self (*attadamatthāya*), for the purpose of the quiescence of the self (*attasamatthāya*), for the purpose of the utter cooling of the self (*attaparinibbānatthāya*). The text shows that some kind of *abhidhamma* was already in existence. The term *attaparinibbāna* is missing in the *Crit. Pāli Dict.,* which mentions only *attaparinibbāpana,* translated as 'complete emancipation of one's self'. In K V, p. 201, Pṭs 1, 3, 3, 28, ten proper aims (*yathattā*) are enumerated, the first three being, *attadamathattho, attasamathatto,* and *attaparinibbānattho.*
62. *Ekamattānaṁ damenti, ekamattānaṁ samenti, ekamattānaṁ parinibbā penti,* where *eka* seems to have the sense of singleness of purpose. A III, p. 188, *Sattakanipāto,* 5, 4, 15. *Ekamattānaṁ dameti, ekamattānaṁ sameti, ekamattānaṁ parinibbāpeti,* occurs in A I, p. 155, *Tikanipāto,* 6, 10. Finally, A II, p. 72, *Catukkanipāto,* 7, 1, 16, uses the same words as A III, p. 188, except that, instead of *parappavādā paṭiviratā,* we find *madappamādā paṭiviratā.*
63. K IV, pt. I, p. 383, Mnd 1, 15, 187. For other passages, see above the section entitled 'He dwells with a self brahma-become'.

NOTES TO CHAPTER 7: 'THE SELF AS RELATED TO *KAMMA* AND REBIRTH'

1. Pe Maung Tin, *The Path of Purity,* (London 1971) p. 726.

2. A I, pp. 129–130, *Tikanipāto,* 4, 6.
3. S I, p. 71, *Kosalasaṁyutta,* 4.
4. K I, p. 18, Dhp 1, 15–16. The following stanzas are also to the point, even though they do not explicitly link *kamma* with *attā.*
5. K III, pt. I, p. 56, J, *Dukanipāto,* 222; and *Ibid.* p. 113, *Pañckanipāto,* 353, 15.
6. M III, p. 280, *Cūḷakammavibhaṅgasutta,* 2. The same words repeated in a similar context at *Ibid.* p. 286, *Cūḷakammavibhaṅgasutta,* 10. An adaptation of the words with a statement in the first person found at A II, p. 336, *Pañcakanipāto,* 6, 7, 6. A similar passage found several times at A IV, p. 338 f., *Dasakanipāto,* 21, 6, 6, where instead of '*Kamma* divides, etc.', we read, 'Whatever *kamma* they do, meritorious or sinful, they become heirs to it'. See also:

   ... because *kamma* does not get annulled.
   Whatever *kamma* a man does, be it good or bad,
   He is an heir to it, whatever be the *kamma* he does.

   K II, p. 266, Tha 2, 12, 143–144. Also, *Ibid.* 2, 13, 146.
7. K II, p. 458, Thi 15, 1, 436.
8. Pe Maung Tin, *Op. cit.,* p. 602.
9. A IV, p. 345, *Dasakanipāto,* 21, 8, 1. Also, *Ibid.,* p. 347, *Dasakanipāto,* 21, 9, 1.
10. K I, p. 193, Itv 1, 22.
11. K I, p. 372, Stn 3, 10, 265.
12. K II, p. 160, Ptv 1, 19, 238. See also:

    Seen by you are hells, animal births, *petas, asuras,* men and gods,
    You yourself (*sayaṁ*) saw the maturing of the *kamma* of your self (*attano*).

    K II, p. 226, Ptv 1, 46, 793. Repeated at *Ibid.,* pp. 226–227, verse 795. The following testimonies can be gathered from the *Vimānavatthu,*

    (a) What *kamma* did you do formerly by your self (*attanā*),
        Being born as a human being in some former birth,
        A choicest gift, or virtue and self-control?
        Due to what, O glorious one, did you acquired such a wonderful destiny?
        Being questioned, O divine being, explain of which *kamma* this is the fruit.

    K II, p. 36, Vmv 1, 30, 298. Repeated at *Ibid.,* p. 71 (1, 48, 810), but with *sīlasaññamaṁ* as v. 1. to *sīlasaṁyamaṁ.* The first two lines repeated at *Ibid.,* p. 98 (2, 14, 181).

    (b) That such (*tadeva*) profitable *kamma* was done by me,
        And now I experience by my self (*attanā*) this happy *kamma.*

    K II, p. 37, Vmv 1, 30, 302 and 303; *Ibid.,* p. 72 (1, 48, 814 and 815); *Ibid.,*

p. 113 (2, 30, 312); *Ibid.*, p. 117 (2, 32, 350) where, instead of *sukhaṁ ca kammaṁ,* we read *sukhaṁ ca dibbaṁ.*

In the *Jātaka,* too, we find a clear reference to the doer and the experiencer, one or the other being linked with *attā*:

(a) I am experiencing my own (*sakaṁ*) *kamma,* the wrong
action formerly done by my self (*dukkaṭamattano*).

K III, pt. I, p. 385, J. *Tiṁsanipāto,* 516, 221. Repeated in the third person plural at K III, pt. II, p. 69, J, *Saṭṭhinipāto,* 530, 125.

(b) As regards the misery that the slave Bījaka sees in his self (*attani*),
Formerly sin was committed by him, that he is experiencing.

K III, pt. II, p. 277, J, *Mahānipāto,* 545, 1252.

(c) You have got a heavenly mansion, owing to the merits of your self (*attano*).

K III, pt. II, p. 232, J, *Mahānipāto,* 543, 807.

Finally we find some testimonies in the *Apadāna*:

(a) I am experiencing my own (*sakaṁ*) *kamma,* this is the fruit of my service.

K VII, p. 18, Apd 2 (44, 2, 19).

(b) There itself was done by me that *kamma,* which was small and of no account,
Due to that *kamma,* I have gone beyond *saṁsāra.*

K VII, p. 77, Apd 2 (50, 8, 80).

13. S II-III, pp. 96–97, *Nidānasaṁyutta,* 67. Similar assertions are made, with pertinent variations in 'conditions', regarding birth, becoming, grasping, craving, feeling, contact, spheres of sense, name-and-shape, consciousness, with the singularity that the last one, *viññāṅa,* is said to be conditioned by *nāmarūpa,* and *nāmarūpa* by *viññāṇa.*
14. A III, p. 140, *Chakkanipāto,* 9, 11.
15. See also:

    One affected by pleasure or pain in village or forest,
    Should not impute them either to self (*attato*) or another,
    Impressions touch [man] due to basis for existence (*upadhi*),
    How can impressions touch one who is without any basis for existence?

    K I, p. 76, Ud 2, 4, 8.
16. K II, p. 124, Vmv 2, 34, 394; K II, p. 207, Ptv 1, 37, 626; K III, pt. II, p. 317, J, *Mahānipāto,* 546, 1591; *Ibid.* p. 320, verse 1615.
17. See, Har Dayal, *The Bodhisattva Doctrine in Buddhist Sanskrit Literature* (Delhi-Patna-Varanasi, 1970), p. 192. Also, *Ibid.* p. 57 and 181.
18. This gives us the right frame of mind to appreciate the following text, 'This body, bhikkhus, is not yours, neither is it of others. It ought to be considered as past *kamma,* previously formed and planned and to be experienced', S II-

III, p. 55, *Nidānasaṁyutta,* 37. Quoted at K IV, pt. I, p. 379, Mnd 1, 15, 186, and *Ibid.,* pt. II, p. 192, Cln 2, 15, 87, where the arisal of the body is not attributed to any actual efficiency of the individual, but reputed to be the result of past *kamma.* But, who is responsible for such *kamma*? Doubtless the individual himself in its previous existences. Therefore 'moral causality' is not excluded.

19. S II-III, pp. 19–20, *Nidānasaṁyutta,* 17.
20. Cf. G. C. Pande, *Studies in the Origins of Buddhism,* p. 194.
21. S II-III, p. 26, *Nidānasaṁyutta,* 21.
22. S II-III, p. 23, *Nidānasaṁyutta,* 19. Diametrically different is the condition of the fool. He does not undertake the brahma-life for the complete destruction of pain, and is one who will be reborn again; he does not become free from pain.
23. M II, p. 64, *Kukkuravatisutta,* 4. A similar exposition is given regarding the question of deeds that are bright and bright in result, of deeds that are dark and dark in result, and of deeds that are neither bright nor dark in result. The exposition ends by declaring that even the cessation of *kamma,* be it dark, bright, or neither dark nor bright, is also intentional. This indirectly points to the existence of an intentional non-doer, which by way of opposition proves the existence of a doer.
24. Pe Maung Tin, *Op. cit.,* pp. 701–702.
25. A II, p. 138, *Catukkanipāto,* 13, 8, 4.
26. S II-III, p. 278, *Khandhasaṁyutta,* 47.
27. M I, p. 190, *Vammīkasutta,* 3.
28. M III, p. 391, *Mahāsaḷāyatanikasutta,* 4.
29. A III, p. 73, *Chakkanipāto,* 5, 8.
30. M II, p. 203, *Nāgaṇḍiyasutta,* 7.
31. S IV, pp. 186–187, *Vedanāsaṁyutta,* 6.
32. Pe Maung Tin, *Op. cit.,* p. 728.
33. The only *khandha* that might have been expected to transmigrate from one existence to another is *viññāṇa.* But in the *Mahātaṇhāsaṅkhayasutta* of the *Majjhima,* Sāti's pernicious view that *viññāṇa* is permanent and passes on from one existence to another, is disowned by the Buddha using very strong language. M I, p. 315 f.
34. D I, p. 122, *Kuṭadantasutta,* 26. The expression *kāyassa bhedā paraṁ maraṇā,* 'at the dissolution of the body, after death', is of frequent occurrence in the *Nikāyas,* always implying a change in the existential conditions with continuity of the individual.
35. D I, p. 71, *Sāmaññaphalasutta,* 95.

36. K VII, p. 309, Bdv 2, 61.
37. M III, p. 184, *Acchariyaabbhutasutta,* 2–3.
38. D II, p. 149–150, *Mahāsudassanasutta,* 30, 32.
39. II, 22:

    Even as a man, casting off his worn-out (*jīrṇāni*) clothes, puts on new ones, Even so, the embodied [self] casting off his worn-out (*jīrṇāni*) bodies, joins himself to other new ones.
40. K VI, Apd 1, p. 416 (40, 7, 431). See also:

    (a) Due to that good work, and to the aspirations of my mind,
    Abandoning (*jahitvā*) the *kinnara* body, I went to the heaven of the thirty-one gods.

    K VII, Apd 2, p. 92 (52, 6, 30). The *kinnaras* are mentioned only in the latest parts of the *Nikāyas.*

    (b) At the time, Vaccha, when a being both discards (*nikkhipati*) this body, and gets another body (*aññataraṁ kāyaṁ anupanno hoti*)... .

    S IV, p. 342, *Abyākatasaṁyutta,* 9.

    (c) Here itself discarding (*nikkhippa*) their bodily form,
    After the breaking up of the body, they go to heaven.

    K III, Pt. II, p. 107, J, *Asītinipāto,* 535, 207.

    (d) *Purā kāyassa bhedā, purā attabhavassa bhedā, purā kaḷevarassa nikkhepā...*

    K IV, pt. I, p. 176, Mnd 1, 10, 84.

    (e) *Pahāya manusaṁ dehaṁ...*

    D II, p. 190, *Mahāsamayasutta,* 2.
41. A I, pp. 124–125, *Tikanipāto,* 4, 4. The same is asserted of the other two: *dosapakata kamma,* and *mohapakata kamma.* There follows the simile of the seed which planted in the best conditions yields an ample harvest. For other passages, where *attabhāva* occurs, see, D III, p. 86, *Sampasādanīyasutta,* 17; M II, p. 257, *Cūḷasakuludāyisutta,* 4; S II-III, p. 361, *Khandhasaṁyutta,* 96, where it is insisted that *attabhāva* is impermanent, unstable, subject to change; A II, pp. 168–169, *Catukkanipāto,* 18, 1, 6; *Ibid.,* p. 201 f., *Catuk,* 20, 2, 4; A III, p. 117, *Chakkanipāto,* 6, 9, 9; K IV, pt. I, p. 176, Mnd 1, 10, 84; K VI, p. 257, Apd 1 (23, 5, 25). In the *Poṭṭhapādasutta* (D I) the reading is *attapaṭilābho,* but the term, as it stands, has no obvious meaning and should be corrected into *attabhāvapaṭilābho,* which appears in some of the texts quoted in this note. Buddhaghosa is of this opinion. Other usages of *attabhāva* connote a miraculous appearance of the person in question, some reincarnation of uncommon size or terrific aspect, or some prodigious creatures many *yojanas* long, supposed to exist in the sea. Cf. A I, p. 259, *Tikanipāto,* 13, 5; K

II, p. 388, Tha 20, 1, 1192; A II, p. 379, *Pañcakanipāto,* 10, 10; S II-III, pp. 211–212, *Lakkhaṇasaṁyutta,* 1; A III, p. 311, *Aṭṭhakanipāto,* 1, 9, etc.

NOTES TO CHAPTER 8: 'A BRIEF GENERAL ASSESSMENT OF THE FIRST PART'

1. *The Collection of the Middle Length Sayings,* Vol. III, p. xi-xiii.
2. Such is, for instance, T. W. Rhys Davids' opinion. Referring to the so-called first sermon, he writes, 'The remarkable fact is that we have here set forth a view of religion entirely independent from the soul theory, on which all various philosophies and religions current in India were based; entirely free from the idolatries and superstitions of the day' (*The History and Literature of Buddhism,* Calcutta, 1962, p. 91).

NOTES TO CHAPTER 9: 'THE DOCTRINE OF *ANATTĀ* CAN CO-EXIST WITH THE REALITY OF *ATTĀ*'

1. F. L. Woodward, *The Book of the Gradual Sayings,* Vol. II (London, 1933), Intr., p. viii.
2. Hiralal Jain and A. N. Upadhye, *Mahāvīra, His Times and His Philosophy of Life* (Varanasi, 1974), pp. 46–47. It has not been satisfactorily proved that the Sāṅkhya system is of non-brahmanic origin. We shall, on occasion afford testimonies of the existing affinity regarding fundamental attitudes in Sāṅkhya-Yoga and early Buddhism.
3. Śrī Kundakunda, *Samayasāra,* With English Translation and Commentary based upon Amṛtacandra's *Ātmakhyāti,* together with English Introduction by Prof. A. Chakravarti (Varanasi, 1971), p. 196, verses 321–322. Kundakunda speaks of some samaṃas who profess the Sāṅkhya doctrine, but it is not clear whether he speaks of Sāṅkhya as being a shramanic domain and therefore non-brahmanic in origin, or whether the samaṇas in question are merely imbued with a doctrine that is non-shramanic. The verse reads:
   Evaṁ saṅkhuvaesaṁ jeu parūvinti erisaṁ samaṇā,
   tesiṁ payaḍī kuvvai appā ya akārayā sabbe.
   Ibid., p. 202, verse 340.
4. *Ibid.,* p. 197. The refutation begins with the following statements: 'But the knowers of the truth speak of an alien thing (*paradravyaṁ*) as "mine", speaking according to common practice (*vyavahārabhāṣitena*), while they know for

certain that there is not a thing that is "mine" even to the size of an atom (*paramāṇu*). Even as a man speaks of "our village, our country, our town, our kingdom", but they are not his, such a person (*ātmā*) speaking out of delusion; in the same way one who knowing an alien thing (*paradravyaṁ*) as "mine" makes it his own self (*ātmānaṁ karoti*), becomes undoubtedly a knower possessed of erroneous belief (*mityādṛṣṭi*)'.

5. From this point of view, the *Upaniṣads* belong to an entirely different world. In the first place, the Upaniṣads profess to a great extent a theistic and creationistic doctrine (Cf. Augustine G. Aranjaniyil, *The Idea of a Personal God in the Major Upaniṣads,* Bangalore, 1975), while shramanism repudiates all belief in a Creator God. Secondly, in the *Upaniṣads* the subject matter for meditation is often enough ritualistic, while shramanism abhorred all sacrifices and their ritual. Thirdly, upanishadic speculation showed an early tendency towards the identification of Brahman, *ātman* and the world, eventually denying reality to empirical existence, while the shramanic systems accepted the reality both of *ātman* and *non-ātman.*
6. Cf. 'By what means, then can liberation be effected? Whenever knowledge of the twenty-five principles, the characteristic of which is knowledge of the distinctness of the soul and body, is attained; or whenever a person knows that this is nature, this intellect, this egotism, these are the five rudiments, these the eleven senses, these the five elements, and this is soul, separate and dissimilar from them all; then from such knowledge proceeds cessation of subtile person, and thence liberation', H. Th. Colebrooke, *The Sāṅkhya Kārikā* (Bombay, 1887), p. 222.
7. Ramjee Singh, *The Jaina Concept of Omniscience* (Ahmedabad, 1974), p. 71.
8. Śri Kundakunda, *Op. cit.,* p. 29, verses 21–23.

NOTES TO CHAPTER 10: 'THE DOCTRINE OF ANATTĀ TAUGHT THROUGH THE DENIAL OF POSITIVE TERMS'

1. S II-III, pp. 280–281, *Khandhasaṁyutta,* 49.
2. Those who hold such opinion may be able to produce some texts where liberation is attributed to *citta.* Thus:

   (a) D I, p. 73, *Sāmaññaphalasutta,* 99, etc., where we read: '*tassa... kāmāsavā pi cittaṁ vimuccati... bhavāsavā pi cittaṁ vimuccati...*'. But who is here the ultimate subject of liberation and the possessor of knowledge of such liberation? Not *citta,* but the bhikkhu to whom *citta* is related, represented by the word *tassa.*

(b) D I, p. 133, *Mahālisutta,* 15, etc., where we read: *'bhikkhu... cetovimuttiṁ paññāvimuttiṁ... upasampajja viharati'.* Here too, the ultimate subject that dwells having attained *cetovimutti* is the bhikkhu in question.

(c) D II, p. 34, *Mahāpadānasutta,* 58, where we read: '*tesam... āsavehi cittāni vimucciṁsu'.* Again the minds that are liberated are not self-subsisting, but *tesaṁ...*

(d) S II-III, p. 282, *Khandhasaṁyutta,* 51, where it is stated: '*cittaṁ vimuttaṁ suvimuttaṁ ti vuccati'.* Even here the ultimate beneficiary of complete liberation is not *citta* itself, but the bhikkhu who regards the *khandhas* as impermanent.

3. S II-III, pp. 80–82, *Nidānasaṁyutta,* 61.
4. Other contexts where the passage: 'What do you think of this: Is material form permanent or impermanent?, etc.' is found:

(a) Mhv, pp. 17–18 (1, 8, 22–23), after a discussion on why the *khandas* are *anattā,* to which we shall refer later on.

(b) M III, pp. 81–82, *Mahāpuṇṇamasutta,* 5. A certain bhikkhu, after having stated that the *Khandhas* are *anattā,* questions the Buddha as to what self do deeds affect, which are done by the non-self. The text will be later discussed.

(c) S II-III, p. 256, *Khandhasaṁyutta,* 8. The text speaks of the worry arising from grasping. Such is the predicament of the unlearned common man who looks at the *khandhas* as: 'This is mine, this I am, this is my self'. When the *khandas* suffer alteration and undergo change, he is subject to pain, lamentation, grief, and mental dejection. Opposite is the condition of the learned ariyan disciple.

(d) S II-III, p. 364, *Khandhasaṁyutta,* 97 (*sutta* 98 is an exact repetition of this one). After the Buddha has replied that there is no *khanda* that is permanent, stable, lasting, unchanging, to stand as it is for ever, he takes a pinch of dust on the tip of his nail, saying that even if that much of material form were permanent, stable, etc., dwelling in the brahma-life for the utter destruction of pain would not be proclaimed. But since it is not so, dwelling in the brahma-life is proclaimed for the utter destruction of pain. The same is repeated of the other *khandhas.* Will any one say that the *khandhas* themselves undertake the brahma-life for the utter destruction of suffering, consequent on the abolition of the same *khandhas*?

(e) S II-III, p. 367, *Khandhasaṁyutta,* 100. After a simile saying that an artist is able to reproduce exactly the figure of a man or woman, it is asserted that in the same way the unlearned common man reproduces the *khandhas* time and again. Here too, the repeated reproduction of the *khandhas* may be immediately due to the process of the *paṭiccasamuppāda,* but the moral responsibility of such a thing occurring again and again is not of the *khandhas* themselves, but of the moral agent, different from them.

5. S II-III, pp. 209–210, *Rāhulasaṁyutta,* 21. Literally repeated at S II-III, p. 354, *Khandhasaṁyutta,* 91; M III, p. 80, *Mahāpuṇṇamasutta,* 4 (different addressee). Other contexts where the passage is found:

   (a) A I, p. 265, *Tikanipāto,* 14, 1, where we are told that a good fighting-man is a far-shooter, and that in the same way a bhikkhu is a far-shooter if he looks at the *khandhas* in this way. The simile of the far-shooter occurs also at A II, p. 216, *Catukkanipāto,* 19, 1.

   (b) A slight variation of the passage is found at M II, p. 100, *Mahārāhulovādasutta,* 1.

   (c) Another variation of the passage at S II-III, p. 379, *Khandhasaṁyutta,* 118–119.
6. A comment and quotation of Horace Hayman Wilson, in H. Th. Colebrooke, *Op. cit.,* p. 123. There is no need to refer in detail to the 'negative' importance of *ahaṅkāra* in the *Bhagavadgītā. Mamaṅkāra* seems to be an original Pāli term coined in imitation of *ahaṅkāra,* corresponding to the Pāli *mamatta.*
7. S II-III, p. 210, *Rāhulasaṁyutta,* 22. A literal repetition of this *sutta* is found at S II-III, pp. 354–355, *Khandhasaṁyutta,* 92.
8. S II-III, pp. 366–367, *Khandhasaṁyutta,* 100.
9. M I, p. 54, *Sallekhasutta,* 1–2. Textual criticism shows that the whole passage is out of place here. Cunda asks the Buddha about the various types of views regarding the self and the world, and how to get rid of them. In the summary of the topics discussed in the *sutta* (*Sallekhasutta,* 12) reference is made to *sallekhapariyāyo, cittuppādapariyāyo, parikkamanapariyāyo, uparibhāvapariyāyo, parinibbānapariyāyo,* five topics in all, while nothing is said of *diṭṭhipahānapariyāyo,* which is the topic discussed in the first place, and the only one about which Cunda is supposed to have questioned the Buddha. To make this more clear, there are some manuscripts that attach a couplet of verses at the end of the *sutta,* where again it is asserted that the topics discussed are five, not six, *sandhayo pañca desitā.* The *sutta,* as it stands, derives its name from the topic most extensively discussed, which doubtless was originally the first one.
10. M I, pp. 180–181, *Alagaddūpamasutta,* 10.
11. A IV, pp. 250–251, *Dasakanipāto,* 10, 3.
12. K IV, pt. I, p. 260, *Mahāniddesa,* 1, 13, 132.
13. S II-III, p. 278, *Khandhasaṁyutta,* 47.
14. S IV, pp. 175–177, Saḷ*āyatanasaṁyutta,* 246.
15. S I, p. 112, *Mārasaṁyutta,* 16.

16. S II-III, pp. 203–204, *Rāhulasaṁyutta,* 1. The same reasoning is applied in the following *suttas* to: the objects of sense (2); the six kinds of sensory consciousness (3); the six kinds of sensorial contact (4); the six kinds of sensory feeling (5); the six kinds of sensory perception (6); the six kinds of intention regarding sense-objects (7); the six kinds of craving related to sense-objects (8). All the five *khandhas* have been mentioned here: *viññāṇa, vedanā, saññā* have been mentioned by name, the objects of sense stand for *rūpa,* and the intention (*sañcetanā*) and craving (*taṇhā*) stand for the *saṅkhārā,* translated in this book as 'inner complexes'. The passage just quoted is repeated at S II-III, p. 208, *Rāhulasaṁyutta,* 11, followed again by a series of *suttas* (12–18) similar to those just enumerated. Other similar contexts:

    (a) To see the six spheres of sensorial contact as: 'This is not mine, this I am not, this is not my self', constitutes the end of pain (*esevanto dukkhassa*). Cf. S IV, pp. 38–39, *Saḷāyatanasaṁyutta,* 71. *Sutta* 72 deals with the same topic and the result of regarding the six spheres of sensorial contact as: 'This is not mine, etc.', is: 'Thus, the sixfold sphere of sensorial contact will have been left aside by you, so as to become again no more in future'. *Sutta* 73 deals again with the same topic, and the result is that one will feel disgust for the sixfold sphere of sensorial contact, feeling disgust he will be detached, etc., as in the stock passage just quoted.

    (b) At M III, p. 362 f., *Nandakovādasutta,* the teaching applies to the senses, sense-objects, sensorial consciousness, and the consequent *vedanā,* etc.
17. S IV, pp. 96–99, *Saḷāyatanasaṁyutta,* 121. Repeated at M III, pp. 376–378, *Cūḷarāhulovādasutta.*
18. M III, pp. 354–356, *Channovādasutta,* 3–6.
19. M III, pp. 382–384, *Chachakkasutta,* 8–9.
20. A II, pp. 175–176, *Catukkanipāto,* 18, 7. Other contexts where the elements are dismissed because of everyone of them one ought to say: 'This is not mine, this I am not, etc.':

    (a) M I, p. 235 f., *Mahāhatthipadopamasutta,* where in the case of each element an enumeration is given of the parts of the body made of such element and their rejection, because of everyone of them ought to be said: 'This is not mine, etc.'. Immediately after that, the possible disturbance of the external element is described, and a question is appended: 'How to say then of this short-lived body, derived from craving, "I" or "mine" or "I am?".' The two preceding passages give us what must have been the number of elements originally admitted, that is to say, four. Of this, there are frequent testimonies in the Nikā yas. Thus for instance, when describing Ajitakesakambala's heresy, man is called *cātumahābhūtiko,* 'made of four elements', but after describing how after death every element merges into the primeval mass of the corresponding cosmic element, it is added that the senses merge into space (*ākāsa*). D I, p. 48, *Sāmaññaphalasutta,* 22. When the *attā* of the annihilationists is being described we are told, *ayaṁ attā rūpī cātumahābhūtiko,* 'this self is material, born of the four elements', *Ibid.,* p. 67 (86). See also '*rūpī cātumahābhūtiko kabaḷīkārāhārabhakkho...*', D I, p. 162, *Poṭṭhapādasutta,* 24; and K IV, pt. II, p. 34, Cln 2, 1, 4.

(b) In the *Mahārāhulovādasutta,* 2 f., (M II, pp. 101–103), 'This is not mine, etc.', as well as the disgust for, and the purification of the mind from the elements is applied not to four but to five elements, *ākāsa* being added. Later on, a *viññāṇadhātu* came to be added to the list of five. See, for instance, S II-III, p. 207, *Rāhulasaṁyutta,* 9; *Ibid.* p. 209 (19).

21. K V, pp. 149–153, Pṭs 1, 2, 1, 2.
22. M I, p. 208, *Nivāpasutta,* 11.
23. *Pathways of Buddhist Thought; Essays from 'The Wheel',* Edited by Venerable Nyānaponika Mahāthera, and selected by M. O. 'C. Walshe (London, 1971), p. 163.
24. S II-III, p. 254, *Khandhasaṁyutta,* 7. The same text repeated at M III, pp. 310–311, *Uddesavibhaṅgasutta,* 8–9, but the text of the *Saṁyutta* appears to be better preserved. A similar reasoning given in an exhortation to a sick man, telling him that by identifying the *khandhas* with the self and being thereby ready to say: 'I am the body', 'the body is mine', 'I am feeling', 'feeling is mine', etc., one is sick in mind and body, due to worries when seing alterations in body, etc. But one who does not identify the self with the *khandhas,* may be sick in body, never in mind (S II-III, p. 242 f., *Khandhasaṁyutta,* 1). Other contexts where this ontological isolation of the self as regards the *khandhas* is taught:

(a) S II-III, pp. 274–275, *Khandhasaṁyutta,* 43, where regarding the *khandhas* as the self, or the self as qualified by the *khandhas,* etc., is said to be the origin of pain, grief, lamentations and mental uneasiness, while regarding the *khandhas,* as they really are, as pain, grief, etc., leads to their abandonment, and by the abandonment of them, the bhikkhu is not troubled, not being troubled he dwells happy, dwelling in happiness, he is one who has attained *nibbāna* in that respect (*tadaṅganibbuto*). Therefore, by isolating himself (his self!) from the *khandhas,* the bhikkhu is said to be *nibbuto,* cooled down.

(b) S II-III, p. 276, *Khandhasaṁyutta,* 44, where we are informed that regarding the *khandhas* as the self, or as qualifying the self, etc., is the way leading to the arisal of samsaric individuality (*sakkāya*), while the opposite view is the way leading to the cessarion of *sakkāya,* and thereby to the end of the samsaric cycle. This indicates also that the *sakkāyadiṭṭhi* as the fundamental *diṭṭhi* in the Nikāyas.

(c) S II-III, pp. 365–366. *Khandhasaṁyutta,* 99, where those who regard the *khandhas* as the self are compared to a dog tied by means of a leash to a stake or a pillar, and going continually round and round. But those who have the opposite view cease being tied to the *khandhas* and going round them, being thus liberated: 'He is entirely free from material form (from feeling, perception, the inner complexes, consciousness), he is entirely free from birth, old-age, death, grief... he is entirely free from Pain'. Who is then the subject of such liberation, but he who does not regard his *attā* as ontologically related to the *khandhas*? Is this not an implicit assertion of the reality of *attā*?

(d) S II-III, pp. 378–379, *Khandhasaṁyutta,* 117, where one holding the view that the *khandhas* are the self, or qualify the self, etc., is said to be 'an unlearned common man bound by the bonds of everyone of the *khandhas*; bound by bonds both internal and external; one who does not see the yonder shore; one who, being bound, grows old; being bound, dies; being bound, goes from this world to another world'. The opposite is asserted of the holder of the contrary view.

(e) M III, pp. 264–265, *Ānandabhaddekarattasutta,* 3, where the view that regards the *khandhas* as the self, etc., is pointed out as the cause of man being caught in present things. The opposite holds in the case of the contrary view. Repeated at *Ibid.,* p. 279, *Lomasakaṅgiyabhaddekarattasutta,* 3; and *Ibid.,* pp. 261–262, *Bhaddekarattasutta,* 4.

(f) See also A II, p. 228, *Catukkanipāto,* 20, 10, 9–10.

25. S II-III, p. 278, *Khandhasaṁyutta,* 47. Such preoccupation with existence and becoming is censured even in other systems which maintain the reality of the self. Thus: '... When there is none of this (*yasya*) [good karma], this has been said "For [*those*] who, after having renounced their own nature [of pondering upon themselves], there is by reason of lack [of good karma], a liking (*ruci*) for the opposing view and no liking for the ascertainment of truth-, [for them there is no sight of the distinction and no cessation of the pondering]", Now-as-to-this (*tatra*), the pondering upon his own states-of-being is in this fashion: "Who was I? How was I? What is this [birth]? How is this [birth]? What shall we become? Or how shall we become?" But this pondering ceases for one who sees the distinction [between *sattva* and the Self]. For what reason is this? Since it is this mind-stuff which undergoes this diversified mutation. But when there is no longer undifferenciated consciousness (*avidyā*), the Self is purified and untouched by the conditions of the mind-stuff. For this reason this skilful person ceases pondering upon his own states-of-being', James Haughton Woods,

The Yoga-system of Patañjali (The Harward University Press, 1927), p. 338. And: 'The mind-stuff which is [borne] down toward nothing but discernment of the difference between *sattva* and the Self, has in its intervals other presented-ideas, either "It is I" or "It is mine" or "I think" or "I do not think",' *Ibid.*, p. 339.

26. K IV, pt. I, pp. 186–187, Mnd 1, 10, 86. Does not the use of the past participle *vivittaṁ,* 'excluded from, separated from, kept apart from, distinguished from, discriminated from, etc.', suggest the reality of both the categories kept apart, excluded from each other, namely, what is empirical, impermanent, changeable and *the self*? We should not forget, as noted previously, that *attā* here stands for the self of the discriminating man, who is engaged here not in a merely mental exercise, but in the process of actual liberation.
27. Undoubtedly the term *phasso* is here connected with the verb *phusati,* used, as indicated in the *P. T. S.'s Pāli-English Dictionary:* 'only in specific sense of attaining to the highest ideal of religious aspiration'. The *Dictionary* refers to passages like, *cetosamādhiṁ phusati* (D I, p. 13, *Brahmajālasutta,* 31), *so nirodhaṁ phusati* (D I, p. 154. *Poṭṭhapādasutta,* 9), *phusanti amataṁ padaṁ* (K II, p. 217, Ptv 1, 38, 706).
28. K IV, pt. I, p. 187, Mnd 1, 10, 86.
29. K IV, pt. I, p. 59, Mnd 1, 3, 18.
30. *Op. cit.,* p. 164.
31. M I, p. 183, *Alagaddūpamasutta,* 14.
32. *Op. cit.,* p. 164.
33. We discover here again the same positive outlook that presides over the 'spiritual' exertion of the bhikkhus, even though we are going to be told that such a possession cannot be had in the world of our experience. When speaking of possession, we imply that there is a subject of possession (*attā*), and a thing possessed (*attaniya*). This is the connection existing between this part of the *sutta* and the passage under discussion, which will soon make its appearance.
34. First to be noted is that the clinging here proposed is not to the self, but to any theory on the self, this clinging being, according to the Nikāyas, the constant companion of such theories. Besides, if there is clinging there is also a feeling of possession and we imply again a subject of possession (*attā*), and the thing possessed (*attaniya*). We ought never to forget that all theories on the self are supposed to have the same background, the identification of the self with the empirical man, i.e., an idea of the self that is wrong. This part of the *sutta* is still more closely connected with the passage under discussion, which ends with a reference to the eternalists' theory.
35. Again, we have here a reference to *diṭṭhi,* and this gives also this part of the

sutta a close connection with the passage under discussion, which will come soon and will be printed in cursive type for greater clarity.

36. In the same *Alagaddūpamasutta* (10) (what we are translating begins with number 13), we find the enumaration of six tenets of speculative opinion (*diṭṭhigatāni*) which identify the self with some empirical factor. But the sixth one reads: 'And even as regards the tenet of speculative opinion: "This is the world, this is the self, I myself shall become after death permanent, stable, perennial, immutable by nature, I shall remain like this unto what is eternal", he [the uninstructed common man] regards it as: "This is mine, this I am, this is my self".'
37. M I, pp. 182–184, *Alagaddūpamasutta,* 13–15.
38. S IV, pp. 50–51, *Saḷāyatanasaṁyutta,* 85. Quoted at K IV, pt. I, p. 381, Mnd 1, 15, 186; and K IV, pt. II, p. 195, Cln 2, 15, 88. Repeated at K V, p. 436, Pṭs 2, 10, 1, 1.
39. K IV, pt. II, pp. 192–193, Cln 2, 15, 88. The *Crit. Pāli Dict.* translates *attasārasāra* as: 'That essence which is called self-essence'.
40. See for the whole passage, K IV, pt. II, pp. 191–196, Cln 2, 15, 88.
41. K I, p. 437, Stn 5, 16, 144. The *Suññakathā* of the *Paṭisambhidāmagga,* whose introduction contains the passage: 'The world is void, the world is void, etc.', distinguishes, with the pedantry so often displayed in the work; twenty-five different kinds of void (*suñña*). The most interesting from our point of view are the following:

    (a) *Suññasuññaṁ* (the absolute void), consisting in the fact that the senses are void of the self, of anything permanent, durable, immutable by nature.

    (b) *Ajjhattasuññaṁ* (the subjective void), consisting again in the fact that the senses are void of the self, etc. (Repetitions do not seem to matter, provided they are given a different name).

    (c) *Bahidhāsuññaṁ* (the external void), which applies the same to sensorial objects.

    (d) *Dubhatosuññaṁ* (the harmful void), which consists in the combination of the two preceding ones. K V, p. 437 f., Pṭs 2, 10, 2. The voidness of self or of what belongs to the self is treated in another section of the book, similar in style to the one just quoted. See *Ibid.* p. 122 (1, 1, 44–49, 251).
42. S IV, p. 264, *Cittasaṁyutta,* 7. Repeated at M I, p. 367, *Mahāvedallasutta,* 13. See also: 'Again, bhikkhus, an ariyan disciple, gone either to the forest or to the root of a tree, or to a lonely spot, reflects thus, "Void is this of the self or of what belongs to the self". The mind of one who thus reflects, who dwells mostly on this, is serene in its proper sphere. Being serene, either attains he to the sphere of no-thing, or by means of superior wisdom is liberated...'. M

III, p. 58, *Aneñjasappāyasutta,* 5. The reflection: 'This is void of the self or of what belongs to the self', constitutes the mental background of (1) the *suññato vimokkho,* because it suppresses all wrong bias (*abhinivesa*); (2) of the *animitto vimokkho,* because it suppresses all mental images; (3) of the *appaṇihito vimokkho,* because it suppresses all selfish aspirations (*paṇidhi*). K V, p. 274, Pṭs 1, 5, 0, 2, 3–5.

43. K V, pp. 206–208, Pṭs 1, 3, 4, 35, 38, 41. See also K II, p. 380, Tha 19, 1, 1120, where *aniccaṁ* is coupled with *dukkhaṁ* and *suññaṁ* with *anattā.*
44. S II-III, pp. 267–268, *Khandhasaṁyutta,* 33. The following *sutta* (34) propounds the same doctrine, without the simile.
45. The *Natumhākasutta* of the *Khandhasaṁyutta* (S II-III, pp. 267–268), which, as has been pointed out, is one of the elements used in the composition of the *Alagaddūpamasutta,* is also quoted at K IV, pt. I, p. 380, Mnd 1, 15, 186. It is to be noted that the quotation comes in a series of texts adduced to illustrate the same point, and should have therefore basically the same import. One of the texts included in the series is precisely the famous Vajirā's utterance, which consequently ought to teach the same kind of *anattā* doctrine as the *Natumhākasutta,* that is to say, relative *anattā.*
46. S IV, pp. 75–76, *Saḷāyatanasaṁyutta,* 101. The same teaching, without the simile, is reiterated in the following *sutta* (102). The same general purport prevails in the *Sakuṇagghisutta,* where the bhikkhus are exhorted not to roam about outside their proper range (*gocara*), because Māra gets access to those who thus roam and gets the opportunity to do them harm. Here the foreign range for the bhikkhus consists in the *kāmaguṇa,* 'the element of sensorial pleasure', found in sensorial objects. But only four senses are mentioned, without the mind. The proper range consists in the four stations of mindfulness. S V, pp. 126–128, *Satipaṭṭhānasaṁyutta,* 6 and 7.
47. S II-III, p. 94, *Nidānasaṁyutta,* 66.
48. M III, p. 127 f., *Bahudhātusutta,* 5 f. The rest of the possibilities and their corresponding impossibilities concern mainly moral matters, except for: the impossibility of there being two Sammāsambuddhas at the same time in the same world-system; a similar impossibility that applies to two 'wheel-turning kings' in the same circumstances; and the impossibility of a woman becoming a Buddha, or Sakka, or Māra. or Brahmā. These impossibilities and their corresponding possibilities are introduced in between the other impossibilities and possibilities regarding moral matters, interrupting the enumeration of things morally possible or impossible, a fact that might indicate their later interpolation. This text is repeated at A I, p. 27, *Ekanipāto,* 15. See also A III, p. 139, *Chakkanipāto,* 9, 9. The last text mentions only 'impossibilities', and

they are distributed in groups of six for every *sutta,* beginning with *sutta* 7 and ending with *sutta,* 11.

49. The reason for this, as given by I B. Horner, *The Collection of the Middle Length Sayings,* Vol. III, p. 108, in a footnote, is that: 'As a category, *dhamma* is wider than *saṅkhārā,* for it includes the uncompounded *nibbāna.* This is *anattā,* but it is neither impermanent nor painful. Everything else is impermanent and painful as well as being *anattā'.* This question will be tackled later on. The only statement of the first two *piṭakas* asserting that *nibbāna* is *anattā* is found in the *Parivāra,* a very late production.
50. S I, p. 188, *Vaṅgīsasaṁyutta,* 4. There is disagreement between the introductory prose and the metrical part. In the introductory prose, Vaṅgīsa is said to resort to Ānanda, while the first stanza of the metrical part is directed to Gotama.
51. A II, p. 20, *Catukkanipāto,* 2, 6. The line seems to be an interpolation, for it disturbs the metrical arrangement of the two *ślokas,* being awkwardly thrust in between them.
52. K II, p. 386, Tha 20, 1, 1169.
53. K II, p. 427, Thi 7, 1, 177.
54. M III, pp. 376–379, *Cūḷarāhulovādasutta,* 2–4.

NOTES TO CHAPTER 11: 'THE DOCTRINE OF NON-SELF TAUGHT THROUGH THE PREDICATION OF THE NEGATIVE TERM *ANATTĀ*'

1. Exceptions to this rule are found in two *sūttas* of the *Sáṁyutta,* where the reading is: *'anattaṁ rūpaṁ "anattā rūpaṁ" ti nappajānāti... anatte saṅkhāre "anattā saṅkhārā" ti nappajānāti'.* It is evident that in *anatte saṅkhāre* the first word is an adjective, but the immediate presence of *anattā saṅkhārā ti,* compared with the previous *anattā rūpaṁ ti,* proves that its translation should *not* be 'not possessing a self', but 'which are non-self'. This means to say that this adjective should be taken as an attributive adjective, not as a possessive compound. The same will apply to *anattaṁ rūpaṁ* of the previous phrase. The passage, therefore, should be translated as follows: 'He does not know, as it really is, material form, which is non-self, thinking as it ought to be [thought] "material form is non-self...'. He does not know, as they really are, the inner complexes, which are non-self, [thinking as it ought to be thought] 'the inner complexes are non-self'. Cf. S II-III, p. 286, *Khandhasaṁyutta,* 55; *Ibid.,* pp. 335–336, *Khandhasaṁyutta,* 85, Cf. H. Günther, *Das Seelenproblem in älteren Buddhismus* (Konstanz, 1949), pp. 16–21.

2. K I, p. 386, Stn 3, 12, 355.
3. S IV, p. 3 f., *Saḷāyatanasaṁyutta,* 1–3. *Suttas* 4–6 assert the same of the objects of sense. *Suttas* 7–12 speak of the senses and the objects of sense being *anattā* in the past, future, and present, the conclusion being: 'Thus discerning, bhikkhus, the learned ariyan disciple remains indifferent regarding the eyes of the past, does not stir with expectation of future eyes, and has attained to disgust, dispassion, cessation, as regards the present eyes'. The same doctrine is taught at S IV, p. 138 f., *Saḷāyatanasaṁyutta,* 204–221, regarding the senses ses and the objects of sense, past, future, and present. See also the same doctrine applied to the *khandhas* at S II-III, p. 259, *Khandhasaṁyutta,* 15, with the consequent disgust, detachment, liberation, and knowledge of liberation. This is repeated in the two following *suttas* (16–17); also at S II-III, pp. 276–277, *Khandhasaṁyutta,* 45, with the speciality that, after asserting that the *khandhas* are *anattā,* there is a reference to *attā* in the expression *paccattaññeva,* which occurs at the end of the *sutta*: 'Bhikkhus, if a bhikkhu's mind is detached from the element of materiality (the element of feeling, the element of perception, the element of inner complexes, the element of consciousness), then it is freed without clinging from the *āsavas.* Due to this freedom it is firm, due to this firmness it is satisfied, due to this satisfaction it is not perturbed, not being perturbed attains *nibbāna* as regards the very self (*paccattaññeva*). He knows...'. The following *sutta* is an exact repetition of *sutta* 45. The same reasoning is applied to the senses and their objects at S IV, p. 138 f., *Saḷāyatanasaṁyutta,* 207–225. Cf. also S II-III, pp. 309–310, *Khandhasaṁyutta,* 76–77.
4. S IV, pp. 151–152, *Saḷāyatanasaṁyutta,* 234.
5. K II, p. 380, Tha 19, 1, 1120. See also: 'The establishment of the void (*suññatā*) is effected by one who meditates with his mind on non-self (*anattato*)', K V, p. 206 f., Pṭs 1, 3, 4, 35 f. (repeated thrice). Also: 'That which is realization of non-self (*anattānupassanā*) and that which is realization of the void (*suññatānupassanā*), these two qualities, have the same meaning, only the expression differs', K V, p. 307, Pṭs 1, 5, 0, 17, 88.
6. M II, p. 118, *Mahāmālukyasutta,* 5. The same holds in the case of the rest of the *jhānas,* and of the three *vimokkhas* relating to the sphere of infinite space, the sphere of infinite consciousness, and the sphere of no-thing. The same teaching is found at A IV, p. 61 f., *Navakanipāto,* 4, 5, with the introductory theme: 'And I declare the destruction of the *āsavas* through the first *jhāna...* through the second *jhāna,* etc.'. See also A II, p. 134, *Catukkanipāto,* 13, 4. The same formula: 'as impermanent, painful, a disease, etc.', occurs in M II, p. 195, *Dīghanakhasutta,* 5, where it applies to the body compounded of the

four elements (*cātumahābhūtiko*); S II-III, pp. 380–382, *Khandhasaṁyutta,* 122, 123, where the formula is applied to the *khandhas*; A II, p. 136, *Catukkanipāto,* 13, 6, where the formula is applied to the *khandhas* in connection with the *brahmavihāras.* A still more elaborate and enlarged formula occurs at K IV, pt. I, p. 45, Mnd 1, 2, 13, where the formula is applied to *phasso,* but without explicitly setting apart any of the metempirical kinds of *phasso (suññato, animitto, appaṇihito, lokuttaro),* in opposition to what we observed was done at K IV, pt. I, pp. 186–187, Mnd 1, 10, 86; *Ibid.,* p. 233 (1, 11, 107), where the subject of discussion is *māna*; K IV, pt. II, pp. 40–41, Cln 2, 1, 8, where every item of the formula is applied to *kusalo sabbadhammānaṁ; Ibid.,* p. 46, (2, 2, 10), where the topic is the knowledge required to attain *nibbāna; Ibid.,* pp. 109–110 (2, 6, 39), where having reached the attainment of the sphere of no-thing and emerging from it, one looks at mental objects as 'impermanent, painful, etc.' (the whole series again). The series found at K V, p. 503, Pṭs 3, 9, 2, 11, is like the one found in the *Mahāniddesa,* but with some modifications at the end. As already indicated there seems to be a conflict between Mnd 1, 2, 13, where after listing all the different kinds of *phasso* we are told of *phasso* (in general, without excepting the metempirical kinds of *phasso*) that it should be regarded as 'impermanent, painful... as something alien, as non-self', and the passage of Mnd 1, 10, 86, where only the empirical kinds of *phasso* are said to be different from the self or what belongs to the self, not the metempirical ones, which, as already said, are intentionally set apart. Even so, the latter passage holds its validity in the face of the apparent contradiction arising from the former passage. The reasons for this are:

(a) In Mnd 1, 10, 86, the author intentionally and on set purpose proceeds setting apart the metempirical *phassā,* while Mnd 1, 2, 13 is a composition of stock passages (repeated at Mnd 1, 11, 107 with reference to *rūpa,* and at Mnd 1, 15, 178 with reference to *māna*), which, as is the case elsewhere are not perfectly adjusted to the new context.

(b) It is evident that Mnd 1, 2, 13 deals on the whole with those *phassā* which are empirical, as it comes in a context that comments upon:

Removing desire as regards both extremes,
Knowing perfectly well [empirical] contact (*phassaṁ*),
Not doing that which results in censure of the self (*attagarahī*),
The wise man is not soiled *regarding what is seen or heard.*

K I, p. 389, Stn 4, 2, 13. Cf. the whole context.

7. S II-III, pp. 94–95, *Nidānasaṁyutta,* 66.
8. M I, p. 338, *Mahātaṇhāsaṅkhayasutta,* 15.
9. S II-III, pp. 258–259, *Khandhasaṁyutta,* 14.

10. S II-III, p. 409, *Rādhasaṁyutta,* 17. The following *sutta* (18) begins with the question: *Anattadhammo, anattadhammo'ti, bhante, vuccati. Katamo nu kho, bhante, anattadhammo'ti?* The term *anattadhammo* is then applied to each one of the *khandhas,* not as an adjective, but as a noun, *'rūpaṁ anattadhammo, vedanā anattadhammo,* etc.', where the rendering of *anattadhammo* cannot be, 'being non-self by nature', but 'a phenomenon that is non-self' (Cf. *The Crit. Pāli Dict. s. v.*). All these phenomena are collectively mentioned in *sabbe dhammā anattā* a dictum which will be discussed later on.
11. S II-III, p. 305, *Khandhasaṁyutta,* 68. The following *sutta* (69) is composed on the same pattern, but instead of *anattā* we read *anattaniyaṁ,* 'belonging to the non-self'. A similar teaching, but given in a simpler form, is found at S II-III, pp. 391–392, *Khandhasaṁyutta,* 143–145. The first of these three *suttas* begins with: 'For whatever is non-self, bhikkhus, you must put away desire (*chando*). And what, bhikkhus, is non-self? Body, bhikkhus, is non-self, etc.'. The other two *suttas* substitute *rāgo* and *chandarāgo,* respectively, for *chando.* The *khandhas* are non-self in relation to the past, the future, and the present: 'Body, bhikkhus, is non-self, both past and future, what then shall we say of the present? Thus discerning, bhikkhus, the learned ariyan disciple remains indifferent for the body that was in the past; is not delighted with any future body; and has attained to repulsion and detachment from, as well as to cessation of, the now existing body'. (The same applies to the rest of the *khandhas.*) S II-III, pp. 257–258, *Khandhasaṁyutta,* 11. All kinds of *khandhas* are non-self: 'All material forms, whether past, future, or present, whether internal or external, whether gross or subtle, whether low or excellent, are ascertained to be impermanent, this is one reflection; are ascertained to be painful, this is one reflection; are ascertained to be non-self, this is one reflection...'. (The same applies to the rest of the *khandhas.*) K V, pp. 58–59, Pṭs 1, 1, 5, 113. The *khandhas* are said to be impermanent, painful, non-self in different ways.
12. K V, p. 206, Pṭs 1, 3, 4, 33. The rest of the *khandhas* are also declared to be impermanent, painful, non-self, but the formula used therein is different. See also *Ibid.,* pp. 343–344 (2, 1, 0, 2, 14 f.), where *anattato anupassanaṭṭhena vipassanā,* is applied to all the *khandhas.*
13. K VII, p. 253, *Therīapadāna,* 3, 6, 236. One who knows the *khandhas* to be non-self, knows them perfectly well, and by knowing them thus: 'he is free from the body, he is free from feeling, he is free from perception, he is free from the inner complexes, he is free from consciousness, he is free from birth, old-age, death, suffering... I say, "he is free from Pain",' S II-III, p. 393, *Khandhasaṁyutta,* 149.

14. S IV, p. 119, *Saḷāyatanasaṁyutta,* 142. Identical reasoning is applied to sensorial objects at *Ibid.,* p. 120, *Saḷāyatasaṁyutta,* 145.
15. S IV, p. 136, *Saḷāyatanasaṁyutta,* 174–176. The same is said of sensorial objects at *Ibid.,* p. 137, *suttas* 183–185. See also: 'Eye, be it past, future, or present is non-self, etc.'. (The same applies to the rest of the senses.) The *sutta* ends up with the stock passage of feeling disgust, a disgust that leads to detachment and ultimate liberation. S IV, p. 138, *Saḷāyatanasaṁyutta,* 192–194. Also *Ibid.,* p. 141, *sutta* 224. The same applies to sensorial objects at *Ibid.,* p. 138, *suttas* 201–203. Also *Ibid.,* p. 142, *sutta* 227.
16. S IV, p. 122, *Saḷāyatanasaṁyutta,* 149. Similar to this is *sutta* 164 (*Ibid.,* p. 133), where the theme is that one should get rid of desire for whatever is non-self. See also: 'How knowing, how seing, Lord, fetters go to their destruction?', 'By knowing, by seing the eye as non-self, bhikkhus, fetters go to their destruction; by knowing, by seing visible forms as non-self...; by knowing, by seing visual consciousness...; by knowing, by seing the eye's sensorial contact as non-self, bhikkhus, fetters go to their destruction. And whatever feeling, be it either pleasant or painful, or neither pleasant nor painful, which arises dependent on this sensorial contact of the eye, by knowing, by seing that also as non-self, fetters go to their destruction'. (The same applies to all the other senses.) S IV, p. 28, *Saḷāyatanasaṁyutta,* 55.
17. S IV, p. 134, *Saḷāyatanasaṁyutta,* 167. Cf. also the negative statement, according to which, the bhikkhu not endowed with certain eleven qualities is unable to see *anattā* in the senses, the objects of sense, etc. A IV, p. 398, *Ekādasanipāto,* 3, 3, etc. The term *anattā,* even if itself negative, has in this context a clearly positive meaning, something that can be seen and known, very much like the *abhāva* of the Naiyāyikas. The same will apply to texts that speak of *anattasaññā* or 'awareness of non-self'.
18. M III, p. 95, *Chabbisodhanasutta,* 3.
19. K VII, Apd 2, p. 238, *Therīapadāna,* 3, 1, 42.
20. A III, pp. 266–267, *Sattakanipāto,* 10.
21. S V, pp. 293–294, *Sotāpattisaṁyutta,* 3.
22. S V, p. 117, *Bhojjhaṅgasaṁyutta,* 78. The *Crit. Pāli Dict.* transaltes *anattasaññā* as 'the conception of *anattā*'. We prefer to give *saññā* here the sense of 'awareness', since it is a thing that can be intentionally fostered and made to grow. The *Crit. Pāli Dict.*'s translation would hold in the case of *anattani, bhikkhave, attā ti saññāvipallāso cittavipallāso diṭṭhivipallāso.* A II, p. 54, *Catukkanipāto,* 5, 9.
23. A I, p. 41, *Ekākanipāto,* 18, 78.
24. A II, pp. 346–347. *Pañcakanipāto,* 8, 2, 1. The same five qualities are pre-

scribed for the perfect knowledge of attachment (*rāga*) at *Ibid.* p. 515 (29, 3). One more quality is added to the preceding five at A III, p. 50, *Chakkanipāto,* 4, 5, where the qualities in question are called '*vijjābhāgiyā*', 'connected with wisdom'. Still one more quality added to the list at A III, p. 268, *Sattakanipāto,* 11, 3, where again the aim is the higher knowledge of attachment. At A IV, p. 32, *Navakanipāto,* 2, 6, the types of awareness to be fostered with great profit, which are conducive to *nibbāna,* and among which is found 'the awareness of non-self in what is painful', are nine. At A IV, p. 183, *Dasakanipāto,* 6, 7, the qualities are ten, with the same purpose as the preceding ones. At A IV, p. 355, *Dasakanipāto,* 23, 1, the qualities are ten, and they are to be fostered for the higher knowledge of attachment.

25. A III, pp. 193–194, *Sattakanipāto,* 5, 6, 8.
26. A III, pp. 170–171, *Sattakanipāto,* 3, 7, 2. Repeated at D II, p. 64, *Mahāparinibbānasutta,* 10.
27. A IV, pp. 184–185, *Dasakanipāto,* 6, 9, 2.
28. See the description of *asubhasaññā* at A IV, p. 186, *Dasakanipāto,* 6, 10.
29. K I, p. 105, Ud 4, 1, 4.
30. Other texts where *anattasaññā* occurs all by itself, without any limitation in the denotation of *anattā* being explicitly stated, are:

    (a) 'He fosters the awareness of impermanence... he fosters the awareness of non-self...', A I, p. 41, *Ekākanipāto,* 18, 82–83.

    (b) Five qualities are to be fostered for the higher knowledge of attachment (*rāga*), among them, 'the awareness of impermanence, the awareness of non-self, the awareness of death...', A II, p. 515, *Pañcakanipāto,* 29, 2. Similarly, at A IV, p. 183, *Dasakanipāto,* 6, 7, where 'the awareness of impermanence, the awareness of non-self, etc.', are among the ten qualities to be fostered with great profit. See also *Ibid.,* p. 355 (23, 2), but in what immediately precedes (23, 1) *anattasaññā* is limited by *dukkhe.*

    (c) 'In the case of one aware of impermanence, the awareness of non-self is established. One who is aware of non-self succeeds in rooting out conceit', A IV, p. 5, *Navakanipāto,* 1, 1, 7. The text coincides exactly with the above quoted passage at K I, p. 105, Ud 4, 1, 4.

    (d) 'For the removal of the heretical view of self (*attānudiṭṭhi*) the awareness of non-self should be fostered', A III, p. 146, *Chakkanipāto,* 11, 6.

    (e) 'He should foster the awareness of impermanence, the awareness of non-self, the awareness of the foul', K II, p. 326, Tha 10, 7, 594.
31. A IV, p. 186, *Dasakanipāto,* 6, 10, 5.
32. K IV, pt. II, p. 33, Cln 2, 1, 4.
33. A III, p. 230, *Sattakanipāto,* 7, 2, 3–9.

34. A I, p. 139, *Tikanipāto,* 5, 7–8. See also K I, p. 53, Dhp 26, 383, where *saṅkhārā* is the opposite of *akaraṁ*.
35. M III, pp. 328–329, *Dhātuvibhaṅgasutta,* 18–19. It is to be noted that 'de-becoming' (*vibhava*) as opposed to becoming (*bhava*) has not here the sense of absolute cessation of becoming consequent to liberation, but a 'de-becoming' that is entirely samsaric, and to be followed by another becoming. This applies to all the contexts where both these terms appear together.
36. S IV, p. 15, *Saḷāyatanasaṁyutta,* 23.
37. S IV, p. 26, *Saḷāyatanasaṁyutta,* 46.
38. S IV, pp. 47–48, *Saḷāyatanasaṁyutta,* 80.
39. A III, p. 143, *Chakkanipāto,* 10, 9.
40. *The Collection of the Middle Length Sayings,* Vol. III, p. 107, n. 1.
41. K II, p. 452, Thi 14, 1, 392–394.
42. '*So yadeva tattha hoti rūpagataṁ vedanāgataṁ saññāgataṁ viññāṇagataṁ te dhamme aniccato dukkhato... samanupassati*', M II, p. 118, *Mahāmālukyasutta,* 5.
43. K I, p. 430, Stn 5, 7, 101.
44. K II, p. 305, Tha 6, 8, 422. See also:
    (a) Truly when the *dhammas* manifest themselves,
    To the ardent, meditating brāhmaṇa,
    Then all his doubts vanish,
    Inasmuch as he comprehends the *dhammas* with their conditions (*sahetudhammaṁ*).

    K I, p. 63, Ud 1, 1. Repeated at Mvg p. 3, *Mahākkhandhaka,* 1.

    (b) There is no fear, chieftain, for one who sees, as it really is,
    The pure and simple causal arisal of *dhammas* (*suddhaṁ dhammasamuppādaṁ*), the pure and simple continuity of compounded things (*suddhaṁ saṅkhārasantatiṁ*).

    K II, p. 341, Tha 16, 1, 716.
45. K IV, pt. II, p. 118, Cln 2, 6, 45.
46. Mvg, p. 11, *Mahākkhandhaka,* 6, 1.
47. A II, p. 459, *Pañcakanipāto,* 18, 9, 7.
48. K I, p. 68, Ud 1, 7, 14.
49. K VI, Apd 1, p. 82 (3, 2, 52). The expression is of very frequent occurrence in the *Apadāna.* For instance: K VI, Apd 1, p. 156 (8, 10, 48); *Ibid.,* p. 421 (40, 10, 484); *Ibid.,* p. 455, (41, 10, 357); K VII, Apd 2, p. 4 (43, 2, 16); *Ibid.,* p. 6 (43, 3, 38), etc.
50. K I, p. 435, Stn 5, 14, 130; *Ibid.,* p. 436, Stn 5, 15, 137.
51. K IV, pt. II, p. 164, Cln 2, 13, 74. Repeated at *Ibid.,* p. 174, Cln 2, 14, 81.

52. A III, p. 142, *Chakkanipāto,* 10, 5. The first part of the *sutta* describes a condition opposite to this one.
53. Cf. also A III, pp. 161–162, *Sattakanipāto,* 2, 6–9.
54. A III, p. 162, *Sattakanipāto,* 2, 8.
55. K I, p. 43, Dhp 20, 279. The three *ślokas* occur also at K II, p. 337, Tha 15, 1, 676–678.
56. K IV, pt. I, p. 78, Mnd 1, 4, 27. Repeated at *Ibid.,* p. 155 (1, 9, 72); *Ibid.,* p. 197 (1, 10, 88), where we read *sabbe dhammā anattā,* but where we also find an assertion of *attā* when, to every item, the following refrain is added, 'Thus he himself knows the *dhamma* and sees it by his very self (*attapaccakkhaṁ*), and does not give faith to any one...'. See also K IV, pt. II, p. 46, Cln 2, 2, 10, etc.
57. K IV, pt. II, pp. 40–41, Cln 2, 1, 8.
58. A II, p. 37, *Catukkanipāto,* 4, 4, 3.
59. A III, pp. 420–421, *Aṭṭhakanipāto,* 9, 3.
60. A IV, pp. 183–184, *Dasakanipāto,* 6, 8.
61. K V, p. 423, Pṭs 2, 8, 1, 1.
62. K IV, pt. II, p. 81, Cln 2, 4, 22–23. For the original text commented here, see K I, p. 427, Stn 5, 5, 78–79. The same applies to another comment that reads, 'By the best *dhamma* is understood the deathless *nibbāna* (*dhammaṁ seṭṭhaṁ vuccati amataṁ nibbānaṁ*)', which is an explanation of:

    And knowing the best *dhamma,*
    Thus you will cross this current.

    K IV, pt. II, pp. 100–101, Cln 2, 5, 33. Original text commented here found at K I, p. 429, Stn 5, 6, 89.
63. Prv, p. 160 (3, 1). Cf. what the Editors of the Nālandā Edition have to say about the place of the *Parivāra* in the *Tipiṭaka*: 'The following two facts must be considered to determine the place of the present volume, the Parivāra Pāli, in the *Tipiṭaka*: (i) in the entire *Tipiṭaka* this is the only book that gives evidence of the practice of committing a text to writing; and (ii) this book gives a list of as many as twenty nine teachers, in succession, of the tradition of the Vinaya in the island of Laṅkā, after the establishment of the Dhamma over there accomplished by the mission led by Prince Mahinda. This indicates that this book must have been compiled somewhere in Ceylon at a much later date, when the practice of writing would have come in vogue. As, perhaps it proved to be very useful for higher studies in the Vinaya, the Elders of the Synods decided to give it the prestige of the word of the Buddha; and just like the *Kathāvatthu,* accepted it as an integral constituent of the *Tipiṭaka.'* (Intr., pp. ix-x).

64. This, notwithstanding the teaching of M I, p. 6 f., *Mūlapariyāyasutta,* 6 f., where all conceit as regards *nibbāna* is condemned. The *nibbāna* which is the object of conceit ceases being the true *nibbāna.*
65. S II-III, pp. 351–352, *Khandhasaṁyutta,* 90.
66. M I, p. 280, *Cūḷasaccakasutta,* 2.
67. M III, p. 382, *Chachakkasutta,* 8–9. The same reasoning applies to all the other senses with their corresponding consciousness, objects, sensorial contact, feeling, craving.
68. *The Bhagavadgītā* (London, 1973), Intr., p. 10.
69. See, for instance, the last *Yogasūtra* of Patañjali, *Puruṣārthaśūnyānaṁ guṇānaṁ pratiprasavaḥ kaivalyaṁ, svarūpapratiṣṭhā vā cittiśaktiriti.*
70. 'The Sāṅkhya soul is described as being devoid of any and every characteristic; but its nature is absolute pure consciousness (*cit*)', S. Dasgupta, *A History of Indian Philosophy,* Vol. I (London, 1932), p. 238. Also: 'Therefore the self, of which we can only say that it is intellect (*citi*), which is other [than the aspects (*guṇa*)], and which is undefiled (*śuddha*) [by objects], is absolutely contrary in quality even to *sattva,* which is mutable', H. Woods, *The Yoga System of Patañjali* (Harward Univ. Press, 1927), p. 262.
71. *Ye suvimuttā te kevalino. Ye kevalino vaṭṭaṁ tesaṁ natthi paññapanāya* (S III, p. 289, *Khandhasaṁyutta,* 56). *Aññena ca kevalinaṁ mahesiṁ, khīṇāsavaṁ kukkuccavūpasantaṁ...* (S I, p. 166, *Brāhmaṇasaṁyutta,* 8). Repeated at K I, p. 282, Stn 1, 4, 82 and *Ibid.,* p. 339 (3, 4, 79). The terms *kevalī* and *kevalajñāna* are frequently used in Jainism, too.
72. S II-III, p. 295 f., *Khandhasaṁyutta,* 59. The whole *sutta* has been incorporated into Mvg, p. 16, *Mahākhandhaka,* 8, 20–23.
73. M I, p. 183 f., *Cūḷasaccakasutta.*
74. S II-III, p. 260, *Khandhasaṁyutta,* 20.

NOTES TO CHAPTER 12: *'ASMIMĀNA, SAKKĀYADIṬṬHI, SASSATAVĀDA* AND *UCCHEDAVĀDA'*

1. Following the line of thought that posits an affinity between early Buddhism and certain other systems, which, even though teaching the doctrine of *anattā,* maintain, nevertheless, the doctrine of the reality of the self, we may quote here *sūtra* 6 of the Second Chapter of the *Yogasūtras* of Patañjali, '*Dṛgdarśanaśaktyorekātmatevāsmitā',* where *asmitā* corresponds with *asmimāna* in the Pāli texts. *Asmitā* is defined, in J. H. Woods' rendering of the *sūtra,* as: 'When the power of seing and the power by which one sees have the appear-

ance (*iva*) of being a single self, [this is] the feeling of personality (*asmitā*)'. Vācaspati Miśra's commentary on the *sūtra* contains the following explanation: 'The seing and that by which one sees are precisely the two powers of the two, the self and the not-self. That undifferentiated consciousness (*avidyā*) which is characterized as being the perception of a self in what is the not-self, and which has the appearance of being a single intended-object, but which, in the strict sense, is not a single self, – this (*avidyā*) is the feeling of personality (*asmitā*)', J. H. Woods, *Op. cit.*, p. 115. This feeling of personality or conceit is represented in the Sāṅkhya system by *ahaṅkāra,* from which the senses and the objects of sense are supposed to proceed. We shall see how, according to the Pāli texts, *asimāna* is rooted in the identification of the self with the activities of the senses and the *khandhas.* In Horace Hayman Wilson's comment on *Sānkhyakārikā* 24, we read: 'The term here given as the synonym and definition of "egotism", *ahaṅkāra,* is *abhimāna,* translated "consciousness". The ordinary sense of both is "the pride or conceit of individuality"; "self-sufficiency"; the notion that "I do, I feel, I think, I am", as explained by Vachaspati: "I alone preside and have power over all that is perceived and known, and all these objects of sense are for my use. There is no other supreme except I; I AM. This pride, from its exclusive [selfish] application, is egotism', H. Th. Colebrooke, *Op. cit.,* p. 123.

2. The whole text is repeated several times, but substituting for *maññitaṁ: iñjitaṁ, phanditaṁ, papañcitaṁ, mānagataṁ,* terms suggestive of instability, confusion, and pride. S IV, pp. 180–182, *Saḷāyatanasaṁyutta,* 248.
3. A II, p. 263, *Catukkanipāto,* 26, 4, 2.
4. A III, p. 144, *Chakkanipāto,* 10, 11.
5. A I, pp. 122–123, *Tikanipāto,* 4, 2. The same ideas are repeated in the following *sutta* (4, 3).
6. A II, pp. 346–347. *Pañcakanipāto,* 8, 1, 6, and 8, 2, 6.
7. M III, p. 331, *Dhātuvibhaṅgasutta,* 26.
8. See: 'I will declare to you, Kappa, the island of those who have gone beyond old-age and death, [the island] which stands in the middle of the worldly current, in this fearsome flood, ... I call that *nibbāna,* the destruction of old-age and death', K I, p. 433–434, Stn 5, 11, 118–119. See also: *'atāri jātiṁ maraṇaṁ asesaṁ', Ibid.,* p. 320 (2, 12, 135).
9. 'Those beings who, knowing this, have attained *nibbāna* in this very life, *being at peace for ever,* they have crossed the entanglement in the world', K I, p. 433, Stn 5, 10, 112. See also: 'I attained the deathless peace, the unfailing state of *nibbāna', Ibid.* p. 298 (1, 11, 206). This utter peace that follows the complete destruction of conceit demands the complete destruction of all doubt, to which

such an importance is given in the Nikāyas. Thus we have a passage that speaks of the incompatibility of a condition where no conceit exists and the survival of doubt. The passage ends: 'This is precisely the escape from the dart of uncertainty and doubt, to wit, the complete rooting out of the conceit "I am",' A III, pp. 14–15, *Chakkanipāto,* 2, 3, 6. The whole passage is repeated at D III, p. 193, *Saṅgītisutta,* 31.

10. K I, p. 154, Ud 7, 1, 2.
11. S II-III, pp. 327–328, *Khandhasaṁyutta,* 83.
12. S II-III, p. 278, *Khandhasaṁyutta,* 47. See *Sāṅkhyakārikā,* 64:

    Evaṁ tatvābhyāsānnāsti na me nāhamityapariśeṣaṁ,
    aviparyayādviśuddhaṁ kevalamutpadyate jñānaṁ.

    Translated by H. Th. Colebrooke as, 'So, through the study of the principles, the conclusive, incontrovertible, one only knowledge is attained, that neither I AM, nor is aught mine, nor do I exist', *Op. cit.,* p. 240. We may quote also H. H. Wilson's reflections appended to this *kārikā*: 'By these expressions therefore, however quaint or questionable, we are not to understand a negation of soul. This would be a direct contradiction to its specification as one of the categories of the system, one of the twenty-five essential and existent principles. It is merely intended as a negation of the soul's having any active participation, individual interest or property, in human pains, possessions or feelings. "I am, I do, I suffer", mean that material nature, or some of her products, (substantially) is, does, suffers; and not soul, which is unalterable and indifferent, susceptible of neither pleasure nor pain, and only reflecting them, as it were or seemingly sharing them, from the proximity of nature, by whom they are really experienced...', *Ibid.,* p. 243. Even though Sāṅkhya and early Buddhism do not agree in all their teachings, who is there that, while reading about the relationship shown here between the self and *prakṛti,* is not reminded of the relationship in early Buddhism between the self and the non-self, i.e., the reality presided and moved by the *paṭiccasamuppāda*?
13. S IV, pp. 36–37, *Saḷāyatanasaṁyutta,* 69.
14. S IV, pp. 81–82, *Saḷāyatanasaṁyutta,* 108.
15. M III, pp. 263–265, *Ānandabhaddekarasutta,* 3. The passage is meant to be an explanation to the verse:

    He should not turn to the past, he should not long for the future,
    What is past is lost, what is to come has not yet been obtained.
    The one who looks at existing things (*dhammaṁ*), as they really are,
    He, immovable, not to be troubled, is the one the wise appreciates.

    The original of this *sutta* seems to be M III, pp. 260–262, *Bhaddekarattasutta.* See also M III, pp. 271–273, *Mahakāccānabhaddekarattasutta,* 7–10, where the same delight in the past, longing for the future, and involvement in the present are described.

16. S II-III, p. 210, *Rāhulasaṁyutta,* 22. Repeated at S II-III, pp. 307–308, *Khandhasaṁyutta,* 72; *Ibid.,* pp. 383–384, *sutta* 125. There is another series of *suttas* worded exactly in the same way, but differing from the previous ones in that they have as their aim the suppression of tendencies to conceit of "I" and "mine". S II-III, pp. 209–210, *Rāhulasaṁyutta,* 21; S II-III, p. 307, *Khandhasaṁyutta,* 71; *Ibid.,* p. 326, *sutta* 82, where the passage in question constitutes only a portion of the *sutta.* M III, p. 80, *Mahāpuṇṇamasutta,* 4, is a repetition of *Khandhasaṁyutta,* 82, just quoted.
17. S IV, pp. 20–21, *Saḷāyatanasaṁyutta,* 30.
18. S IV, pp. 21–22, *Saḷāyatanasaṁyutta,* 31.
19. S IV, pp. 22–24, *Saḷāyatanasaṁyutta,* 32.
20. The consideration of impermanence and pain, without any reference to *anattā* is also pointed out at times as a remedy against conceit. Cf. S II-III, p. 279, *Khandhasaṁyutta,* 49, where the incongruity is noted of holding views such as: "Better am I", "equal am I", "worse am I", as regards everyone of the *impermanent and painful khandhas.* All the same, the *sutta* ends with the consideration of non-selfhood regarding the *khandhas* by means of the stock passage: 'What do you think, Soṇa, is material form permanent or impermanent...'. See also M III, p. 179, *Mahāsuññatasutta,* 7, where the consideration of the rise and fall of the *khandhas* conduces to removal of *asmimāna.* See also S II-III, p. 370, *Khandhasaṁyutta,* 102, where the awareness of impermanence, well developed, is expected to remove all *asmimāna.*
21. A IV, p. 5, *Navakanipāto,* 1, 1, 7; also *Ibid.,* p. 9, (1, 3, 17) and K I, p. 105, Ud 4, 1, 4.
22. M III, p. 106, *Sappurisasutta,* 12.
23. M III, p. 108, *Sappurisasutta,* 13.
24. M I, p. 372, *Cūḷavedallasutta,* 6.
25. M III, p. 58, *Aneñjasappāyasutta,* 5, 6. In the second half of the quotation a *mama* has been filled in, on the analogy of another *mama* which occurs in a very similar text of the *Aṅguttara,* in a context where conceit regarding the sphere of no-thing is also discussed, *...na ca mama kvacani...* A II, p. 188, *Catukkanipāto,* 19, 5.
26. S II-III, p. 450, *Sāriputtasaṁyutta,* 1.
27. One cannot but see in the last *vimokkha* an achievement similar to what in the *Yogasūtras* of Patañjali, Ch. I, *s.* 51, is called *nirbīja samādhi,* the final result of such condition being described in the *Vyāsabhāṣya* as: 'Consequently, its task ended, together with the subliminal impressions which are conducive

to Isolation, the mind ceases (from its task). When it ceases, the Self abides in himself and is therefore called pure and liberated', J. H. Woods, *Op. cit.*, p. 98.

28. M I, p. 369, *Cūḷavedallasutta,* 2. Also S IV, p. 231, *Jambukkhādakasaṁyutta,* 15, where the speaker is Sāriputta.
29. The transmigrational character of *sakkāyo* is also taught in the following passage: 'The fire of lust burns mortal men, addicted to sensual pleasures, infatuated. The fire of ill-will burns also malevolent men, who kill living beings. The fire of delusion burns also men bewildered, ignorant of the ariyan *dhamma.* People who know not these fires, addicted to their existential aggregate, make hell swell, as well as animal wombs, and the devilish abode of ghosts, unfree from Māra's bonds', K I, p. 244, Itv 3, 44.
30. *Sakkāyo,* its arisal, its cessation, and the way conducive to its cessation, are explained in a very similar way at S II-III, pp. 372–373, *Khandhasaṁyutta,* 103. See also *Ibid.,* p. 373, *sutta* 105.
31. M I, p. 370, *Cūḷavedallasutta,* 3. The same description of *sakkāyadiṭṭhi* is found at S II-III, p. 323, *Khandhasaṁyutta,* 82, and M III, p. 79, *Mahāpuṇṇamasutta,* 2. In both the last cases, the speaker is the Buddha.
32. S II-III, p. 398, *Khandhasaṁyutta,* 155. The nex *sutta* (156) follows the same pattern, but instead of *sakkāyadiṭṭhi* it discusses *attānudiṭṭhi,* which, as we shall see, is practically a synonym of *sakkāyadiṭṭhi.* To verify the central position in early Buddhism of the polarity between self and non-self, we can examine the whole series of *suttas* in this part of the *Saṁyutta.* All follow the pattern shown in the quotation, and deal, among other things, with the heresy of eternalism, with the heresy of annihilationism, with *micchādiṭṭhi* in general, and finally with *sakkāyadiṭṭhi* and *attānudiṭṭhi,* proving thereby the affinity prevailing among them all, as all of them depend for their arisal on the identification of the non-self with the self.
33. M III, pp. 385–386, *Chachakkasutta,* 10–11.
34. K I, p. 437, Stn 5, 16, 144. Also at K VII, Apd 2, p. 136 (54, 10, 353–354). Quoted at K IV, pt. I, p. 380, Mnd 1, 15, 186. Commented on in the *Cullaniddesa,* as we shall presently see.
35. K IV, pt. II, pp. 196–197, Cln 2, 15, 88.
36. K V, pp. 159–161, Pṭs 1, 2, 5, 21–24. The equivalence of *sakkāyadiṭṭhi* and *attānudiṭṭhi* is confirmed later on when to the question, *sakkāyadiṭṭhiyā katamehi vīsatiyā ākārehi abhiniveso hoti*?, the answer given is the same as the one given to a similar question on *attānudiṭṭhi. Ibid.,* p. 171 (1, 2, 5, 44–46).
37. K V, pp. 181–182, Pṭs 1, 2, 5, 74.
38. S II-III, pp. 311–312, *Khandhasaṁyutta,* 78. The whole *sutta* is repeated at A II, pp. 36–37, *Catukkanipāto,* 4, 3. The sway of *sakkāyo* extends even to

Brahmaloka. There is a *sutta* in the *Saṁyutta* that teaches how a sick man should be comforted. First, he should be detached from all love for relatives, for love for sensual pleasures, he should be instilled every time with desire for a higher sort of heaven, till *Brahmaloka* is reached. Then he should be exhorted like this: 'Friend, even the Brahma-world is impermanent, unstable, entirely immersed in the existential aggregate (*sakkāyapariyāpanno*). Well, reverend one, rousing your mind out of the Brahma-world, focus it on the cessation of the existential aggregate. And if he were to say, "my mind is roused from the Brahma-world, and I focus it on the cessation of the existential aggregate", I say, Mahānāma, that there is no difference between a lay disciple whose mind is thus freed, and a bhikkhu whose mind is emancipated from the *āsavas,* inasmuch as there is freedom by means of freedom', S V, p. 351, *Sotāpittisaṁyutta,* 54.

39. A III, pp. 136–137, *Chakkanipāto,* 9, 1.
40. The same striking opposition is found in the following context, where first we find the description of a bhikkhu who enjoys activity, given to talk, sleep, companionship, etc. He is heading for an unhappy end. The description ends with: 'Such one, friends, is said to be a bhikkhu addicted to the existential aggregate (*sakkāyābhirato*), he does not leave aside the existential aggregate for making a complete end of Pain'. While the bhikkhu who behaves in the opposite way: 'Such one, friends, is said to be a bhikkhu who finds delight in *nibbāna* (*nibbānābhirato*), he leaves aside the existential aggregate for making a complete end of Pain', A III, pp. 15–16, *Chakkanipāto,* 2, 4. Repeated in the following *sutta* (2, 5).
41. A II, p. 485, *Pañcakanipāto,* 20, 10, 5. The description of the five factors of deliverance is repeated at D III, pp. 186–187, *Saṅgītisutta,* 26 and at D III, pp. 215–216, *Dasuttarasutta,* 6. Similar to the previous one is the following text, where first the negative instance is given and then the parallel case is stated in a positive way: 'Herein, bhikkhus, a bhikkhu dwells having attained to a certain calm release of mind. He reflects on cessation of the existential aggregate; while he is reflecting on cessation of the existential aggregate his mind rejoices in it, is pleased with it, finds satisfaction in it, lets itself go regarding it. Bhikkhus, the cessation of the existential aggregate is to be expected in the case of such a bhikkhu', A II, p. 176, *Catukkanipāto,* 18, 8, 1–2.
42. M III, p. 60, *Āneñjasappāyasutta,* 10.
43. 'The wrong view of the existential aggregate, doubt and clinging to morality and religious practices – these are the three fetters cast off in the stage of the stream-winner', K V, p. 341, Pṭs 2, 1, 0, 1, 10.
44. S II-III, pp. 414–415, *Diṭṭhisaṁyutta,* 1.

45. S II-III, p. 472, *Vacchagottasaṁyutta,* 1.
46. The *suttas* continue being composed on this same pattern and attribute the arisal of the manifold speculative theories to: lack of insight regarding everyone of the *khandhas,* the same as before (6–10); incomprehension (*anabhisamayā*) (11–15); lack of understanding (*ananubodhā*) (16–20), etc.
47. S IV, pp. 255–256, *Cittasaṁyutta,* 3.
48. S IV, pp. 335–338, *Abyākatasaṁyutta,* 7.
49. K IV, pt. I, p. 42, Mnd 1, 2, 12.
50. S II-III, p. 352, *Khandhasaṁyutta,* 90.
51. S II-III, pp. 351–353, *Khandhasaṁyutta,* 90. The Kaccāna incident, to which reference is made here, occurs in its original setting at S II-III, p. 17, *Nidānasaṁyutta,* 15, where the query is: 'How far is there right view?'
52. All these questions occur also at S II-III, p. 25, *Nidānasaṁyutta,* 20, where it is said that such questions do not arise in the mind of one who knows by right wisdom the *dhammas* of the *paṭiccasamuppāda.*
53. M I, pp. 12–13, *Sabbāsavasutta,* 5–6.
54. S I, p. 135, *Bhikkhunīsaṁyutta,* 10.
55. M III, p. 81, *Mahāpuṇṇamasutta,* 5.
56. It will not be out of place to quote here H. H. Wilson's comment on the above quoted *kārikā*: 'The doctrine here laid down seems at variance with what has preceded, and with the usual purpot of the notions that attach the accidents of bondage and liberation to the soul. Apparently, however, the difference is one of words only. Soul is incapable of action, consequently is not liable to change. It cannot be bound, as the consequence of acts which it does not perform; and as it is never in bondage it cannot be set free. The application of these terms to soul, therefore, is to be understood in a relative not in a positive sense; and their positive signification is properly restricted to nature. It is nature that is bound, nature that is liberated, nature that undergoes change or migration. When nature attaches itself to soul, when she separates from it, the converse is equally true, soul is attached to, or is separated from, nature; and is consequently said to be bound, to be set free, to undergo change. But soul is passive in all these things; it is nature that is active, that binds, loosens, or changes form. Gauḍapāda's explanation of these subtleties is not very clear, but such appears to be his understanding of the texts', H. Th. Colebrooke, *Op. cit.,* p. 237. Later Jainism had a similar idea of the ultimate nature of the self: 'He who beholds the self as not-bound (*abaddha*), not-touched (*apṛṣṭa*), not-other (than itself) *(ananyaka),* permanent (*nitya*), undifferentiated (*aviśeṣa*), unattached (*asaṁyukta*), know him to be a holder of the right point of view', Srī Kundakunda, *Op. cit.*, p. 25, v. 14. To say that the self is not bound is to

say that is free by nature. But this will not impair Kundakunda's zest to describe man's bondage and to persuade him to attain liberation. In the texts quoted, both the *Sāṅkhyakārikā* and Kundakunda view the self from a metaphysical perspective. This was never the perspective taken by the Buddha. His aim was definitely practical he intended only to preach salvation and to exhort men to free themselves from the misery of mundane existence. It was of no practical use, from such point of view, to say that man was by nature a liberated being. Buddha spread his message not looking down from the peak of perfection, where few have the courage to climb, but from the valley of old-age and death, of existential pain, where most men seem willing to stay for ever. Hence his constant insistence not on what the self is, but on what the self is not, and should, therefore, be discarded.

57. A further confirmation of the point made in Chapter 11, that *sabbe dhammā anattā* does not apply to *nibbāna,* which is no part of the *paṭiccasamuppāda.* Taking hold of the sentence just quoted an *anattavādin* would say that the Buddha is teaching here that all *moral* activity should be attributed to the *dhammas* of the *paṭiccasamuppāda.* It is true that all activity, *as such,* implying as it does change, falls within the realm of the *dhammas.* But there is nothing in the *dhammas* that gives the reason, the cause, for a *moral* activity that strives to break the chain. The chain, left to itself, will never stop, but will ever renew itself, and keep itself moving. This sentence, therefore, needs the corrective of all those texts, so numerous and so eloquent, in which the activity of the *moral self* is emphasized. The one-sided insistence on the *paṭiccasamuppāda* doctrine, with the resulting neglect of the activity of the *moral self,* was responsible for the denial in later times of the reality of the moral agent. The teaching of this passage seems rather to be that whatever *speculative* difficulties may be experienced, and to which a true bhikkhu should never pay attention, one should never come to the conclusion that the *dhammas* of the *paṭiccasamuppāda* are in any way the self.

58. M III, pp. 81–82, *Mahāpuṇṇamasutta,* 5. This incident is reported also at S II-III, pp. 326–327, *Khandhasaṁyutta,* 82. This version of the incident seems to be later than the one occurring at M III. It is also possible that both versions depend on a common source which they reproduce differently. The fact is that the variant readings in M III, give place in S II-III to a neat version which seems the work of a later compiler who even combines different readings. Thus in S II-III we read, *paṭipucchāvinitā kho me tumhe, tatra tatra tesu tesu dhammesu,* where there seems to be no reference to the *paṭiccasamuppāda.*

59. M I, p. 283, *Cūḷasaccakasutta,* 6. Either the Jain position is misrepresented, or Aggivesana oversimplifies matters, or, finally, displays ignorance of his own

faith. From the metaphysical point of view, the self of the Jainas, no less than the self of early Buddhism, is not the body, nor the senses and their functions. Thus:

Jīvassa ṇatthi vaṇṇo ṇavi gandho ṇavi raso ṇavi phāso,
ṇavi rūpaṁ, ṇa sarīraṁ ṇavi saṇṭhāṇaṁ ṇa saṁhaṇaṇaṁ.

Srī Kundakunda, *Op. cit.,* p. 50, v. 50. All these realities are said to belong to the self only from the *vyavahāra* point of view, not from the point of view of reality (*niścayanaya*):

Vavahāreṇa du ede jīvassa havanti vaṇṇamādīyā
guṇaṭhāṇantā bhāvā ṇa du keī ṇicchayaṇayassa.

Ibid., p. 55, v. 56. We dare say that this distinction is in the Nikāyas in a latent, not developed, condition. When this distinction was made explicit, it served only to deny the reality of the moral agent. In Jainism, the *vyavahāra* point of view in no way detracts from the reality of the self. That *vedanā* is not the self is clear from:

Jo vedadi vedijjadi samae samae viṇassade uhayaṁ,
taṁ jāṇago du ṇāṇī ubhayamavi ṇa kaṅkhai kayāvi.

Ibid., p. 141, v. 216. See A. Chakravarti's comment on this, *Ibid.,* pp. 141–142. Where early Buddhism parts company with Jainism is in the question of perception and knowledge. Thus we read in A. Chakravarti's comment on the corresponding *gāthās*: 'No, perception and knowledge are not attributes to be transcended by the supreme consciousness, because they are the attributes of the supreme consciousness itself'. But even in this matter, the writer makes the following reservation: 'Of course it should not be misunderstood that these properties of perception and knowledge are the same as the process of perceiving and knowing associated with the empirical ego', *Ibid.,* pp. 183–184. Consequently, the real difference between early Buddhism and Jainism is in the fact that the former never predicated consciousness as an attribute of the self.

60. Against what is asserted at D I, p. 100, *Soṇadaṇḍasutta, 5, samaṇo khalu bho Gotamo kammavādī kiriyavādī.* See also, A I, p. 60, *Dukanipāto,* 4, 3, 3.
61. Another confirmation, again, of the opinion that the saying, *sabbe dhammā anattā,* does not refer to *nibbāna.*
62. S IV, p. 343, *Abyākatasaṁyutta,* 10.
63. It is worth comparing the conclusion to which we arrive, by applying the principle established above to the passage under discussion, with the conclusion to which Oldenberg arrives: '… If the Buddha avoids the negation of the existence of the ego, he does so in order not to shock a weak-minded hearer. Through the shirking of the question as to the existence or non-existence of the

ego, is heard the answer, to which the premises of the Buddhist teaching tended: The ego is not. Or, what is equivalent: The Nirvāṇa is annihilation', H. Oldenberg, *Buddha: His Life, His Doctrine, His Order* (Delhi, 1971), p. 273. The Buddha was not 'shirking the question', he was answering it with what, according to our interpretation, was a meaningful silence. It was useless for the Buddha to speak if he knew for certain he was going to be misunderstood. It was, besides, his policy never to state anything positive on the metaphysical self. The reason for this will be indicated in the next chapter.

64. K V, p. 172, Pṭs 1, 2, 5, 47–48.
65. K V, pp. 172–173, Pṭs 1, 2, 6, 50–52.
66. M III, pp. 24–25, *Pañcattayasutta,* 5.
67. S II-III, p. 395, *Khandhasaṁyutta,* 152.
68. M I, pp. 181–182, *Alagaddūpamasutta,* 12.
69. M III, pp. 24–25, *Pañcattayasutta,* 5.
70. K I, pp. 211–212, Ivt 2, 22.
71. S II-III, p. 17, *Nidānasaṁyutta,* 15. This incident is included in S II-III, pp. 353–354, *Khandhasaṁyutta,* 90.
72. This makes it evident that H. Kern was not right when he held that even the Buddishm of the Nikāyas was a kind of 'nihilism'. See: 'In our view Buddhism was from the very beginning *essentially* such as we find it in the Tripiṭaka, a creed aptly characterized in the following words: "As a philosophy, Buddhism thus seems to be an Idealistic Nihilism...",' *Manual of Indian Buddhism* (Varanasi, 1972), p. 50.
73. See S II-III, p. 22, *Nidānasaṁyutta,* 18.

NOTES TO CHAPTER 13: 'SELF AND NON-SELF AFTER LIBERATION'

1. *Buddhist Philosophy* (Varanasi, 1963), pp. 61–62.
2. As I. B. Horner writes: 'MA, ii, 117 says here, "tathāgata means both a being, satta, and the highest person, one who has destroyed the cankers". Cf. UdA, 340, which explains tathāgata by attā', *The Collection of the Middle Length Sayings,* Vol. I, p. 179, n. 4. In M I, p. 185, *Alagaddūpamasutta,* 16, the equivalence in meaning between the perfect bhikkhu and the Tathāgata is clearly indicated: 'The devas, bhikkhus, together with Indra, Brahmā, and Prajāpati, even when looking for him, do not find *a bhikkhu so liberated in mind* [being able to say]. "Here has settled the consciousness of *the Tathāgata".* Why so? I say, bhikkhus, that a Tathāgata is untraceable even in this very life.'

3. See for the whole *sutta,* S II-III, p. 331 f., *Khandhasaṁyutta,* 85.
4. *The Book of the Kindred Sayings,* Vol. III, p. 93, n. 3.
5. It is surprising to see that the customary questions which usually follow this first one are not found here:

   And what is impermanent is pleasant or painful?
   Painful, friend.
   And what is impermanent, painful, mutable by nature, is it fitting that one should regard it as, 'This is mine, this I am, this is my self'?
   Not so, friend.

   As a matter of fact, the stock passage, in this abbreviated form, is repeated in the two previous *suttas* (84 and 85), but occurs in its habitual full version in *sutta* 82. And if we go on reading forward we see that it reappears again in its full version in *suttas* 86 (which deals exactly with the same topic as the present one) and 87. This seems to indicate that, unless there is a positive reason for the suppression of the missing questions, they must be supposed to have been there originally. In point of fact, there are positive reasons for their inclusion, not their suppression, as they describe the fundamental attitude of mind required as a remedy against a mentality that was under the influence of the *sakkāyadiṭṭhi,* which indentifies the self with the *khandhas.* Let it be added that this separation of the self from the *khandhas* is a necessary assumption for the right understanding of what follows.
6. Thus we read in the *Brahmajālasutta,* 147 (D I, p. 40): 'The body of the Tathāgata, bhikkhus, stands before you with all that leads to a new becoming having been destroyed. So long as the body will stand, gods and men will see him. After the dissolution of the body, beyond the end of life, gods and men do not see him.' We see, also, king Pasenadi prostrating himself at the feet of the Buddha, kissing them, and touching them with his hands. The Buddha questions the king's attitude: 'But, mahārāja, in view of what significance do you pay such homage and make an offering of friendliness *to this body*?' The answer of the king was: 'Keeping in mind my gratitude and thankfulness, I pay such a homage and make an offering of friendliness *to the Blessed One'.* In what follows, the king proclaims ten reasons for his behaviour, all referring to outstanding qualities of the Blessed One – not of his body – ending with his attainment of *nibbāna*: 'And, besides, Lord, the Blessed One, by the destruction of the *āsavas,* dwells having obtained in this very life a liberation of mind, and a liberation through higher wisdom, that is free from the *āsavas*, having realized it by himself. It is seing this significance that I pay such a homage and make an offering of friendliness *to the Blessed On',* A IV, p. 150 f., *Dasakanipāto,* 3, 10. To note, that 'this body' in Buddha's question turns into 'the

Blessed One' in the king's answer. King Pasenadi was not paying homage merely to Buddha's body, but through it, to the outstanding personality of the Buddha, recognising thereby that the body bore a special relationship to such personality. This provides us with the rationale for the special veneration paid to the remains of the Buddha in the *Mahāparinibbānasutta,* a veneration often mentioned in the *Apadāna* as an action of outstanding merit.

7. Woodward has chosen the second meaning, which certainly is the meaning of the verb in passages such as: *'Yassa ubho ante ca bhavābhavāya ca idha huraṁ ca paṇidhi taṇhā natthi na santi nupalabbhanti',* K IV, pt. I, p. 92, Mnd 1, 5, 36. See also *Ibid.,* pp. 205–206 (1, 10, 91), and *Ibid.,* pp. 206–207 (1, 10, 92 and 93).
8. This is also the conclusion to which Oldenberg arrives: 'Thus are all attempts to define dialectically the ego of the Perfect One, repelled. The idea is certainly not that some other attempt might prove successful, but is kept in concealment by Sāriputta; no more does the unavailingness of all these attempts to find a solution imply that the Perfect One does not exist at all. Thought, Sāriputta means to say, has here reached the unfathomably deep mystery, on the solution of which it must not insist. The monk who seeks the happiness of his soul, has something else to pursue', *Buddha: His Life, His Doctrine, His Order* (Delhi, 1971), p. 282. See also T. V. Murti, *The Central Philosophy of Buddhism* (London, 1960), Chapter Two, where topics as the following are dealt with: 'The Antinomical Character of the Avyākṛta', and 'The Real is transcendent to Thought'. But Dr. Murti accepts unconditionally the doctrine of absolute *anattā* as being the genuine teaching of the Nikāyas. Thus on page 49 we read: 'For Buddha however, the self is a primary wrong notion...', and a little below, 'This can only mean that for him knowledge is the self-conscious awareness of the world process; to realize the inexorability of the Causal Law (pratītya-samutpāda) is to stand aside from it'. We may ask who is it that by realizing the inexorability of the Causal Law stands aside from it. Certainly not that self which according to the illustrious author was for the Buddha a primary wrong notion, because that wrong notion is precisely a product of the Causal Law and identifies itself with the world process. Therefore the liberating *self*-awareness cannot belong to the self that is merely a wrong notion and nothing more.
9. See for the whole *sutta,* S II-III, p. 331 f., *Khandhasaṁyutta,* 85.
10. *Sutta* 86 (*Anurādhasutta*) has been mentioned above as following the *Yamakasutta* and as a *sutta* where the stock passage: 'What do you think of this, is body permanent or impermanent, etc.', reappears in its full version, including the question: 'And what is impermanent, painful, mutable by nature, is it fit to consider it as, "This is mine, this I am, this is my self?"' It so happens

that the topic discussed in *Anurādhasutta* coincides with the topic discussed in *Yamakasutta,* that is to say, the incomprehensibility of the self even in this very life, much more so after the death of the perfect man. Anurādha is accosted by many wanderers of other faiths with the words: 'Friend Anurādha, he who is a Tathāgata, the best of men, the highest of men, the winner of the highest gain, him the Tathāgata is wont to declare in these four ways, "The Thatāgata exists after death, the Tathāgata does not exist after death, etc. Is it not so?" Anurādha replies: "He who, friends, is a Tathāgata, the best of men..., him the Tathāgata is wont to declare in a way different from those four ways...".' The wanderers left Anurādha saying that the latter was either a fool or new in the Order and ignorant. When alone, Anurādha reflected that if they had pressed him with further questions he might have misinterpreted the Buddha's teaching. He therefore applies to the Buddha. The latter confronts Anurādha with the same antinomies as those pressed by Sāriputta on Yamaka in the previous *sutta.* The dialogue, and together with it the *sutta* end with: 'Then, Anurādha, if the Tathāgata is not comprehended by you in this very life as he truly and really is, is it fitting for you to explain things in this way, "He who, friends, is a Tathāgata, the best of men..., him the Tathāgata is wont to declare in a way different from those four ways...?"' 'Not so, Lord'. 'Very well, Anurādha. Both previously and at present I declare only pain and the cessation of pain', S II-III, pp. 337–340, *Khandhasaṁyutta,* 86. This seems to have been the original *sutta. Yamakasutta* seems to be both an elaboration and an explicit generalization of this one. It is an elaboration, because it contains more elements; and it is an explicit generalization, because the Tathāgata in *sutta* 86 becomes in *sutta* 85, 'a bhikkhu with *āsavas* destroyed', and 'a bhikkhu who is an arahant, with *āsavas* destroyed'.

11. M I, p. 185, *Alagaddūpamasutta,* 16. It is to be noted that among the gods mentioned in the text, the god of the kṣatriyas comes first, even as when the four castes are enumerated the kṣatriya caste gets preference over the brāhmaṇas, and even as the samaṇas are mentioned always before the brāhmaṇas.
12. D I, p. 30, *Brahmajālasutta,* 84.
13. A IV, p. 253, *Dasakanipāto,* 10, 4. 4.
14. A III, p. 289, *Aṭṭhakanipāto,* 2, 1, 8. Repeated at *Ibid.,* p. 296 (2, 2, 21).
15. A II, pp. 171–172, *Catukkanipāto,* 18, 3. The next *sutta* (4) is an exact replica of this one, but with Ānanda as the questioner, and Mahākoṭṭhika as the instructor.
16. K I, p. 347, Stn 5, 16, 144. Repeated at K VII, Apd 2, p. 136 (54, 10, 353–354). Commented upon at K IV, pt. II, p. 190 f., Cln 2, 15, 88. '*Na pas-*

sati' is explained as *na dakkhati, nādhigacchati, na vindati, na paṭilabhati,* combining the lack of vision with the impossibility to find or to approach.

17. S I, p. 112, *Mārasaṁyutta,* 16.
18. K I, p. 21, Dhp 4, 46.
19. K I, p. 22, Dhp 4, 57.
20. S I, p. 133, *Bhikkhunīsaṁyutta,* 7.
21. M I, pp. 207–208, *Nivāpasutta,* 11, Quoted at K IV, pt. II, p. 198, Cln 2, 15, 88.
22. S I, pp. 120–121, *Mārasaṁyutta,* 23, and S II-III, p. 344, *Khandhasaṁyutta,* 87.
23. K I, p. 26, Dhp 7, 92–93. Both the stanzas have three verses, but the first one seems to be a later addition. The second *śloka* is repeated at K II, p. 255, Tha 1, 92.
24. D II, pp. 54–55, *Mahānidānasutta,* 32. In our translation we have omitted the words *'itissa diṭṭhī ti'* from *'na jānāti na passati itissa diṭṭhī ti'*, because the sense postulates such suppression and the words in such a place can be accounted for as a result of the previous repetition of them at the end of the four *diṭṭhis,* which cannot be attributed to the emancipated bhikkhu.
25. K I, p. 384, Stn 3, 12, 348. For health being a synonym of *nibbāna* see M II, p. 206 f., *Māgaṇḍiyasutta,* 9 f., particularly, 'So you have not the ariyan eye, by which you might know health (*ārogiyaṁ jāneyyāsi*), you might see *nibbāna', Ibid.,* p. 207, *Māgaṇḍiyasutta,* 12.
26. K I, p. 219, Itv 3, 14. 'A sage is no more a subject of designation', corresponds in the text to *saṅkhyaṁ nopeti vedagū.* See also: 'When all the *dhammas* have been swept away, all the ways of talking have been removed', K I, p. 430, Stn 5, 7, 101.
27. K I, p. 177, Ud 8, 10. Repeated at K VII, Apd 2, p. 215 (2, 7, 286–287).
28. That *saṅkhā* or *saṅkhyā* has in these texts the meaning of 'name' or 'designation' is proved by the use of the word at M II, pp. 444–445, *Esukārīsutta,* 6, where the underlying thought is that there is no essential difference between the members of different castes, the only difference being that of the name, which depends on the extrinsic circumstance of the family into which one is born. Thus: *'khattiyakule ce attabhāvassa abhinibbati hoti khattiyo tveva saṅkhyaṁ gacchati'.* Then the illustration of fire is given, which receives its designation from the kind of fuel employed in its production; if the fire burns by reason of dry sticks is called a dry-stick-fire, etc.
29. See D I, p. 48, *Sāmaññaphalasutta,* 22.
30. K IV, pt. II, pp. 115–116, Cln 2, 6, 43.
31. See commentary, K IV, pt. II, p. 117, Cln 2, 6, 44.

32. K I, p. 430, Stn 5, 7, 98–101.
33. Such is the explanation given in the commentary to 'all *dhammas*'. This confirms again that the dictum *sabbe dhammā anattā* does not refer to *nibbāna*. K IV, Pt. II, p. 118, Cln 2, 6, 45.
34. S IV, pp. 344–345, *Abyākatasaṁyutta,* 11.
35. The same reasoning is applied to the rest of the *khandhas*. S IV, pp. 321–326, *Abyākatasaṁyutta,* 1.
36. In contrast with the Buddhist position, we are told that the teachers of other faiths: Pūraṇa Kassapa, Makkhali Gosāla, Nigaṇṭha Nāṭaputta, Sañjaya Belaṭṭhaputta, Pakudha Kaccāna, and Ajita Kesakambala, tended to describe the fate of the perfect after death, with the same words used to describe the fate of those who were reborn, namely: '*Asu amutra upapanno, asu amutra upapanno',* while the Buddha was using such words only in the case of those who were reborn; regarding the man who died in a state of absolute perfection, the Buddha used to describe his destiny as: 'He has destroyed craving, he has cast off all bonds, by a perfect comprehension of conceit he has made an end of Pain', S IV, pp. 341–342, *Abyākatasaṁyutta,* 9. In what concerns the Jains, this seems to be a misrepresentation, as they also recognize the ineffability of the liberated ones. We shall quote a clear testimony of this later on.
37. M III, p. 134, *Isigilisutta,* 4.
38. K III, pt. II, p. 168, J, *Mahānipāto,* 539, 143.
39. K II, p. 56, Vmv 1, 35, 656.
40. K II, p. 57, Vmv 1, 36, 664.
41. M II, p. 467, *Vāseṭṭhasutta,* 6. Repeated at K I, p. 367, Stn 3, 9, 243. We have already quoted elsewhere these two passages:

    (a) 'The devas, bhikkhus, together with Indra, Brahmā, and Prajāpati, even when looking for him, do not find a bhikkhu so liberated in mind, [being able to say]: "Here has settled the consciousness of the Tathāgata". Why so? I say, bhikkhus, that a Tathāgata is untraceable even in this very life', M I, p. 185, *Alagaddūpamasutta,* 16.

    (b) 'The body of the Tathāgata, bhikkhus, stands before you, with all that leads to new becoming having been destroyed. So long as the body will stand, gods and men will see him. After the dissolution of the body, beyond the end of life, gods and men do not see him', D I, p. 40, *Brahmajālasutta,* 147.
42. K VII, Apd 2, p. 213, *Therīapadāna,* 2, 7, 256–258. The 'Five-eyed One' is the same as 'The Leader', that is to say, the Buddha. He is called the 'Five-eyed One' because he is the possessor of five kinds of vision, or, as it is given in the Pāli texts, the possessor of five eyes, namely: *maṁsa-cakkhu* or 'physical eye'; *dibba-cakkhu* or 'deva-eye', all pervading and seing all that goes on in

hidden worlds; *paññā-cakkhu* or 'eye of wisdom', by which he can know all that can be known; *Buddhacakkhu* or 'eye of a Buddha', by which he sees the heart of man; *samanta-cakkhu* or 'the eye of all round knowledge', the eye of a Tathāgata, of a being perfected in all wisdom. See *P. T. S.*'s *Pāli English Dictionary,* s. v. *cakkhu.*

43. Thus we read in the Jain scriptures: '[The liberated] is not long, nor small, nor round, nor triangular, nor quadrangular, nor circular; he is not black, nor blue, nor red, nor green, nor white; neither of good or bad smell; not bitter, nor pungent, nor astringent, nor sweet; neither rough, nor soft; neither heavy, nor light; neither cold, nor hot; neither harsh, nor smooth; he is without body, without resurrection, without contact [of matter]; he is not feminine, nor masculine, nor neuter; he perceives, he knows, but there is no analogy [whereby to know the nature of the liberated soul]; its essence is without form; there is no condition of the unconditioned. There is no sound, no colour, no smell, no taste, no touch – nothing of that kind. Thus I say', Herman Jacobi, *Jaina Sūtras* (Oxford, 1884), p. 52. And immediately before the quoted passage we read: ' "All sounds recoil thence, where speculation has no room", nor does the mind penetrate there. The saint knows well that which is without support', *Ibid.* The quotation within the text seems to coincide with the upanishadic saying: *'yato vāco nivartante, aprāpya manasā saha...', Tait. Up.* II, iii, 1 and II, ix, 1. As to the mind being unable to reach to trascendent reality we read also: *'naiva vacā na manasā prāptuṁ śakyo...', Kaṭha Up.* II, iii, 12, and: *'na tatra cakṣurgacchati na vāggacchati no manaḥ...', Kena Up.* I, 3.

44. In this question of the indefinability of the emancipated self, or of the self in its metaphysical reality, we are in agreement with H. Günther, *Das Seelenproblem in älterem Buddhismus* (Konstanz, 1949), p. 28: 'Auch in diesen Zitaten wird nur gegen die Bestimmungen des ātman polemisiert, die ihn als körperlichkeit oder als einzelne psychische Funktionem fassen wollen, wärend es von dem ātman selbst nur heist, das er eine unerkennbare Wesenheit ausdrückt, die wir als solche nicht erfassen und über deren Inhalte wir nichts aussagen können, weil sie unser Fassungs- und Vorstellungs- vermögen übersteigen.... Hieraus erkennen wir also, das der ātman für den Buddha eine irrationale Gröse, etwas undefinierbar war'.

45. S IV, pp. 330–331, *Abyākatasaṁyutta,* 3.

46. S IV, pp. 331–332, *Abyākatasaṁyutta,* 4.

47. S IV, pp. 332–333, *Abyākatasaṁyutta,* 5.

48. S IV, pp. 333–335, *Abyākatasaṁyutta,* 6. In the same *sutta,* three more reasons are given why one holds the views, 'the Tathāgata exists after death, etc.'.
(a) When one rejoices in becoming (*bhava*), when one is in love with becom-

ing, when one takes delight in becoming, when one does not know, does not see, as it really is, the cessation of becoming, one holds the view, 'the Tathāgata exists after death, etc.'.

(b) When one rejoices in grasping (*upādāna*)...

(c) When one rejoices in craving (*taṇhā*)....

49. K V, pp. 177–179, Pṭs 1, 5, 65–66.
50. S IV, pp. 335–338, *Asaṅkhatasaṁyutta,* 7.
51. S IV, pp. 338–341, *Asaṅkhatasaṁyutta,* 8.
52. A III, pp. 204–205, *Sattakanipāto,* 6, 1, 2–3.
53. M II, p. 107 f., *Cūḷamālukyasutta.* Even a hurried perusal of the Nikāyas will convince anyone of the emphasis laid in them on pain and liberation from pain here and now, in this very life. Against the wastefulness of the *diṭṭhis,* this simple formula, pregnant with meaning, and containing in its brevity and apparent simplicity all the philosophy of life, is proposed as the *sammādiṭṭhi* or 'right view'. Thus: 'And what, your reverences, is right view? The knowledge regarding pain, the knowledge regarding the arisal of pain, the knowledge regarding the cessation of pain, the knowledge regarding the way leading to the cessation of pain. This, your reverences, is called right view', M III, p. 337, *Saccavibhaṅgasutta,* 8, etc. There are several other passages where the same reasons, worded in the same way, are given for leaving the *abyākata pañhā* unexplained and for explaining in their stead the four Noble Truths:

(a) This dialogue about the unexplained questions and the reasons for leaving them unexplained, as well as for the four Noble Truths being what the Buddha has explained, forms the contents of the *Parammaraṇasutta* at S II-III, pp. 185–186, *Kassapasaṁyutta,* 12.

(b) This dialogue is also found at D I, pp. 156–157, as part of the *Poṭṭhapādasutta* (16).

(c) S V, pp.. 358–359, *Saccasaṁyutta,* 8, is an exhortation to the bhikkhus not to entertain the sinful thought of the unexplained questions, because such thought is 'not connected with the goal, etc.', and to think of the four Noble Truths, because such thought is 'connected with the goal, belongs to the beginning of the brahma-life, etc.'.

(d) The same exhortation is a part of the *Lokacintāsutta* at S V, pp. 382–383, *Saccasaṁyutta,* 41.

(e) Another example of idle questions to which the Buddha refuses to answer is found at A IV, pp. 256–257, *Dasakanipāto,* 10, 5. The wanderer Uttiya comes to the Buddha and asks everyone of the unanswered questions, to which he gets the usual answer: 'This, Uttiya, has not been explained by me'. Then the wanderer asks the Buddha what is it that has been explained by him, and gets an answer similar to that found in the previous passages: 'Having fully known it, Uttiya, I teach *dhamma* to my disciples for the purification of beings, for the transcending of sorrow and lamentation, for the cessation of pain and mental uneasiness, for the attainment of the Way, for the realization of *nibbāna'*. Then the wanderer insists on asking the Buddha whether the whole world is led to salvation by the *dhamma,* or only half of it, or a third part of it. The Buddha answers, as on other occasions, with silence. Ānanda is the one who undertakes to explain to Uttiya that such a question is of no interest to the Buddha. What the Buddha is interested in, is that: 'All those who have been saved from the world, or are being saved, or will be saved, all of them attain salvation by relinquishing the five hindrances, by knowing the defilements of the mind that weaken it, with their minds well established in the four stations of mindfulness, by developing in the proper way the seven limbs of wisdom.... But that question which the Blessed One was asked [by you], was asked with a different mentality'.

54. *Diṭṭhaṁ*, a form etymologically related to *diṭṭhi*, but yielding an experiential, not speculative meaning.
55. M II, pp. 176–179, *Aggivacchagottasutta,* 1–4.
56. A IV, pp. 259–260, *Dasakanipāto,* 10, 6, 4.
57. *'Ekaṁ hi saccaṁ na dutiyamatthi'*, K I, p. 405, Stn 4, 12, 119.
58. *'Na heva saccāni bahūni nāna'*, K I, p. 405, Stn 4, 12, 121.
59. M II, p. 196, *Dīghanakhasutta,* 5.
60. As we have remarked somewhere else, existence and non-existence are terms of a merely samsaric import. That is why we have deliberately avoided referring to the metaphysical self's existence, preferring to speak rather of its reality.

NOTES TO CHAPTER 14:'RECAPITULATION'

1. *The Central Philosophy of Buddhism* (London, 1960), p. 23.
2. *The Early Buddhist Theory of Man Perfected* (London, 1936), p. 42.
3. *Op. cit.,* p. 24.
4. *Op. cit.,* p. 17.

Selected Bibliography

A. LIST OF SOURCES AND ABBREVIATIONS, see p. XI

B. TRANSLATIONS CONSULTED

Vinaya Piṭaka

I. B. Horner, *Book of the Discipline* (London)
Part I, 1949;Part II, 1957; Part III, 1957; Part IV, 1962; Part V, 1963.

Sutta Piṭaka

1. *Dialogues of the Buddha* (London)
   T. W. Rhys Davids, Part I, 1956; T. W. and C. A. F. Rhys Davids, Part II, 1910; T. W. and C. A. F. Rhys Davids, Part III, 1921.
2. I. B. Horner, *The Collection of the Middle Length Sayings* (London). Vol. I, 1954; Vol. II, 1957; Vol. III, 1959.
3. *The Book of the Kindred Sayings* (London)
   Mrs. Rhys Davids, Vol. I, 1917; Mrs. Rhys Davids, Vol. II, 1922; F. L. Woodward, Vol. III, 1924; F. L. Woodward, Vol. IV, 1927; F. L. Woodward, Vol. V, 1930.
4. *The Book of the Gradual Sayings* (London)
   F. L. Woodward, Vol. I, 1932; I. B. Horner, Vol. II, 1957; E. M. Hare, Vol. III, 1934; E. M. Hare, Vol. IV, 1935; F. L. Woodward, Vol. V, 1935.
5. *The Minor Anthologies of the Pāli Canon* (London)
   Mrs. Rhys Davids, Part I, 1931; F. L. Woodward, Part II, 1948; Bimala Churn Law, Part III, 1938; Jean Kennedy and Henry S. Gehman, Part IV, 1942.

Other translations

Bhikkhu Nānamoli, *The Minor Readings,* London, 1960.

E. M. Hare, *Woven Cadences of the Early Buddhists,* London, 1947.
Mrs. Rhys Davids, *Psalms of the Early Buddhists,* Vol. I: Psalms of the Sisters, London, 1909.
Mrs. Rhys Davids, *Psalms of the Early Buddhists,* Vol. II: Psalms of the Brethren, London, 1913.
K. R. Norman, *The Elders' Verses,* I: Theragāthā, London, 1969.
Pe Maung Tin, *The Path of Purity*, London, 1971.

C. SOME ARTICLES ON *attā* AND *anattā*

Anuruddha, Thera, 'Warum Anattā?', *Einsicht,* 1956, pp. 34–41.

Allen, James, 'The Illusion of the Ego', *Mahābodhi,* May–June 1966, pp. 119–123.

Aver, Albert van, 'Dualism as a Presiding Principle in some Major Indian Masterpieces', *Darshana International* (Moradabad), April 1963, pp. 46–60.

Battacharya, V., 'The Doctrine of Ātman and Anātman', V, *All-India Oriental Conference* (Lahore), 1928.

Chatterji, J. C., 'The Buddha and the Ātman', *Prabudha Bhārata*, March 1963, pp. 91–98.

Chaturvedi, Giridhar Sharma, 'Baudda Darśana men Ātma-vicāra', *Gaveshana* (Moradabad), I, 4, Feb. 1965, pp. 1–5.

Choudury, R. P., 'Interpretation of the Anattā Doctrine of Buddhism', *Indian Historical Quarterly*, 1955, pp. 52–67.

Falk, M., 'Nairātmya and Karman' (The life-long problem of L. de la Vallée Poussin), *Indian Historical Quarterly,* 1940, pp. 429–464.

Groth, A., 'Kausalität und Anattā', *Einsicht*, 1956, pp. 11–15.

Horner, I. B., 'Attā et Anattā dans les Textes du Canon Pāli', *La pensée Bouddhique, Bulletin des Amis du Bouddhisme*, Janv. 1949, pp. 6–13.

Horsch, P., 'Le principe d'individuation dans la philosophie indienne', 2e. partie, Études Asiatiques (Berne), 1957–1958, 1–2, pp. 29–41 (Theravāda and other schools of the Hīnayāna); 3e. partie, *E. A.* (Berne), 1957–1958, pp. 119–142 (Mādhyamika, Vijñānavada, Jaina, Ājivaka, Orthodox Hindu Schools).

Jayatilleka, K. N., 'The Buddhist Conception of Truth', *Ceylon Today*

(Colombo), May 1965, pp. 18–24.

Kar, S., 'Buddhist Sarvaśūnyavāda', *Indian Culture*, 1947, pp. 175–177.

Karpelès, S., 'Anicca-Dukkha-Anattā', *La pensée Bouddhique*, Avril 1950, pp. 16–19.

Khanghe, S. T., 'The Aṭṭhakavagga and the Theory of Soul', *Summaries of All-India Oriental Conference* (Ahmedabad), 1953, p. 58.

Kropatsch, A., 'Body Soul Problem in Modern Psychology and in Buddhism', *Mahābodhi*, 1956, p. 198.

Ladner, M., 'die Anattā-Lehre', *Einsicht*, 1954, pp. 102–107 and 114–116.

La Fuente, M., 'Études sur le Dharma', III et IV, *La Pensée Bouddhique*, Avril 1947, pp. 13–20.

Lorenzo, G. de, 'Instability and Non-entity of the World', *East and West*, III, 4, 1953, pp. 205–213 and IV, 1, 1953, pp. 24–29.

Lounsbery, G. C., 'La personalité dans le Bouddhisme. La science et la doctrine d'Anattā', *La pensée Bouddhique, Bulletin des Amis du Bouddhisme* (Paris), Juillet 1939, pp. 14–23.

Malasekara, G. P., 'The Unique Doctrine of Buddhism', *Mahābodhi*, May–June 1966, pp. 63–69.

Mitchel, Donald W., 'The No-self Doctrine in Theravāda Buddhism', *International Philosophical Quarterly*, 1940, pp. 429–464.

Pérez-Remón, J., 'Comments Upon the Brahmajālasutta', *Boletín de la Asociación Española de Orientalistas*, 1978, pp. 61–96.

Pérez-Remón, J., 'The Simile of the Pith (*sāra*) in the Nikāyas and its bearing on the Anattavāda', *Boletín de la Asociación Española de Orientalistas*, 1979, pp. 71–93.

Rhys Davids, C. A. F., 'Groth of Non-man in Buddhism', *Indian Historical Quarterly*, Sept., 1928, pp. 405–417.

Rhys Davids, C. A. F., 'Buddhism not Originally a Negative Gospel', *Hibbert Journal Quarterly* (Oxford and London), July 1928, pp. 624–632.

Rhys Davids, C. A. F., 'How does Man survive?', *Prabudha Bhārata or Awaken India*, May 1931, pp. 226–229.

Rhys Davids, C. A. F., 'The Self: An Overlooked Buddhist Simile', *J. R. A. S.*, 1937, pp. 259–264.

Shastri, Shrinivas, 'Bauddha Darsana kā Anātmavāda', *Gaveshana* (Moradabad), Feb. 1965, pp. 80–85.

Shukla, Karunesha, 'Ātman in Buddhist Philosophy', Chapter II: 'The Upaniṣadic Ātman and the conception of Attā in the Teachings of the Buddha', Poona Orientalist, July–Oct. 1962, issued April 1965, pp. 114–132.

Story, Francis, 'The Search for the Self is Vain', *World Buddhism* (Colombo) No. 9, 1970, pp. 223–225.

Vallée Poussin, L. de la, 'The Ātman in the Pāli Canon', *Indian Culture*, April 1936, pp. 821–824.

Glossary of terms

abhidhamma: Name of the third group of canonical books.
abyākatā pañhā: Applied to certain questions which the Buddha refused to answer or explain.
ajjhattaṁ: Regarding the self; interior or subjective.
anāgamī: One who after death will not be reborn in the world; he will appear in heaven and there attain *nibbāna.*
anattā: Non-self.
anupādāparinibbāna: Utter *nibbāna* without rebirth basis.
arahant: A perfect man who has destroyed the *āsavas* and is bearing a body for the last time.
arūpa: Immaterial.
asaṅkhata: Not compounded; not a mental creation or composition.
āsavas: The states of radical perversion that have to be extinguished for the attainment of *nibbāna.*
asuras: The mythological enemies of the gods.
asmimāna: Lit. 'the conceit (*māna*) "I am" (*asmi*)', It connotes pride or a morbid preoccupation with self.
ātman: Sanskrit for self.
attā: The self.
attadiṭṭhi: The eternalist view that identifies the self with man's empirical factors and believes that such a self is eternal.
attānudiṭṭhi: Attadiṭṭhi q. v.
āyatana: Sphere, extent; exertion, practice.
bahiddhā: External, objective.
bala: Spiritual power (of faith, of energy, of mindfulness, of complete concentration, of wisdom).
bhāshya: Commentary.
bhava: Samsaric becoming.
bhāvanā: Spiritual progress or development.
bhikkhu: A Buddhist mendicant, member of the Buddhist religious order.

bhikkhunī: A female mendicant, member of the Buddhist religious order for women.

bodhisatta: A being destined to attain Buddhahood.

bojjhaṅga: Lit. constituent of wisdom (mindfulness, investigation of the Doctrine, energy, rapture, mental quiescence, complete concentration, equanimity).

brahmacariya: The holy life of one who has renounced the world and works zealously for spiritual perfection.

dhamma: Buddha's teaching, taken either partially or in its entirety; good and bad state; phenomenal attribute of man; thing in general.

dhamma cakkhu: Lit. the eye of dhamma. The power to realize that whatever is of a nature to arise is also of a nature to cease.

dhātu: Primary physical element; basic condition or potentiality.

diṭṭhi: Lit. view. It refers mostly to a misguided or purely speculative opinion of no soteriological value.

diṭṭhigataṁ: A matter of *diṭṭhi* q. v.

dosa: Blemish or ill-will.

dukkha: Suffering. It often summarizes whatever is samsaric.

esanā: Longing, desire.

iddhi: Personal endowment; psychic power, mystic wonder.

indriya: Sense-faculty; potency in general.

issara: God as creator and ruler of the world.

kamma: A deed; moral liability to punishment and reward; actual punishment and reward.

kasiṇa: A phenomenal aid to mystic contemplation.

khandhas: The empirical factors in man (*rūpa* or living body as the substrate of the six spheres of sense, *saññā* or perception, *vedanā* or feeling, *saṅkhārā* or inner activities, complexes formed as a response to perception and feeling, *viññāṇa* or partial and global consciousness).

kilesa: Impurity, depravity.

māna: Pride, conceit.

manomaya: Made of the mind stuff.

Māra: The embodiment or personification of evil.

moha: Confusion, infatuation.

nibbāna: The highest aim of Buddhist spiritual training and practice, the extinction of all liability to samsaric existence.

nikāya: One of the five sections of the second group of canonical books.
nīvaraṇa: Lit. hindrance, obstacle (sensuality, ill-will, torpor, worry, wavering).
ogha: The flood of *saṁsāra*. In plural stands for: lust, ill-temper, stupidity, conceit, idle speculation.
oḷarika: Material, gross.
paccekasambuddha: One who has attained perfection but is not concerned with the salvation of others.
paccattaṁ: Regarding the very self or in the very self.
paññā: Wisdom.
pāramārthika: (Pāli, *paramatthika*), ultimately real.
paramattha: The 'summum bonum' or highest good.
pāramitā: The perfect exercise of ten perfections by the Bodhisatta.
parinibbāna: Complete *nibbāna.*
paṭiccasamuppāda: 'The wheel of becoming'. A formula that explains the genesis and cessation of human samsaric phenomena in one existence after another. A chain of twelve *nidānas* or root-causes in mutual dependence: the first producing the second, the second producing the third and so on until the last which produces the first.
peta: Wandering spirit.
phasso: Sensorial contact; any kind of spiritual achievement.
rāga: Passion, attachment.
sakkāya: Empirical, samsaric individuality consituted by the *khandhas* q. v.
sakkāyadiṭṭhi: The view that identifies the self in man with the *khandhas* q. v.
saṅkhāra: Anything compound and perishable; in plural, one of the *khandhas* q. v.
saṅkhata: Mentally constructed or put together.
sammāppadhāna: Right exertion.
saṁyoga: Fetter, bond.
samaṇa: A religious wanderer, opposed generally to *brāhmaṇa.*
sammutisacca: Apparent or conventional truth.
saṁsāra: Transmigration, series of rebirths and deaths.
sassatavāda: The view that identifies the self in man with the empirical factors and believes that such a self will become eternal and unchange-

able.

satipaṭṭhāna: Application of mindfulness (to body, sensations, the mind and mental objects or states).

satto: Being in general; a person.

sīla: Moral behaviour; code of moral behaviour.

sotāpanno: A converted man. One who is free from all forms of transmigrational punishment and sure to obtain the highest enlightenment.

sotāpatti: The condition of a *sotāpanno*; the first step towards perfection.

sūtra: Teaching given in a summary form and to be explained more fully.

sutta; A chapter of the second group of canonical books, composed in a narrative form, containing some teaching of the Buddha or his closest companions.

suttapiṭaka: Name of the second group of canonical books.

taṇhā: Graving, specially for saṁsaric becoming.

tathāgata: Title of the Buddha; in general, one who has attained the highest possible perfection.

thera: A senior *bhikkhu.*

therī: A senior *bhikkhunī.*

tipiṭaka: The three divisions of the Buddhist scriptures.

ucchedavāda: The annihilationist theory that identifies the self in man with the empirical factors and holds that the self perishes at death.

upādāna: Saṁsaric grasping, the fuel on which the flame of becoming is fed.

vinayapiṭaka: Name of the first group of canonical books.

vy*āvahārika:* Conventional.

Table of Scriptural Passages Commented or Quoted

Note. Figures within brackets refer to pages and, in most cases, also to the notes where the corresponding quotations are found. A few corrections have occasionally been introduced.

Index of Names and Subjects